# Culture and Equality

To
Mrs Anni Parker
as the most eminently qualified
of all persons known to the author
either to originate or to appreciate
speculation on social improvement,
this attempt to explain and diffuse ideas
many of which were first learned from herself
is
with the highest respect and regard
dedicated

# Culture and Equality

## An Egalitarian Critique
## of Multiculturalism

Brian Barry

Harvard University Press
Cambridge, Massachusetts

First Harvard University Press paperback edition, 2002

First United Kingdom Publication in 2001
by Polity Press in association with Blackwell Publishers Ltd

**Library of Congress Cataloging-in-Publication Data**

Barry, Brian M.
  Culture & equality: an egalitarian critique of multiculturalism / Brian Barry.
    p.   cm.
  Includes index.
  ISBN 0-674-00446-9 (cloth)
  ISBN 0-674-01001-9 (pbk.)
    1. Multiculturalism.  2. Equality.  3. Assimilation (Sociology).  I. Title: Culture
  and equality.  II. Title.

HM1271 .B37  2001
306—dc21                                                         00-063366

# Contents

# Preface

This book takes its origins in the many occasions on which Anni and I would linger over the dinner table finishing a bottle of wine (or two) while talking about the latest piece of foolishness, and sometimes bestiality, perpetrated somewhere in the world and defended by somebody in the name of multiculturalism. A form commonly taken by these conversations was imagining even more absurd things that looked as if they could be justified on the same basis. Not infrequently, these flights of fancy later came home to roost, illustrating the point that the *reductio ad absurdum* is a difficult argument to make against multiculturalism. It was Anni who first said that I should write a book about it, and convinced me that it was worth doing now, rather than later, despite its postponing the completion of my *Treatise on Social Justice*. Since then, she has continued to discuss the ideas with me as it has proceeded and has come up with additional examples. She has also tried to keep in check the inveterate academic propensity to qualify every statement to death, and sometimes succeeded.

These were all ways in which, according to my understanding of the matter, Harriet Taylor helped to bring John Stuart Mill's projects to fruition, so I have taken the liberty of borrowing for this book the dedication that he intended for her. Mill's plan was that it would be printed at the beginning of *The Principles of Political Economy*. In the event, however, it was only 'pasted in a few gift copies to friends', because of the opposition of Harriet Taylor's estranged husband, John.[1] With ten days to go until publication (those were the days!) she wrote to him asking for his advice. Such dedications, she suggested 'are not unusual, even of grave books, to women', and she offered as a precedent (with less than perfect tact, perhaps) August

Comte's having dedicated some tome on political economy to Madame de Sismondi – who was, though Harriet did not mention this, Comte's lover.[2] John Taylor's furious reaction scuppered the project, but the dedication seemed to me too good to let go to waste.[3]

The technology of authorship has, of course, moved on a lot since Mill's day. He would have employed a steel-nibbed pen and an inkpot, whereas writing this book used up several hundred felt-tipped pens. Mill, however, had the advantage of being able to send off his handwritten manuscript to the printer, and was then able to revise what he had written at the proof stage. Nowadays, publishers expect typescripts – even disks – and do not look with favour on authors who have second thoughts once the book is typeset. The gap between what I produce and what they want has been filled by Anni, who (among other things) deciphered some four hundred pages of fax from the Alto Adige while also superintending our move from London to New York in the summer of 1998, and then set up amid the packing cases to process a couple of rounds of revision after lugging a so-called portable computer across the Atlantic. A fortnight later came the start of the academic year. Between furnishing an apartment, teaching several new courses and working on the book, something would have had to give if Anni had not thrown herself into keeping the show on the road. Unquestionably, what would have had to give would have been working on the book, so it is in every way as much hers as mine.

Anni likes to tell the story about the occasion, about a month after we first met, on which I expounded the crux of the paper given that afternoon to an LSE political philosophy seminar by some visiting speaker. More or less as soon as the words were out of my lips, Anni gave the answer which it had taken about fifteen academics and graduate students twenty laborious minutes to arrive at. I said 'You know, you're really quite bright.' Despite this, we are still together and for that, among all the other things, this book is dedicated to her.

I should also like to thank my history teacher at Taunton's School, Southampton, who suggested, when I said I was wondering about putting in for Philosophy, Politics and Economics rather than History at Oxford, that I should try *Language, Truth and Logic* and *On Liberty* and see if I liked them. I liked them both tremendously, but took to *On Liberty* more, and inside a week had turned in an essay arguing that Mill had got it about right – a view that, as will be apparent in this book, I still retain. I am, at any rate, glad to take the opportunity of expressing my gratitude for a piece of advice that has enabled me to get paid, first as a student and then as an academic, to spend the last thirty-five years doing political philosophy.

Like the cat on Shackleton's *Endurance*, Gertie oversaw the entire operation, and made much the same kind of contribution as Mrs Chippy, her speciality being to hide the scissors and stapler (essential tools of the trade if you write the way I do) by settling down on top of them and yielding them up only under protest.[4] More conventional, but no less sincere, thanks are owed to Elizabeth and Hans Mair and Inge and Iska Brandstätter at the Hotel Sonnenhof in Merano, where several chapters of the book were drafted in July, 1998 and much of the final revision carried out in the summer of 1999. I am particularly grateful to Inge Brandstätter for putting so many pages of draft through the fax machine – a job way beyond the call of duty to any ordinary hotelier.

I am also grateful to the organizers of a number of lectures and seminars at which some of the ideas were presented, and to the audiences for their questions and comments. These were as follows: the E. H. Carr Memorial Lecture at University College, Aberystwyth (University of Wales); the Austin and Hempel Lecture at Dalhousie University in Halifax, Nova Scotia; the Annual Meeting of the Conference for the Study of Political Thought, UK (Oxford, January 1998); the IIS Institute at the University of Bremen; the Center for Ethics and Public Policy at Harvard University; the Center for Human Values at Princeton University; the Murphy Center for Political Economy at Tulane University; the Department of Law at Edinburgh University; and the Department of Politics at the University of Newcastle. On the last occasion, Peter Jones and Simon Caney were both kind enough to give me comments in writing, and Peter Jones has also provided me with some valuable comments on the whole draft. In addition, portions of the manuscript have been discussed at various stages along the way by the Rational Choice Group in London and the Washington Square Consensus in New York.

I have been aided in the process of revision by a reader's report on the draft manuscript commissioned by Polity Press and by two (one by Ian Shapiro and one by Steven Macedo) commissioned by Harvard University Press. In addition, the following have read the draft and commented on some or all of it, in a number of cases extensively: Bruce Ackerman, Rainer Bauböck, Harry Brighouse, Chris Brown, Vittorio Bufacchi, Keith Dowding, Robert Goodin, Amy Gutmann, Jacob Levy, David Little, Andrew Mason, Philip Parvin, Alan Ryan and Stuart White. I am very grateful to all of them, and also to Oonagh Reitman and Kent Greenawalt, both of whom put their expertise unstintingly at my disposal, thus saving me from several errors of fact and interpretation in chapter 5. I should say (more emphatically, perhaps, than usual) that none of those whose names are listed above should be assumed to endorse the arguments contained in this book. Indeed, a couple of them half-seriously suggested that I would be doing them a favour by omitting their names from the acknowledgements. I am glad, however, that they were only half-serious about it.

I was fortunate during the academic year 1998–9 to be able to co-teach two graduate courses at Columbia University both of which advanced my work on the book. In the Fall semester, chapters of the book draft were discussed in successive weeks in a seminar on 'Multiculturalism' given jointly with Jeremy Waldron. I am very grateful to him and also to the students for their penetrating comments and criticisms. Also valuable was the incentive to finish the draft created by the promise to circulate in advance chapters as yet not finished or in some cases begun. Then, in the Spring semester, I co-taught a course with Akeel Bilgrami on 'Nationalism, Secularism and Liberalism'. The lively discussions, involving him and the other participants, helped me to clarify the ideas about identity which are presented in chapter 3. In the same context, I should like to acknowledge, since it did not in the end get cited, the stimulus provided by David Laitin's book *Identity in Transition*.[5] As a member of the jury appointed by the American Political Science Association to recommend the recipient of its David Easton Prize for the most significant theoretical contribution to political science in the four years 1994–8, I am glad to have been associated with its public recognition.

Because of the critical nature of this book, it contains a lot of quotations, and it is important that the views under discussion should be accurately quoted. The indispensable job of checking quotations from the authors most often cited was undertaken by Katherine Rein. I am grateful to her for her care in checking my quotations and her enterprise in following up doubtful-looking quotations in the work of other authors. Last, but by no means least, Sarah Dancy was everything an author hopes for in a copy-editor. The readers of this book, as well as I, have reason for being grateful to her.

London – Merano – New York

OF Equality – as if it harm'd me, giving others the same chances and rights as myself – as if it were not indispensable to my own rights that others possess the same.

Walt Whitman, *Leaves of Grass*

# PART I

Multiculturalism and Equal
Treatment

# 1

# Introduction

## I. Losing Our Way

'A spectre is haunting Europe – the spectre of Communism.'[1] That is the famous first sentence of the *Communist Manifesto*, which was given to the world just over a century and a half ago. In the course of time, the spectre came to life, but it has now been laid to rest, apparently for good. It is not simply that 'real existing socialism' has been abandoned everywhere except North Korea, which is scarcely an advertisement for it. Equally significant for its long-term prospects is the way in which within academia it has lost ground to the point at which it is not even attacked any more, let alone defended.

Both developments are to be welcomed in themselves. What concerns me is the manner in which the void left by communism and Marxism has been filled. The spectre that now haunts Europe is one of strident national-ism, ethnic self-assertion and the exaltation of what divides people at the expense of what unites them. Moreover, the precipitate dismantling of command economies has resulted in a massive expansion of material inequality and the collapse of the public services. The same trends in less extreme forms are also apparent in the affluent countries of Western Europe and North America, and in the southern hemisphere in Australia and New Zealand. Claims for special treatment are advanced by groups of all kinds while material inequality grows and the postwar 'welfare state' shows increasing signs of strain.

These developments have their counterpart, not surprisingly, in the world of ideas. Only now that it has been so thoroughly marginalized has it become clear how important Marxism was as a bearer of what one might describe as the left wing of the Enlightenment. What I mean by this is that Marx shared with contemporary Victorian liberals the notion that there was a universally valid notion of progress. He believed that the key to the emancipation of human beings from oppression and exploitation was the same everywhere. Although Victorian liberals would have disagreed about the institutional implications, they too would have held that the conditions for the self-development of human beings did not vary from place to place, though in many places entrenched beliefs and practices put the achievement of those conditions a long way off in the future.

In the course of the twentieth century, liberals have increasingly come to squirm at the dogmatic confidence of their Victorian forebears. They have had some reason to, since there is no doubt that the Victorians tended to attribute universal value to some purely local cultural prejudices, as we can see with the advantage of hindsight. Nevertheless, Marxism, so long as it remained an intellectual force, provided a stiffening of universalism to the liberal cause: the best response to the Marxist vision of universal emancipation was an alternative liberal one. With the collapse of Marxism as a reference point, however, there was nothing to prevent the loss of nerve among liberals from turning into a rout. With some distinguished exceptions, the ex-Marxists themselves led the way by embracing various forms of relativism and postmodernism rather than a non-Marxist version of universalistic egalitarianism.

Does this matter? It matters to the extent that ideas matter, and in the long run they do. It is true that the French Revolution would not have occurred without pervasive discontent with the *ancien régime* or the Russian Revolution without the disintegration of the Czarist empire under the impact of war. Similarly, it was the dislocation due to hyperinflation and mass unemployment that paved the way for the triumph of the Nazis in Germany. But there was nothing inevitable about the way in which the raw materials for upheaval were channelled into particular forms of political movement. Anti-Semitism, it has been said, is the socialism of fools. Whether racist scapegoating or universalistic measures to succour the needy are the response to a slump is not socially or economically predetermined. It depends on the persuasiveness of alternative diagnoses and prescriptions. Similarly, there is nothing inevitable about the way in which today discontent increasingly flows into the channels of fundamentalism, nationalism and ethnocultural chauvinism. The wiseacres who say that there is something 'natural' or 'primordial' about these forces merely reveal their historical and sociological illiteracy. It was said of the Bourbons when they were restored to the throne of France in 1815 that they had learned nothing and forgotten nothing. The same may be said of those who pursue policies of ethnocultural nationalism and particularism, and also of those who lend them intellectual support.

Many of those who (like myself) lived through the Second World War hoped that the ideas underlying the Fascist and Nazi regimes were permanently discredited. Never again, we thought, would the world stand by while people were slaughtered simply because they belonged to a certain ethnic group; never again would the idea be seriously entertained that obligations to the nation overrode obligations to humanity. The Nuremberg trials at the end of the Second World War established the principle that there were crimes against humanity that could be punished by an international tribunal even though they did not necessarily violate the laws of the state in which they were committed. Then, in 1948, the Universal Declaration of Human Rights seemed to betoken a new era marked by the general acknowledgement of certain standards of decent treatment that were the birthright of all human beings, standards to which all states should be held internationally accountable.

These hopes have not proved altogether delusory. The notion of an 'international community' has become far more of a reality than it ever was before, as international agencies and non-governmental organizations have proliferated. The appeal to state sovereignty as the response by a government to external criticism is increasingly becoming perceived as 'the last refuge of a scoundrel'. The machinery for the prosecution of crimes against humanity is finally falling into place. Yet at the same time as all this is happening, western philosophers are apparently less and less confident of the universalistic moral ideas that alone make sense of efforts to enforce human rights and punish violators of them. An illustration is provided by the annual series of lectures held in Oxford that has been sponsored and published by Amnesty International. Although the subject is supposed to be human rights, what is striking is how few of the eminent philosophers who have delivered these lectures have offered a forthright statement of the case for their universal applicability.

My focus in this book is on ideas that are distinctly more benign than those underwriting genocide, xenophobia and national aggrandizement. They are, nevertheless, also anti-universalistic in their thrust. My concern is with views that support the politicization of group identities, where the basis of the common identity is claimed to be cultural. (The point of the last clause is to exclude cases in which group identity is based on a shared situation that does not arise from cultural difference, for example a common relation to the labour market.) Those who advocate the politicization of (cultural) group identities start from a variety of premises and finish up with a variety of policy prescriptions. Nevertheless, there is enough overlap between them to make it feasible to discuss them within a single book. The views in question are known as the politics of difference, the politics of recognition or, most popularly, multiculturalism.

Will Kymlicka has recently suggested that there is a 'possible convergence in the recent literature... on ideas of liberal multiculturalism'.[2] This view, which he also calls 'liberal culturalism', has, he says, 'arguably become the dominant position in the literature today, and most debates are about how to develop and refine the liberal culturalist position, rather than whether to accept it in the first place'.[3] What Kymlicka says is true, but also in a certain way misleading. Thus, when he tells us that 'liberal culturalism has won by default, as it were' because there is 'no clear alternative position', he implies that almost all (anglophone) political philosophers accept it. My own private, and admittedly unscientific, poll leads me to conclude that this is far from being the case.

What is true is that those who actually write about the subject do so for the most part from some sort of multiculturalist position. But the point is that those who do not take this position tend not to write about it at all but work instead on other questions that they regard as more worthwhile. Indeed, I have found that there is something approaching a consensus among those who do not write about it that the literature of multiculturalism is not worth wasting powder and shot on. The phenomenon is by no means confined to multiculturalism. On the contrary, it is merely an illustration of a pattern that occurs throughout moral and political philosophy (and elsewhere). By and large, those who write about environmental ethics believe that the human race needs to change its ways so as to preserve the environment, while those who do not think this write about other things they regard as more important. Similarly, the philosophical literature on the claims of non-human animals is more tilted towards giving them a high priority than is the distribution of opinion among all philosophers. These are both causes to which I am myself sympathetic, but this does not prevent me from recognizing the built-in bias in the philosophical literature on them.

In my naively rationalistic way, I used to believe that multiculturalism was bound sooner or later to sink under the weight of its intellectual weaknesses and that I would therefore be better employed in writing about other topics. There is no sign of any collapse so far, however, and in the meanwhile the busy round of conferences (followed by journal symposia or edited volumes) proceeds apace in the way described by David Lodge in *Small World*. There are, indeed, wide-ranging criticisms of multiculturalism from outside political philosophy, such as Robert Hughes's splendidly dyspeptic *Culture of Complaint* and Todd Gitlin's *The Twilight of Common Dreams*.[4] I have learned from both, but their focus is that of an art critic and a sociologist respectively. What is still lacking is a critical treatment of a similarly broad kind from within political philosophy, and that is what I have undertaken to provide here.

In the piece by Will Kymlicka from which I have quoted (as it happens, the introduction to the proceedings of a conference), he says, as we have seen, that there is 'no clear alternative position' to the multiculturalist one espoused by himself and his itinerant band of like-minded theorists. He then immediately outlines one alternative, which 'would be to show that the earlier model of a unitary republican citizenship, in which all citizens share the identical set of common citizenship rights, can be updated to deal with issues of ethnocultural diversity, even though it was originally developed in the context of much more homogeneous political communities'.[5] There is nothing in the least 'unclear' about this position: what Kymlicka means is merely that he disagrees with it. In my view it is not only clear but right.

The core of this conception of citizenship, already worked out in the eighteenth century, is that there should be only one status of citizen (no estates or castes), so that everybody enjoys the same legal and political rights. These rights should be assigned to individual citizens, with no special rights (or disabilities) accorded to some and not others on the basis of group membership. In the course of the nineteenth century, the limitations of this conception of equality came under fire with increasing intensity from 'new liberals' and socialists. In response, liberal citizenship has, especially in this century, come to be supplemented by the addition of social and economic elements. Universalism (categorical entitlements and social insurance) replaced the old poor law, which targeted only those with no other means of support; and the removal of legal prohibitions on occupational advancement was supplemented by a more positive ideal of 'equality of opportunity'.

Although there was never a complete consensus on these ideas, and the practice fell short (to varying degrees) in different western countries, I think it is fair to say that political philosophers were reflecting widespread sentiments when they articulated notions such as these in their work. John Rawls's *A Theory of Justice* can clearly be seen in retrospect to be the major statement of this conception of citizenship in all its aspects, including the assumption built in at the outset of an already existing 'society' whose members constitute a state in which the government has the power to determine such matters as the nature of the economic system and the distribution of wealth and income.[6] Rawls's first principle of justice, which called for equal civil and political rights, articulated the classical ideal of liberal citizenship, while his second principle gave recognition to the demands of social and economic citizenship. The first part of this second principle set out a very strong conception of equality of opportunity, while the second part (the 'difference principle') made the justice of social and economic institutions depend on their making the worst-off socio-economic group in the society as well off as they could be made under any set of institutional arrangements.

Hegel said that the Owl of Minerva takes its flight at dusk, and Rawls's theory of justice provides a perfect illustration. Even in 1971, when *A Theory of Justice* was published, there were already (especially in 'new left' and feminist circles) attacks being made on the individualistic nature of liberal citizenship. Similarly, even back then books were being written about the 'crisis of the welfare state' – again more often at this time by those on the left than those on the right. Since then, criticisms of the liberal paradigm have grown in volume and vehemence: it is widely believed to be deeply flawed in principle. If anything even more widespread is the assumption that the postwar social democratic settlement represented by the so-called welfare state is unsustainable as a consequence of international competition and mobility of capital, the inability of states to run macroeconomic policies that will reliably produce full employment, the disappearance of jobs in manufacturing due to technical change, and so on. There is unquestionably some validity in the claim that the ability of a nation-state to transform market outcomes in line with an egalitarian political agenda is more circumscribed than it was in the era of exchange controls and import quotas. But the massive increase in the extent of inequality in Britain and the United States in the last twenty years is largely the result of the anti-egalitarian policies deliberately pursued by Thatcherite and Reaganite governments and maintained (even in some respects intensified) by their nominally distinctive successors, Blair and Clinton. These policies could have been different. If they had been, the context of the current debate about multiculturalism would be different.

I shall argue in the final chapter of this book that a politics of multiculturalism undermines a politics of redistribution. Until then, I shall focus on criticisms of the liberal paradigm as misconceived in principle. As a political philosopher, I shall direct most of my attention to the forms in which the thesis is presented in the work of other political philosophers. But I am pretty sure that these ideas also have a considerable resonance beyond the ranks of those whose academic speciality they fall under. I am not suggesting that the crisis of liberal citizenship is the staple of conversation in the average pub. Nevertheless, those who read the *Times Literary Supplement* and *The New York Review of Books* or sample journals of opinion (across a wide ideological range) will have been exposed to a steady stream of popularized versions of the same themes, and it would be surprising if this had no effect over the years. I hope that this book will be read by at any rate some of those who have found such claims persuasive, because my object is, in broad terms, to provide an antidote. As will become apparent in subsequent chapters, I do not wish to maintain that there is nothing to be learned from the critics of the liberal conception of citizenship. But I shall argue that whatever objections are valid can be met by formulating it more carefully and making its underlying assumptions more explicit. Most of the criticisms, however, cannot be accommodated in this way, and I believe that these should be rejected.

## 2.  The Flight from Enlightenment

Strange as it may seem for academics to repudiate enlightenment, it is noteworthy how popular the sport of Enlightenment-bashing has become in recent years. Especially among the pop academics and their journalistic hangers-on, it is now a commonplace that something they call the 'Enlightenment project' has become outmoded.[7] But ideas are not like designer dresses. There, the latest fashion is the most desirable simply in virtue of being the latest. There is only one parallel to ideas: new fashions in ideas help to sell books as new fashions in *haute couture* help to sell clothes. But in the case of ideas we can ask a question that does not make sense in the case of clothes: is the latest fashion right or wrong? It is my contention that the anti-Enlightenment bandwagon is misdirected.

During most of the nineteenth and twentieth centuries, attitudes to the Enlightenment marked the main division between left and right in many Western European countries: the left embraced the universalism of the Enlightenment, while '[critics] from the right argue[d] that, by reducing all social relations to a set of abstract and impersonal rights, [universalism] tears the fabric of society to pieces'.[8] Now, however, a variant on the same refrain has gained currency among those who see themselves as being on the left. These 'have charged that [the Enlightenment's] talk of universal rights remained oblivious to inequalities in gender, race and class'.[9] According to them, the conception of equal citizenship embodied in equal rights needs to be replaced by a set of culturally differentiated rights.

The critique from the right is profoundly opposed to the whole set of ideas underlying and (more or less) embodied in the French Revolution. Without eliding the differences between, for example, Burke, de Maistre and Hegel, we can nevertheless trace a Counter-Enlightenment current of thought that has been represented in the middle of this century by Michael Oakeshott in England and in the United States by a number of more wholeheartedly reactionary figures exiled from the continent of Europe. None of these would have wished to say that the Enlightenment had become outmoded, because that would imply that there was some previous era in which it was appropriate. This would equally be denied by contemporary foes of Enlightenment such as (in different ways) Alasdair MacIntyre and Roger Scruton, for whom the whole idea was a mistake all along.

There is no unified line among thinkers of the anti-Enlightenment right towards policies that might give legal recognition to culturally based differences. However, where the culture in question is itself fundamentally opposed to the values of the Enlightenment, its claims for special treatment tend to attract a good deal of sympathy. In the United States, the Amish and cognate conservative Christian groups such as the Mennonites have benefited from right-wing financial and political support. (I shall discuss the Amish extensively in chapter 5.) Orthodox Judaism is in some degree the product of a reaction against the moves in the second half of the nineteenth century to liberalize Jewish doctrines and practices that led to the breaking away of Conservative and Reform Judaism. (The Roman Catholic Church similarly redefined itself as self-consciously opposed to liberalism in the same period.) Claims of Orthodox Jews to special exemptions from generally applicable laws to accommodate their distinctive ideas about diet, clothing and the observance of the Sabbath also therefore attract the sympathy of those who approve of the existence of anti-liberal enclaves as the closest attainable approximation to the complete destruction of liberal institutions.

The French Revolution swept away the special privileges of the clergy and the nobility, and abolished the innumerable special arrangements with respect to taxation extorted by towns and cities over the centuries in return for temporarily relieving the financial embarrassments of the King. In the face of all these complex traditionally sanctioned differences, it introduced a system of uniform laws and taxes. Similarly, the Revolution introduced a uniform system of weights and measures, which facilitated trade between different areas and also circumvented the problem that the local measures were subject to manipulation. Previous efforts by the French state to standardize had foundered on the lack of common citizenship: 'As long as each estate operated within a separate legal sphere, as long as different categories of people were unequal in law, it followed that they might also have unequal rights with respect to measures.' Thus, 'the simplification of measures... depended on that other revolutionary political simplification of the modern era: the concept of a uniform, homogeneous citizenship' which 'can be traced to the Enlightenment and is evident in the writings of the Encyclopedists.'[10] In the same spirit, the Revolution swept away the patchwork of historic jurisdictions and replaced it with the uniform grid of *départements* that still survives today virtually unchanged.

All of these examples of administrative rationalization were anathema to conservative critics of the Revolution as an outward expression of the spirit of the Enlightenment. Their contemporary heirs have no principled objection to the creation of a mass of anomalies and special cases to accommodate cultural minorities, as advocated by multiculturalists, because they are well aware that uniformity of treatment is the enemy of privilege. Some multiculturalists even share the enthusiasm of the thinkers of the Counter-Enlightenment for pre-modern political forms. Thus, in his book *Strange Multiplicity*, James Tully writes of 'the victorious modern language of constitutional uniformity' as embodying an 'error' in that it 'serve[s] to exclude or assimilate cultural diversity'.[11]

Much of what Tully has to say about 'modern constitutionalism' is a travesty. But it is true that it can be defined in terms of a 'contrast with the irregularity of an ancient constitution'.[12] Thus, 'because it is the incorporation of varied local customs, an ancient constitution is a motley of overlapping legal and political jurisdictions', whereas a modern constitution is one 'that is legally and politically uniform: a constitution of equal citizens who are treated identically rather than equitably'.[13] What is doing the rhetorical work in this sentence is, of course, the presupposition that identical treatment is to be contrasted with equitable treatment. That is a core assumption of multiculturalism, and one of my primary purposes in this book is to challenge it. In advocating the reintroduction of a mass of special legal statuses in place of the single status of uniform citizenship that was the achievement of the Enlightenment, multiculturalists seem remarkably insouciant about the abuses and inequities of the *ancien régime* which provoked the attacks on it by the Encyclopaedists and their allies. It is not so much a case of reinventing the wheel as forgetting why the wheel was invented and advocating the reintroduction of the sledge.

In other ways, too, the anti-liberal rhetoric of multiculturalists is not uncongenial to the reactionary right. Thus, exponents of the 'politics of difference' typically inveigh against the 'abstract universalism' that they attribute to liberalism. A good example of this is Iris Young, to whom I shall return a number of times in the course of this book.[14] On similar lines, Tully (as we shall see in chapter 7) draws strong anti-universalistic conclusions from an extended metaphor in which different cultural groups are represented by different species of animal. Ethnic groups, it has been said, are seen by multiculturalists as 'self-evident, quasi-biological collectives of a reified "culture" '.[15] In much the same way, it has been suggested, 'the logic of Young's proposal for group representation seems to require an essentialized and naturalized conception of groups as internally homogeneous, clearly bounded, mutually exclusive, and maintaining specific determinate interests'.[16] All this fits in nicely with the essentialism of the Counter-Enlightenment, encapsulated in de Maistre's well-known remark that he had seen Frenchmen, Italians and Russians, and so on, but that 'as for *man*, I declare I have never in my life met him; if he exists, he is unknown to me'.[17] While the new left took over from German romanticism the idea that each ethnic group can flourish only by maintaining the integrity of its own distinctive culture, 'in the 1970s and 1980s the new right reworked the historic themes of racial difference and hierarchy through a discourse of culture'.[18] The notion that groups should retain their racial purity was thus recoded as the claim that each group should maintain its own cultural integrity.[19]

The proliferation of special interests fostered by multiculturalism is, furthermore, conducive to a politics of 'divide and rule' that can only benefit those who benefit most from the status quo. There is no better way of heading off the nightmare of unified political action by the economically disadvantaged that might issue in common demands than to set different groups of the disadvantaged against one another. Diverting attention away from shared disadvantages such as unemployment, poverty, low-quality housing and inadequate public services is an obvious long-term anti-egalitarian objective. Anything that emphasizes the particularity of each group's problems at the expense of a focus on the problems they share with others is thus to be welcomed. If political effort is dissipated in pressing for and defending special group privileges, it will not be available for mobilization on the basis of broader shared interests.

I shall not address myself any further in this book to those whose support for the multiculturalist agenda derives from the way in which it lends itself to the maintenance and even the deepening of social hierarchy. My target is, rather, those multiculturalists who would be happy to embrace the watchwords of the French Revolution: liberty, equality and (in some appropriately non-sexist rendition) fraternity. What unites them is the claim that, under contemporary conditions of cultural heterogeneity, 'classical' or 'difference-blind' liberal principles fail to deliver on either liberty or equality: only by adopting the tenets of the 'politics of difference', it is said, can we hope to achieve real liberty and equality. Against this, I shall argue that multiculturalist policies are not in general well designed to advance the values of liberty and equality, and that the implementation of such policies tends to mark a retreat from both. Even when there are reasons for introducing group-differentiated rights based on membership in cultural groups, these do not include the advancement of equal liberty. Rather, the case has to be that these are departures from equal liberty that can be supported pragmatically.

How does all this connect up with the Enlightenment? I have quoted James Schmidt as saying that 'critics from the left have charged that its talk of universal rights remained oblivious to inequalities in gender, race and class'. This statement, while true, leaves open a variety of possible responses to the alleged failings of the Enlightenment. One is the response that I have already endorsed: that the universal civil and political rights of citizens envisaged (if far from completely instantiated) by the French and American Revolutions were indeed insufficient, and need to be supplemented by universalistic social and economic rights. This line of thought, which does not denigrate universal civil and political rights but seeks to build on them, is in my view a development fully within the tradition of the Enlightenment.

A second response would go along the same lines most of the way but add that it may be possible to make out a case for certain group-based measures, such as 'affirmative action' in relation to jobs, or special funding for education, to help groups whose members suffer systematic disadvantage. As long as 'disadvantage' is defined in universal terms – as the lack of things (resources and opportunities) whose possession would generally be agreed to be advantageous – this too is a potential way of realizing the values of the

Enlightenment. This is not to say that group-based programmes are in any particular set of circumstances a good idea. It is simply to say that the question is not to be foreclosed by saying that any such programmes are contrary to basic liberal principles. It follows that we have to qualify the statement that classical or 'difference-blind' liberalism cannot countenance any deviation from universal rights. For there may be cases in which a system of group-based rights for those suffering from systematic disadvantage will be a way of helping to meet the egalitarian liberal demand that people should not have fewer resources and opportunities than others when this inequality has arisen out of circumstances that they had no responsibility for bringing about. However, special treatment for members of disadvantaged groups is justifiable only for as long as the inequality persists. We may say, therefore, that the objective of special treatment for members of disadvantaged groups is to make the need for that special treatment disappear as rapidly as possible. (I shall return to this in chapter 4.)

It is instructive to contrast this with the case made by multiculturalists for granting special rights to groups defined by their distinctive cultural attributes. These special rights will, according to their advocates, be needed permanently – or at any rate as long as the group retains its cultural distinctiveness. Moreover, if the group did no longer need special rights, that would not be regarded as a cause for celebration, because it would be taken to suggest that the support for the group's culture had been insufficient to prevent its members from assimilating to that of some larger or more powerful group.

This distinctive argument for group rights may be said to constitute a third response to the perceived failings of the original 'Enlightenment' model of liberalism. Unlike the second response, it does not rest the case on lack of resources or opportunities. Members of minority cultures may, indeed, suffer from a paucity of resources or opportunities, but the case for culture-based special rights does not depend on its being so. Rather, the argument is that, even where resources and opportunities are equal, the members of a group are entitled to special rights if their distinctive culture puts them in a position such that they are in some way less well placed to benefit from the exercise of the rights that provide the standard resources and opportunities than are others. This position will, in a number of guises, occupy me over much of this book. I shall also, however, have to spend some time with a fourth response to the perception that the Enlightenment's 'talk of universal rights remained oblivious to inequalities in gender, race and class'. This is the response best known in the form that was given to it by Marx, and in that form it has been tragically influential in the twentieth century. Despite their disagreements, the three responses considered so far share something significant: the idea that rights are important. This is what Marx denied.

I said earlier that Marx represented the left wing of the Enlightenment. This is so in two respects. First, Marx did not reject the slogan 'liberty, equality, fraternity'; on the contrary, he claimed to take it more seriously than did those who originated it. And second, he was just as much of a universalist as was any Enlightenment figure: he was as fully persuaded as was Condorcet that all societies would pass through the same stages and finish up at the same destination, though Marx's conception of the stages and the destination was different from that of Condorcet, and he envisaged the process as being driven by different forces.[20] Where Marx was distinctive was in his position on civil and political rights: he was not content to point to their limitations in the face of great economic inequalities; rather, he denounced them as suitable only to 'egoistic man'.[21] The solution was not to supplement these universal rights with others, but to abolish rights altogether. In the society of the future, social solidarity and spontaneous cooperativeness would obviate the need for 'bourgeois rights'.

It is not necessary to hold Marx responsible for every crime against humanity committed by Lenin, Stalin and Mao to recognize that his con-temptuous attitude to standard liberal rights provided an ideological under-pinning for the monstrous abuses of the legal system perpetrated by the regimes that they ran, and by other regimes modelled on theirs. Even under conditions of crude, unrestrained capitalism, the equal freedom of all to sign a contract still puts the proletarian in a different position from the serf, the slave, or the worker in a Soviet-style command economy. (Apologists for slavery in the American South were fond of the suggestion that slaves fared better than northern workers; but this did not persuade northern workers to clamour for the extension of slavery.) The defects of the primitive capitalist labour market are better met by adding other rights to the right of contract: health and safety measures, maximum hours, protections against dismissal, trade union rights, rights to an income outside the labour market, and so on. Similarly, a system of legal rules that gives everyone formally equal rights needs to be supplemented by the provision of legal aid, but even without that it is still preferable to a system of estates in which different categories of people have more or fewer rights, or a Soviet-style system in which judges are encouraged to ignore legal procedures in order to pursue what are taken to be the overall objectives of the government.

Sentimentalists of right and left join hands in the condemnation of liberal rights. Those on the right hold up the vision of a society (which many claim to believe actually existed in some place in the past) in which people knew their place. Motivated on one side by *noblesse oblige* and on the other by gratitude and deference, the different ranks formed an organic whole whose integrity would have been destroyed by strident assertions of individual rights. The left version, as we saw in the case of Marx, is essentially the same picture but with an egalitarian twist. The family, that 'haven in a heartless world', is for sentimentalists of all stripes a paradigm of a community within which rights are out of place. In the right-wing version, the wife obeys the husband, the children in turn obey both, and conflict is avoided by adherence to well-specified roles. In the left-wing version, the bond between equals makes an appeal to rights unnecessary – even the possibility of appealing to them diminishes the quality of the relationship. It would not be a bad definition of a gut liberal (as against one whose liberalism is purely cerebral) to say that it is somebody who feels an inclination to throw up when confronted by this kind of stuff, in either its right or left manifestations.

What has all this to do with multiculturalism? The answer, it turns out, is that it has quite a lot to do with it. For an important strand within the school of thought that advocates a 'politics of difference' downplays the significance of legal rights, emphasizing instead the necessity for cultural change. We shall see in chapter 7, for example, how equal rights for gays and lesbians (including comprehensive measures against discrimination in the labour market, the housing market, and so on) are dismissed by Iris Young as 'merely civil rights'. What Young wishes to focus on instead of legal rights is the need for a public affirmation of the value of a gay or lesbian lifestyle. The anti-liberal animus of this approach is brought out clearly in Young's stated approval for the 'continuing effort [of new left movements] to politicize vast areas of institutional, social and cultural life'.[22] Lest we be in any doubt: 'Politics in this sense concerns all aspects of institutional organization, public action, social practices and habits, and cultural meanings insofar as they are potentially subject to collective evaluation and decisionmaking.'[23] Has she ever, I am led to wonder, read *The Scarlet Letter* or, to come further up to date, *Wild Swans*?[24] Perhaps she has and likes what she has read: she talks without a trace of irony about the need for a 'cultural revolution', and her account of 'the process of politicizing habits, feelings and expressions of fantasy and desire that can foster cultural revolution' is chillingly reminiscent of *Nineteen Eighty-Four*.[25]

So far, I have accepted without demur the assumption common to the critics of the Enlightenment that there was a single 'Enlightenment project' that can be captured in a few airy remarks about 'Reason' and so on. In fact, this assumption is groundless.

The 'Enlightenment project' remains too ill-defined a notion to serve as an object either of allegiance or condemnation. What is needed instead is a careful weighing up of the variety of different commitments and intentions – not all of them reconcilable – that have been carelessly lumped together under the label of the 'Enlightenment project.' But ... to undertake a critical examination of these different claims is to take up a task that ... might well be characterized as the 'Enlightenment project.'[26]

In spite of this, I think we may be fairly safe in saying that there were some things the Enlightenment was against, so that the Enlightenment can be defined negatively even if it is illegitimate to talk about an 'Enlightenment project' of a positive kind.

Thus, different strands of the Enlightenment would have given somewhat different answers to the question of how institutions were to be justified. But there was a broad agreement that institutions did need to be justified, and that the reasons adduced in favour of an institution must explain its virtues in terms of general principles – that it served the public good, was equitable, and so on. On this basis, we could argue about what is a good system of taxation, but it would be common ground that people who were identically situated in relation to the relevant criteria – same income, same property, same number of dependants, and so on – should be treated in the same way within any given polity. The notion that there was an 'Enlightenment project' which proposed to deduce everything a priori from the demands of Reason is a fiction put about by the critics. But consistency of treatment, according to intelligible criteria, could be not unaptly described as a demand of Reason. It is, we may say, revolting to Reason in this sense that (as in the *ancien régime*) people who are identically situated in relation to any conceivable criterion that could be rationally defended should have different tax liabilities depending on the negotiating skill of the burghers in their town and the incompetence or desperation of the king's representatives when they agreed, perhaps centuries earlier, to some permanent alleviation in the town's tax burden in return for a short-term boost to the treasury. The contrast is not with uniformity in the sense that everybody pays the same amount of tax but with uniformity in the sense that everybody faces the same tax system. A good deal of anti-Enlightenment rhetoric depends on systematically confusing these two senses of uniformity.

When we move on from a negative characterization of the Enlightenment to a positive one, Schmidt's strictures are entirely valid. Any attempt to distil it into a single 'Enlightenment project' is bound to pick out aspects developed in some countries, and by some thinkers, at the expense of others. Fortunately, however, what I want to defend in this book is something not unrecognizably different from what is called 'the Enlightenment project' by its critics. Thus, whenever they want a name to represent what they think is wrong with the 'Enlightenment project', the one that they almost invariably come up with is that of John Rawls, and in particular the Rawls of *A Theory of Justice*. The egalitarian liberalism that I shall lay out here is influenced by, and related to, Rawls's theory of justice, at any rate on my interpretation of it. If Rawls is taken to epitomize the contemporary state of the 'Enlightenment project', this book constitutes a defence of it.[27] The reader who is impatient for an exposition of the grounds of liberal universalism is invited to turn to section 5 of chapter 7. For those who are prepared to trust me, however, I undertake in the course of the book to develop the theory of egalitarian liberalism as and when it is needed in order to explain my objections to multiculturalism.

## 3.  A Brief Overview

The book is divided into three parts. Following this introductory chapter, the rest of Part I consists of a critical analysis of the frequently made claim that public policies of the kind supported by advocates of the 'politics of difference' can be justified by an appeal to the value of equal treatment. If public policy treats people differently in response to their different culturally derived beliefs and practices, the argument runs, it is really treating them equally. To appreciate this, it is said, we need a more subtle understanding of what is involved in equal treatment than that which underlies 'difference-blind' liberalism, according to which people are treated equally when they are treated in the same way.

The public policies defended in these terms are of two kinds, negative and positive. Negative policies are those that provide individual exemptions from generally applicable laws on the basis of cultural practices or (very often) religious beliefs. A familiar example is the exemption granted to turban-wearing Sikhs in many jurisdictions from the requirement to wear a crash helmet when riding a motorcycle. The argument that exemptions of this sort are demanded by a suitably sophisticated conception of equal treatment will be the subject of chapter 2. Chapter 3 will then take up the parallel argument that deviations of a positive kind from prima facie equal treatment are necessary for the achievement of equal treatment in some superior sense of the expression. I distinguish positive public policies from negative ones as follows: whereas negative policies simply provide relief from the burden imposed by some law, positive policies provide advantages to individuals (on the basis of their membership in some culturally defined group) that are not available to others. An example would be a policy of reserving a certain proportion of the places in professional schools or in certain occupations for members of groups defined (or alleged to be defined) in terms of their distinctive culture.

In Part II, the focus of the inquiry shifts from individuals to groups. The argument to be considered here is that egalitarian liberal principles, unless modified in ways proposed by exponents of the 'politics of difference', are liable to be destructive of the independence of associations and communities that are the bearers of minority cultures. Since these principles do not impose similar constraints on the associations and communities of the mainstream society, it is suggested that they have an unfair impact on cultural minorities and thus again fail the test of mandating really equal treatment.

Chapter 4 offers an exposition of this claim, and then attempts to develop a coherent egalitarian liberal theory of group rights. The remaining two chapters in Part II apply this theory to two important topics, chapter 5 to religion and chapter 6 to education.

Part III, which comprises chapters 7 and 8, raises some questions about the broader significance of multiculturalism. The gist of chapter 7 is that many moves that deploy 'culture' as a justification of actions and practices make sense only on the assumption that moral universalism is false. Some of those who appeal to 'culture' acknowledge this, while others do not. Either way, my claim in this chapter is that moral universalism is valid, and that as a consequence there are only certain very limited contexts (the criteria for which can be precisely specified) in which 'This is the way we do things here' can operate as a justification for going on doing the thing in question. (This is not to say, of course, that there may not be plenty of good reasons for continuing in our customary ways, only that in general merely pointing out that it *is* our custom is not one of them.) Finally, chapter 8 addresses the politics of multiculturalism. There are two main theses. One is that, to the extent that the advocates of multiculturalism have succeeded in getting their policies adopted, this does not shed a very flattering light on the workings of liberal democratic institutions. The other is that these particularistic policies do little to help (and sometimes do a lot to harm) members of their target groups, while at the same time tending to stand in the way of the kinds of universalistic policies that would be of far more benefit to most members of minority groups.

This is a quite substantial book, and I recognize that not everybody is as uniformly interested in the topics discussed in it as I am. It therefore occurs to me that it may be helpful to give some indication of the extent to which chapters in different parts of the book can be read independently of one another. On the assumption that anybody reading this has already completed chapter 1, I estimate that it should be possible, without too much loss, to go straight from here to any of chapters 2, 3, 4, 7 or 8. (The later chapters contain references to relevant earlier material that can be followed up if desired.) Chapters 5 and 6 can also be read independently of one another, but it would be advisable before tackling either of them to read chapter 4, or at the very least the final section of it.

# 2

---

# The Strategy of Privatization

## 1. Cultural Diversity

In every society, differences are socially recognized. The distinction between male and female is everywhere a basic building block of social organization, and most societies have far more elaborate and differentiated expectations of behaviour appropriate to the sexes than do contemporary western societies. Similarly, every society distinguishes age groups – at the minimum the young, the old and those in between – and attaches different expectations to each. The blind and the deaf, the physically handicapped and the severely mentally retarded are always socially recognized as different, and as requiring special treatment – though not necessarily benign treatment. Again, every society recognizes relations of marriage and kinship, and attaches normative expectations to the roles of husbands and wives, parents and children and often many additional relationships within extended families.

The fact of difference is universal and so is its social recognition. As far as that goes, there is nothing different about contemporary western societies. What is, however, true is that in these societies differentiation tends to be more complex and to have a larger optional component than is characteristic of traditional societies. The whole concept of a 'lifestyle', as something that can be deliberately adopted and may demand some sort of recognition from others, is indicative of a society in which the consumer ethic has spread beyond its original home. Somewhere on the interface between the more or less serious commitments involved in a lifestyle and the realm of pure consumption are modes of dress: when visiting other parts of the world, western visitors are bound to be forcibly reminded of the cultural peculiarity of their own societies in the wide range of clothing that is socially acceptable. What line, if any, public policy should take in relation to this proliferation of divergent lifestyles is a question that is addressed by this book.

Most countries have always contained people with different religious beliefs and other divergent ideas about the right way to behave: these are typically transmitted within the family or some wider social group from one generation to the next. Here, too, there is nothing new. Nor is there anything new about conflict arising from difference. Conflicts between different Christian denominations, and between Christians and Jews, have been endemic in Europe. Adding to the religious and cultural mix Muslims, Hindus, Sikhs, Buddhists, Rastafarians and others in the last half century has undeniably created tensions which have given rise to harassment and occasionally lethal violence in Britain, for example. However, these phenomena do not appear to be motivated to a significant extent by doctrinally based hostility. Saying this is not, of course, to suggest that violence fuelled by racism or xenophobia is any less to be deplored than violence stemming from religious or cultural antagonism. It is only to make the simple but (as we shall see throughout this book) often neglected point that religious or cultural difference may be a marker of group identity without being the reason for the members of the group to suffer physical abuse or discrimination. It is doubtful that the louts who set out in a British city for an evening's 'Paki-bashing' see themselves as the spiritual descendants of the mediaeval Christian knights who set out to fight the Paynim.

It is, I suggest, precisely because the *odium theologicum* has not held the centre of the stage that the violence generated by the influx of widely divergent religious and cultural groups has been on a totally different scale from that which different Christian denominations managed to produce all by themselves in centuries of religious wars and persecutions. The one sizeable non-Christian group in Europe, the Jews, suffered over the centuries from segregation, discrimination and sporadic violence that was largely inspired by the Christian belief that the Jews were responsible for killing Jesus Christ. (It is curious that this should have been thought to be a bad thing, since Christians believe that somebody had to do it if mankind was to be redeemed.) The Holocaust was a different matter – a horrific reminder that racism too has a potential for unleashing massive destruction. It is instructive to contrast racialist ideology with the driving force behind the introduction of the Spanish Inquisition, which was the fear that Jewish *conversos* still harboured non-Christian beliefs in the inner recesses of their minds. It was thus premised on the assumption that there was nothing in principle preventing Jews from being good Christians – otherwise the inquiry into beliefs would have been pointless – whereas it followed from Nazi racist doctrine that Jews could never become Aryans: 'Germanism was in the blood, and this blood made possible the sentiments and capacities of the German spirit.'[1]

In the previous chapter, I quoted Will Kymlicka as saying that 'the earlier model of a unitary republican citizenship, in which all citizens share the identical set of common citizenship rights . . . was originally developed in the context of much more homogeneous political communities', and as denying that this earlier model 'can be updated to deal with issues of ethnocultural diversity'.[2] In fact, this model of citizenship was developed in response to the *dear* wars of religion that made much of Europe a living hell in the sixteenth and seventeenth centuries. If it could bring those conflicts to an end – and on the whole it did – it is not at all apparent why it should not be up to the task of coping with religious and cultural differences now. In direct opposition to Kymlicka, indeed, I maintain that the relatively peaceful incorporation of a wide range of religions and cultures in the past half century is a tribute to the ability of what he calls the 'earlier model' to 'deal with issues of ethnocultural diversity'. For, whether the exponents of multiculturalism like it or not, no country – even Canada – has so far departed very far from the model of 'common citizenship rights'. Naturally, it is the sore spots that get the attention – from both politicians and academics – and I shall be discussing a number of them later in this chapter. But what tends to get forgotten is that the problems thrown up by a uniform system of liberal laws have been relatively few. In contrast, the 'politics of difference' is a formula for manufacturing conflict, because it rewards the groups that can most effectively mobilize to make claims on the polity, or at any rate it rewards ethnocultural political entrepreneurs who can exploit its potential for their own ends by mobilizing a constituency around a set of sectional demands.

Diversity is a fact and is here to stay – assuming (as I do) that we rule out, as possible 'solutions' to ethnic and cultural diversity, such drastic measures as compulsory sterilization, genocide, mass expulsion and Taliban-style methods of enforcing cultural conformity. The point is worth emphasizing if only because of the intellectually corrupting role played in contemporary discourse by the word 'multiculturalism'. One objection is that it has built into it the idea that the basis of all social groups is cultural – an assumption that does a lot of work but is in many instances simply bad anthropology. Thus, for example, Will Kymlicka's *Multicultural Citizenship* is largely about the phenomenon of multinational states.[3] But national identity may or may not be based on a sense of cultural distinctiveness; and the demand for a degree of national autonomy may or may not be bound up with the desire to control the institutions responsible for cultural reproduction, such as the schools and the media, so as to ensure the perpetuation of the national culture. Scotland lies at one extreme, Quebec at the other. In the course of this book, I shall be calling attention in a variety of contexts to the way in which the analysis of groups (including ethnic and national groups) is distorted by defining groups so that their basis must be some distinctive cultural identity rather than some other distinguishing feature.

An even more potent source of confusion is the use of terms such as 'pluralism' and 'multiculturalism' to refer simultaneously to a state of affairs and a political programme. Thus, we may speak descriptively of 'a view of society first depicted as "pluralism" and later as "multiculturalism"'. The former term points to the socio-cultural diversity that one may find in contemporary society; the latter indicates that this diversity has become an essential attribute of society itself.'[4] At the same time, 'some writers emphasize an ideological and normative aspect'.[5] The trouble is that one and the same writer is liable to switch between the two uses without notice. Thus, the author of the first of these two quotations cites as an illustration of the descriptive use of 'multiculturalism' Charles Taylor's essay on 'The Politics of Recognition'.[6] But in that essay Taylor also uses 'multiculturalism' to refer to a set of public policies that would give different cultures some kind of official 'recognition'. Similarly, 'pluralism' can be used not only descriptively but also prescriptively to advocate a programme of group separation that I shall discuss in the next section.

What makes the conflation of the descriptive and prescriptive uses of words such as 'multiculturalism' intellectually corrupting is that it can license an unargued shift from the one to the other. Recognition of the fact of multiculturalism can easily be taken to entail a commitment to the multiculturalist programme; conversely, anybody who dissents from normative multiculturalism automatically stands accused of blindness to the fact of multiculturalism. A fine example of this kind of *non sequitur* can be found in an essay on Canadian multiculturalism by three academics based in Quebec. 'In English Canada, multiculturalism as policy is criticized in the name of equality, the latter being contrary to the promotion of distinction or differentiation. Such criticism advocates a unity that is impossible to reconcile with the constant insistence on the population's ethnic diversity.'[7] This compounds both of the errors I have been talking about. First, ethnic diversity – especially in the North American usage of 'ethnicity' – is not the same thing as cultural diversity. People belong to an ethnic group to the extent that they identify themselves as descended from immigrants who saw themselves as belonging to some nationality, whether or not it had a state of its own. The identity may linger on for many generations even if after the first or second generation it has little cultural content and none that could form a basis for any special demand on the polity. (I shall have more to say about ethnicity of this kind in the next chapter.)

The second error embodied in the quotation is the unargued move from fact to norm. Even if 'ethnic diversity' (i.e. the fact of a number of ethnic groups in the sense just laid out) could be equated with cultural diversity, it does not follow that there is anything wrong with the criticism of multiculturalism (considered now as a programme) quoted by the authors. That is to say, it would be perfectly possible to accept the reality of cultural diversity while still maintaining that the multiculturalist programme is incompatible with equality, on the ground that equality is 'contrary to the promotion of distinction or differentation'. The sleight of hand involved in moving from fact to norm is accomplished via the assertion that 'such criticism [of the multiculturalist programme] advocates ... unity'. But there is nothing in the advocacy of a system of rules equally applicable to all citizens that commits one in any way to advocating 'unity', if that is taken to mean anything over and above (tautologically) the policy of equal treatment itself. Just as the whole point of liberal institutions with respect to religion is to give different religions a chance to flourish on equal terms, so an enormous range of cultural differences can be accommodated within a common framework of liberal laws.

Charles Westin, whom I quoted as drawing attention to the equivocation between multiculturalism as fact and multiculturalism as norm, goes on to make a terminological proposal: 'Some of the confusion may be cleared by consistently using the term "multiculturalism" for normative, programmatic approaches, and the term "multiculturality" for empirical conditions of cultural plurality.'[8] I have too much respect for the English language, bruised and battered as it already is by so much of the multiculturalist literature I shall have to discuss, to accede to the second half of this suggestion. I do, however, accept the spirit of the proposal and will reserve the term 'multiculturalism' for the political programme of the 'politics of difference' – or, more precisely, the variety of programmes (not all necessarily consistent with one another) that have been advocated in its name. I shall not, however, engage in the pedantry of modifying quotations to fit this usage, nor will I draw attention to deviant uses on the part of others unless there is some special reason for doing so.

Similarly, of the numerous contemporary uses of pluralism (several of which, unfortunately, will have to be encountered in the course of this book), I shall allow myself the pleasure of eliminating one of them: that which describes a situation of cultural diversity. I shall reserve 'pluralism', in contexts such as the present one, for a political programme that aims to institutionalize cultural difference by segmenting society. If we were to call the realization of this programme the creation of a 'plural society', we would be in line with a distinguished tradition of sociological analysis, according to which 'in a condition of cultural plurality, the culturally differentiated sections will differ in their internal organization, their institutional activities, and their system of belief and value. Where this condition of cultural plurality is found, the societies are plural societies.'[9]

In terms of the vocabulary that I am adopting, then, the argument of this book is not that the fact of multiple cultures is unimportant (or in most

instances regrettable) but that the multiculturalist programme for responding to it is in most instances ill-advised. Indeed, it is just because the fact of
multiple cultures is important that the politicization of group identities and
the development of group-specific policies should be resisted. The liberal
doctrine that the same law should apply to all, so far from being obsolete in
contemporary conditions, is especially well adapted to meeting the challenges that they throw up. Of course, the liberal doctrine is not that any
old law is satisfactory merely on condition that it has uniform application.
The liberal commitment to civic equality entails that laws must provide
equal treatment for those who belong to different religious faiths and different cultures. Much of what follows will be devoted to asking precisely
what equal treatment means.

## 2.  Privatization and Pluralism

So far in this chapter, I have made a good deal of the role of religion in
inciting people to conflict, some of it of enormous magnitude. It is therefore
important, for the sake of balance, to add that there is nothing inherent
in the phenomenon of religion as such that inevitably leads to conflict
between adherents of different deities, cults or sects. In Edward Gibbon's
famous words: 'The various modes of worship which prevailed in the
Roman world were all considered by the people as equally true; by the
philosopher as equally false; and by the magistrate as equally useful. And
thus toleration produced not only mutual indulgence, but even religious
concord.'[10] The key to this happy state of affairs was the non-exclusivity
of religious faith: 'The devout polytheist, though fondly attached to his
national rites, admitted with implicit faith the different religions of the
earth.'[11] Contrary to the much-touted claim of Samuel Huntington, there
is no reason why adherents of different belief systems cannot coexist
peacefully.[12] 'Civilizations', which Huntington largely identifies with major
religions, will 'clash' only if there is something specific to fight about.
Difference as such is not a source of conflict. What causes conflict among
adherents of different religious faiths is their leading to incompatible
demands. Thus, the belief in a divinely sponsored mission to convert
others, if necessary by force, is an obvious recipe for conflict. So is a claim
made by the adherents of some religion to possess a particular holy
place when this claim is contested by others. (Jerusalem is the prime example.) Finally, where members of different religious faiths have incompatible ideas about the way in which a polity and a society should be
organized, and at least one group seeks to impose its ideas on a territory
containing other groups, that is bound to result in conflict. Given that these
are the conditions for conflict, it is scarcely surprising that the two prosely-

tizing monotheistic religions, Christianity and Islam, have been implicated in so much of it.

Liberal principles are not some sort of 'magic bullet' that can somehow create harmony without any need for sacrifices by the parties. If we want a medical analogy, we might better make the less agreeable comparison with a course of chemotherapy: it holds out the hope of destroying the malignant features of religion, but only with side-effects that are liable to be experienced as debilitating by believers. In other words, if the parties want peace enough to make the concessions that are needed to reduce their demands so that they become compatible, liberalism proposes a formula for doing so. More than that, liberal principles can make a moral appeal as a fair way of solving conflict, because they offer the parties equal treatment. There is, however, no guarantee that either peace or equity will be regarded by everybody as more important than winning – that is to say undertaking courses of action destructive of civility that are derived from religious beliefs.

The liberal formula for the depoliticization of differences first arose as a way of dealing with the strife between Protestants and Roman Catholics that the Reformation brought about, and that remains an important reference point. The prior assumption in Europe was that civil peace required the imposition of a single religion within each state, and that international peace required the mutual recognition by states of the rule 'Cuius regio, eius religio': to each realm its own religion. Religion was thus politicized up to the hilt: it was a matter of prime public concern, in as far as conformity to the state religion and loyalty to the state were regarded as inseparable. The liberal move – stated at first with qualifications and later more boldly – consisted in throwing all of this into reverse. The source of conflict, it was now suggested, was the very attempt to create religious conformity that was supposed to eliminate conflict. Only if the state took no official line on religion would religious passions be calmed and peace assured. As we now know, the gamble paid off, and religious toleration brought an end to holy warfare. Residual attempts to suppress a well-entrenched religious faith (as in Ireland well into the nineteenth century) simply reinforced the lesson by creating massive and lasting disaffection from all the state's institutions.

Nevertheless, the liberal proposal is controversial, and is bound to be. A common charge is that it assumes the unimportance of religion in people's lives. In this form, the objection is misguided. On the contrary, it can be replied, it is precisely because liberals recognize the important role that religion plays in many people's lives that they emphasize the importance of neutralizing it as a political force. There is, however, a more carefully phrased version of the objection that must, I think, be accepted as valid in its own terms. According to this, the liberal solution to religious conflict, in relegating religion to the private sphere, fails to accommodate all those whose beliefs include the notion that religion ought to have public expression.

In virtue of the unworldly teachings of its founder, Christianity has at base a certain affinity with the privatization of religion. Many Protestant sects, indeed, find the detachment of religion from public life entirely congenial, while a few carry detachment to the point of refusing to 'render unto Caesar the things that are Caesar's', such as authority over road safety or sanitation. (I shall return in chapter 5 to the problems that they pose.) However, the founder – assuming him to have been accurately reported – appears to have assumed that the Last Trump would be heard by some of his audience in person. The failure of this prophecy, like the failure of subsequent prophecies on the same lines, did not undermine belief in the rest of the doctrine, but it left ample room for reinterpretation. Beginning as a cult whose members desired nothing except to be free of persecution, it in time developed towering structures such as the Roman Catholic Church and its Orthodox counterparts. Doctrinal development to legitimate them occurred alongside. All of these churches made claims to (direct or indirect) secular authority, and so in their turn did Lutherans and Calvinists. There is no way of denying, then, that the liberal formula fails to satisfy the understandings of the role of religion that have formed a central element in most mainstream variants of Christianity. The complaint is undeniably valid, as far as it goes. The only question is how far it does go.

Pressure on the legitimacy of official state neutrality has increased as a result of the permanent settlement in the past half century of substantial Muslim populations in France, Germany and Britain. The political pretensions of Christian churches are lent little support by the New Testament. Thus, for example, the temporal authority of the Pope rested only on 'what was arguably the most momentous – and the most successful – fraud of the Middle Ages: that known as the Donation of Constantine'.[13] In the ironic words of Gibbon: 'This fiction was productive of the most beneficial effects. The sovereignty of Rome no longer depended on the choice of a fickle people; and the successors of St Peter and Constantine were invested with the purple and prerogatives of the Caesars.'[14] In contrast with this, it is widely thought that (as one Indian scholar has expressed it) 'a Hindu or a Sikh, or a Muslim for that matter, would find it more difficult to make sense of the notion of "privatization of religion" than, perhaps, a Christian does'.[15]

At the same time, however, it is also widely agreed

that Hinduism as traditionally practised in India is for the most part accommodative of the coexistence of plural religions, and [that]... Hindu nationalism of the current sort... is a distortion and perversion of Hinduism because it has *politicized religion*, mobilizing and exploiting religion instrumentally for political ends, thereby making it a divisive force providing no meeting ground for followers of different faiths.[16]

The position of Islam is rather different. It is true that here, too, we can distinguish the core doctrine from characteristically modern forms of politicized Islam, which are themselves pathological reactions to modernity.[17] But to describe them as 'fundamentalist' is misleading if it is taken (on analogy with fundamentalism within Christianity) as siting their distinctive feature in a belief that the Koran is the literal word of God. For this is a standard, though not defining, feature of Islam. Although the Koran does not (as is sometimes supposed) underwrite a theocracy, it does contain a set of prescriptions for the way in which the community of the faithful is to be organized that has no counterpart in the Gospels.[18] This body of doctrine, subsequently elaborated by generations of interpreters, sets up a strain between Islam and liberal norms a sign of which is that no polity with a Muslim majority has ever given rise to a stable liberal democratic state.[19] It is also significant that the one that comes closest, Turkey, was subjected to what could without exaggeration be described as a 'cultural revolution' under Kemal Atatürk, following the overthrow of the Ottoman empire. Yet even this effort to create a secular state has not been sufficient to create a stable democracy observing the rule of law or to avoid a tension between secular and Islamic forces, as is evident today.

What follows from all of this? The lesson commonly drawn by multiculturalists is that 'liberalism can't and shouldn't claim complete cultural neutrality'.[20] This is a lazy response because no attempt is made to specify what 'complete cultural neutrality' might look like or to explain why it should ever have been supposed that liberalism is committed to it. The evidence against liberalism's having this property appears to consist in nothing except its incompatibility with some other (obviously incompatible) beliefs. Charles Taylor, from whom the quotation is taken, emphasizes the incompatibility of liberalism with Islam.[21] But liberalism is also, as I have been at some pains to point out, incompatible with most versions of organized Christianity too, as they have existed during most of their history. If this is the evidence that constitutes the case against liberalism's cultural neutrality, we have to ask how on earth the condition of cultural neutrality could ever possibly be instantiated. It would seem that for liberalism – or any other doctrine for that matter – to be culturally neutral, there would have to be no existing (or possible?) world-view with which it conflicts. Since this is manifestly absurd, the assertion that liberalism is not culturally neutral asserts something that could not conceivably be denied.

Unless you take it as axiomatic that liberals are complete cretins, prudence might counsel caution here. If the claim to offer 'neutral ground' can be dismissed as easily as Taylor supposes, would it ever have been put forward?

The alternative, which Taylor does not consider, is that there must be some other sense in which liberals claim that they can offer 'a neutral ground on which people of all cultures can meet and coexist'.[22] The answer is that the way in which liberalism is neutral is that it is fair. This is a general claim, but let us stick for now to the paradigmatic case of religion. What can be said about the liberal proposal for privatizing religion, then, is that it is the only way in which religions can be given equal treatment, and equal treatment is what in this context is fair. This contention is, of course, open to dispute. But it cannot be proved wrong merely by observing that the kind of settlement it recommends will be inimical to the beliefs of some people. A fair distribution of property will be inconvenient to those who have an unfairly large amount. Similarly, a fair way of dealing with religions will incommode those who wish to make claims on behalf of their own religion that cannot be accommodated within the constraints prescribed by fairness. There is nothing surprising in this.

The objection to privatizing religion was, let us recall, that there are many faiths that assign religion a more central role than is permitted by the strategy of privatization. From their point of view, the proposal demeans religion by denying it the public position that it ought to have. But the demand that the public arena should be suffused by religion is not, of course, a demand that it should be suffused by religion in general. Rather, it is a demand that one particular set of doctrines, or one particular religious authority, should be granted a privileged position. It may be a matter of outright proscription of rivals, a prohibition on their building places of worship, a ban on proselytizing, or some other form of discrimination, but the intention as well as the effect is unequal treatment. Similarly, if the society's major institutions are modelled on the prescriptions handed down by one religion, that must necessarily mean that the views of other believers (and non-believers) will not be equally incorporated.

Tariq Modood has written, with feigned innocence, that 'it is surely a contradiction to require both that the state should be neutral about religion, and that the state should require religions with public ambitions to give them up'.[23] But the point is, as he understands very well, that the giving up of public ambitions is precisely what neutrality between religions does require, to the extent that those ambitions would, if realized, violate the conditions of equal treatment. As Modood remarks, 'it is interesting that Prince Charles has let it be known he would as a monarch prefer the title "Defender of Faith" to the historic title Defender of *the* Faith.'[24] But it is mainly interesting for the light it throws on the Prince's ideas about religion: given that his guru was Laurens van der Post, we can guess that it is equated by him with some kind of vague spirituality devoid of doctrinal content. Actual *faiths* cannot all be defended unconditionally, because their demands are likely to conflict. Fortunately, the monarchy has done nothing to defend *the* faith since the conscientious scruples of William IV held up the enactment of Roman Catholic Emancipation, but it would be better to perpetuate an anachronism than replace it with a piece of nonsense. Taking the monarchy out of the faith business altogether would be even better, of course, though best of all would be to get rid of the monarchy.

Neutrality is, then, a coherent notion that defines the terms of equal treatment for different religions. It is compatible with neutrality, however, that religions should be publicly recognized: the only constraint is, again, that they should be treated equally. Thus, almost every liberal democratic polity (the United States is a notable exception) provides public funding on some basis or other for schools run by or on behalf of religious denominations. This kind of pluralism can be questioned for its tendency to reinforce communal boundaries and disserve the interests of children in being well educated. (I shall say more about this in chapter 6.) But there is no doubt that such policies can be carried out in a way that is compatible with equal treatment. It should be noticed, however, that what we have here is the pursuit of privatization by other means. Parents are treated as having a preference for one sort of school over another, and they then get their proportional share of the total school budget in order to satisfy their preference. Religion is thus still depoliticized, and dealt with as a private matter; all that happens is that education is also depoliticized and treated as a private matter (at least within limits). Similarly, giving churches charitable status for tax purposes is not to be deemed inconsistent with privatization, even though it requires the fiscal authorities to determine (subject to an appeal to the courts) what is a church, and hence entails state recognition of churches for this purpose. The point is that charitable status or subsidy does not involve public endorsement of the activities carried out by the organization.

We can say, then, that such policies are neutral, in the sense that they are even-handed, and that is the only sense that matters. The educational policy is not 'culturally neutral' in the impossible sense presupposed by Taylor, because it must displease those who would prefer no state funding of religious schools, those who would prefer all state funding to go to schools run by their own religious denomination, and those who would like all schools except those of their own religious denomination closed down by the state. Similarly, some would prefer no tax breaks for religions to tax breaks all round, and others would prefer that they should be selective.

A policy of pluralization could be carried even further and made not merely facilitative but compulsory. Thus, parents might not merely be offered an opportunity to send their children to the schools of their own religion but made to do so. There is an obvious objection to this on the basis of freedom, but it could still be regarded as equal treatment. (Indeed, Charles Taylor is prepared to support parallel measures in relation to language and culture on the ground that this is a superior interpretation of equal treatment.) The final stage would be for a society to 'require its citizens to remain loyal to whatever system of belief they were brought up in, or first committed themselves to.... That would be consistent with pluralism even though it would run counter to liberal principles.'[25] It would also (like the previous proposal) go beyond privatization in that it would shift the state away from the passive accommodation of religious demands towards the role of an enforcer of pluralist policies. If the refusal to countenance the enforcement of diversity makes liberalism 'inhospitable to difference', as Taylor claims, that is a complaint whose validity must be acknowledged. (I shall explore Taylor's argument on this score in the next chapter.)

To conclude this discussion, it is worth noticing that the pluralist approach of protecting religious beliefs at the expense of liberty could be pursued in relation to the law of blasphemy. The current situation in Britain, which puts Christianity (and in particular the Church of England) in a uniquely privileged position, is manifestly indefensible on the most element-ary conception of equal treatment. At least taking a short-term view, the conflictual potential of religion would plausibly be minimized by the prohi-bition of any attack on a religion that its adherents might find offensive. Thus, Lord Scarman, the most vociferous advocate among the judiciary of multicultural policies, argued at the time of the Rushdie affair in favour of 'legislation extending [the offence of blasphemy] to protect the religious beliefs and feelings of non-Christians', on the ground that it would 'safe-guard the tranquillity of the Kingdom'.[26] (So would putting Valium in the water supply.) There is also an argument for pluralism as intellectual insula-tion on the ground that, because beliefs are constitutive of persons, 'to undermine and despise their beliefs is simultaneously to undermine and despise their selves. Freedom of speech should be devoted to, and also limited by, the promotion of mutual understanding between different com-munities of believers.'[27]

The case against all this is that a society owes its members the opportunity – whether they choose to avail themselves of it or not – of changing their minds in matters of religious belief, and that this entails more than the absence of legal sanctions against apostasy. The basic argument for freedom of expression is travestied when it is represented as a way of indulging authors. If, as Bhikhu Parekh has suggested, 'the traditional liberal defence' was simply that free speech benefits intellectuals, perhaps at the expense of what is 'good for society as a whole', it would indeed be weak.[28] Parekh tells us that 'advocates of free speech [such] as Milton, Locke, J. S. Mill, Kant and Schelling universalized [the interests of] the poet, the philosopher, the scientist or the artist.' Their high-minded protestations were a mere disguise for the pursuit of filthy lucre: 'the illustrious defenders of free speech ... earned their living by, and had a vested interest in, free speech.'[29]

Let us concede, for the sake of the argument, the claim made that James Joyce put into the mouth of Stephen Dedalus in chapter 9 of *Ulysses*: the claim that Shakespeare liked money – and very likely wrote for money. Still, there is something rather breathtaking in the idea that the chief gainer from the existence of Shakespeare's plays is Shakespeare's bank account. Yet it is absolutely clear that, when Parekh writes that 'liberal writers have tended to concentrate on the beneficiaries, ignoring those who stand little chance of enjoying these rights and for the most part bear only the corresponding burdens', he means to identify the creators with the beneficiaries of free speech and to identify the rest of the population with those who mainly stand to suffer burdens from its being exercised by others.[30]

If this is where 'respect for culture' takes us, it is scarcely necessary to spell out its illiberal implications. The chief beneficiaries of the world's literature, philosophy and science are those whom it enables to break out of the limited range of ideas in which they have been brought up. There is no reason for exempting religion from this. Indeed, since religions (as against culturally transmitted practices) claim a truth value, there is even more reason for saying that the members of all religious faiths should be able to find out what can be said against them. Moreover, it is not enough that only polite and respectful criticisms should be available. Parekh complains that the contributions of (other) political philosophers to the discussion of the Rushdie affair were largely irrelevant to the terms in which the public debate was carried on. 'They asked if the Muslim demand for the restriction of free speech was justified. In fact Muslims were asking to know if and why the right to examine beliefs critically included the right to mock, ridicule and lampoon them.'[31] There are two answers to this. The obvious one is that the right to mock, ridicule and lampoon is inseparable from the right of free speech. Seeking to ban *The Satanic Verses* on the grounds that it mocked, ridiculed and lampooned Islam was therefore demanding a restriction of free speech, and the political philosophers were simply doing their job by treating it as such. Parekh's attempt to suggest that there were two different issues, one discussed by political philosophers and the other by Muslims, is completely spurious.

A more substantive answer is that few people have ever been converted to or from a religion by a process of 'examining beliefs critically'. Religious fanaticism is whipped up by non-rational means, and the only way in which it is ever likely to be counteracted is by making people ashamed of it. If Christianity has in the past fifty years finally become compatible with civility (at least in most of Western Europe), that is the long-term consequence of an assault on its pretensions that got under way seriously in the eighteenth century. Gibbon employed the stiletto, while Voltaire resorted to the rapier. But in both cases the core of their deflationary strategy was mocking, ridiculing and lampooning. Voltaire, however, lived openly at Ferney and died in old age of natural causes, even though religious zealots would have had no difficulty in assassinating him. The fate of Rushdie, forced to live in hiding with a price on his head, unfortunately suggests that the Islamic equivalent of Voltaire may still be some time off.

I wrote several years ago that we might be 'headed for a new Dark Age' and was roundly abused by Parekh for it: 'although Barry thinks "the evidence is there for all to see", he does little more than point to fascist and fundamentalist movements, none of which really threatens the fabric of Western civilization.'[32] I remain uncontrite about the evidence, which seems to me to show that in many parts of the world liberal institutions and liberal ideas are on the defensive, and in some cases actually in retreat. But it is not necessary to go far afield to look for evidence. There is quite enough of a threat from within. To appreciate this, we need only ask what would be the prospects for freedom of speech if ideas such as those put forward by Parekh became dominant in currently liberal societies.

## 3.   Equal Treatment

The strategy of privatization entails a rather robust attitude towards cultural diversity. It says, in effect, 'Here are the rules which tell people what they are allowed to do. What they choose to do within those rules is up to them. But it has nothing to do with public policy.' A simple model of rational decision-making, but one adequate for the present purpose, would present the position as follows: the rules define a choice set, which is the same for everybody; within that choice set people pick a particular course of action by deciding what is best calculated to satisfy their underlying preferences for outcomes, given their beliefs about the way in which actions are connected to outcomes. From an egalitarian liberal standpoint, what matters are equal opportunities. If uniform rules create identical choice sets, then opportunities are equal. We may expect that people will make different choices from these identical choice sets, depending on their preferences for outcomes and their beliefs about the relation of actions to the satisfaction of their preferences. Some of these preferences and beliefs will be derived from aspects of a culture shared with others; some will be idiosyncratic. But this has no significance: either way it is irrelevant to any claims based on justice, since justice is guaranteed by equal opportunities.

None of this means, of course, that people will not in fact feel hard done by and complain that the system of uniform laws treats them unfairly. Many such complaints are, indeed, made. The question that has to be asked is what merit there is in these complaints. That will be the subject of the rest of the chapter. The main conclusion for which I shall argue is that a popular political response – and one that multiculturalists would like to see made more common – is actually very hard to justify in any particular case, even though it cannot be ruled out a priori. This is the approach that keeps the rule objected to for most of the population but allows members of cultural or religious minorities to opt out of the obligation to obey it. More precisely, I shall concede that this approach, which I shall call the rule-and-exemption approach, may sometimes be defensible on the basis of political prudence or an estimate of the balance of advantages. But I shall reject the characteristic case made by the supporters of multiculturalism, that a correct analysis would show exemptions for cultural minorities to be required in a great many cases by egalitarian liberal justice.

An example of the rule-and-exemption approach is the exemption from humane slaughter regulations that many countries have enacted to accommodate the beliefs of Jews and Muslims. Another is a family of exemptions from laws designed to reduce head injuries which have the effect of permitting turban-wearing Sikhs to ride motorcycles, work in the construction industry, and so on. I shall discuss both of these in the next section. Most, though not all, of these exemptions are claimed on the basis of religious belief. Indeed, Peter Jones has gone so far as to suggest that, if we leave aside the 'religious components of culture', there should be 'few, if any problems of mutual accommodation' arising from cultural diversity.[33] We shall see in the course of this book how often demands for special treatment – by individuals and by organizations – are based on religious belief. This is, perhaps, to be expected if we recognize the tendency for religious precepts to be experienced as more peremptory than norms that are supported only by custom.

We should at the same time, however, appreciate that claims based on religion are more likely to be sympathetically received by outsiders than claims based on custom, especially in largely Protestant (or ex-Protestant) countries, in which there is a traditional reluctance to 'force tender consciences'. This tendency is reinforced in the United States by the constitutional guarantee of 'freedom of religion', which encourages the packaging of custom as religion. The result is, for example, that wearing a *yarmulke* (skull cap) is presented as a religious obligation rather than as the traditional practice that it is for some Orthodox Jews. Even without this incentive, however, it is perceived as advantageous to press claims on the basis of religion wherever possible. Thus, it is questionable that the wearing of a turban is a religious obligation for Sikhs, as against a customary practice among some.[34] In the parliamentary debate on the proposal to exempt turban-wearing Sikhs from the requirement that all motorcyclists must wear a crash helmet, those who favoured the exemption thought it important to insist on the religious standing of the turban, while those who were opposed to it argued for its customary status.[35] There is, however, a countervailing force in Britain, as we shall see below: outside Northern Ireland, discrimination on the basis of religion is not illegal, but discrimination on the basis of race or ethnicity is. This means that there is an incentive to code what may plausibly be a religious obligation (e.g. the wearing of some kind of head-covering by Muslim women) as an ethnic cultural practice, so as to bring it within the scope of the Race Relations Act.

The strong claim made by many theorists of multiculturalism is that special arrangements to accommodate religious beliefs and cultural practices are demanded by justice. The argument is that failure to offer special treatment is in some circumstances itself a kind of unequal treatment. For, it is said, the same law may have a different impact on different people as a result of their religious beliefs or cultural practices. Thus, the liberal claim that equal treatment is generated by a system of uniform laws is invalid. What can be said of this argument? There can be no question that any given general law will have a different impact on different people. But is there anything inherently unfair about this? The essence of law is the protection of some interests at the expense of others when they come into conflict. Thus, the interests of women who do not want to be raped are given priority over the interests of potential rapists in the form of the law that prohibits rape. Similarly, the interests of children in not being interfered with sexually are given priority over the interests of potential paedophiles in the form of the law that prohibits their acting on their proclivities. These laws clearly have a much more severe impact on those who are strongly attracted to rape and paedophilia than on those who would not wish to engage in them even if there were no law against them. But it is absurd to suggest that this makes the laws prohibiting them unfair: they make a fair allocation of rights between the would-be rapist or paedophile and the potential victim.

The point is a completely general one. If we consider virtually any law, we shall find that it is much more burdensome to some people than to others. Speed limits inhibit only those who like to drive fast. Laws prohibiting drunk driving have no impact on teetotallers. Only smokers are stopped by prohibitions on smoking in public places. Only those who want to own a handgun are affected by a ban on them, and so on *ad infinitum*. This is simply how things are. The notion that inequality of impact is a sign of unfairness is not an insight derived from a more sophisticated conception of justice than that previously found in political philosophy. It is merely a mistake. This is not, of course, to deny that the unequal impact of a law may in some cases be an indication of its unfairness. It is simply to say that the charge will have to be substantiated in each case by showing exactly how the law is unfair. It is never enough to show no more than that it has a different impact on different people.

All of this bears on a line of thought in recent political philosophy according to which a legitimate claim for additional income can, in principle at least, be made by those with expensive tastes – people who have to eat plovers eggs and drink vintage claret (to take a famous example) if they are to achieve the same level of satisfaction as others can achieve with sausages and beer. The usual reaction to the idea that those with expensive tastes should get extra resources is that it is absurd, and such a reaction is perfectly sound. This is not simply because the proposal is unworkable: those who put forward the idea are usually quite willing to concede that. The error lies in thinking that, even as a matter of principle, fair treatment requires compensation for expensive tastes. To explain what is wrong with the idea, we have to invoke the fundamental premise that the subject of fairness is the distribution of rights, resources and opportunities. Thus, a fair share of income is a fair share of income: income is the stuff whose distribution is the subject of attributions of fairness. Suppose that you and I have an equal claim on society's resources, for whatever reason. Then it is simply not relevant that you will gain more satisfaction from using those resources than I will. What is fair is that our equal claim translates into equal purchasing power: what we do with it is our own business.

If we rule out the claim that equal treatment entails equal impact, there may still be other arguments for special arrangements to accommodate cultural practices or religious beliefs. But what are they? One natural recourse is to suggest that what I have said so far may be all very well for costs arising from preferences, but that costs arising from beliefs are a different kettle of fish. It is very hard to see why this proposition should be accepted, however confidently it is often advanced. Consider, for example, the way in which people's beliefs may make some job opportunities unattractive to them. Pacifists will presumably regard a career in the military as closed to them. Committed vegetarians are likely to feel the same about jobs in slaughterhouses or butchers' shops. Similarly, if legislation requires that animals should be stunned before being killed, those who cannot as a result of their religious beliefs eat such meat will have to give up eating meat altogether.

Faced with a meatless future, some Jews and Muslims may well decide that their faith needs to be reinterpreted so as to permit the consumption of humanely slaughtered animals. And indeed this has already happened. According to Peter Singer, 'in Sweden, Norway and Switzerland, for example, the rabbis have accepted legislation requiring the stunning [of animals prior to killing] with no exceptions for ritual slaughter'.[36] The case for saying that humane slaughter regulations are not unfair does not, however, depend upon the claim that beliefs are a matter of choice, so that it is somehow people's own fault if they are incommoded by their beliefs. (That is not the point about expensive tastes either.) If we want to say, as Yael Tamir does, that people should be 'free to adhere to cultures and religions of their choice', that should be taken to mean only that they should not be penalized for changing their minds about the value of their current religious or cultural commitments.[37] It should not be interpreted to mean that these commitments are the product of choice. It makes no sense to say that we can decide what to believe. Similarly, we can say if we like that people are responsible for their own beliefs, but that should be understood simply as a way of saying that they own them: their beliefs are not to be conceived of as some sort of alien affliction. (The same may, again, be said in general about preferences.) Talking, as Michael Sandel does, about people being 'encumbered' by their beliefs feeds this sense of alienation.[38]

The position regarding preferences and beliefs is similar. We can try to cultivate certain tastes (by, for example, developing a familiarity or skill), and we can try to strengthen certain beliefs (by, for example, deliberately exposing ourselves to messages tending to confirm them), but in neither case is there any guarantee of success. Moreover, the decision to make the attempt must come from somewhere: we must already have a higher-order preference for developing the taste or a higher-order belief that it would be a good thing to strengthen the belief. Choice cannot, in either case, go all the way down. I suspect that one source of the idea that many preferences are easily changeable is a result of a tendency to muddle together preferences and choices. Suppose, for example, that I have a preference for vanilla over strawberry ice cream, other things being equal. That entails that, if other things are actually equal, I will choose vanilla. But this preference may be a weak one, which means that things do not have to be very unequal before my choice switches to strawberry. The weakness of my preference would be revealed by my willingness to pay only a little more for vanilla and my lack of reluctance to let somebody else have the last vanilla ice cream. Even so, the preference itself, even if weak, may be solidly based in physiology and almost impossible to change. The upshot is, then, that beliefs and preferences are in the same boat: we cannot change our beliefs by an act of will but the same can be said equally well of our preferences. It is false that the changeability of preferences is what makes it not unfair for them to give rise to unequal impact. It is therefore not true that the unchangeability of beliefs makes it unfair for them to give rise to unequal impacts.

Beliefs are not an encumbrance in anything like the way in which a physical disability is an encumbrance. Yet precisely this claim is sometimes made. Thus, Bhikhu Parekh argues that giving people special treatment on the basis of their beliefs 'is like two individuals who both enjoy the right to equal medical attention but who receive different treatments depending on the nature of their illness'.[39] A disability – for example, a lack of physical mobility due to injury or disease – supports a strong prima facie claim to compensation because it limits the opportunity to engage in activities that others are able to engage in. In contrast, the effect of some distinctive belief or preference is to bring about a certain pattern of choices from among the set of opportunities that are available to all who are similarly placed physically or financially. The position of somebody who is unable to drive a car as a result of some physical disability is totally different from that of somebody who is unable to drive a car because doing so would be contrary to the tenets of his or her religion. To suggest that they are similarly situated is in fact offensive to both parties. Someone who needs a wheelchair to get around will be quite right to resent the suggestion that this need should be assimilated to an expensive taste. And somebody who freely embraces a religious belief that prohibits certain activities will rightly deny the imputation that this is to be seen as analogous to the unwelcome burden of a physical disability.

The critical distinction is between limits on the range of opportunities open to people and limits on the choices that they make from within a certain range of opportunities. Parekh deliberately blurs this distinction by writing that 'opportunity is a subject-dependent concept', so that 'a facility, a resource, or a course of action' does not constitute an opportunity for you, even if it is actually open to you, unless you have 'the cultural disposition ... to take advantage of it'.[40] This proposal actually destroys the meaning of the word opportunity, which originally related to Portunus, who was (and for anything I know to the contrary still is) the god who looks after harbours.[41] When the wind and the tide were propitious, sailors had the opportunity to leave or enter the harbour. They did not have to do so if they did not want to, of course, but that did not mean (as Parekh's proposal would imply) that the opportunity then somehow disappeared. The existence of the opportunity was an objective state of affairs. That is not to say that opportunity could not be individualized: whether a certain conjunction of wind and tide created an opportunity for a particular ship might depend on its build and its rigging. But it did not depend on the 'cultural disposition' of the crew 'to take advantage of it'. They might, perhaps, have chosen not to sail because setting out on a voyage was contraindicated by a religious omen, but that simply meant that they had passed up the opportunity.

Lily Bart, the heroine of *The House of Mirth* (in the sense in which Becky Sharp is the heroine of Thackeray's *Vanity Fair*), spends a lot of time in the novel bemoaning the way in which the wealth of her relatives and friends provides them with opportunities – a word she uses several times in this context – that they do not take up because their horizons are limited by the stifling culture of upper-crust New York, and she reflects on the advantage she would be able to take of the same opportunities. If Parekh were right, we would have to convict Miss Bart and her creator, Edith Wharton, of committing a conceptual mistake. On Parekh's analysis, Lily Bart would have had to think that, if she had the wealth of her relatives and friends, she would have had a lot of opportunities that they did not have. But this would be, I submit, to lose the point of her complaint, which was precisely that they had the opportunities yet did not use them. Similarly, the opportunity to read a wide range of books is ensured by literacy plus access to a public library or (provided you have the money) a bookshop. If you belong to some Christian sect that teaches the sinfulness of reading any book except the Bible, you will choose not to avail yourself of this opportunity. But you still have exactly the same opportunity to read books as somebódy who is similarly placed in all respects except for not having this particular belief.

The peculiar implications of Parekh's analysis are well illustrated by his treatment of one example of 'giving people special treatment on the basis of their beliefs'. At issue here is the exemption that Sikhs enjoy from the 'provisions designed to penalize those who carry knives and other sharply pointed objects' contained in the Criminal Justice Act of 1988, which 'specifically states that it is a defence for an accused to prove that he had the article with him in a public place "for religious reasons" ', a provision that was 'introduced ... to permit Sikhs to carry their *kirpans* (swords or daggers) in public places without fear of prosecution'.[42] Parekh asks if non-Sikhs can 'legitimately complain of discrimination or unequal treatment' and replies that 'there is no discrimination involved both because their [i.e. non-Sikhs'] religious requirements are not ignored, and because they [i.e. non-Sikhs] do not suffer adversely as a result of the law respecting those [religious requirements] of the Sikhs'.[43] However, the rationale of a law against the carrying of knives in public must be that unarmed citizens (pleonastically) 'suffer adversely' if some other people are going around carrying weapons. Unless a knife confers an advantage on its possessor, there is no point in having a law restricting the carrying of knives at all. Assuming that the law's rationale is sound, it is absurd to deny that granting an exemption to it for members of one group inevitably reduces the personal security of all the rest of the population.

Parekh also argues that 'as for the complaint of inequality, there is a prima facie inequality of rights in the sense that Sikhs can do what others cannot. However the alleged inequality grows out of the requirements of the principle of equal respect for all, and it is not so much inequality as an appropriate translation of that principle in a different religious context.'[44] But the inequality of rights is not prima facie – it is real. The right to carry knives amidst a population none of whom can legally do the same is an inequality of rights, however we look at it. Whether or not it is a justifiable inequality is another matter. But it is playing with words to suggest that it is really a superior form of equality to the liberal one that says we have equal rights when we have the same ones.

I have argued so far that the differential impact of a general law cannot in itself found a claim that the law is unjust. But justice is not the only basis on which the argument for an exemption from the law might be made. If it is true that a law bears particularly harshly on some people, that is at the very least a reason for examining it to see if it might be modified so as to accommodate those who are affected by it in some special way. Prudence or generosity might support such a move. From a utilitarian point of view, we could pose the question by asking if it is worth giving up some of the benefits of the law in order to reduce the costs of complying with it. It does not follow, though, that the best approach is to keep the general rule unchanged and simply add an exemption for the members of some specific group. The alternative is to work out some less restrictive alternative form of the law that would adequately meet the objectives of the original one while offering the members of the religious or cultural minority whatever is most important to them. This avoids the invidiousness of having different rules for different people in the same society. In practice, however, it is the rule-and-exemption approach that is usually followed.

We can understand how this comes about if we think for a moment about the politics involved. Any open political system (not only one with formally representative political institutions) is inevitably subject to lobbying by minority groups with a special interest in some aspect of public policy. It very often happens that there is no similarly well-organized group on the other side. Governments and legislatures are naturally tempted, therefore, to take the path of least resistance and cave into these minority group demands. To a politician, the attractions of a general law with exemptions for members of specific groups are almost irresistible. No creative effort is required; and, while those who are concerned with the objective of the law may grumble at the special dispensations, they will at least be satisfied that they have achieved most of what they want. At the same time, the articulate special interests that are most opposed are bought off by permission to opt out. Sikhs, whose relatively small overall numbers in Britain are offset by their concentration in a small number of parliamentary constituencies, have been remarkably successful at playing this game, as we shall see.

Once we accept, however, that the case for exemptions must be based on the alleviation of hardship rather than the demands of justice, it seems to me much more problematic to make it out than is widely assumed. I do not wish to rule out the possibility that there will be cases in which both the general law and the exemption are defensible. Usually, though, either the case for the law (or some version of it) is strong enough to rule out exemptions, or the case that can be made for exemptions is strong enough to suggest that there should be no law anyway. Consider, for example, the claim that 'the core of Rastafarian religiosity resides in the revelatory dimensions induced by the sacramental use of *ganja* [cannabis], in which a new level of consciousness is attained. Adherents to the movement are enabled more easily to perceive Haile Selassie as the redeemer and to appreciate their own identities.'[45] It might perhaps be said of many other religious truths that they too would be more easy to believe in under the influence of mind-altering substances.[46] However, there would obviously be insuperable practical problems in legalizing the use of cannabis for Rastafarians only, such as the difficulty of restricting its use to Rastafarian religious ceremonies, the absurdity of trying to distinguish 'genuine' from 'opportunistic' Rastafarians, and the virtual impossibility of preventing Rastafarian cannabis from 'leaking' into the general population.[47] For the same reasons; claims for religiously based exemptions to laws prohibiting use of marijuana in the United States have been ruled out even by those Supreme Court judges sympathetic to such exemptions in general: 'the Ethiopian Zionist Coptic Church... teaches that marijuana is properly smoked "continually all day"', and even if its use were officially prescribed only within the context of a religious ceremony, 'it would be difficult to grant a religious exemption without seriously compromising law enforcement efforts'.[48] The best case for making cannabis legal for Rastafarians or members of the Ethiopian Zionist Coptic Church would be to argue that it is far less harmful than either alcohol or tobacco, both of which are legal.[49] But this is an argument whose scope is not confined to Rastafarians. Rather, if it is valid, it constitutes a case for legalizing the consumption of cannabis by anybody.

## 4. The Rule-and-Exemption Approach

Because it tastes better and is less likely to contain antibiotics or growth hormones, but also out of feelings of guilt (since I can see no answer to the moral case for vegetarianism), I try to buy only meat from animals that have been reared under conditions appropriate to them, fed only food that forms part of their natural diet, and have been slaughtered humanely. This is, literally, an expensive taste. A metaphorically expensive taste (since it might actually end up saving money) would be that of somebody who is a vegetarian out of moral conviction but misses the taste of meat and would still be buying it if they had not come across Peter Singer. A variant on this would be a vegetarian on religious grounds (a Brahmin, for example) or somebody whose religion forbade them to eat pork, such as an observant Jew or Muslim, if they hankered for what was not permitted. Provided we are prepared to extend the conception of 'expensive taste' to include costs that arise from moral convictions or religious beliefs, these are all cases of expensive tastes. They are also, I shall take it, all cases in which nobody would suggest that those with the expensive taste should be compensated out of public funds or granted some waiver from generally applicable laws.

I mentioned earlier that humane slaughter regulations will have the effect of ruling out the consumption of meat for Orthodox Jews and observant Muslims, unless their religious authorities declare that the traditional precepts do not have to be followed, as has occurred among Jews in Norway, Sweden and Switzerland. These religious precepts may also be said to create an expensive taste, in conjunction with humane slaughter legislation, at any rate among those who would eat meat as long as it was kosher or halal. Unlike the previous cases, however, this is one in which the expensive taste is widely held to justify the demand that Jews and Muslims should be given special treatment in the form of an exemption from humane slaughter legislation so that they can go on eating meat consistently with their beliefs. Moreover, campaigns to secure such an exemption have been successful in almost all western countries, the exceptions being the three already listed. In Britain, for example, 'under the Slaughter of Poultry Act (1967) and the Slaughterhouses Act (1979) Jews and Muslims may slaughter poultry and animals in abattoirs according to their traditional methods'.[50] 'Traditional methods' is a euphemism for bleeding animals to death while conscious, rather than stunning them prior to killing them, as is otherwise required.

There are two possible approaches to ritual slaughter that would not lead to the making of an exemption to a general rule. The first would be a libertarian one. It can be argued that, just as the decision to eat meat at all is currently left to the individual conscience, decisions about the way in which animals are killed should be left to the conscience of the consumer. In effect, the job of weighing animal welfare against human carnivorous tastes would be left for each person to perform. This argument is parallel to one used to oppose the prohibition of bloodsports to the effect that their moral acceptability should be left to the individual conscience. Alternatively, the case of ritual slaughter might be assimilated to the ban on cockfighting and dogfighting, customs in their time just as deep-rooted as hunting or hare-coursing but prohibited nonetheless on animal welfare grounds. Taking this line, the implication would be that there is a certain point beyond which cruelty to animals is a legitimate matter for collective decision-making, and that kosher/halal butchery is over that line.

The current situation in Britain is indefensible on libertarian grounds because it is fundamental to the libertarian position that consumers should have clear information on the basis of which to make choices. This condition is not met. There is no requirement that meat from animals killed while still conscious should be labelled to indicate this. Moreover, there is a conspiracy of silence maintained by government and retailers to conceal from consumers the fact that meat displayed on supermarket shelves may come from animals killed in this way. I have never seen this information provided at point of sale and my own informal survey indicates that it is a well-kept secret. In practice, 'a substantial proportion of meat produced by means of religious slaughter is marketed to the general public without any indication of its origins'.[51] The reason for selling most of this meat (as much as two-thirds, according to Singer) on the general market is the cost of preparing meat that is to be sold as 'kosher'.

For meat to be passed as 'kosher' by the Orthodox rabbis, it must, in addition
to being from an animal killed while conscious, have had the forbidden tissues,
such as veins, lymph nodes, and the sciatic nerve and its branches removed.
Cutting these parts out of the hindquarters of an animal is a laborious business
and so only the forequarters are sold as kosher meat.[52]

Does this matter? I think it does. Already 'by 1983 a National Opinion Poll
[in Britain] revealed that 77 per cent of respondents were altogether opposed
to religious slaughter'.[53] Since then, there is much evidence that public
opinion has moved ahead of the politicians in concern about the welfare of
farm animals. There has, for example, been a big swing away from purchase
of eggs from hens in battery cages, and survey evidence suggests that more
explicit labelling would have created a bigger swing still. It is therefore
reasonable to assume that a very large proportion of the population would
shun meat from animals killed by ritual slaughter if they were aware of its
provenance.

At the opposite pole from the libertarian position is the proposal to
require all animals to be stunned before death. This was advocated by
the British government's own Farm Animal Welfare Council in its 1985
*Report on the Welfare of Livestock when Slaughtered by Religious
Methods.* 'The Report's principal conclusion was that, although there was
a dearth of scientific evidence to indicate at precisely what stage in
the process of losing consciousness animals cease to feel pain, loss of
consciousness following severance of the major blood vessels in the neck is
not immediate.'[54] In their own words: 'The up-to-date scientific evidence
available and our own observations leave no doubt in our minds that
religious methods of slaughter, even when carried out under ideal conditions, must result in a degree of pain, suffering and distress which does
not occur in the properly stunned animal.'[55] On similar grounds, 'the
Commission of the European Communities Scientific Veterinary Committee
recommended to the European Parliament in 1990 that the legal exemptions from stunning should be abolished in all the Community's member
states.'[56]

In the face of this, it seems to me virtually impossible to provide an
intellectually coherent rationale for the rule-plus-exemption strategy, even
though it is easy enough to understand its political success. The libertarian
line is that there should be no collective view about the demands of animal
welfare. Individual consumers should be put in a position to make informed
choices, according to their own religious beliefs, ideas about the importance
of animal suffering, taste preferences, and anything else that comes into the
equation. The alternative line is that there is a legitimate collective concern
with the welfare of animals which underwrites the requirement that all
animals be stunned prior to being killed.

What do we have to think in order to finish up with neither of these but rather with the notion that the general rule should be that stunning must take place yet at the same time that there should be a special exemption for religious slaughter? Clearly, we have to accept two things: first, that it is legitimate to take collective decisions in pursuit of animal welfare, and, second, that animal welfare is better served by stunning. (If we did not believe the second, there would be no point in having a restrictive policy that makes stunning the rule.) We then have to hold that an inferior method is nevertheless to be tolerated, so long as its practice is restricted to those for whom it has religious significance. A rough analogy would be to allow hunting but restrict it to those who could show that it was part of their culture. However, it is implausible that a fox would feel better about hunting if it knew that it was to be chased by the Duke of Beaufort than if it knew it was to be chased by Roger Scruton, whom it might regard as a parvenu unable to claim hunting as part of his ancestral way of life.[57] Similarly, it is hard to see why some cows and sheep should have to suffer in ways that are unacceptable generally in order to enable people with certain religious beliefs to eat their carcasses. To withstand that objection, it is necessary to postulate that, although ritual slaughter is far from being best practice, it is nevertheless above some threshold of cruelty below which prohibition would be justified. This then has to be taken to legitimate some sort of collective decision about the relative weight of the interests involved in which those of the animals lose out. I would not be so bold as to say that nobody could in good faith maintain such a position. I do, however, wish to claim that it requires a capacity for mental gymnastics of an advanced order.

It is worth adding this: the rule-plus-exemption regime is predicated on the assumption that the total amount of suffering due to ritual slaughter is to be minimized – consistently with not prohibiting it, of course. But then it is inconsistent with that logic to permit the sale of any part of the carcass of an animal killed by ritual slaughter as anything except kosher meat. A requirement that all the meat must be marketed as kosher would cut in three the number of beasts killed without prior stunning if the demand for kosher meat remained the same. Since, however, the expense of removing the forbidden parts would have to be reflected in the price of kosher meat, there would presumably be some reduction in demand for it, so the total number of beasts killed under the exemption would decline even further. This kind of provision, which as far as I am aware has never been proposed, cannot reasonably be resisted by anyone who seriously accepts the premises that are required for the derivation of the rule-plus-exemption system.

Some will no doubt think that I have overlooked the most compelling argument in favour of an exemption, the argument from freedom of religion. Thus, Sebastian Poulter cites in support of the right to kill animals while conscious Article 9 (1) of the European Convention on Human Rights, which 'provides that everyone has a right to freedom of religion, including the right to manifest this religion in practice and observance', and Article 27 of the International Covenant on Civil and Political Rights, which says that members of minority groups 'shall not be denied the right . . . to profess and practise their own religion'.[58] However, an appeal to religious liberty provides only spurious support for this and other similar exemptions, because the law does not restrict religious liberty, only the ability to eat meat.

However insubstantial it may be, the argument from religious liberty is often put forward in this kind of context and has been found persuasive by the British parliament.

> In 1976 Parliament enacted a special exemption for turbaned Sikhs from the statutory requirement that all motorcyclists must wear crash helmets. . . . Parliament voted in favour of the special exemption with little debate because it wished to safeguard the religious freedom of the Sikh community in Britain even though there was a strong counter-argument about the need for safety on the roads.[59]

In the discussion within a Standing Committee of the House of Commons, 'the value of religious freedom was stressed by several speakers', so the question was conceived as one of 'whether the right to religious freedom should predominate over the principle of equal treatment in the enforcement of measures promoting road safety'.[60]

The requirement that drivers and passengers should wear helmets was introduced in 1971 with no exemptions. This was challenged in court on the ground that 'the regulations [requiring a helmet] were null and void as being in contravention of the guarantee of freedom of religion enshrined in the European Convention of Human Rights'. Lord Widgery disposed of this claim with the crisp remark: 'No one is bound to ride a motor cycle. All that the law prescribes is that if you do ride a motor cycle you must wear a crash helmet.'[61] The European Commission on Human Rights rejected a similar claim based on freedom of religion, saying that 'the compulsory wearing of crash helmets is a necessary safety measure for motor cyclists. The Commission is of the opinion therefore that any interference there may be with the applicant's freedom of religion was justified for the protection of health in accordance with article 9 (2).'[62] If the regulations could be said to have interfered with freedom of religion, it was an interference justified by (as the judgement continued) 'the valid health considerations on which the regulations are based'.[63] But the wording leaves it open whether or not the regulations could properly be counted as an interference at all. Lord Widgery's argument was that they did not, because the inability to ride a motorcycle does not prevent a Sikh from observing any demands of his religion. This is the right answer.

Lord Widgery continued by saying that Sikhs were 'prevented from riding a motor cycle, not because of the English law but by the requirements of their religion'.[64] Poulter criticizes this by saying that he was 'transparently wrong in stating that their faith precluded the riding of motor cycles when it clearly did not. It was the provisions of English law which had this effect.'[65] This is as silly as asking if it is the upper or lower blade of a pair of scissors that cuts the paper. The essential point is that the practice of their religion entails that turbaned Sikhs cannot ride a motorcycle without exposing themselves to a risk of preventable head injuries. The question is then whether or not they should nevertheless be allowed to assume that risk. The important point made by Lord Widgery in this context is that if they are not given an exemption they are not discriminated against by the law, as they would be if there were a law that said 'No Sikh may ride a motorcycle.' To say, as Poulter does, that it is the law that precludes Sikhs from riding motorcycles assimilates a crash helmet law to this quite different kind of law, which could quite correctly be said to be discriminatory.

Once again we must insist on the crucial difference between a denial of equal opportunities to some group (for example, a law forbidding Sikhs to ride motorcycles) and a choice some people make out of that from a set of equal opportunities (for example, a choice not to ride a motorcycle) as a result of certain beliefs. Those who believe that, even with a crash helmet, riding a motorcycle is too dangerous to be a rational undertaking are (in exactly the same, misleading, sense) 'precluded' from riding one. We all constantly impose restrictions on ourselves in choosing among the options that are legally available to us according to our beliefs about what is right, polite, decent, prudent, professionally appropriate, and so on. Atheists are entitled to feel offended at the idea that the only restraints on self-gratification derive from religious belief.

It is interesting to note that, in the parliamentary debates, the ritual slaughter exemption was drawn on as an argument for the exemption of Sikhs from the requirement of wearing a crash helmet.[66] We thus see how one dubious case is deployed to support another. The claim that exemptions for ritual slaughter are about religious freedom, as members of parliament seem to have believed, is just as bogus as in the crash helmet case, and for exactly the same reason: to adapt Lord Widgery's lapidary words, nobody is bound to eat meat. (Some Orthodox Jews are vegetarians.) Assuming that killing animals without prior stunning falls below the prevailing standards for the humane treatment of animals, the point is that those who are not prepared to eat meat from animals killed in any other way cannot eat meat without violating these minimum standards. It is not the law but the facts (assuming the facts bear it out) of neurophysiology that make this so. The law may condone the additional suffering of animals killed without prior stunning, but if it does we should be clear that what it is doing is accommodating the tastes of a subset of carnivores, not observing the demands of religious freedom.

As in the ritual slaughter case, it is hard to steer a path between the conclusion that wearing a crash helmet is so important that all motorcyclists should have to do it and the alternative of saying that this is a matter that people should be left free to decide for themselves. There is one argument for making turbans a special case that would be valid if its premises were true. However, the minor (factual) premise of the argument is not true. The major premise has been put forward by Parekh as follows: 'if another headgear served the purpose [of avoiding death and injury] equally well [as a crash helmet], there was no reason to disallow it.'[67] This is undoubtedly true, and if turbans did serve this purpose equally well there would be no need to stipulate that the right to wear a turban instead of a crash helmet should be restricted to Sikh motorcyclists: the law could simply specify either a crash helmet or a turban. The minor premise consists in the claim that 'the turban largely satisfied that criterion' (that is to say, the criterion that whatever headgear was worn should avert death or injury as well as a crash helmet), and the conclusion is then drawn that, in virtue of this equivalence, the turban 'was accepted as legally equivalent to the helmet'.[68] This is an imaginative reconstruction of the terms of the parliamentary debate, such as it was. In fact, the government's spokesman denied explicitly, on the basis of test results, 'that a properly tied turban in itself provides adequate protection in the event of an accident involving a blow to the head'.[69] The choice was presented as one between 'road safety criteria' and 'religious tolerance', and this way of structuring the issue appears to have been generally accepted.[70] Thus, Parekh's argument is invalidated by the falsity of its factual premise.

The relevance of the test results for the incidence of death and injury among motorcyclists could be challenged by suggesting that they assume no difference in behaviour between those wearing helmets and those not wearing them. Thus, if it said that 'by wearing a helmet the risk of death could be reduced by 40 per cent and the risk of serious injury by 10 per cent', the reply might be made that these figures translate into actual deaths and serious injuries only if those with and without helmets have accidents at exactly the same rate.[71] Perhaps those lacking the protection of a helmet drive more safely, so that their rate of death and serious injury is no higher than that among those wearing helmets. If there is anything at all in this idea, it may be noted that it depends upon those who do not wear helmets being in possession of accurate information about their much greater exposure to death or serious injury from an accident of any given degree of gravity. Those who, like Parekh, propagate the myth that turbans are as safe as helmets will have a lot to answer for in this case.

Suppose, however, that people did have accurate information about risks and (consciously or unconsciously) adapted their behaviour to keep constant the level of risk of death or serious injury to which they exposed themselves. Then the conclusion would still not be that there should be a special exemption for turban-wearing Sikhs. Rather, it should be concluded that there is no point in imposing any safety measures that can be offset by changes in behaviour, because they are bound to be self-defeating. The hard-core version of this 'risk-budget' theory would suggest, indeed, that even safety measures that cannot be offset will fail to alter the death rate in the long run: if flying became less safe because airlines spent less money on maintenance, people would adapt (even if they flew as often as before) by being infinitesimally more cautious in overtaking or infinitesimally more careful when crossing the road so as to keep their 'risk budget' in balance. Quite apart from its limited a priori plausibility, this theory appears to be contradicted by the facts: in 1976, when the crash helmet law had been running for five years without any provision for an exemption, 'the Ministry of Transport estimated that compulsory helmets were saving around 200 fatal and serious casualties each year' – and this despite the fact that 80 per cent of motorcyclists had already been wearing crash helmets before the legislation became effective.[72]

A more direct, and more defensible, argument against a compulsory crash helmet measure is that the legislation is paternalistic, and that if people choose not to wear crash helmets the resultant injuries are (literally) on their own heads. Libertarians may object on principle to having to adhere to such a law. Others may object not on general principle but on the ground that the thrill of riding a motorcycle at high speed is severely compromised by having to wear a crash helmet: a former colleague in North America once assured me that nothing matches riding a Harley-Davidson at full throttle down a deserted freeway, and that a bare head is essential to the value of the experience. These may add their voices to those of Sikhs in demanding to be allowed to decide for themselves what risks to take.

It is sometimes suggested that the case for a compulsory crash helmet measure can be made without appealing to paternalistic considerations. The argument is that the extra cost to the National Health Service arising from injuries that could have been avoided by wearing a helmet justifies the imposition of the rule. I strongly suspect that those who put forward this argument are for the most part actually moved by the paternalistic desire to reduce the toll of death and paralysis resulting from preventable head injuries but are deterred by the bogeyman of paternalism from saying so. In any case, the argument is superficial. If we really want to pursue the kind of macabre analysis proposed, we should bear in mind that a helmet is estimated as reducing deaths by 40 per cent but injuries by only 10 per cent. Deaths – provided they occur before arrival at the hospital – are cheap, involving only the cost of transport to the mortuary; in comparison, the last months of people who die of natural causes are often very expensive. Moreover, if we carry through this grisly calculus to the end, we have to reckon that healthy people who die suddenly in the prime of life are an excellent source of organ donation, thus saving other lives and also expense, since organ transplants are highly cost-effective in comparison with other forms of treatment. If we do the benefit-cost analysis right, it will perhaps turn out that crash helmets should be prohibited! If we do not believe that any such conclusion should be drawn, however the calculation comes out, then we cannot believe that the case for making crash helmets compulsory rests on benefit-cost considerations either.

Suppose we accept that it is a valid objective of public policy to reduce the number of head injuries to motorcyclists, and that this overrides the counter-argument from libertarian premises. Then it is hard to see how the validity of the objective somehow evaporates in the case of Sikhs and makes room for an exemption from the law requiring crash helmets. As in the ritual slaughter example, the argument for a general rule coupled with a specific exemption has to be made on balance-of-advantage grounds. Perhaps it is actually more plausible in this case, because the balance of gains and losses has Sikhs on both sides of the computation, rather than the desires of Orthodox Jews and Muslims on one side and the suffering of cows and sheep on the other. Nevertheless, it is still necessary to walk a fine line to make the desired answer emerge.

To finish up with a rule-plus-exemption regime, the injury-saving rationale of the law has to be conceded to be powerful enough to justify compulsion of the majority, while at the same time being deemed not powerful enough to outweigh the desire of the minority to ride a motorcycle without a crash helmet. From the other side, if we are too highly impressed by the point that those who choose to avail themselves of the exemption are not harming others but merely undertaking a self-imposed risk, we are liable to conclude that the same privilege should be available to all. Thus Poulter writes that

> there is force in the argument that the people whose safety is principally put at risk are the turbaned Sikhs themselves.... If they decide that the practice of their religion outweighs the greater risk of physical injury, the values of a liberal democracy are hardly imperilled in the way in which they might be if a significant degree of harm was being inflicted upon others.[73]

But why should not anybody else make a similar claim? Religion appears to play no essential part in what is in essence a simple argument to the effect that people should be free to decide for themselves what risks of injury to accept. The case is thus analogous to the one involving the Rastafarians and cannabis discussed at the end of the previous section: if it is valid, the argument implies that the restrictive law should be repealed, not that it should be retained and some people allowed an exemption.

The persuasiveness of the balance-of-interests argument for exemption depends on the context. If not being able to ride a motorcycle ruled out a significant proportion of all the jobs in an area open to somebody with a certain level of trained ability, that would be relevant. But it does not. It would also be a matter of specific concern if the inability to ride a motorcycle prevented Sikhs from joining the police force, because it is important that the police should be open to all, and should in fact contain representatives of all minorities. This is not so much a matter of doing a favour to Sikhs as one of pursuing a benefit to all of us. But there is nothing to prevent police forces from organizing themselves so that Sikh members are not assigned to duties that entail riding a motorcycle. (The police already, quite rightly, permit Sikhs to wear turbans.)[74]

Where turbans create a real employment problem is in the construction trade, which is the largest single source of employment for Sikhs, because 'the traditional occupation of the Ramgarhia "caste" was skilled work as artisans (carpenters, blacksmiths, bricklayers etc.)'.[75] There is an extremely strong case based in industrial safety for requiring hard hats on construction sites, and 'the turban provides generally poor protection'.[76] Even with a special exemption for Sikhs, the hard hat requirement reduced fatalities within two years of coming into operation from 26 to 15 per year and halved the number of major injuries from 140 to 70.[77] The exemption for Sikhs from the hard hat regulation is, furthermore, in violation of a directive from the Council of the European Communities of 1989 which specifically mandated that 'helmets for head protection on building sites' were to be required for all workers by the end of 1992.[78]

While the case for a universally applicable rule is strong, the particular circumstances make the balance-of-advantage argument for an exemption rather powerful. There is no official figure for the number of Sikhs in Britain but it is estimated at between 300,000 and 500,000.[79] There are 'reckoned to be around 40,000' who are building workers.[80] Assuming that Sikhs have now been settled long enough to have a more or less normal age and sex distribution and that the building workers are all males, this implies, if the lower figure for the total population is correct, that almost half of all male Sikhs of working age are engaged in construction work. Even the high figure for total numbers makes it over a quarter. Clearly, ending this employment for whatever (unknown) proportion of Sikh construction workers who wear turbans could be seriously disruptive socially, especially because Sikhs tend to live in geographically concentrated areas. Employment is important not only as a source of income but also as a means of social integration, so there is a strong argument against the sudden termination of the exemption. At the same time, it is hard to deny that the improvement in safety justified the compulsion of the 70 per cent of construction workers who were not wearing hard hats before the requirement was brought in.[81] Perhaps the most sensible course would be to restrict the exemption to those already employed in the construction trade, and possibly in addition those already embarked on acquiring relevant qualifications. This would accept that those who have already availed themselves of the exemption have acquired a sort of vested interest in the job, while gradually phasing out the inherently dangerous business of working on a construction site with only the protection of a turban.

## 5.　A Pragmatic Case for Exemptions

My argument has been that there is a possible case for letting everybody do what they please and a possible case for constraining everyone alike, but that a great deal of finagling is needed in order to support a general rule with exemptions based on religious beliefs. In the cases considered here, I have made clear my own opinion that the case for having a restrictive law is a strong enough one to tip the balance in favour of universal constraint, apart from a continuation of the exemption from hard hat regulations for existing beneficiaries. Nothing turns on that as far as the validity of the general argument is concerned, and some readers may well think that in some cases the libertarian solution is the appropriate one. There is, however, one asymmetry between the two logically coherent positions. This involves the practical problems of moving from a currently anomalous situation to either of the internally consistent ones.

Anyone who believes that the case for having a restrictive law is strong enough to justify universal constraint is bound to believe, of course, that repealing a version of the law that contains exemptions so that there were no constraints at all would have bad consequences: more animal suffering, more tragic victims of motorcycling accidents, and so on. But it would not have bad effects on relations between members of different religious groups. It might even if anything have good effects in eliminating the cause of any resentment that the majority may feel about special privileges for minorities. In contrast, retaining the law but rescinding the exemptions would have good direct effects but would probably have bad effects on relations between different religious groups and would give an encouraging signal to racists who peddle nostalgic dreams of cultural homogeneity. At the same time, it would be widely regarded by members of religious minorities as representing some kind of attack on their position within the polity, and would thus increase the alienation that they already feel as a result of racially motivated harassment and job discrimination.

There is no need here to weigh the pros and cons to decide where the balance of advantage lies. Suppose, however, that the conclusion reached is that – at any rate in the current parlous state of race relations in Britain – rescinding the existing exemptions would over all do more harm than good. What then should be the position of those who nevertheless think that the constraints now enforced are valuable? The answer is surely that it is preferable to give up on consistency than abandon the advantages of the present legislation. The objectives are, after all, being met quite extensively, and these are not situations in which non-compliance with a general rule undermines the efforts of those who do comply. The good done is in direct proportion to the amount of compliance. If the current amount is the most that is desirable, taking account of side-effects, then the present state of affairs is the best attainable.

Does this mean that the entire argument up to now lacks any practical import? Not at all. For the way in which the existing exemptions are viewed has important policy implications. The usual context in which exemptions such as those discussed above are cited is as illustrations of some general principle mandating respect for religious differences. The suggestion is then made that following through this principle consistently would entail more exemptions for more groups. However, if (as I have maintained) there is no such principle, these cases are not the thin end of the wedge – they are the wedge itself. In other words, they are anomalies to be tolerated because the cure would be worse than the disease. But they provide no support for any extension to new cases. If the argument is made (as it surely will be) that it is inconsistent to have these exemptions and not others of a similar kind, the answer that can be given is that the current exemptions were a mistake that is awaiting rectification at an opportune time, so it would be absurd to add to their number in the meanwhile. Moreover, those that do exist should be limited as tightly as possible.

I can illustrate what I have in mind by going back to my other example involving Sikhs – the exemption that they have been granted from the general prohibition on the carrying of knives in public. There is no doubt that this was introduced, as Poulter says, 'to permit Sikhs to carry their *kirpans* (swords or daggers) in public places without fear of prosecution'.[82] However, it may be recalled that the law was couched in general terms, 'stat[ing] that it is a defence for an accused to prove that he had the article with him in a public place "for religious reasons" '.[83] A consequence of this open-ended exemption was the following case.

In the legend, the young Arthur claimed his 6th-century birthright by answering a challenge where all others had failed. 'Whoso pulleth out this sword of this stone and anvil is rightwise King born of all England.' Yesterday, the man who believes he is Arthur's 20th-century reincarnation wrestled his Excalibur

from the grip of the law. After seven months apart, Arthur Uther Pendragon –
otherwise titled Honoured Pendragon of the Glastonbury Order of Druids,
Official Swordbearer of the Secular Order of Druids and Titular Head of the
Loyal Arthurian Warbands – was reunited with the 3ft-long, double-edged
sword by a judge at Southwark crown court. Dressed in flowing white robes
and a green velvet cloak, the former biker heard Judge Stephen Robbins
declare himself satisfied that Pendragon was a genuine druid who used the
sword for ceremonial purposes.... The sword and a ritual dagger were taken
from Pendragon when he was arrested at a demonstration in Trafalgar Square
in April. The prosecution had argued the weapons should be confiscated for
good. But after reading reports from Ronald Hutton, professor of history at
Bristol university and the country's leading authority on druids, Judge Robbins dismissed the charges. He said 'Professor Hutton leaves this court in no
doubt that this defendant's druid credentials are genuine. It is not in the public
interest to pursue the case.'[84]

As I observed earlier in this chapter, states cannot, if they are going to give
privileges to religions impartially, avoid taking some decision about what is
to count. 'For American witches, a watershed event occurred in September
1986, when a Federal appeals court ruled that Wicca was a religion protected
by the constitution.'[85] Wicca is a broad, but rapidly growing, church:

given the movement's diversity, without essential texts, no central authorities
and many solitary practitioners, estimates of how many people fit under the
pagan umbrella vary widely, from 100,000 to three or more times that number.
Some have found historical antecedents for their beliefs and work to re-create
ancient Egyptian or Greek religions; some call themselves Druids.[86]

In Britain, 'paganism, which embraces a colourful mix of druids, witches and
followers of the Viking god Odin, is recognised as a "faith" by the Home
Office'.[87] As a result, 'the Home office pays for 30 pagans to visit devotees in
jail'.[88] Similarly, 'the Department of Health pays the expenses of 50 pagan
chaplains who visit hospitals under the "right to solace" enshrined in the
patient's charter'.[89] Despite this official recognition, however, 'the country's
fastest-growing religion has been stripped of its charitable status by the
Charity Commission and has consequently lost lucrative tax perks'.[90]

This reverses a decision taken ten years earlier that 'first granted charitable status to a [sic] openly pagan trust'.[91] The Commission's arguments for
taking this step are remarkably weak. One is that 'paganism has many
strands and there is a difficulty in its definition and identifying teaching
which it promotes'. The other is that 'any charity must be established for
public benefit. This is not apparent in the case of paganism.'[92] I cannot see
that paganism is any less of a public benefit than any other religion: neither
in Britain nor in the USA do religions normally have to prove, in order to

acquire favourable tax treatment, that they provide public benefits over and above those presumed to flow from their simply being religious. Moreover, the charities that have been deregistered are far more clearly beneficial to the public (as against benefiting their own adherents solely) than any churches: these include a charity 'created to raise money to buy threatened woodlands associated with ancient rituals' and the Pagan Hospice and Funeral Trust, which 'had been a charity for a year, tending to sick people of all faiths without complaint' (according to its former head) when it was denied charitable status.[93]

As far as content is concerned, the 'former chaplain-general at the Home office' told the Charity Commission that paganism 'is a valid religion, having a deity and a clearly defined system of beliefs and practice'.[94] This is, perhaps, putting it a bit too strongly. Nevertheless, the credentials of paganism will certainly bear comparison with those of any other religion. Its cult antedates that of Christianity in Britain. Moreover, the propitiation of the chthonic deities or spirits is the closest thing there is to a universal religion, and is probably the oldest. (It has been suggested that neolithic cave-paintings may have had something to do with it.) Indeed, in the absence of belief in a special revelation, its claims seem rather strong, since nobody who is not wholly lacking in sensibility can fail to be moved by a sense of awe at the forces of nature. The worst that can be said of contemporary pagans is that they do not altogether dispel an air of postmodern irony. But that is not a sufficient basis for dismissing the judge at Southwark Crown Court as a buffoon and the expert witness as a dupe. Those who are unhappy with the outcome in the case of Arthur Pendragon's sword should admit that dignifying a pragmatic concession to Sikhs with the trappings of a general rule defined in terms of a religion was a mistake. It would be wiser to beat an unprincipled retreat, amending the legislation so that it refers only to Sikhs.

Alternatively, here as elsewhere, the need to worry about exemptions to a general rule could be avoided by abolishing the rule altogether. The case for doing so might be put by arguing that the existence of a law prohibiting the carrying of knives will not actually prevent the ill-intentioned from carrying them anyway, and that there is nothing to fear from those who are not ill-intentioned. This is parallel to the case that the American gun lobby has pressed (successfully in a number of states) for legislation permitting the carrying of concealed firearms in public. I believe that the argument is equally flawed in both instances, for two reasons. First, if the ill-intentioned are stopped by the police before using their illegal weapons, they can be disarmed and also charged with an offence. And, second, intentions are not always decisive: you may not plan to get into a drunken brawl when you set out for the evening, but if you are carrying a knife (and even more, of course, a gun) the brawl has a greater potentiality of leading to serious injury.

Moreover, you are more likely to carry a knife just in case you might need it if you think that others are likely to be carrying them, and they are more likely to do so if they think people like you will... and so on in a vicious spiral. Even if a law prohibiting the carrying of knives has mainly a declaratory effect (and this is a more important function of law than is commonly recognized), it may still succeed in coordinating expectations at the non-knife equilibrium rather than at the equilibrium at which the carrying of knives in public is widespread. Provided that the exemption for Sikhs does not do too much damage to the achievement of the non-knife equilibrium, there is a clear case for preferring it to the alternative of repealing the law altogether.

## 6.   Culture and Job Discrimination

There are a variety of jobs outside the construction industry in which injuries to the head are to be feared. These are not covered by the legislation that exempts turban-wearing Sikhs from the requirement imposed on other workers to wear a hard hat. Let us suppose that an employer whose business is not covered by the legislation imposes a hard hat requirement on all workers deemed to be in danger of head injuries. He may cite in defence the raised insurance premiums to which he would otherwise be liable, the greater risk that work will be disrupted due to injury if not all workers are protected, and the danger that somebody who incurs a head injury poses to fellow workers by falling on them or dropping things on them from a height. Does a Sikh who is thereby prevented from wearing his turban on the job have good grounds for claiming that he has suffered from discrimination? Such cases have been litigated in Britain, and it has been decided that the employer is justified in imposing the hard hat requirement. As a consequence, the employer has won in these cases, because a charge of discrimination is annulled if the condition of employment imposed is held to be justifiable.[95]

In this concluding section, I shall focus on cases such as these: that is to say, cases in which there is no specific exemption deriving from primary legislation but in which the claim is made, on the basis of general anti-discrimination law, that some condition of work imposed by an employer constitutes job discrimination. Let me begin at the beginning by asking what, from an egalitarian liberal point of view, is wrong with job discrimination. This will make it easier to see why some things should count and others not. A central principle of egalitarian liberalism, it may be recalled, is equality of opportunity. But the concept of equal opportunity is a difficult one, and it has to be interpreted differently in different contexts. Thus, in its most general signification, equality of opportunity may be characterized as equality of choice sets. In the context of employment, however, it requires a narrower definition. It is not a violation of equality of the opportunity to be employed as a brain surgeon if only those who are qualified as brain surgeons are considered, even though this eliminates an element from the choice sets of all others. What equality of opportunity means in relation to employment is that those who are equally well qualified to do a job have an equal chance of getting the job. If some people who are as well qualified as others are denied an equal chance of employment in some job, they can complain of (unfair) discrimination.

In some instances, establishing the existence of discrimination entails statistical tests, comparing the proportion of qualified applicants in different racial groups (for example) with the proportion appointed. This is a use of group-based measurements that is, incidentally, entirely compatible with the principles of liberal individualism. For the objective is to ensure that individuals are not treated unfairly. In other cases, discrimination is so blatant that there is no need of statistical tests to establish its presence. All that is needed is to send a candidate with certain qualifications for a job, and compare his or her experience with that of another with the same qualifications but different ascriptive characteristics. Thus, if the black candidate is told that the job is filled while the white candidate is offered it, that amounts to virtual proof of discrimination. Unhappily, such experiments regularly demonstrate the existence of pervasive discrimination in the United Kingdom.

Equal opportunity entails that each applicant for a job should be considered on his or her individual merits. Thus, even if the possession of some job qualification is associated statistically with some characteristic, this does not excuse the blanket exclusion from employment of those with this characteristic. For example, if some job genuinely requires a certain degree of physical strength to perform it satisfactorily and men are much more likely than women to have this degree of strength, it would be quite efficient for an employer to refuse to consider women for it, since this would reduce the cost of selecting workers. But taking the decision on an individual basis is a cost that employers have to bear in order to provide equality of opportunity. Statistical discrimination of this kind is an example of a practice that may be said to have a rational basis from the point of view of the employer, but is still ruled out as unfair. For it clearly fails to provide everybody equally capable of doing a certain job with an equal chance of getting it.

Similarly, employers cannot cite pure prejudice on the part of fellow workers or customers in justification of a refusal to employ members of certain ascriptive groups. Even if it is true that many customers in some area prefer to be served by white shop assistants, and that some will choose a shop catering to their prejudices over one that does not, permitting firms to base employment criteria on these facts would clearly subvert any notion of equal opportunity. For it would mean that people could be denied a job simply on the basis of ascriptive characteristics. Hence, the notion of a relevant qualification must be construed in terms of relevant behaviour, as distinct from identity as such. This does not mean, however, that the criteria must be purely technical or mechanical. For some jobs, for example, it may be perfectly reasonable to say that a certain quality of personal charm is highly desirable. (I shall return to this issue in the next chapter.)

In Britain, discrimination on the basis of race or ethnicity is illegal, though penalties are inadequate and enforcement insufficiently vigorous. On the mainland of Britain, though not in Northern Ireland, discrimination on the basis of religion is not illegal. There is a certain rationale for treating religion in Northern Ireland as the equivalent of ethnicity because it is a place in which 'Protestant' and 'Catholic' are the names of communities. To find out which community somebody belongs to involves an inquiry about their family background. A scrutiny of their precise views about transubstantiation is not required. In this context, discrimination on the basis of religion is the equivalent of discrimination on the basis of any other ascriptive characteristic. What needs to be emphasized, since it will be important later, is that religion here has nothing to do with any kind of behaviour related to ability to do the job. Thus, Harland and Wolff, the shipyard that was a major source of employment in Belfast, was notorious for not employing Roman Catholics. This could not be justified by saying that Roman Catholics refused to wear safety equipment on religious grounds or wished to break off work at inconvenient times to pray. It was simply an expression of domination by the Protestant community. If there was any ulterior motive, it was to encourage Catholics to emigrate disproportionately, thus preventing their higher birthrate from changing the ethnic balance within Northern Ireland to the disadvantage of Protestants.

What I have been discussing so far is direct discrimination: treating people differently on the basis of certain ascriptive characteristics. However, the cases that are of interest here have arisen as claims of indirect racial discrimination. The concept of indirect discrimination was incorporated into English law by the 1976 Race Relations Act, which

> renders unlawful certain apparently neutral acts done by employers and others, which are not designed to discriminate against ethnic minorities but which nevertheless have a disproportionate impact on them because of their cultural and religious backgrounds. In particular, the Act's provisions have the effect of making it unlawful for employers and educational establishments to impose standardized rules about uniforms, dress and appearance with which members of minority groups cannot conscientiously comply, unless such rules can be demonstrated to be 'justifiable'.[96]

The question that I shall take up to illustrate the application of the idea of indirect discrimination is this: could a woman who was dismissed from her job – working in an office in London, say – for wearing a headscarf claim to be a victim of unfair discrimination?

Countries that are predominantly Muslim vary enormously in the prevailing norms concerning the appropriate dress for women in public. (This is leaving aside those in which the norm is that women should not appear in public at all.) Within a single country, urban norms are often more liberal than rural ones. Whatever the norms are, they are also enforced differently in different places: sanctions may have the force of law, or they may be imposed arbitrarily by vigilantes (with or without police connivance), or they may take the form of social disapproval and rejection. Muslim immigrants to Britain tend to have been drawn from unsophisticated rural environments, within which it has been a customary practice for women to cover their heads in public. It is also worth bearing in mind the point that diasporas are liable to be culturally conservative, clinging to ways of behaving that have been abandoned in their countries of origin. (A Scandinavian Lutheran from the 1870s would find Lake Wobegon a good deal more congenial than contemporary Oslo or Stockholm.) The claim that wearing some kind of head covering is a customary practice can therefore be brought forward to show that forbidding it is illegal discrimination, unless the employer can prove that it is justifiable.

One authority, Professor Gordon Conway, has suggested along these lines that 'a young Asian woman might be successful in arguing in court that a headscarf is a custom of Pakistan, where her parents came from'.[97] He complains, however, that a convert to Islam from a Christian family background would not have any case under the Race Relations Act, because religious discrimination is not illegal in Britain. Muslims have been ruled not to constitute an ethnic group, so Muslim religious practices cannot claim protection *per se* under the Race Relations Act.[98] However, immigrants and their descendants who are of Pakistani or Bangladeshi origins are undeniably an ethnic group, and can therefore claim indirect discrimination based on their membership of that group. If a ban on the wearing of a headscarf were held to be disproportionately disadvantageous to members of this group, it would follow that it could be treated as prima facie indirect racial discrimination.

Even if religious discrimination were outlawed, Conway's hypothetical convert to Islam might still fail in court if the norm requiring the wearing of a head covering were held to be customary rather than religious. For it could then be concluded that only those whose traditional culture contained the norm could claim the protection of the law. I shall suppose, however, that it could be argued successfully that a conscientious Muslim convert could reasonably feel an obligation to cover her head, even if other converts could reasonably reach a different conclusion. (Whether reasonableness is needed or whether it is enough simply to hold the belief sincerely is a question I shall postpone until chapter 5.)

Clearly, the situation complained of by Conway constitutes an 'anomaly' (as he suggests it does) only on the assumption that religious discrimination should be prohibited as such. Should it be? It can be argued that giving protection to people on the strength of religion is to open a can of worms. However, the expansive conception of ethnicity adopted by the House of Lords has already opened that can, and faced courts with adjudicating claims of indirect discrimination arising from religiously mandated practices. Moreover, most of the work of industrial tribunals and the courts reviewing their decisions turns around questions about what kind of behaviour by employees can and cannot reasonably be treated by employers as grounds for dismissal. While, therefore, 'justifiability' is a vague notion in itself, legislation outlawing indirect religious discrimination that cannot be justified could latch on to a formidable body of existing case law.

How might the question of justifiability be argued in the case of headscarves? It is consistent with everything said so far that the reason for wishing to wear a headscarf is relevant. If wearing a headscarf were a purely personal preference, it is doubtful that it would be appropriate to bring to bear the ponderous machinery of the law in order to enforce a right to wear one. Specifically, there could be no reasonable basis for describing a ban on headscarves as constituting unfair job discrimination in such circumstances. This still leaves the question: should a ban on headscarves count as unfair discrimination if wearing one has customary or religious significance? Those who are anxious to be on the side of the angels will regard the case as an open and shut one. All the more reason, then, for putting the other side. Dress codes are a matter of convention: what is appropriate for praying in a mosque is one thing, what is appropriate for working in an office is another. Immigrants have always accepted that some accommodation with the host society will be necessary – the most obvious accommodation being to learn its language. (I shall take this up in the next chapter.) An Englishwoman who chose to work in Pakistan would be expected to conform to local sensibilities in the way of dress. Why should not those who want a job in the mainstream economy leave the customs of Pakistan behind in Pakistan?

One way of posing the question is to ask if headscarves are within the scope of the response 'This is the way we do things here.' There are unquestionably some things that are covered by it, the traffic code being the most straightforward and most commonly cited. There are also unquestionably some things that are not: Christianity is an equally obvious example on that side. The argument against the appropriateness of 'This is the way we do things here' in the headscarf case is fairly clear. All dress codes are, in the last analysis, conventional. These conventions are, nevertheless, heavily freighted with symbolic import. That they could have been otherwise is neither here nor there: what matters is the way that they actually are. To abandon a long-established custom that enjoins women not to appear in public with uncovered heads is no trivial matter. Since there is no non-trivial reason in support of a ban on headscarves, the ban is rightly to be regarded as a denial of equal opportunity, or at the very least an unreasonable infringement of the right to make a living without having to make a gratuitous sacrifice.

Professor Conway, whom I quoted in introducing this topic, is clearly locked into the paradigm of exemptions for specific groups from general rules. For it is on the basis of this that he wishes to extend the exemption from 'ethnic' Muslims to Muslim converts. This is fair enough as far as it goes. It is the implication of my overall argument, however, that it does not go far enough because the whole rule-and-exemption approach is suspect. It seems to me as obnoxious that an employee who had converted to Islam might have to produce a certificate from a mosque before she was allowed to wear a headscarf as it would be if she had to produce a record of regular church attendance before being allowed to wear a crucifix. The essential question is whether or not the wearing of headscarves can legitimately be claimed by an employer to interfere with the operations of the business. If this claim cannot be sustained, it is hard to see why employers should be licensed to carry out intrusive investigations into their employees' religious affiliations simply in order to be able to deny permission to 'rogue' headscarf-wearers. It is one thing to say that the right to wear a headscarf would be weakly founded if it were never more than a matter of personal preference. Once the right has been won, however, why should not those for whom it is a matter of personal preference be able to take advantage of it?

I specified in raising the example that the context was employment in an office. Would it make a difference if it were changed to employment as a shop assistant in a department store? Those who manage these emporia operate on the assumption that what customers want is a service but not necessarily a personal statement, and therefore tend to have rigid codes specifying dress and prohibiting personal adornments. They may fear that some of their customers will prefer to take their business to some rival establishment in which the experience of shopping does not include confrontation with a form of dress that they may regard as having not only religious significance but also as symbolizing the inferior status of women. The customers could be wrong about this: according to two Canadian political philosophers, 'one could make a plausible case that French *haute couture*, by constructing female identity in terms of a women's [*sic*] ability to dress in ways that are attractive to men, has contributed more to the subordination of women – think of short skirts and high heels – than the *hijab* ever did'.[99] I am inclined to doubt that this view is ever likely to be

found plausible outside the circles moved in by Canadian political philosophers, but that is beside the point. Whether a distaste for headscarves
could be held to have a rational basis or not, the implication of the maxim
that 'the customer is always right' will be that those who run shops should be
entitled to take account of the prejudices of their customers in deciding
whom to employ. But I have already argued that this principle cannot be
endorsed unless we are going to let employers drive a coach and horses
through anti-discrimination legislation. For then they could legitimately
appeal to the racial prejudices of their customers as a justification for
reflecting those prejudices in their hiring policies.

As far as the headscarf case is concerned, I think we have to say bluntly
that one of the costs of cultural heterogeneity is that, in implementing anti-
discrimination legislation, we simply cannot afford to ask if negative reactions to behaviour are well-founded or not, provided the behaviour in
question does not actually get in the way of the efficient discharge of the
task in hand, narrowly defined. That proviso, it need hardly be said, leaves a
lot of room for interpretation. The principle, however, is clear: culturally
derived characteristics that do not demonstrably interfere with the ability to
do the job cannot be accepted as a basis for job discrimination.

The headscarf question has been the centre of a controversy in France,
where the symbolic significance of the headscarf was the key to the position
of both sides. *L'affaire du foulard* was precipitated when some Muslim
schoolgirls in the town of Creil, north of Paris, went to school wearing
headscarves. When they were sent home by the school, a major dispute
erupted which eventually drew in the public intellectuals and the politicians.
Among those whose self-perception put them on the left, there was a sharp
division between on one side those who inveighed against an action that they
saw as expressing or at any rate fostering anti-Algerian prejudice and on the
other side those who saw the headscarf as a symbol of female subjection,
hinting darkly at family pressure, especially from fathers and brothers.
However, the issue as it presented itself to those charged with running the
schools did not turn on any of these things. The key for them was the *laïcité*
of the French public school system.[100] The headscarf, as a religious symbol,
was claimed to be a threat to this lay status. When it was pointed out that no
objection was made to the wearing of a crucifix, the defenders of the headscarf ban resorted to a distinction between discreet and prominent religious
symbols. Needless to say, the opponents found this distinction contrived.

To put this dispute into perspective, a couple of things should be borne in
mind about France. The first is that the republican tradition has throughout
been non-racist but assimilationist. Anybody could become French, but the
entrance ticket was fairly high: command of the French language, absorption into French culture, a knowledge of (and the right attitude towards) the
major events in French history, and so on. The second is that schools, along

with the army, have been the institutions entrusted with the major role of creating French citizens on this model. This has been largely a matter of homogenizing the linguistically and culturally disparate regions of France itself, but it has also included the assimilation of immigrants. The militantly lay status of the schools is an aspect of this republican mission.

The point of interest here is that in the British context the religious significance of the headscarf counts in its favour, but in the French context it is precisely the religious significance of the headscarf that condemns it. The position is almost that in France headscarves would be fine if there were nothing to wearing them except an expression of personal taste – the precise opposite of conventional British rule-and-exemption thinking. Secular public schools are a possible form of the privatization of religion, provided that attendance at them is not compulsory. However, the difficulty of the French position seems to me to be that it is simply not very plausible to suggest that headscarves will really undermine *laïcité*. A less vulnerable argument would be, I believe, a version of the one advanced earlier on the anti-headscarf side in Britain: that dress codes are a matter of convention and schools can legitimately decide on the convention to be observed in them. It has to be conceded, however, that this is open to the counterargument that wearing or not wearing a headscarf cannot simply be declared to be a matter of convention if for some people it manifestly is not because it has religious or customary significance.

In Britain, it may be noted, the conventionalist case for imposing a school dress code has been decisively rejected by the House of Lords. The leading case involved a turban-wearing Sikh boy aged thirteen who was refused admission to a private school in Birmingham on the ground that he failed to comply with the school's rules, which 'prescribed a particular uniform, including a cap, and required boys to have their hair cut short so as not to touch the collar'.[101] This was the leading case that established Sikhs as an ethnic group for the purposes of the Race Relations Act on the ground that they were a 'separate and distinct community'.[102] Once this hurdle had been cleared, it was straightforward that the school rule was discriminatory, since it was unquestionably one 'which was such that the proportion of Sikhs who could comply with it was considerably smaller than the proportion of non-Sikhs who could so comply', in the sense that fewer could not comply with it 'consistently with the[ir] customs and cultural conditions'.[103] The only remaining question was: could the rule nevertheless be held to be justifiable? The headmaster put forward (among others) the argument 'that the school was seeking to minimise the external differences between boys of different races and social classes, to discourage the competitive fashions which tend to exist in a teenage community'.[104] But this (along with the other arguments) was dismissed by Lord Fraser as failing to 'provide a sufficient justification for what was *prima facie* a discriminatory school rule'.[105]

The examples considered in this section have been ones in which the case against enforcing a rule that worked to the detriment of religious or cultural minorities was strong. On the one side was a denial of equal occupational or educational opportunity, and on the other side no interest that was worthy of protection. Wearing a headscarf to work or a turban to school threatened no danger to the public or to the individuals concerned, nor could it plausibly be said to interfere with the effective functioning of the business or the school. The only question that they raised was, therefore, whether the rule-and-exemption approach was the appropriate one or whether the libertarian alternative was better. In the employment case, I argued that, if once the employer's demand for complete uniformity had been rejected, there seemed little to be said for restricting the right to wear a headscarf to certified Muslims. For this would invest discretionary power in religious officials and employers while serving no plausibly legitimate (i.e. job-related) purpose.

In the school case, there is more to be said for the rule-and-exemption approach. The headmaster's argument in favour of a school uniform is, at the very least, one that many parents find persuasive. That is, perhaps, a good enough basis for saying that parents who want to send their children to a school that enforces the wearing of a uniform should be entitled to do so. And that, obviously, entails that schools must be allowed to make the wearing of the uniform a condition of attendance. Under these circumstances, it seems reasonable to say that the breach in uniformity to accommodate minority religious beliefs or cultural practices should be kept as small as possible. This is the kind of case in which the rule-and-exemption approach comes into its own.

To sum up, the rule-and-exemption approach has a role to play in accommodating minority beliefs and practices, but it is far from being the panacea that it is commonly represented as by multiculturalists. To make sense, it requires a combination of very precise conditions that are rarely satisfied all together. It must be important to have a rule generally prohibiting conduct of a certain kind because, if this is not so, the way in which to accommodate minorities is simply not to have a rule at all. At the same time, though, having a rule must not be so important as to preclude allowing exceptions to it. We are left with cases in which uniformity is a value but not a great enough one to override the case for exemptions. The case of the Sikh boy whose turban contravened the school rules is a good example of this, but I do not believe that there are too many others.

# 3

## The Dynamics of Identity: Assimilation, Acculturation and Difference

### 1. Vive la Différence?

The thesis that public policies should not be designed to mete out special treatment to members of groups defined by their cultural characteristics has been ascribed by Charles Taylor to something he calls 'difference-blind liberalism'.[1] The differences to which Taylor refers are not those between rich and poor, employed and unemployed, well-educated and ill-educated, and so on. The egalitarian liberal conception of justice is not blind to these or to their importance: on the contrary, it will condemn as unjust much of the inequality along those dimensions to be found in contemporary societies. Taylor, in common with the other exponents of the 'politics of difference' addressed in this book, sees himself on the left. Yet, as Todd Gitlin has observed (with the United States especially in mind), 'the politics of identity is silent on the deepest sources of social misery: the devastation of the cities, the draining of resources away from the public and into the private hands of the few.'[2]

Specifically, there has in the past two decades been a large increase in the concentration of wealth and in the disparity of incomes – both those arising from earnings and those arising from holdings of capital – while at the same time taxes on income and capital gains have become less progressive and estate duties have become almost voluntary. These trends have affected most western countries, but Britain and the United States the most. Since 1977, three-fifths of all households in the United States have become poorer, with the poorest losing the most. Over 90 per cent of the increase in the national income over this period has gone to those in the top 1 per cent of the distribution, and the rest to those in the top two-fifths. 'The gap between rich and poor has grown into such an economic chasm that this year the richest 2.7 million Americans, the top 1 per cent, will have as many after-tax dollars to spend as the bottom 100 million.'[3] Right at the top, the gains have been even more remarkable. In 1980, 'the typical C.E.O. of a big American company was taking home about forty times the annual earnings of a typical worker on the factory floor'.[4] By 1990, 'they took in about eighty five times as much as factory workers'. Then 'between 1990 and 1998, . . . the annual "compensation" of C.E.Os. at large firms rose from $1.8 million to $10.6 million. . . . Last year, big-league C.E.Os. pocketed, on the average, four hundred and nineteen times the earnings of a typical production worker.'[5]

At the same time, especially in Britain, there has been a greater spread in the quality of education and health care available to people with different incomes: as the gap between rich and poor widens, those at the top can increasingly afford to buy their way out of the system of publicly provided schools and hospitals. These public services are then liable to deteriorate further in response to pressure from wealthy and influential people for keeping down the taxes that pay for services they do not use. Within the universities, the academic multiculturalists exhaust their energies in arguing about the content of reading lists, but nobody seems to care much about the increasing inequality of opportunity to go to a university, especially the sort that offers the best prospects of entry into elite occupations. In England, not only Oxford and Cambridge but also the London School of Economics (which does not have their traditional connection with the elite private schools) recruit over half their undergraduate intake from private schools, while in the United States the increase in unequal opportunity has been even more striking: 'In 1979, a student from the top quarter of American families had four times the chance of earning a B.A. degree at the age of 24 as a student in the bottom quarter. In 1994, a student from the top quarter had nineteen times the chance.'[6]

If (God forbid!) I were inclined to engage in polemics, I might feel drawn to expressing the view that it is the multiculturalists who are blind to the ever-widening differences that are such a deplorable feature of most contemporary western societies. As it is, however, I shall accept the epithet 'difference-blind' for the position that I am defending in this book. To say that it is blind to difference is, of course, intended pejoratively. Let us recall, however, that the figure of justice is traditionally represented as blindfold. The basis for this is that justice is supposed to be dispensed in a way that takes no account of factors that are irrelevant to reaching a just verdict. If liberalism is indeed blind to cultural differences, we should not assume immediately that this must be a fault: it may in some circumstances be precisely what is required.

The gist of Taylor's complaint is that the egalitarian liberal position is 'inhospitable to difference'.[7] Only in the form of a 'more hospitable variant' that he favours can it be 'cleared of the charge of homogenizing difference'.[8] I agree with Taylor that 'this form of liberalism is guilty as charged by the proponents of a politics of difference' on a number of counts.[9] But this is a virtue: it is 'difference-blind' liberalism that gets the right answers and the 'politics of difference' that should be rejected. For example, justice demands that under some conditions state services should be offered in more than one language. (I shall take up the specification of these conditions at the end of this chapter.) But it may still be that a language becomes extinct, simply because those speaking it take decisions that in aggregate result in its disappearing. Very many languages have done just that in the past and doubtless many more will do so in future: two thousand of the world's six thousand languages have fewer than one thousand speakers, and are unlikely to survive. A liberal society cannot adopt policies designed to keep a language in existence if those who speak it prefer to let it go. Thus, Taylor is quite correct in saying that liberalism 'can't capture the full thrust of policies designed for cultural survival'.[10] But why should it be expected to?

What liberalism can accommodate is precisely the kind of thing that Taylor says is inadequate: 'having the French language available [in Quebec] for those who might choose it'.[11] Policies that make it illegal for the children of francophone parents to attend any except francophone public schools put the power of the state behind 'those who value remaining true to the culture of our ancestors' while making it difficult or impossible for 'those who might want to cut loose in the name of some individual goal of self-development' to pursue their aspirations.[12] The notion that birth is fate – that simply in virtue of being born into a certain ethnic group one acquires the (potentially enforceable) duty to maintain its 'ancestral culture' – is continuous with a kind of ethnic nationalism that is profoundly at odds with liberalism. What we are faced with here has been decried by Gitlin as 'the cant of identity', which 'proposes to deduce a position, a tradition, a deep truth, or a way of life from a fact of birth, physiognomy, national origin or physical disability'.[13]

We may say that liberalism is, both historically and logically, the result of generalizing the proposition that it is no business of the state to enforce the observance of the true religion – however and by whomever that is defined. Conversely, the notion that the state may (and perhaps should) deploy its coercive powers to ensure the maintenance of the ancestral culture can be seen as what we get by 'culturalizing' the proposition that the legitimate tasks of the state include the enforcement of the true religion. There is, however, one important respect in which 'culturalization' changes the nature of the original doctrine. In its original form, the proposition was that the state should enforce the observance of the *true* religion, and the truth claim was essential to the case for enforcement. In contrast, the proposal to put the state's power behind the maintenance of 'culture' does not rest on any claims about the objective value – truth value or any other value – of the culture in question. (I shall follow up the implications of this idea in chapter 7.) In practice, the idea that tradition is somehow self-validating provides a virtual *carte blanche* for the politicians who define the tradition to decide on the content of education, the arts and the media. It is scarcely surprising, therefore, if the traditions favoured by politicians turn out to promote deference to the powers that be: the 'neo-Confucianism' that scholars tell us was invented out of whole cloth at the behest of Lee Kuan Yew is exceptional only in its blatancy. Taylor himself illustrates the negotiability of the concept of the ancestral culture. True to his allegiance to Herder, he focuses on language; but the ancestral culture of ethnic French Quebecois could with equal authenticity have been defined in terms of adherence to the Roman Catholic Church.[14]

Liberals must stand up for the rights of those who wish to pursue individual goals of self-development. Contrary, however, to a frequently heard claim, liberals are not committed to the attempt to eradicate all traditional ways of life in order to further some ideal of free-floating personal autonomy. (I shall endeavour to lay to rest this *canard* in the next chapter.) The point here is simply that the complaint made by liberals is not against the objective of remaining true to some ancestral culture but against the coercion of those who do not share that objective. If that position makes liberalism 'inhospitable to difference', it is not something to be ashamed of. From Slovakia to Singapore, it is clear that liberal institutions are not safe in states in which the maintenance of a (supposedly or actually) traditional culture is accepted as part of the political agenda.

Taylor asks rhetorically: 'if we are concerned with identity, then what is more legitimate than one's aspiration that it never be lost?'[15] The answer is, of course, that this is a perfectly legitimate aspiration. Similarly, perpetuating one's genes is a perfectly legitimate aspiration. But there are legitimate and illegitimate ways of going about it: rape, for example, is excluded. The aspiration that a collective identity should never be lost is unquestionably one that can legitimately be pursued in a whole number of ways. On the assumption, for example, that a fair (i.e. pro rata) system of state funding was already providing for the support of the French language in Quebec, enthusiasts would be able to add to it from their own pockets, participate in organizations devoted to advancing French culture and language, and so on. There are other means that would be illegitimate, some involving individual action (e.g. defacing English books in libraries) and some collective. Among the latter are the kind of 'measures designed to ensure [group] survival through indefinite future generations' supported by Taylor.[16]

The fundamental error, which is central to Taylor's project, is encapsulated in the title of a collection of essays edited by Will Kymlicka: *The Rights of Minority Cultures*.[17] Cultures are simply not the kind of entity to which rights can properly be ascribed. Communities defined by some shared cultural characteristic (for example, a language) may under some circumstances have valid claims, but the claims then arise from the legitimate interests of the members of the group. On similar lines, Peter Jones has pointed out that

> cultures are not moral entities to which we can owe obligations of fairness. Insisting that we should be fair to cultures merely as cultures is like insisting that we should be fair to paintings or to languages or to musical compositions.... So, if we seek to deal fairly with cultural diversity, it is not cultures that will be the ultimate objects of our concern but the people who bear them.[18]

What follows from neglecting this is illustrated by a case cited by one of the contributors to Kymlicka's own collection of essays. The legislature of the Province of Quebec passed legislation that violated the constitutional provision that 'a parent has the right to have his or her children educated in the minority language [i.e. French or English] of the province in which they reside, provided that the parent was educated in that language in Canada'. The legislation would have allowed the right to choose an education in English for their children 'only to those who were educated in English *in Quebec*'.[19] In response to a legal challenge, counsel for the Quebec government argued that the guarantee 'is intended to ensure the survival of the minority group in each province. Hence, it must not be understood as conferring on every person falling within its terms an individual right to education in the minority language, but rather on the whole minority group a collective right to sufficient educational establishments to ensure its survival.'[20] Taylor claimed, as we have seen, that 'having the French language available for those who might choose it' is not enough if the goal is its indefinite survival – regardless of the desires of the individual speakers of the language. And this is obviously true. The impeccably Taylorian reasoning of counsel for Quebec gives us the other side of the coin. What it shows is that, if we define the objective as cultural survival, it is not even necessary that education in the English language should be available for all those who can claim their ancestral culture to be bound up with English.

This perversion of common sense is bound to happen once the goal of cultural survival is elevated to the status of an end in itself. Human beings then become mere cyphers, to be mobilized as instruments of a transcendent goal. Thus, the logic of counsel's reasoning would suggest that if – as may well happen – the anglophone community in Quebec dwindles at some time in the future (due to further emigration and increased assimilation) to the point at which its survival is threatened, its remaining members could legitimately be compelled to use English-speaking public schools, as their francophone counterparts are now compelled to use French-speaking ones. Some may doubt if the solicitude of a Quebec government for the survival of English would really prove so great if the situation arose. That is neither here nor there. The point is simply that this is the kind of nonsense that follows from attributing an intrinsic value to cultural survival, detached from the interests of the individual bearers of that culture.

## 2.   Liberalism and the 'Ideal of Assimilation'

A popular way of expressing the complaint that liberalism is 'inhospitable to difference' is to say that it is 'assimilationist'. This complaint can take a number of forms. The strongest version maintains that liberalism presupposes the non-existence of any differences between people. The subject of liberal political philosophy, according to this contention, is an abstract being with no distinctive characteristics such as age, sex, ethnocultural identity or nationality. This charge goes right back to the beginning of the Counter-Enlightenment: as I mentioned in chapter 1, Joseph de Maistre said that he knew about Frenchmen and Germans, and so on, but had never come across *man*. The idea that liberalism denies the existence of difference, proceeding as if its principles applied to units of undifferentiated humanity, has become something of a mantra among anti-liberals. Its truth is often, indeed, so taken for granted that it is not considered necessary to offer any evidence for it.

I hope that what has already been said suffices to give the lie to this oft-repeated claim. The liberal notion of equality before the law, so far from resting on the assumption that differences do not exist, is proposed as the fairest way of accommodating them. To rehearse the historically central example once again: demanding that churches and other religious bodies should fit their activities within a uniform legal framework that puts them on an equal footing is actually a way of responding to the importance of the role that religion may play in people's lives. It is precisely because they recognize the potential for destructive conflict inherent in religion that liberals have insisted on a legal regime that depoliticizes religious identity and is in that sense 'difference-blind' with respect to religion. Indeed, in his critique of liberal rights (mentioned in chapter 1), Marx adduced as evidence of their inadequacy the fact that freedom of religion in the United States was associated with the flourishing of religion.[21] For a liberal, however, that provides evidence for the proposition that freedom of religion does not belittle the significance of religion.

When it is not treated as a dogma, the idea that liberalism presupposes the insignificance of difference is usually supported by citing John Rawls's theory of justice.[22] The surprisingly frequent claim that Rawls's theory is designed for disembodied beings and not for real people, with particular commitments and attachments, rests on a complete misunderstanding of Rawls's motives and methods. What the critics seize upon is Rawls's proposal that principles of justice are those that would be chosen to regulate their lives together by people who were temporarily deprived of information about their identities.[23] His invocation of this so-called Original Position, it is said, shows that Rawls fails to recognize the importance to people of gender, ethnocultural identity, religious affiliation, physical and intellectual abilities, and so on. But what it actually shows is the opposite. It is precisely because such things are important to people that it is essential for a theory of justice to take account of them in the right way. To stick to my example, if religion were of trivial significance in people's lives, it could scarcely matter how the polity handled it. Even a state religion, accompanied by civil disabilities (such as lack of access to educational or professional opportunities) or criminal penalties for deviation from it, would be of little import if nobody cared much one way or the other.

What is the right way to deal with difference? Rawls's basic idea is that a sign of our having achieved a just answer is that it is one that can be endorsed as fair by each person, whatever his or her personal characteristics, endowments and commitments may be. The Original Position is put forward as a construction that can generate principles of justice satisfying this criterion. There is no need, for the present purpose, to ask if the Original Position is really well adapted to doing the work that Rawls wants it to do.[24] The point is simply that, so far from overlooking or wishing away difference, Rawls builds his entire structure around the assumption that the main business of a theory of justice is to deal with difference in a manner that can be shown to be fair.

A more subtle but in the end equally perverse thesis about the assimilationist impulse behind liberalism has been put forward by Iris Young. According to this line of analysis, liberalism does not actually assume away the existence of difference, but it is committed to hoping that all the differences constituting people's distinctive social identities will some day disappear. Indeed, liberal principles of equal treatment are, Young alleges, inextricably bound up with this 'ideal of assimilation'. Thus, for example, an 'ideal of assimilation' with regard to race and sex would be realized by a state of affairs in which race and sex were no longer categories with any social meaning. Such a state of affairs would have been achieved when 'the race or sex of an individual would be the functional equivalent of eye color in our society today. While physiological differences in skin color or genitals would remain, they would have no significance for a person's sense of identity or how others regard him or her.'[25]

Where Young muddies the waters is in contrasting this 'ideal of assimilation', which she takes from Richard Wasserstrom, with what she calls an 'ideal of diversity'.[26] For whereas the 'ideal of assimilation' describes a state of affairs that might (or might not, depending on one's point of view) be ideal, the 'ideal of diversity' is defined not in terms of a state of affairs but in terms of a public policy: one in which group identities are given an explicit role in relation to both the inputs and outputs of political decision-making.[27] Without any need for argument, the effect of this categorization is to identify the liberal principle of equal treatment (which is the denial of Young's 'ideal of diversity') with the ideal of assimilation. But any attempt to make the argument for this identification explicit would immediately reveal the fallacy that arises from treating her two positions as if they exhausted the possibilities when in fact they both exclude the core liberal position. Young is right to say that, in a society that was non-racist and non-sexist in the sense required by the ideal of assimilation, it would have to be the case that 'no political rights or obligations would be connected to race or sex, and no important institutional benefits would be associated with either'.[28] But it would be perfectly possible for somebody to support the 'difference-blind' conception of equal treatment while regarding the ideal of assimilation as a bit of a nightmare.

Liberal societies already approximate fairly closely to the liberal principle of equal treatment in relation to sex, at least as far as public policy is concerned, and it is hard to believe that the remaining exceptions (for example the requirement that marriage must be between a man and a woman) are all that stands in the way of the full realization of the ideal of assimilation. Barring science fiction scenarios, there is obviously an ineluctable biological basis for the social recognition of difference in relation to reproduction. And even if we give whatever credence is due to the idea that the categories of heterosexual and homosexual are social constructions, that is still a long way from saying that sexual attraction might be entirely disconnected from sexual identity. Richard Wasserstrom, from whom Young took the 'ideal of assimilation', carries it through consistently at this point:

> the normal, typical adult in this kind of nonsexist society would be...as indifferent to the sexual, physiological differences of other persons for all significant interpersonal relationships [as normal, typical adults are now to eye color]. Bisexuality, not heterosexuality or homosexuality, would be the typical intimate, sexual relationship in the ideal society that was assimilationist with regard to sex.[29]

The point I wish to emphasize is that the case for a system of universal rights does not stand or fall on the attractiveness of the ideal of an assimilationist society set before us by Wasserstrom. Advocating public policies that give equal rights and opportunities to men and women does not require any commitment to the view that these policies are desirable because they may contribute to the realization of an ideal of assimilation of this kind. For egalitarian liberals, equal treatment is required by justice. It is an expression of the equal rights to which citizens of a liberal state are entitled.

Classifying people in terms of race is inherently suspect, because it is almost inevitably tied up with bogus biology and psychology and almost always presupposes (on the part of those who create the categorization) an assumption that some races are superior to others. Often it imposes an identity on people that has nothing to do with their own self-understanding: the typical British lumping together of Afro-Caribbeans and South Asians as 'blacks' illustrates this. Anyone with an ounce of good will must therefore hope for the disappearance of 'race' as a basis of identity. However, cultural or religious identifications are not inherently objectionable in the same respects, even when the culture is closely associated with some ethnic group. Thus, it is simply false to generalize from the obnoxiousness of 'race' as a social classification to suggest that 'liberal individualism . . . claims that social group categorisations are invidious fictions whose sole function is to justify privilege'.[30]

Liberals will certainly deny that in a just society members of different groups should have different 'political rights and obligations', and that 'important institutional benefits' should be available to some while being denied to others. If that constitutes being opposed to what Young calls an 'ideal of diversity' then they are against it. Yet it would be quite consistent with this to anticipate (with anything from equanimity to enthusiasm) that within this common institutional framework members of different groups would observe different customs, emphasize different values, spend their leisure time differently and perhaps have a tendency to cluster in different occupations. I have to confess myself baffled by Young's assumption that she is affirming anything a liberal has to deny when she says that people 'find significant sources of personal friendship, social solidarity, and aesthetic satisfaction in their group based affinities and cultural life'.[31] Those who believe that this kind of differentiation is positively desirable may be said to have an 'ideal of diversity'. Liberals as well as non-liberals can hold such an ideal. What distinguishes a liberal from a non-liberal is a principled objection to any attempt to promote such an ideal by the creation of group-specific public policies – the kind of thing that Young misleadingly calls an 'ideal of diversity'. For liberals, the right amount of diversity – and the right amount of assimilation – is that which comes about as a result of free choices within a framework of just institutions.

## 3.   Assimilation: Good, Bad or Indifferent?

Leaving behind objections to 'difference-blind' liberalism that are based on misconceptions, we can now focus on one that has more substance: the complaint that it demands assimilation of those who migrate permanently to liberal democratic societies, even if this requires a change in the culture that the immigrants have brought with them from their own society of origin. This is one of those cases in which I am quite willing to agree that there are limits to the amount of hospitality to difference that liberalism can accept. To say that liberalism is 'inhospitable to difference' constitutes a criticism of liberalism only if we have determined how hospitable any political philosophy should be and have found liberalism wanting when measured against this standard. There is, after all, such a thing as the abuse of hospitality. If I am right, the limits of liberal toleration for difference correspond to the point at which the legitimate enjoyment of hospitality turns into its abuse.

I believe that it is an appropriate objective of public policy in a liberal democratic state to facilitate the achievement of a state of affairs in which all immigrants – or at least their descendants – become assimilated to the national identity of the country in which they have settled. But I make that claim only to the extent that national identity is understood in a certain way that I shall in due course explain. I can anticipate one feature of it, however, by saying that I chose my words carefully in talking about immigrants or their descendants 'becoming assimilated' rather than about their 'assimilating'. The latter implies that it is the immigrants who have to do all the work; the former leaves it open that the task may at least as much involve the host population in having to change its attitudes and its practices.

What is it to assimilate? The *Oxford English Dictionary* distinguishes two primary meanings. The first, which is tied tightly to the etymology, is 'to make or be like'. The second is 'to absorb and incorporate', and especially to turn food into part of one's bodily substance. It is interesting that the dictionary takes social assimilation to be a figurative extension of this process of digestion, rather than simply a direct application of the idea of becoming alike. This connects assimilation to identity: for the members of a group to have been assimilated, they must have become absorbed or incorporated in some other (normally larger or more powerful) group. One way of making the distinction would be to define the process of becoming more similar culturally as 'acculturation', while reserving the term 'assimilation' for the complete disappearance of the group's identity, so that it ceases to function as a reference point either for the members of the group or for others outside the group. On this conception of the relation between acculturation and assimilation, we may think of assimilation as a state that can be reached only when acculturation is so complete that members of the two groups have become culturally indistinguishable. This is clearly the conception upon which the following statement by the Israeli sociologist Eliezer Ben-Rafael is based:

> As part of a larger society, [a culturally distinct minority] group necessarily experiences some degree of acculturation in the sense that it is influenced by its environment and becomes increasingly similar to the strata that embody the values and norms predominant in society. Eventually, the group might even undergo assimilation, which means that acculturation comes to include identity.[32]

Even if we were to regard complete acculturation as a necessary condition of assimilation (in the sense of the disappearance of a distinct identity), we would still have to acknowledge that it is not a sufficient condition. As Rainer Bauböck has pointed out, 'assimilation is different from acculturation in that the former requires some ratification by the [receiving] group'.[33] Thus, if 'acculturation' is 'the process by which an individual comes to acquire cultural practices belonging to the tradition of another group', then 'assimilation' is a further step 'indicat[ing] a change of membership which makes an individual similar to a receiving community in the sense that the members recognize her as one of their kind'.[34] The best (and most fateful) illustration of the possible disjunction between acculturation and assimilation, understood as the merging of identities, is the case of German Jews in the interwar period. Almost all were thoroughly acculturated in that they had absorbed German culture (on average probably rather better than their non-Jewish compatriots) and many belonged to families that had been Christian for more than one generation. Despite all this, the Nazi definition of German nationality, eventually embodied in the Nuremberg Laws, made Jewish descent incompatible with membership in the German nation.[35]

Criteria of ethnic identity vary. Racist criteria, which are obsessed with 'blood', and are imposed by the dominant racial group, normally take the form of confining membership of the dominant group to those of 'pure' descent. One Jewish grandparent made somebody a Jew in the eyes of the Nazis. In theory, anyway, anti-miscegenation laws in the American South counted as black anybody with a black ancestor, however remote. As the sheriff of Natchez, Mississippi, puts it in *Show Boat*: 'One drop of nigger blood makes you a nigger in these parts.'[36] In practice, some people were able to 'pass', but they were constantly at risk. In *Show Boat*, again, Miss Julie, whose father was white and her mother black, passes as white. But her less than perfect acculturation is displayed by her revealing knowledge of a song that Queenie says she 'didn't ever hear anybody but colored folks sing';

and she and her (white) husband are later denounced to the sheriff as being in violation of the law against miscegenation.[37] Other ethnic groups have precise rules governing the acquisition and loss of membership by marriage and birth. A widespread rule, for example, is as follows: if a man marries somebody outside the group, his wife will become a member of the group and so will their children; but if a woman marries outside the group, she ceases to be a member and their children will not be members. Obviously, this rule reflects the patriarchal notion that a man 'owns' his wife and children, so they 'naturally' acquire his ethnicity.

If ethnic or racial boundaries do not have legal force or significance, the idea that groups must have clearly defined memberships is unlikely to persist, even if ethnic or racial identities are salient within civil society. As a result of intermarriage, more and more people are likely to be regarded, and to regard themselves, as 'mixed', and this category itself will be fluid: to some extent people can adopt an identity and get it accepted by others by their choice of an accent, a way of dressing, a set of leisure activities, a place of residence, and above all a set of associates. (The obverse of the saying that birds of a feather flock together is that those who flock together will tend to count as the same kind of bird.) England is a place in which 'race' has been a salient but informal category: English colonialism was, of course, another matter; but the formalized racialism that returning colonials brought with them never infected the main body of the population. For example, in the late eighteenth and early nineteenth centuries, it was considered rather chic among well-to-do families in London (especially if they had West Indian connections) to have a black servant or two. Scattered as they must necessarily have been by this employment, it is scarcely surprising that they long ago disappeared as a group due to intermarriage with the native population. Recently, some people have been digging into their family records and have discovered a black ancestor from this period. In the society of *Show Boat*, they would have been anxious to hush this up. In fact, however, they regarded it as an interesting fact and were happy to be interviewed by reporters about it.

Ethnic or racial criteria of group membership, even if they leave some leeway for individuals to move in and out of the 'mixed' group, present the most resistance to assimilation. Where the criteria of membership do not stipulate descent, relatively small groups may disappear into the wider population very easily. In fact, this is the most likely outcome unless the descendants consciously try to maintain a separate identity, and even then they may not succeed. For example, it is doubtful that there is now a sense of distinctive identity among the grandchildren of the Poles who were recruited to cope with the shortage of miners after the Second World War or the grandchildren of the Italian prisoners of war who chose to remain in Britain when the war ended. If we want to insist that all actions that are not carried out under coercion or compulsion are to count as voluntary, we shall have to say that these are examples of voluntary assimilation. But to call the process voluntary is liable to mislead in as far as it suggests a transformation consciously willed. We need a third category of things that just happen, being neither deliberately brought about nor deliberately resisted. Unless we believe that there is something inherently suspect about changes in people that come about without being consciously willed by them (a view for which there seems to me little to be said), it is hard to see why anybody should deplore assimilation that occurs naturally in the kind of way I have just described.

Let us now consider voluntary assimilation in the sense of assimilation deliberately aimed at by one group and (in Bauböck's term) 'ratified' by the other. Much assimilation has always occurred as a result of groups or individual members of groups acting on the judgement that they – or perhaps only their descendants – will have better life prospects if they can shed their present identity and acquire another. What makes such voluntary choices potentially problematic, morally speaking, is the context in which they are made. Especially where whole groups attempt to assimilate, there are good reasons for suspecting that the motivation is a desire to escape stigmatization and discrimination. Then the real objection is to those conditions, not to a rational adaptation to them. But we cannot simply assume that conditions in which there are incentives for assimilation are necessarily unjust. Even if the institutional background satisfies the demands of justice, it may well still be that the culture (for example, the language) of a group puts it at a disadvantage in pursuing ends valued by its members. Linguists and anthropologists may well have professional regrets if as a result a certain language ceases to be spoken or a certain cultural trait disappears. But preferences of these kinds are surely not an adequate basis on which to force people to perpetuate the language or cultural traits against their own judgement as to where their advantage lies.

The third possibility is that assimilation may be brutally enforced, and a great deal of assimilation (religious, linguistic and cultural) has been of this kind all through history. It still goes on. Thus, in Sudan, 'the processes of state incorporation are at present extremely violent' – a rather antiseptic description of a bloody conflict amounting virtually to genocide on the government's part.

> To 'become Sudanese,' an inhabitant of one of the marginalized areas of Sudan must accept a particular interpretation of Islam; adopt a certain code of dress, eating, and housing; and participate in the monetary economy.... 'Sudanization' was once primarily a peaceful process, but today certain peripheral groups in northern Sudan...face the choice between submission to this process on very unfavourable terms and a fight to the death.[38]

Again, in Australia 'up to a third of Aboriginal children were forcibly removed from their families between 1910 and 1970.... The stolen boys were sent to sheep and cattle stations and paid in rations and pennies. The girls, who were the majority, were sent for training as domestic servants, then "indentured" to "masters" in white middle-class homes.' John Pilger remarks that, when he was growing up, 'this was known as "assimilation." '[39]

It is cases such as these that give 'assimilation' the negative connotations that it commonly carries and give potency to the accusation that some policy (or the absence of a policy) is 'assimilationist' in effect even if not in intent. But if it is assimilation of this kind that is objectionable – and it surely is – we should not conflate it with assimilation that occurs in the absence of coercion within a context of just institutions. The thesis of 'difference-blind' liberalism is that it would be an improper interference with individual liberty to design public policies aimed at frustrating the wishes of those who would like to assimilate under those conditions. What of cases in which the pressures on people to assimilate amount to an unjust imposition? The answer that flows from the 'difference-blind' conception of liberalism is that compulsion to prevent these pressures from being effective is at the best a very inferior alternative to taking measures aimed at ending the unfair treatment that is at the root of the problem.

To conclude this discussion, it is worth asking what is the relation between assimilation (understood as loss of distinct identity) and the egalitarian liberal conception of equal treatment. It is a necessary truth that people who are indistinguishable from one another cannot be treated differently in a systematic way. (They may individually be treated arbitrarily; but this must, in the absence of any distinguishing characteristics, be a fate to which all are equally exposed.) However grossly the rules may discriminate between members of different groups, defined along some dimension or other, they can have no discriminatory impact among the members of a single group. Suppose, for example, that the law decrees burning at the stake for everybody in the country who is not a Roman Catholic. This will not result in unequal treatment of people according to their religious affiliations if everybody who was previously anything other than a Roman Catholic has undergone conversion. I have just suggested, indeed, that much of the assimilation that has occurred in history has been precisely of this kind: a response to a situation in which the possession of a distinct identity is strongly disadvantageous. The whole point of egalitarian liberalism, in contrast with this, is to ensure that people who are different are treated equally. Assimilation is not therefore necessary to ensure equal treatment. By the same token, any assimilation that does occur cannot be objected to on any grounds recognized by 'difference-blind' liberals.

## 4.   Varieties of National Identity

The demand that immigrants should take on the national identity of their new country is regarded by supporters of the 'politics of difference' as oppressive and perhaps counterproductive in creating loyalty to it. I wish to argue that whether this is so or not depends on what goes into the idea of a common national identity. There is, indeed, one conception of common nationality that appeals to most multiculturalists, and it is one that is also important to liberals. This is nationality as defined in passports. For this purpose, of course, a 'nation' is simply a state: to be a 'national' of some country is to be a citizen of it. Where liberals part company from multiculturalists (or should do) is in denying the common multiculturalist claim that this purely legal conception of common nationality is all that is needed.

Unquestionably, membership of this kind is of enormous significance to everybody: not to have a nationality – to be a 'stateless person' – is an international form of social death. Moreover, it is clear that a country which does not have an inclusive definition of citizenship cannot by definition be a democracy, because the set of people who have the full range of legal and political rights constitutes only a subset of those whose fates are inextricably bound up with the functioning of the country's institutions. Citizenship has to be available to all permanent residents in order to satisfy 'the basic liberal principle of equal concern and respect for everybody who depends on a government for a guarantee of her or his rights'.[40] On the same grounds, citizenship should also be available at the age of majority to those who have been born within the national borders and have lived in the country since then, even if neither parent was a citizen of the country. Some countries, such as the United States, go further than this, giving citizenship unconditionally to anybody born on their soil. But this is not required by the liberal conception of citizenship, and it is actually rather inimical to its spirit in that it divorces citizenship from any kind of attachment to the country.

My thesis is that an inclusive conception of nationality as citizenship is not sufficient to give any assurance of 'equal concern and respect', even though it is a necessary condition. To see why the formal conception of nationality is inadequate, let us consider a state whose territory is regarded by the members of an ethnically defined *Staatsvolk* as their 'homeland'. Even if citizenship is granted to those who do not belong to the ethnic group that conceives of itself as 'owning' the state, there is nothing to prevent the numerically and politically dominant ethnic group from discriminating against citizens who do not belong to it by, for example, disqualifying them from eligibility for positions that are regarded as too important to entrust to them. The justification for doing this, that their loyalty cannot be trusted, is likely to become a self-fulfilling prophecy. The state may also, without setting it out as a formal policy, subject those who do not belong to the majority nationality to brutal treatment by the police and discriminate against them in the allocation of public housing and other services, such as roads, hospitals and schools. Where the state takes the lead in employment discrimination, it can scarcely legislate against it in the private sector. If most of the desirable jobs are within the control of the majority ethnic group, it is not likely to be inhibited in discriminating vigorously against others. (If discrimination is practised rigorously enough, especially in relation to jobs and housing, the majority may be able to achieve a certain amount of 'ethnic cleansing' without resort to violence – or, more precisely, with resort only to the violence that maintains a state of affairs in which those outside the *Staatsvolk* are reduced to such a degree of frustration and despair that they choose to emigrate.) Finally, citizenship can be reduced to a charade on the side of input to the state as well as the side of output from the state: even if those outside the majority ethnic group have the vote, its effect can be nullified if the party or parties representing the majority exclude other parties from power. Two cases that between them illustrate all of these points are Northern Ireland during the half century from its creation in 1921 until the Stormont regime was wound up in 1973 and Israel during the half century from its creation in 1947 until now.

Admittedly, the problem of ethnically based discrimination among citizens will not arise if the state territory is occupied exclusively by people who belong to the ethnic group that claims it as its homeland. In the large literature on this topic, however, there is just one example of such a state that recurs constantly, that of Iceland. With this possible exception, all countries are ethnically mixed, and the only way in which this can be changed is for the government (or private agencies condoned by the government) to engage in either genocide or 'ethnic cleansing'. (The two policies are in fact complementary in as far as the plausible threat of genocide will create the terror that results in 'ethnic cleansing'.) As Alfred Stepan has put it:

> Some parts of the world's map are of course more culturally homogeneous in the 1980s than they were in the 1930s, but in Poland and in Czechoslovakia this was 'helped' first by Nazi genocide of Jewish and Gypsy minorities and later by the Soviet-backed expulsion of the Germans, an expulsion which the Allies accepted. As the millennium turns, Croatia is now nearly homogeneous, but at the cost of ethnic cleansing and the creation of an ethnocracy. These are not useable templates for the practice and theory of democracy.[41]

Liberal democracy is a relatively rare form of government in the world. Almost all of the countries that gained independence from a colonial power in the last half century, for example, were endowed at their creation with impeccably liberal democratic constitutions. Yet almost every one has fallen (usually quite quickly) into dictatorship or anarchy, or some combination of the two either sequentially or simultaneously. This suggests that the conditions for maintaining liberal democracy must be quite stringent. There is certainly no guarantee that outcomes that an egalitarian liberal would salute will arise from liberal democratic institutions. But they are extraordinarily unlikely to arise from political institutions other than those of liberal democracy; and, even if they did so by a fluke in some instance, the lack of liberal democratic institutions would in itself constitute a failure to instantiate egalitarian liberal principles, because these concern the proper distribution of political authority as well as the distribution of individual rights. It follows, therefore, that the creation and maintenance of the conditions under which liberal democratic institutions will survive must be a very high priority for an egalitarian liberal. If there are further conditions that make not only for their survival but for their tending to produce just outcomes, egalitarian liberals will be keen to see these too created where they do not exist and maintained when they do.

What might be the conditions that we are looking for? To begin with, we cannot expect the outcomes of democratic politics to be just in a society that contains large numbers of people who feel no sense of empathy with their fellow citizens and do not have any identification with their lot. This sense of solidarity is fostered by common institutions and a spread of incomes narrow enough to prevent people from believing – and with some reason – that they can escape from the common lot by buying their way out of the system of education, health care, policing and other public services that their less fortunate fellow citizens are forced to depend upon. Joseph Raz has suggested, along similar lines, that limiting the spread of incomes is likely to increase empathy because it will make the experience of citizens more similar: 'restricting inequalities of income and wealth helps to limit gaps in life-expectancy, in health and in general expectations, gaps which often make people on opposite sides of the social and economic divide incapable of understanding and empathizing with one another.'[42] This may be described as a limitation on cultural diversity, but it is very different from the kind of thing that it is usually thought to be worth protecting under that head. Perhaps, indeed, 'the very rich are different from you and me', and Ernest Hemingway was wrong in thinking that they were different only in having more money. But egalitarian liberal justice is incompatible with great inequalities of wealth and income. It is not a legitimate objection to redistribution to claim (even if it is true) that your 'culture' depends on the possession of great wealth, any more than it would be a legitimate objection to the abolition of slavery to claim that your 'culture' depends on the ownership of slaves. (I shall return to this point in chapter 7.)

More broadly, liberal democracies are very unlikely to produce just outcomes unless their citizens have certain attitudes towards one another. It must be accepted on all hands that the interests of everyone must count equally, and that there are no groups whose members' views are to be automatically discounted.[43] Equally important is a willingness on the part of citizens to make sacrifices for the common good – which, of course, presupposes that they are capable of recognizing a common good.[44] Moreover, citizens do not just as a matter of fact have to be willing to make sacrifices; it is also necessary that citizens should have firm expectations of one another to the effect that they will be prepared to give up money, leisure and perhaps even life itself if the occasion arises. What shall we call this cluster of attitudes towards fellow citizens? I propose to define it as a sense of common nationality, distinguishing the appropriate concept of nationality from both the formal one embodied in a passport and also the ethnic interpretation of nationality. In contrast with either of these, I shall describe the relevant sense of nationality as civic nationality.

There are, of course, dangers in appropriating the word 'nationality' for my purpose, because it is so often defined either in ethnic terms or in terms of an all-encompassing homogeneous culture. Andrew Mason, in an article whose general drift is congenial to the position argued for here, concludes that what a liberal democracy needs in order to function well is not 'sharing a national identity' but 'a sense of belonging to a polity'. He argues as follows:

> a sense of belonging to a polity is needed to underpin a politics of the common good, but a shared national identity is often unnecessary. If there is a widespread sense of belonging of this kind, then citizens will feel part of the polity of which they are members, and as a result they are likely to have a sense of sharing a fate with others who are also part of it.[45]

My substantive objection to this is that talking about 'a sense of belonging to the polity' is too subjectivistic an account of what is needed: it is not enough for people to feel that they belong themselves unless they also feel that others belong and those others feel that everybody else belongs. Talking about a shared identity emphasizes that there must be mutuality of recognition and not merely a lot of people who harbour in their breasts similar feelings about their personal relation to the polity. With that revision, however, what Mason wants to call 'a sense of belonging to a polity' is in essence what I am proposing to call civic nationality. Despite its dangers, this usage has the great advantage that it reflects the way in which people actually think and speak, whereas 'a sense of belonging to a polity' is unlikely to trip off the tongue of anybody who is not a political theorist.

What is involved in assimilation to a certain civic nationality? The model of assimilation that I have relied upon so far says, in a nutshell, that complete acculturation plus ratification equals assimilation in the sense of the disappearance of a distinctive identity. But the specification of civic nationality that I have just been developing does not include any reference to acculturation. It may well be that, in order to meet the requirements that have been set out, the acquisition of some cultural traits (especially the national language) is essential. But that still leaves it open that people may be able to assimilate (or be assimilated) to the common nationality without giving up distinctive cultural attributes and – equally important – without losing a distinctive identity. The key to all this is, again, the conventional aspect of identity – what I have called 'ratification'. We have seen that complete acculturation to a group is not a sufficient condition of ratification as a member of that group. It is equally true, however, that, just because identity turns on a decision (though not necessarily one consciously taken), complete acculturation is not a necessary condition of ratification. How culturally 'thick' are the necessary conditions of identity will be one of the defining characteristics of the group. But we should bear in mind that these conditions are not fixed once and for all: they are constantly subject to renegotiation. 'In the process of inclusion, both the minority ethnic groups and the majority group can be seen to be involved in a give-and-take.'[46] As Aristide Zolberg has said, we need 'a more interactive model of incorporation'.[47]

The crucial point is that, just as the acquisition of a new identity may not require complete acculturation, so it may not require the giving up of an old identity. Clearly, we are dealing here with a sense of 'assimilation' different from that discussed in the previous section. We may call the earlier one 'absorptive assimilation' and contrast it with 'additive assimilation', defining this (with Bauböck) as 'retaining a previous cultural membership while acquiring a new one'.[48] Zolberg, along similar lines, has written that we should not think of 'identity-formation as a constant-sum game, whereby the acquisition of a new identity occurs at the expense of the original one' but should rather acknowledge 'the uniquely human capacity for additive identities, as manifested by the capacity of any member of the species to learn and use more than one language, and for transforming many aspects of the self'.[49] In the next section, I shall look back over some historical examples of the development of additive identity and ask what lessons can be drawn that may be relevant to contemporary conditions.

## 5. National Identity in Practice

In the United States, a country formed largely by immigration, the notion that national identity is compatible with a distinctive ethnic identity is commonplace. Just as one can have a Texan identity, say, as well as an

American identity, so one can combine an American identity with one as a member of an ethnic group, defined in terms of the nation from which one's ancestors come – or, more precisely, for most Americans today, the nation of whichever ancestors one chooses for the purpose.[50] There have, almost from the beginning, been 'nativist' sentiments – sometimes giving rise to political movements – among people whose ancestors arrived earlier against those who have arrived more recently. ('Nativism' in this sense has never been carried through consistently to recognizing the prior claim of those who are now called Native Americans.) But attacks on the notion of 'hyphenated Americans' have never succeeded in driving out the idea that being, say, an Irish-American or Italian-American is a way of being an American, not an alternative to it.

Identity does not have to have a distinctive cultural content at all. It may be defined purely in terms of descent. Ethnicity in the United States is increasingly vacuous culturally. Even in the past its most important role was as a building-block in the creation of coalitions in urban politics. (I shall return to the significance of this in chapter 8.) The cultural manifestations were secondary, and they existed in the forms of cuisine, modes of family organization, churches (often differentiated according to ethnicity even when they were all Roman Catholic), and so on. Will Kymlicka informs us that it is only since the 1970s that it has been 'accepted that immigrants should be free to maintain some of their old customs regarding food, dress, religion, and recreation and to associate with each other to maintain these practices. This is no longer seen as unpatriotic or un-American.'[51] This may be true of a parallel universe, or perhaps of Canada, but it is certainly not true of the United States, where people were doing all those things long before the 1970s and have at most times and in most places experienced no difficulty in doing so.[52] Indeed, it is precisely in the past thirty years that these cultural differences have thinned out. This depletion of cultural content is not, incidentally, inconsistent with making a big issue out of the vestiges that remain: this is the phenomenon that Michael Ignatieff (following Freud) has called 'the narcissism of minor differences'.[53]

None of this is to deny the truth of Zolberg's claim that concerns about the consequences of immigration led to 'a concerted program of forceful "Americanization", which imposed recitation of the Pledge of Allegiance on every school child, brought the national anthem to every baseball game and music-hall, and flags on every public building every day of the week as well as from private homes on holidays'.[54] This 'outpouring of patriotic rituals, which is now taken for granted as a routine feature of American life' inevitably strikes visitors from Western Europe as rather oppressive.[55] Nevertheless, it must be emphasized that only public behaviour is affected: Kymlicka's claims about food, dress, religion, recreation and association remain beyond rescue.

Moreover, the downplaying of 'patriotic rituals' in Western Europe does not necessarily entail greater acceptance of immigrants: it may, on the contrary, reflect the lack of any will to incorporate them in the nation. Zolberg remarks that a similar 'outpouring of patriotic rituals...would raise more than eyebrows throughout Europe and abroad were it to be encouraged, say in Germany today, as a strategy for speeding up the Germanization of former guestworkers and their offspring'.[56] Given, however, the ethnic conception of nationality that prevails in Germany, there is no way in which Turks, say, can be 'Germanized'. This is reflected in the contrast between automatic eligibility for citizenship of people who may not even speak German provided they have German 'blood' and the difficulties facing those who were born in Germany (and have spent all their lives in the country) in acquiring naturalization if they are not of German descent. That Turks are not 'encouraged' to take part in 'patriotic rituals' does not reflect such a high level of enlightenment in Germany that engagement in them is not thought to be needed for the incorporation of Turks into the German nation; rather, it means that there is no project for incorporating them at all.

As far as Britain is concerned, waving union jacks and singing jingoistic songs is an activity now largely relegated to the increasingly postmodern Last Night of the Proms. Immigrants are not, therefore, subjected to much pressure to take part in 'patriotic rituals'. At the same time, however, the situation is in several crucial respects different from that obtaining in Germany: almost all immigrants from the 'new commonwealth' (and their children) are British citizens, and British nationality is not defined in ethnic terms. The problem is, rather, that the criteria for membership in the British nation may be so undemanding as to render membership incapable of providing the foundation of common identity that is needed for the stability and justice of liberal democratic polities.

As Linda Colley has pointed out, the attractions of a British identity that were manifest when it denoted a privileged position in relation to the British Empire have disappeared but not been replaced by any others.[57] Already, 'British' seems to be largely a legal conception tied up with formal British citizenship rather than one with significant affective, cognitive or behavioural connotations. In future its salience is likely to be further reduced as it is eroded on one side by a larger, European identity and on the other by an increase in the significance of the component nationalities in the UK and perhaps even regions within those national areas. Experience in the rest of Europe would in any case support such expectations, but we also have direct indications in Scottish (and to a lesser degree Welsh) devolution and a prospect (at the time of writing) of more distinctive institutions in Northern Ireland. If British identity appealed only to ethnic minorities and unreconciled Ulster Protestants, it would clearly not serve the purposes I laid out for a concept of civic nationality. Survey evidence suggests that two-thirds of 'new commonwealth' immigrants and their descendants 'felt British, and these proportions were, as one might expect, higher amongst young people and those who had been born in Britain', yet at the same time 'most of the second generation...were not...comfortable with the idea of being British being more than a legal title'.[58] These findings reinforce the sense that British nationality is a very thin glue to rely on if one is concerned about social cohesion.

It is a familiar phenomenon that the break-up of nationally heterogeneous states creates increased problems for minorities in the successor states.[59] It would be foolish to ignore the applicability of this rule to the UK. In recent decades, it has come to be the conventional wisdom of the race relations industry that immigrants from the Caribbean and the Indian subcontinent – and their descendants born in Britain who make up an increasingly large part of the 'immigrant' population – can reasonably aspire to being only British. Englishness, for example, is thought to carry with it so much cultural baggage that it would be oppressive to place on 'new commonwealth' immigrants and their descendants the expectation of becoming English. If I am right, however, we would do well to pay attention to the way in which membership in the English nation has already expanded over the centuries. Enoch Powell's notorious claim that immigrants and their descendants would never become integrated into English society depended on a conception of integration that made it equivalent to what I have called absorptive assimilation: 'To be integrated into a population means to become for all practical purposes indistinguishable from its other members.'[60] There are, indeed, some examples of this in English history, as I have pointed out, but they are the exception rather than the rule. Most assimilation has been additive assimilation. Typically, the process has been one in which the criteria for membership in the English nation have become more relaxed.

A good example of this dynamic is the relation between religious affiliation and membership in the English nation. Thus, for a long time after the break with Rome in the sixteenth century, there was a widespread feeling that a necessary condition of being truly English was to be a Protestant. Indeed, for much of the period Roman Catholics were suspected of disloyalty – not altogether groundlessly – and pride in the foiling of 'Popish plots' (still commemorated on Guy Fawkes Day) became an aspect of patriotism. The decisive defeat of the Stuart cause in 1745 did a lot to allay fears that Roman Catholics constituted a potential 'fifth column'.[61] Then the Napoleonic Wars showed how far religion had been replaced as a uniting and dividing force, pitting Protestant, Catholic and Orthodox forces against France: with Nelson recommending that British forces should come to the aid of the Pope, and Wellington collaborating with Spain, the hereditary enemy, things had come a long way in two centuries. Roman Catholic

Emancipation in 1829 could be said to have put the formal seal of ratification on the incorporation of Roman Catholics in the nation.

The point of this historical excursion is to emphasize that assimilation to English identity did not involve Roman Catholics in abandoning their religious allegiance: national identity was additive, not absorptive. The cultural threshold of incorporation was lowered – the cultural content of 'Englishness' thinned – by dropping the connection with Protestantism. Yet at the same time it is equally important to see that this change in the criteria was not a unilateral move: it was a response to a change in the significance of Roman Catholicism within European politics. This phenomenon of the depoliticization of Roman Catholicism is not perhaps captured very happily by the concept of acculturation. Nevertheless, the case surely exemplifies the larger point that assimilation is typically a two-way street.

By the middle of the nineteenth century, then, there was no doubt that Christians of any stripe (including, of course, non-religious people of Christian ancestry) could be English. But this left the question: could people be English as well as being Jewish, or were these mutually exclusive identities? A factor that told against the 'assimilationist' answer was the rise of racist thinking. Looking back now, our attention is captured by racism as the legacy of colonialism and black slavery and the form of it represented by the Nazis' doctrine of the superiority of the Aryan 'race'. We thus tend to overlook the pervasiveness of racist thinking in every western country in the late nineteenth and early twentieth centuries. Thus, for example, Horace Kallen, who is regarded as a hero by contemporary multiculturalists for his espousal of pluralism – a 'democracy of nationalities' – actually based his position on crude racialism.[62] There could not be a new American identity subsuming those of immigrants because 'in historic times so far as is known no new ethnic types have originated'.[63] 'Intermarriage or no intermarriage, racial quality exists and is identifiable.... Different races responding to the same stimuli are still different, and no environmental influence...can ever remold them into an indifferent sameness.'[64] And it should be borne in mind that 'in the early twentieth century, race meant the different immigrant groups in the United States; Italians, Jews and Poles were often considered to constitute their own races.'[65] Similarly, within Europe, cultural differences between nations were typically assumed to correspond to different 'races', so that there were, for example, English, French and German 'races'.

As far as Jews were concerned, there was a long-standing belief that they were potentially disloyal citizens. Even those who would have disdained paranoid notions of an international conspiracy led by Jewish financiers might well have felt some inclination to agree with the nationalist French historian Michelet, who wrote: 'The Jews, whatever is said of them, have a country – the London Stock Exchange; they operate everywhere, but are rooted in the country of gold.'[66] In the later part of the nineteenth century, such characteristics were cast in explicitly racial terms. 'Between 1870 and 1914, antisemitism was invented. The English, searching for their true origins as they engaged in a romantic mission to take their civilization throughout the world, contributed to the idea of social evolution, hereditarism and eugenics.'[67] In France, anti-Semitism coagulated around the Dreyfus affair. 'For the anti-Dreyfusards the pertinent fact about Dreyfus was simply that he was a Jew. Everything followed from that.'[68] 'That Dreyfus was a traitor', wrote the anti-Dreyfusard Barrès, 'I conclude from his race.'[69] Yet at the same time, he added, 'since Dreyfus does not belong to our nation, how could he betray it? The Jews' fatherland is wherever they find a profit.'[70] Here we see the old cultural stereotype given a racial underpinning.

Although anti-Semitism in England was less virulent than in France during the same period, the anti-Semitic sentiments that are rife in the popular novels of the period illustrate the notion that Jews had various hereditary characteristics, such as untrustworthiness and cowardice, which contrasted unfavourably with the inherited English traits of honesty and bravery. Thus, George du Maurier's Trilby (from, as George Orwell pointed out, the period of the Dreyfus case) contrasts Svengali, who has 'genius', with the English figures who 'have "character", and "character" is what matters. It is the attitude of the rugger-playing prefect towards the spectacled "swot", and it was probably the normal attitude towards Jews at that time.'[71] More generally, Orwell also remarked in 1943 that 'in the minor novels of [thirty years ago] you find it taken for granted far oftener than you would nowadays that a Jew is an inferior and a figure of fun'.[72]

Over just the same period, the massive decline in the salience of religion was making the social significance of Jewish or Christian religious affiliation less and less all the time. What this account illustrates is, however, that the ratification of identity has more to do with perceptions about trustworthiness, loyalty and commitment than it has to do with culture. The Second World War changed things in two ways. As the true extent of the Nazi evil sank in, it became almost impossible to express anti-Semitic racialist ideas in public. Independently, it seems clear in retrospect that the heightened sense of social solidarity induced by a sense of sharing a common fate and joining in a common purpose during the war included Jews within its scope. Jewish identity is now unquestionably compatible with English identity. Furthermore, the social distance between secular Jews and gentiles of the same social class is essentially non-existent, and intermarriage rates are so high that a good deal of assimilation in the strong sense of disappearance of distinct identity is occurring. Community leaders are, indeed, beginning to worry about the disappearance of Jewish identity within a few generations outside the ranks of the Orthodox.[73]

What can we learn from the troubled course of assimilation to English identity in the past that might throw light on the situation of immigrants from the Caribbean and the Indian subcontinent and their descendants? I shall eschew speculation and prophecy as far as possible, limiting myself to an attempt to draw whatever lessons seem to follow directly from past experience with the expansion of English nationality. One initial point that is worth reiterating is that the incorporation of new groups absolutely requires that nationality should not be defined in terms of descent. Over almost the whole of the history of England as a separate entity, Englishness cannot have been defined in that way: otherwise it would be impossible to explain how the English could be descended from such a heterogeneous collection of invaders and migrants. In relation to this whole history, the racism of the last part of the nineteenth and the first part of the twentieth centuries is best seen as an unfortunate 'blip'. There is, no doubt, still some sympathy for the idea, especially associated with Enoch Powell, that English people can be descended from anybody as long as they are sufficiently 'white'.[74] Because any such belief is incompatible with the effective operation of liberal democratic institutions, its extirpation is a legitimate objective of public policy, to the extent that it can be accomplished by means that are compatible with liberalism itself.

An encouraging conclusion that can be drawn with confidence from the foregoing is that English nationality cannot today be taken with the remotest plausibility to exclude anybody simply on the basis of the religion that they profess. Where additive identity is concerned, acculturation is neither a necessary nor a sufficient condition, and religion illustrates this point well. Nevertheless, cultural similarity between groups must in general increase the amount of social integration. (If, however, the majority group regards the acculturating group as racially inferior, it may code the appropriation of its culture as 'uppity' behaviour: this again brings home the harmfulness of racialism.) 'Ethnic identification is no longer necessarily connected [in Britain] to personal participation in distinctive cultural practices, such as those of language, religion or dress.'[75] Thus, we see what has already occurred in the United States happening in Britain: ethnic identification persists but becomes increasingly drained of cultural content. Even more important, perhaps, is the widespread failure of the older generation to instil in the younger an anxious concern for public opinion in their place of origin. The closing of social distance between those of Afro-Caribbean descent and the mainstream population is helped by the absence of religious distinctiveness, except in the case of Rastafarians. Good evidence for the degree of social integration is the finding that 'among the British-born, of those who had a partner, half of Caribbean men,[and] a third of Caribbean women ... had a white partner'.[76]

The lesson that is suggested by my two historical examples is that culture is not the heart of the matter. Provided that assimilation to a common identity is not ruled out by descent-based criteria, the core of common national identity is a common commitment to the welfare of the larger society made up of the majority and the minority (or minorities), and mutual trust in others to abide by that commitment even when it entails sacrifices. Todd Gitlin has spelled out the implications for multiculturalism as follows:

> Democracy is more than a license to celebrate (and exaggerate) difference.... It is a political system of mutual reliance and common moral obligations.... If multiculturalism is not tempered by a stake in the commons, then centrifugal energy overwhelms any commitment to a larger good. This is where multiculturalism has proved a trap even – or especially – for people in the name of whom the partisans of identity politics purport to speak.[77]

Multiculturalism is especially a trap when it takes the form of devolving public functions on to minority groups. Pluralism of this kind was carried to considerable lengths in the Ottoman system of communal self-government (millets) and the similar arrangement for Jews in Europe (kahals) that persisted in Russia until the middle of the nineteenth century. It is significant that these institutions flourished in authoritarian societies, and that 'over time the millet and the kahal systems broke down, with awful consequences for all groups but especially for minorities'.[78] Along similar lines, Ralph Grillo has remarked on

> [the] sobering thought that what are now recalled as some of the most horrifying episodes of ethnic violence of the twentieth century (Armenian massacres, expulsions from Asia Minor, Cyprus, Lebanon, Palestine, and, by no means least, Bosnia [we can now add Kosovo – BB]) all occurred in territory which formed part of the 'Divinely protected well-flourishing absolute domain of the House of Osman.'[79]

It is axiomatic that no large-scale historical phenomenon has only one cause. Nevertheless, it is not hard to appreciate the relation between institutional pluralism and the potential for group conflict: a situation in which groups live in parallel universes is not one well calculated to advance mutual understanding or encourage the cultivation of habits of cooperation and sentiments of trust. For what it is worth, it may be noted that experiments by social psychologists find evidence for the proposition that 'superordinate identification [what I am calling the creation of an additive identity] can be encouraged[by] increas[ing] task interdependence or a feeling of sharing a common fate'.[80] In a much-cited experiment by Sherif et al., for example, a party of eleven-year-old children in a summer camp was divided into two competing groups, which 'produced in-group friendships and hostility toward the other group'.[81] But then the set-up was changed, so that 'both groups were required to work together to achieve mutually beneficial goals. For example, the two groups had to pool their money to rent a film both groups wanted to see. The joint cooperation lessened hostility.'[82] What is, perhaps, as significant as this result is that it would have been very surprising if it had been any different. The psychodynamics at work are entirely familiar to everybody.

In the light of all this, it is hard to imagine anything more ill-conceived than proposals put forward by multiculturalists such as Bhikhu Parekh for parcelling out public functions to ethnic communities. 'The state', he suggests, 'can adopt group-related welfare policies and invite minority communities to participate in planning community centres, health and social services and so on.'[83] Echoing Kallen, Parekh suggests that the state should become 'a community of communities'. In accordance with this, he argues that 'there is no obvious reason why [decentralization] should be based only on territorial and occupational and not on communal grounds as well'.[84] I believe, on the contrary, that there is every reason for making deliberate attempts to draw up geographically based administrative units that cut across communal boundaries. Gitlin, it may be recalled, emphasized the importance of everyone's having 'a stake in the commons', and the most basic way of providing people with one is to ensure that there actually is a 'commons' in the form of shared institutions upon which all depend alike.

Equally important is cooperation in shaping that fate. It must be believed on all sides that a concession made today by one party will be matched with a concession by another party tomorrow, and that can come about only if members of minority and majority groups actually share in the running of their common institutions. A sense of commitment to a common good can over time arise out of this kind of patient, unglamorous work that goes on mostly behind the scenes. It has nothing to do with Norman Tebbit's 'cricket test'. The mark of a good politician is the ability to take a stupid idea and make it sound (at least for a short while) plausible. Tebbit, in suggesting that to be English you had to cheer the English cricket team, managed to do the opposite: he took an idea that was in essence sound and contrived to make it sound stupid. The non-stupid version involves the development of trust and of sentiments conducive to mutual aid.

Above all, it should go without saying, the suppression of group-related harassment and violence must be given the highest priority. It is sometimes argued that the liberal conception of equal treatment cannot countenance the concentration of police resources on the prevention of attacks based on ethnic identity or the imposition of higher penalties on those convicted of them. This kind of formalistic understanding of 'equal treatment' would, indeed, invite condemnation as 'difference-blind'. Many jurisdictions have laws making it an aggravating feature of an offence that the victim was a police officer. Here, the identity of the victim is allowed to make a difference to the gravity of the crime, presumably on the ground that assaults on the police are peculiarly threatening to public order. It may be said, along parallel lines, that attacks based purely on ethnic identity have especially serious import because they are peculiarly destructive of relations of trust and solidarity between members of different ethnic groups. It is also instructive to compare 'hate crime' with genocide. The United Nations does not define the crime of genocide in terms of the number of people killed but rather in terms of their being killed simply on the basis of their group identity. Murder based solely on the group identity of the victim might be thought of as a kind of individualistic genocidal enterprise and hence worthy of special condemnation.

It does not follow from all this that the best approach is to define a special legal offence of 'hate crime'.[85] The law already leaves room for a variety of facts about the crime and about the criminal to be taken account of in determining the sentence for an offence. One of these could be the fact, if it had been clearly established, that a crime had no other object than that of inflicting injury on the basis of ethnic group membership. What matters most is that the police, the Director of Public Prosecutions and the courts should all manifest a commitment to taking ethnically based harassment and violence seriously. The biggest danger of 'hate crime' legislation is that it will be seen as an alternative to the hard task of eradicating racism from the police force – a task barely yet begun either in Britain or in many parts of the United States.

## 6.    The Dodo's Dictum

Immigrants to contemporary liberal democracies will not suffer criminal penalties if they retain their customary ways of dressing, cooking, associating, communicating or living – as long, of course, as it does not bring them into conflict with generally applicable laws. Nor will they suffer any civil disabilities, except that failure to learn the language of the country may prevent them from qualifying for naturalization. For all that, immigrants are under pressure to make some adaptations to the extent that they want to obtain good jobs in the mainstream economy. Nathan Glazer quotes from the entry on 'Americanization' in the (1930) *Encyclopedia of the Social Sciences* as follows: 'A conspicuous force which makes for adjustment is the urge to material success, which makes the immigrant adapt himself to the American ways of work and business. This usually involves learning the English language as quickly as possible.'[86] Glazer remarks that the same forces are still at work and this is certainly true: whatever clothes you wear and whatever language you speak at home, if you want a job on Wall Street you will need to speak English and wear a suit. This has nothing to do (directly, anyway) with identity, but it does relate to the second meaning of 'assimilation' that I extracted from the *Oxford English Dictionary*, which made assimilation a matter of becoming more alike. I have proposed that we should distinguish this from assimilation (in either its absorptive or additive forms) and follow a common usage in calling it 'acculturation'. What we are talking about, then, is a form of partial acculturation that manifests itself only in certain contexts. (It may as a matter of fact extend beyond those contexts, but 'material success' does not demand that it should.)

The point can be extended so that it no longer applies only to immigrants. We can state it as a general proposition that cultural differences are quite likely to be related to the positions that their bearers hold in the hierarchy of kinds of employment. This is an exemplification of the way in which any uniform set of criteria for success in a competition will place those who possess certain traits at an advantage in comparison with those who lack these traits. The criteria for winning the hundred yards dash favour those who can run fast over short distances. What is rewarded here is a physiological capability enhanced by training. In other contexts, traits that make for success may have a cultural basis. Some cultures, for example, value and encourage academic achievement in children, while others place little value on it or even disparage it. Obviously, positions that are open only to those with high academic qualifications will tend to be filled disproportionately by those who grew up within the first kind of culture. There are jobs for which an ability to get on with people is a prerequisite, and it is likely that people from some cultural backgrounds will tend to be better suited to such jobs than those from others.

The suggestion to be considered here is that this way of appointing to desirable positions is unfair because members of cultures with a tendency not to produce success-making traits are put under pressure to transform themselves in ways that will undermine their cultural distinctiveness. The price of their failing to do this is that group members will tend to cluster in occupations at the lower end of the hierarchy of money, status and power. To put the objection in the vocabulary made familiar by Taylor, criteria of merit applied to all alike are 'difference-blind' in that they take no account of the different cultural characteristics of different groups. I shall organize my discussion around Iris Young's version of the argument in favour of group-specific criteria, though it should be made clear that it is a staple of the 'politics of difference' literature.

I have denied that the case for the standard 'difference-blind' liberal approach to the distribution of rights, resources and opportunities depends on the notion that they are valuable only as means to the realization of an 'ideal of assimilation'. This approach can be defended, I have argued, without any recourse to such an ideal: on egalitarian liberal premises, equal treatment of a 'difference-blind' nature is what is called for by fairness. It is precisely this claim that Young denies. In other words, the objection now is not to the 'assimilationist ideal' but to the 'principle of equal treatment or non-discrimination' with which Young mistakenly identifies it.[87] Young's alternative to this conception of equal treatment amounts to a conception of equality of outcome, defined over groups: ' "Equality", defined as the [equal] participation and inclusion of all groups in institutions and positions, is sometimes better served by differential treatment.'[88] I have inserted the word 'equal' in the quotation so as to exclude 'tokenism', and Young makes it clear elsewhere that this is a correct interpretation. Thus, she writes that 'unless one begins with the assumption that all positions of high status, income, and decisionmaking power ought to be distributed in comparable numbers to women and men, finding that very few top corporate managers are women might not involve any question of injustice.'[89] If one does begin with such an assumption, of course, the statistics settle the issue straight off: no further inquiry is needed.

The egalitarian liberal position is that justice requires equal rights and opportunities but not necessarily equal outcomes defined over groups. It is certainly true that many liberals have as a matter of fact hoped that, once women had the same rights and opportunities as men, there would be a long-run tendency for the profile of choices made by women and the profile of choices made by men to converge. But what must be emphasized is that it is perfectly possible to believe that justice demands equal rights and opportunities for men and women while at the same time neither hoping nor expecting that this will result in the career choices of women tending to become statistically indistinguishable from those of men.

A good example of somebody who held this position is John Stuart Mill. As a matter of justice, he argued, women should cease to have special legal disabilities laid upon them, should be able to vote and participate on equal terms in politics, and should have open access to educational and occupational opportunities: 'even if we could do without [the contributions of women], would it be consistent with justice to refuse to them their fair share of honour and distinction, or to deny to them the equal moral right of all human beings to choose their occupation (short of injury to others) according to their preferences, at their own risk?'[90] At the same time, Mill was prepared to accept the possibility that 'women have a greater natural inclination for some things than for others'.[91] At one point, he went a bit further and talked about 'the preference always likely to be felt by the majority of women for the one vocation in which there is nobody to compete with them'.[92] But he insisted that such speculations about the choices that women would make under a regime of equal opportunity could have no bearing on the strength of the case for offering women equal opportunities.

As he pointed out, if women do turn out to 'have a greater natural inclination for some things than for others, there is no need of laws or social inculcation to make the majority of them do the former in preference to the latter'.[93]

Not surprisingly, Mill has in the last few decades been hauled over the coals for failing to be 'in tune... with present day feminism'.[94] But he was right on the essential point that the argument for equality of opportunity as an intrinsically fair arrangement can and should be detached from any expectations about the patterns of choice that will arise from its implementation. Unless this is done, the consequence is that equality of opportunity will have to be branded a failure if it fails to bring about one particular pattern. If women disproportionately choose to give up full-time paid employment for a few years while their children are young, for example, they should not have to be burdened by the fear that they are somehow undermining the case for equal access for equally qualified people to all positions. That case is entirely sound, as Mill insisted, regardless of the pattern of choices that arises from the implementation of liberal equality. Whatever outcomes occur as a result of free choices made within just institutions are the outcomes that should occur.

Having said all that, I would not for a moment wish to deny the great plausibility of a claim that the lack of women in 'top corporate positions' strongly suggests the existence of discrimination. But that is not Young's claim: according to her, the fact that fewer than half of all 'top corporate positions' are filled by women actually *constitutes* discrimination. Suppose we say, instead, that the underrepresentation of women is prima facie evidence of discrimination. Then we are saying that we expect to be able to find specific processes that cause women to do less well in the competition for 'top corporate jobs' than equally qualified men. There are certain background assumptions that underlie the suspicion that unequal outcomes here arise from discrimination: we are talking, for example, about countries in which women are on average as well educated as men and have similar aspirations. Suppose that one or other (or both) of these conditions did not hold. Then, the lower proportion of women in 'top corporate jobs' could be explained without invoking discrimination in the workplace. Of course, there might well actually be discrimination in the workplace, and in such a society it is very likely that there would be. The point is, however, that in these circumstances there would be a plausible alternative explanation of the fact that women were statistically underrepresented in 'top corporate jobs', which did not invoke discrimination.

Let us consider a society in which women were statistically underrepresented in 'top corporate jobs' because they had, on average, fewer qualifications than men had, and let us assume that this in turn had arisen from the operation of an educational system that granted females inferior educational opportunities to those available to males. An egalitarian liberal would still, of course, describe this society as unjust. Suppose, instead, however, that women were as highly qualified as men but disproportionately chose to devote their lives to activities incompatible with reaching the top of a large corporation. An egalitarian liberal could not then complain of injustice if, as a result, women were underrepresented in 'top corporate jobs'. To illustrate the point, in an admittedly rather fanciful way, let us ponder Young's claim that there has in recent years been a growing tendency in the United States for women to revive some earlier ideas about the distinctive role of women, 'drawing on images of Amazonian grandeur, recovering and revaluing traditional women's arts like quilting and weaving, or inventing new rituals based on medieval witchcraft'.[95] As a full-scale 'alternative lifestyle', this is presumably too much of a minority affair to affect the occupational statistics significantly. Let us imagine, however, that it did grow so as to become pervasive. Anyone who wanted (to paraphrase Marx) to do weaving in the morning, quilting in the afternoon and witchcraft after dinner would have little time – or presumably inclination – for a high-flying business career.

Young's claim is, in essence, that 'more just patterns in the distribution of positions' would entail equal success rates for all groups.[96] Even 'strong affirmative action' programmes would be inadequate to achieve this, she says, because they still require that 'racially and sexually preferred candidates be qualified, and indeed often highly qualified'.[97] Notice, however, that special group-based policies would not be required to achieve 'just patterns' if two conditions were both met. First, all the groups picked out by Young (defined by ethnicity, gender, sexual orientation, age, disability or class) would have to have the same profile in terms of professional and educational qualifications. And second, all these groups would have to display the same distribution of achievement-orientated dispositions. Under these conditions, all groups would contain the same proportion of qualified applicants for all jobs. In the absence of discrimination, therefore, all groups would enjoy equal success rates.

Public policy can contribute to meeting the first condition by making equality of educational opportunity more of a reality. (The United States scores especially poorly on this, in comparison with other western liberal democracies, because of the way in which school funding tends to reflect the taxable capacity of the jurisdiction within which the school is located.) But even equal opportunities for groups do not guarantee equal group outcomes, because some groups may have a systematic tendency to take more or less than average advantage of those opportunities. Certain of Young's groups, moreover, present special problems. 'The disabled' are an immensely heterogeneous group, whose boundaries are ill-defined. But it is surely to be expected in the nature of the case that, across the group as a whole, its members will be less qualified than the average, even if the amount of money spent on their education is the average or more than the average. As far as the working class is concerned, this is a group defined by its members' occupations, so it seems to be a conceptual error to include it in a list of groups whose members suffer from 'cultural imperialism' or 'oppression', if that is taken (as it appears to be by Young) to entail that justice requires them to be represented in all occupations in proportion to their numbers.

The second condition – an identical distribution of achievement-motivations within each group – is not directly within the legitimate scope of public policy in a liberal society. If, however, the aspirations of group members tend to rise in line with the opportunities open to them, an improvement in the extent to which equality of educational opportunity is realized should help here too. What is apparent in any case is that, for the foreseeable future, Young will continue to be right to claim that 'more just patterns in the distribution of positions', as she understands them, will entail a very radical departure from a conception of justice according to which the most qualified people should get the job and any falling away from that standard constitutes unjust discrimination.

The driving force behind Young's advocacy of group proportionality is the idea that different ways of life pursued by different groups should have no effect on their collective success: the processes by which institutions such as those of the market and democratic political competition produce winners and losers in accordance with differential behaviour are to be overridden in the name of equality for groups. After the Caucus Race in *Alice in Wonderland*, the Dodo proclaimed 'Everybody has won, and *all* must have prizes.'[98] What we have here is a group-related version of the Dodo's principle, according to which it is all right for some people to win and others to lose, but members of all groups should get prizes in the same proportion. A statement of the principle that Young applauds, which is due to Kenneth Karst, runs as follows: 'As full members of the larger society, [members of cultural minorities] have the option to participate to whatever degree they choose. They also may look inward, seeking solidarity within their cultural group, without being penalized for that choice.'[99] If 'penalized' meant what it normally means (i.e. subject to the deliberate imposition of a penalty) this would be unexceptionable. But the intention is clearly that the choice of solidarity within one's cultural group should not give rise to any sort of relative disadvantage, compared with participation in the mainstream society.

Young vastly expands the scope of Karst's claim, in the process creating the list that I have already itemized. Thus, she writes that, 'if "cultural minority" is interpreted to mean any group subject to cultural imperialism, then this statement applies to women, old people, disabled people, gay men and lesbians, and working-class people as much as it applies to ethnic or national groups.'[100] Karst's original identification of ethnic and national groups as 'cultural minorities' already had built into it the questionable assumption that these groups are always defined by a distinctive culture. Young compounds the problem many times over by assuming implicitly that all the other groups that she adds are culturally constituted. Indeed, her formal definition of a social group actually stipulates that all social groups have a cultural basis: 'A social group is a collective of persons differentiated from at least one other group by cultural forms, practices, or way of life.'[101] Yet none of the groups she wishes to add is defined in this way.

The group consisting of women makes up half the human race, but (except for rare cases parasitic upon the general practice) membership of it is defined on the basis of physiology, not cultural characteristics. Old people are defined by age, not by sharing some 'old people's culture'. 'The disabled' simply describes the group made up of people with disabilities. It is true that there may be said to be a 'deaf culture' built around sign language.[102] But we still have to say that deafness is, as a matter of definition, a physical condition rather than a cultural trait. Gay men and lesbians are defined by their sexual orientation: some choose to adopt a 'gay lifestyle' while others do not. Class is defined by position in the class structure, and it may or may not be associated in a certain country or region with something recognizable as a distinctive 'working-class culture'. Moreover, the ethnic and national groups that were the subject of Karst's own statement are themselves primarily identified within the United States by (notional) descent rather than cultural attributes, as we saw earlier.

Even where there is a cultural component, it is unwarranted to assume that any discrimination suffered by members of such a group must be based on its culture. Let us suppose, for example, that old people in Britain have to some degree a shared culture – depending, perhaps, on their having in common the experience of having lived through the Second World War. It is not in virtue of this that people in their fifties or older find it difficult to get jobs for which they are qualified. There is an irresistible case for making discrimination based on age illegal. But if this is done the vast majority of cases brought will, I have no doubt, be complaints of direct discrimination, not indirect discrimination based on some cultural attribute distinctive to those over some age.

As Young observes, 'many legal theorists' have put forward the proposal that 'a policy or practice should be found discriminatory if it results in a disproportionate exclusion of women or people of color, whatever the intent of its makers'.[103] Although she indicates sympathy for this proposal, however, Young concedes that 'neither courts nor the general public have appeared willing to accept such an expanded concept of discrimination'.[104] Others would perhaps stop to wonder if this reluctance might stem not simply from queasiness about stretching the concept of discrimination but from reluctance to accept that there must necessarily be something wrong with differential group outcomes, regardless of their cause. Young, however, is undeterred by any such qualms. She simply suggests that the conclusion should be retained (and indeed extended) but furnished with a new rationale. 'Thus the primary argument for policies that consciously aim to increase the participation and inclusion of women, Blacks, Latinos, or disabled people in schools and offices and in positions of high reward and authority is that these policies intervene in the processes of oppression.'[105] The obvious problem with this proposal is that it is liable to reproduce the difficulty that led Young to give up on 'discrimination'. If the term 'oppression' were to retain its standard condemnatory force here, it would have to be shown for any particular case of statistical underrepresentation that it arose from some identifiable mechanism of oppression, in the ordinary sense of the word – that is to say, that it resulted from the illegitimate use of power. We are not entitled to deduce that there must be something wrong whenever we find that different groups have different success rates. We need to distinguish between processes giving rise to unfair outcomes and those that bring about disproportionate outcomes in ways that are not unfair. Let me describe three processes of each kind.

The first possible explanation of differential achievement, which clearly falls into the category of illegitimate causes, is direct discrimination. Thus, for example, if as many women as men were qualified applicants for some type of job or for some position such as that of parliamentary candidate, women would be underrepresented if employers or constituency selection committees chose fewer women. The second possible explanation of disproportionality is unjustifiable indirect discrimination. Illegitimate underrepresentation of a group would occur here if, for example, its members were as able and willing to do some job or hold some position as the rest of the population, but were disproportionately affected for religious or cultural reasons by some demand that was not necessary to the effective performance of the task. The third possibility is the legitimate counterpart to the second. Here we have requirements that disproportionately impinge on the members of some group as a result of their distinctive religious beliefs or cultural practices but can be justified because they are genuinely relevant to ability to do the job.

We can distinguish between a fourth and fifth possibility along lines parallel to those used to distinguish between the second and third. Thus, there will frequently be educational or professional qualifications for jobs. Some of these (our fourth case) may be unfairly discriminatory in that they disproportionately rule out members of certain groups and cannot be shown to be closely enough related to the ability to do the job to be justifiable. The fifth case is then parallel to the third: this is one in which the demand for certain formal qualifications can be justified as necessary. It should be borne in mind, however, that the outcome may still be unjust at one remove if there was a denial of equal opportunity to acquire the relevant qualifications.

The sixth and final possibility is that there may be group-related preferences for certain occupations. I gave an example of this in the previous chapter: the propensity of Sikhs in Britain to work in the construction industry is said to reflect the fact that the traditional occupation of the Ramgarhia 'caste' has been work of this kind. Young herself, we may recall, emphasized the importance to people of 'group based affinities and cultural life', and I commented that (contrary to her assumption) liberals were not committed to slighting the importance of such things or hoping that their importance would diminish. She can surely not wish to say that there is anything necessarily unfair or oppressive going on if one aspect of the importance of 'group based affinities and cultural life' is that members of different groups tend to cluster in different occupations by choice. To the extent that this is the explanation of differential group outcomes, there is no question of 'oppression'.

## 7.  The 'Myth of Merit'

Once we abandon Young's assumption that lack of group proportionality automatically entails injustice, we cannot avoid an element of judgement in determining what are fair criteria for employment, retention or advancement. We cannot sensibly deny that employers are entitled to give a preference to job candidates who have the ability and motivation to do the work over candidates who do not. Thus, by far the largest part of the explanation for the fact that American blacks are not represented in middle-class occupations proportionally to their numbers is simply that fewer than average have the educational qualifications needed for such occupations. This in turn reflects conditions that undermine equality of educational opportunity. Improving these conditions is a pressing demand of egalitarian social justice. But in the current situation we cannot properly describe as unfair discrimination the lack of 'willingness of employers, including Afro-American entrepreneurs, to hire unqualified persons further burdened by poor soft skills'.[106]

Or can we? Orlando Patterson (from whom that quotation comes) refers to 'poor soft skills', but does not enlarge on this. What employers will reject as 'poor soft skills' may indeed be cultural traits. We then have to ask, as with all discrimination on the basis of cultural traits, how far employers and co-workers can reasonably be expected to accommodate them. Thus, the employment record of young black males is even worse than would be predicted from their educational qualifications, and increasingly contrasts with the relative success of black women in moving up the occupational hierarchy. One explanation that has been offered is that there is a tendency for young black men to be perceived as having an 'in your face' attitude that makes for difficult relations with superiors and co-workers in the organization.[107] It may well be that this kind of attitude constitutes a survival trait in the Hobbesian state of nature that the most deprived black neighbourhoods approximate.[108] But that still leaves us with the question: is it a case of unfair discrimination if those who display it are not hired or are hired and then fired? To address this question we need to ask how the notion of job performance can be deployed in a way that does not warrant charges of unfairness.

This way of posing the question presupposes that the notion of job performance is not inherently flawed. Young attacks what she calls the 'myth of merit', but what she has to say on this score seems to me to fall far short of what would be needed to establish a case for believing that the whole idea of some people being better at doing things than others is almost entirely a social construction. Thus, she says that many jobs – for example that of a travel agent – are 'too complex and multifaceted to allow for a precise identification of their tasks and thus measurement of levels of performance of those tasks'.[109] But this does not mean that there are not good and bad travel agents, or that customers would have much difficulty in agreeing on which were which. Similarly, anyone who has ever tried to buy an interval drink at a theatre will be acutely aware of the extraordinary range of ability that lies between a good and a bad bartender. It may well be difficult to specify the qualities needed in advance and test for them, but after three months in the job it can scarcely fail to be clear who is up to it and who is not. I have noticed, incidentally, that even the most strenuously postmodern academics tend to agree that some departmental secretaries are a lot better than others at the job.

Young appears to believe that the 'merit principle' can be sustained only if there are 'normatively and culturally neutral measures of individual job performance'.[110] But why on earth should it be supposed that the relevant criteria must be narrowly technical? Thus, she thinks she has a knock-down argument against the 'neutrality' of education as a criterion of competence by saying: 'Much of what schools teach is not technical skills, but cultural values and social norms such as obedience, attentiveness, and deference to authority. Students are often graded according to how well they have internalized these values and norms rather than how well they are able to perform certain tasks.'[111] But employers would surely be perfectly reasonable if they regarded grades as relevant to hiring decisions, on the assumption that Young is right about what grades are a proxy for. An employee who is *able* to 'perform certain tasks' is of little value unless that ability is deployed effectively on the job. It is a safe prediction that an employee disposed to disobedience and inattentiveness will not get the job done very well. There is nothing mythical about a conception of merit that includes characteristics such as diligence, conscientiousness, reliability and cooperativeness.

Young would be on much more solid ground if she were to denounce the 'myth of merit' that takes broad academic qualifications and performance on general tests as the sole basis of appointment to desirable jobs. The reasoning of the Supreme Court in the case of *Griggs* v. *Duke Power Company* is instructive here.[112] This power company, located in North Carolina, had in 1955 instituted a policy that made graduation from high school a condition of employment in the more desirable jobs. However, it applied this criterion only to new recruits: those without high school diplomas who were already in these jobs were allowed to stay in them and also to gain promotion. Ten years later, the company offered an alternative to high school graduation in the form of a certain level of performance on a test purporting to measure intelligence and a 'mechanical comprehension test'. Again, existing workers who had not graduated from high school were retained in the desirable jobs and were not required to take the tests. Also in 1965, when the Civil Rights Act came into effect, the company for the first time opened up the more desirable jobs to black applicants on condition that they met one or other of the criteria for appointment.[113]

This was the background. What gave rise to the case was the fact that very few blacks satisfied either of the criteria for appointment to the more desirable jobs. The argument was made that the criteria had a racially discriminatory effect (whether intended or not), because they prevented many blacks who could have done those jobs from being appointed to them. How could anyone claim to know that blacks would have been able to do these jobs without satisfying the company's criteria for appointment to them? The answer given by the Court was that the company had created a natural experiment by changing the rules in 1955 in the precise way that it did. According to the Court, 'the evidence shows ... that employees who have not completed high school or taken the tests have continued to perform satisfactorily and made progress in departments for which the high school and test criteria are now used'.[114] Even promotion from these jobs to the next level up appeared to be unrelated to the firm's newly introduced criteria for appointment to them: 'the percentage of white employees who were promoted but who were not high school graduates was nearly identical to the percentage of nongraduates in the entire white work force.'[115] The Court declared, on the basis of these facts, that 'neither the high school completion requirement nor the general intelligence test is shown to bear a demonstrable relationship to successful performance of the jobs for which it was used'.[116]

It appears to have been thought unnecessary to defend the assumption that the data on white employees could be used to derive the implication that blacks without a high school education would do the jobs in question as well as whites without a high school education – and therefore as well as whites who were high school graduates. Only on the basis of this assumption could it have been deduced that blacks were being prevented by the company's criteria for appointment from doing jobs that they would prove themselves able to do if given the chance to show it. This assumption could be challenged. The Court itself drew attention to the fact that 'because they are Negroes, petitioners have long received inferior education in segregated schools'.[117] This could have meant that black employees who had not completed a high school education were a lot worse educated than whites who had not completed a high school education: quite likely the blacks would not have attended a high school at all. However, the well-established finding that graduating from high school made no difference to the ability of whites to do the jobs could surely support at least the conclusion that blacks should not be denied the opportunity of showing what they could do, and if necessary given some extra training to bring them up to speed.[118]

The *Griggs* decision has subsequently been greatly weakened by the Supreme Court.[119] For the present purpose, however, what is of concern is the basic point that people who do well at acquiring general qualifications and taking general tests may simply be good at whatever it is that is needed to do well at them, and that this may have little to do with the proven ability to do some specific job well. The *Griggs* case was in one way exceptionally easy because there was evidence that (at any rate among white employees) there was a complete lack of any connection between high school graduation and success in the desirable jobs within the power company. The more usual situation is one in which there is some correlation between general qualifications or test scores and the ability to do a certain job, but only a weak one: 'test scores explain only about 10 to 20 per cent of the variation in job performance'.[120] However, this very low correlation has the implication that, if appointment to desirable jobs is made contingent upon qualifications and test scores, enormous numbers of people who are bad at acquiring qualifications and passing tests will be kept out of jobs that they could do well if they were given a chance.

For reasons that are not at all well understood, blacks have a strong tendency to underperform on tests in relation to their abilities to do specific jobs.[121] 'The predictor that social scientists can measure most accurately – namely cognitive skills – is the predictor on which blacks are most disadvantaged.'[122] The point is not that the tests are biased or that better tests are available. It is simply that, even though there is a genuine correlation between test scores and job performance, it is so low that many blacks (and other low scorers) who could do the job are excluded at the outset if only cognitive tests are used as a means of selection. 'The test score gap between black and white job applicants has traditionally averaged about one standard deviation. When employers do not screen workers [i.e. select by test scores], the performance gap is likely to be much smaller – typically more like two-fifths of a standard deviation.'[123] On these figures, a firm with six hundred applicants for a hundred jobs that hired all of them and retained the hundred who did best would finish up with thirty-six black workers, whereas one that simply hired the hundred with the best scores and hung on to them all would employ only thirteen.[124]

It is crucial to recognize that the criticism of the use of formal qualifications and test scores as criteria for appointment to desirable jobs rests on the presupposition that there really is such a thing as being good or bad at a job. Before we can sensibly say that test scores are poor predictors of performance in a job, we must think that we have some way of assessing performance in a job. The Supreme Court was extremely clear about this in *Griggs*: 'if any employment practice which operates to exclude Negroes cannot be shown to be related to job performance, the practice is prohibited.'[125] And again

> Congress has not commanded that the less qualified be preferred over the better qualified simply because of minority origins. Far from disparaging job qualifications as such, Congress has made such qualifications the controlling factor, so that race, religion, nationality, and sex become irrelevant. What Congress has commanded is that any tests used must measure the person for the job and not the person in the abstract.[126]

Some of Young's criticisms of the 'myth of merit' seem to have as their target the inappropriate use of general qualifications and tests to screen out candidates for desirable jobs. But most of her attack on the 'myth of merit' suggests that what she is mainly against is the idea of job performance itself – the whole notion that some people are better at a job than others. Thus, she says that what is wrong with 'the ideology of merit' is that it 'seeks to depoliticize the establishment of criteria and standards for allocating positions and awarding benefits'.[127] By the same token, then, the politics of difference seeks to politicize appointments. According to Young, 'democratic decision making about [the filling of jobs and offices] is a crucial condition of social justice'.[128] But once it becomes the orthodox view that the criteria for filling jobs are up for grabs, jobs will go to the members of whichever faction or coalition comes out on top.

To be fair, it should be said that Young wishes to impose some limits: 'People with particular group affinities, social positions, or personal attributes may be preferred, but only to undermine oppression or compensate for disadvantage, and never to reinforce privilege.'[129] However, this proviso would be extremely hard to enforce through any system of judicial review. In any case, Young's list of the oppressed is so comprehensive as to amount to open season on white middle-class males who are straight, able-bodied, and neither young nor old. Consistently with doing in the members of this minority, there would obviously be no end of room for infighting for positional advantage among advocates of different groups among the rest. I find it hard to conceive that, if the concept of justice is to retain any independent signification, the results of a politicized appointment process along the lines advocated by Young could have anything to do with justice.

Employers must discriminate among job candidates if they are to take any decisions at all. Discrimination becomes a pejorative term only when the criteria are inappropriate. Liberals cannot afford the postmodern luxury of saying that the relevance of a criterion is in the eye of the beholder. The liberal conception of fairness in employment depends on the possibility of reasoned argument about the appropriate criteria. Thus, the answer in the case that I raised at the beginning of this discussion must turn on the relevance of an 'in your face' attitude to job performance. That this is a cultural trait does not make it unfair *per se* to reject those who display it. I mentioned in chapter 2 a variety of culturally derived characteristics that would make people unsuited to specific jobs: there is no reason why there might not be cultural characteristics that made their bearers poor prospects for almost any job. At the same time, it would be unfair if the difficulties experienced by employers and workmates that led to dismissal arose from nothing more than a failure to adapt to a certain style of self-expression. (The disproportionate rate of exclusion of Afro-Caribbean children from state schools in Britain raises many of the same issues.)

To determine whether the problem is one of cultural decoding or a deeper one that really involves job performance would be a delicate business. But that is the question which has to be addressed. There may in the end turn out to be a grey area, where one side claims with some plausibility that certain behaviour impedes cooperation and the other side argues with equal plausibility that it would not do so if everybody else were to adapt to it. A case law will then have to be built up by courts and tribunals, based on some notion of what it is reasonable to demand of each side. Perhaps within this grey area it may properly be said that there is no 'objective' answer, and that Young's contention is borne out to that extent. However, saying that at some point a decision has to be made about where the burden of adaptation should lie is very far from conceding Young's central contention that the whole idea of some people being better at jobs than others is a mere device for oppression.

## 8. Language and Opportunity

If we take seriously Karst's suggestion, endorsed by Young, that people should not be 'penalized' (that is to say, disadvantaged) by looking inward and seeking solidarity within their cultural group, we shall have to conclude that nobody should be placed at a disadvantage by lack of fluency in the language already established as the standard medium of politics, public administration and business. 'Many Spanish-speaking Americans', Young says, 'have asserted their right to maintain their specific culture and speak their language and still receive the benefits of citizenship, such as voting rights, decent education, and job opportunities.'[130] It goes without saying that speaking Spanish and maintaining Spanish culture (by reading Spanish books, attending churches in which the liturgy is in Spanish, and so on) should not be a bar in itself to being enabled to enjoy rights and opportunities such as those listed by Young. The intention is, however, to suggest that one should be able to enjoy all these benefits without also having to be fluent in English. Whereas the first demand is completely unexceptionable, satisfying the second cannot reasonably be held to be a requirement of egalitarian liberal principles.

Curiously, when she gets into a more detailed discussion of language, Young says that 'few advocates of cultural pluralism and group autonomy in the United States would deny that proficiency in English is a necessary condition for full participation in American society'.[131] The earlier and later statements could be true together only if the 'many Spanish-speaking Americans' whose demands were expressed in the first quotation are not counted among the 'advocates of cultural pluralism and group autonomy' among whom few, according to the second quotation, make such demands. However the puzzle is resolved, I believe that those whose opinions are reported in the second quotation are the ones with the right answer.

In earlier times, it was perfectly feasible (as in parts of the Austro-Hungarian empire) for the towns to be linguistic enclaves surrounded by a peasantry that spoke another language. It was enough if there were some economic intermediaries and public officials who could speak both languages. Life could go on quite satisfactorily for all concerned under those conditions, so long as everybody accepted the political and economic status quo. But the specifics of the conditions under which this occurred actually make the case for linguistic uniformity in liberal societies. For economic relations in these societies violated elementary liberal precepts by being stratified and segmented: Germans, for example, would settle in the towns (and upwardly mobile locals assimilated), while peasants spoke some vernacular that might not even have a written form. There was, moreover, no need for political cooperation – or room for political conflict – because the form of government was authoritarian.

Egalitarian liberalism is committed to equality of opportunity. As I explained in the previous chapter, this does not in the present context mean that all have the same choice sets: it is not unfair if only qualified brain surgeons are considered for a position as a brain surgeon in a hospital. There is some room for disagreement about what is entailed by equality of opportunity in education. Fortunately, however, I can finesse this dispute for the purpose of the present discussion. All that I need to say is that it is, at any rate, fairly clearly a violation of equal opportunity for members of different groups within a society to have systematically different prospects of educational and occupational achievement, even where they have comparable levels of native ability and motivation. The existence of different linguistic communities within a single country is compatible with equality of opportunity understood in this way, on condition that these communities are able to maintain educational and economic institutions capable of providing a range of opportunities of roughly equal value. It would be pedantic to insist that the two sets of opportunities must be absolutely identical. What matters is that the prospects facing people with the same aptitudes and inclinations in the two communities should be equally good. Belgium (for French and Dutch speakers), Canada (for English and French speakers) and Switzerland (with regard at least to speakers of French and German) all meet these conditions adequately.[132] The politics of wonderland begin to encroach only where such conditions are not fulfilled.

Manifestly, an Inuit in Canada who does not speak English or French is at a severe disadvantage in the national job market. Anyone who wants to participate fully in the mainstream Canadian economy will have to learn English or French. But it should be noted that there is no demand in Canada for the creation of an entire parallel economy for those whose only language is that of one of the 'first nations'. What those who choose to identify with a Native American group want is to have a quite different set of options from those offered in the mainstream economy. It will not be regarded as an objection that a career as a player in a symphony orchestra or as a nuclear physicist is not going to be available within the group. On the conception of opportunity put forward by Bhikhu Parekh and discussed in the previous chapter, we could say that monoglot Inuit do not miss out on any opportunities, even though so many jobs in the mainstream economy are closed to them, because nothing counts as an opportunity unless the person concerned has 'the cultural disposition to take advantage of it'.[133] But this would, as I have argued, drain the concept of opportunity of any independent significance. If we stick to the notion that opportunities are available options, we shall have to say that people who speak only a Native American language have only a very truncated range of opportunities open to them but that this is nevertheless not unfair. To achieve what they want calls for measures to give them control over the resources they need for a distinctive way of life, not the creation of an entire parallel economy operating in their own language and offering the full range of opportunities open to other Canadians.

The point to be made here is that nothing in this case carries over to that of immigrants. Immigrants to liberal societies (which are the only sort with which I am concerned here) are normally attracted by job opportunities in the mainstream economy: they have no wish to create a completely distinctive, self-enclosed economy, on the lines of a Native American band. There are a few exceptions such as the Hutterites and the Amish in North America. These raise some questions about equal opportunity in as far as their educational practices place those who choose to leave the community at a disadvantage in the mainstream job market; but, for those who stay, nobody would regard it as an objection that membership is incompatible with a career in ballet or banking. The singularity of these cases (which I shall take up in chapter 5) highlights the difference between such groups and the general run of immigrants.

A firm in the mainstream economy may be able, by using a bilingual supervisor as intermediary, to accommodate linguistic minorities in jobs such as sewing jeans, working at checkout counters or collecting rubbish. But it cannot reasonably be accused of unfair employment practices if it makes fluency in the standard language a condition of getting a job that requires communication with others in the firm or with the public. Similarly, those who do not learn the language of public life cannot reasonably complain if they are disadvantaged in dealing with the law and the bureaucracy and are marginalized politically. Even where lack of fluency in the language of business and politics imposes these limitations, there may well still be community leaders who urge the maintenance of linguistic enclaves. This is, however, more plausibly seen as an intergenerational conflict of interest within the immigrant group than as a straightforward conflict between the interests of that collectivity and those of the host society. For the older generation, there is the advantage of not having to adapt. In addition, there are for the community leaders the power and other rewards that come from being needed as the intermediaries between the ordinary group members and the political and administrative structures of the wider society. (Characteristically, the community leaders do not practice what they preach in that they are themselves bilingual.) For the children, there is much less to lose and much more to gain from the acquisition of the means of moving freely in the larger society.[134]

Compelling children to learn a minority language as a second language is, obviously, much less damaging to their job prospects than not ensuring fluency in the mainstream language. Even here, however, 'the opportunity costs that are involved in studying a regional language are often equivalent to the non-acquisition of a foreign language that may be of greater practical use'.[135] Thus, 'Wales is linguistically the most "Celtic" strand in the United Kingdom's "Celtic fringe", with approximately 20 per cent of the population still speaking Welsh.'[136] This is, on the basis of the principles laid out here, a reason for ensuring that the Welsh language is available to be taught in the schools: the nineteenth-century practice of beating children for speaking

Welsh even in the school playground is precisely the kind of compulsory 'assimilation' that I repudiated earlier in this chapter. At the same time, it has to be recognized that the great majority of people in Wales do not speak Welsh at home, and for them learning Welsh in school from scratch is in direct competition for time with learning a major foreign language. It is therefore scarcely surprising that compulsory instruction in Welsh in the schools has aroused opposition from English-speaking parents; and the principles put forward here would lend support to their case.[137] The labour market advantages of those with an educational qualification in the Welsh language have been boosted by policies adopted by local authorities that require knowledge of Welsh as a condition of employment. Cases have been brought under the 1976 Race Relations Act challenging such policies, though without success.[138] Unless knowledge of Welsh can be shown to be related to the effective discharge of the duties of the job, however, requiring it is clearly unfair discrimination. Creating an artificially protected labour market in order to motivate acceptance of compulsory instruction in Welsh in the schools is simply to compound one abuse of state power by another.

Where language is concerned, a state cannot adopt a neutral stance: it must provide its services in one or more languages, decide if a linguistic test for employment is to count as illegal discrimination, and so on. At the same time, however, it can be said of language as of no other cultural trait that it is a matter of convention. No doubt every language has its own peculiar excellences, but any language will do as the medium of communication in a society as long as everybody speaks it. This is one case involving cultural attributes in which 'This is how we do things here' – the appeal to local convention – is a self-sufficient response to pleas for the public recognition of diversity.

When we say, then, that equality of opportunity is a criterion on which an egalitarian liberal society can properly be judged, this must be taken to mean that everybody should have an opportunity to acquire the country's language, to achieve educational success in that language, and to gain employment on the basis of those qualifications without suffering discrimination. These are hard enough to achieve, and most countries have at best a spotty record in ensuring them. But they are objectives whose validity nobody who accepts egalitarian liberal principles can deny. In contrast, the provision of genuine equality of opportunity without linguistic assimilation by immigrants would be, if not absolutely impossible, almost unimaginably burdensome.

It has to be admitted frankly that this has the implication that the first generation of immigrants may well find themselves at a disadvantage if they are unable to become fluent in the language of business and public affairs in their new home. But many newly arrived immigrants are in any case at a disadvantage as a result of coming in with an education that restricts their occupational opportunities. They themselves are normally content if their lot has improved over the one that they left behind. Where equality of opportunity is relevant is among those who are born and grow up in the host country. Fortunately, the experience of immigrants all over the world testifies to the ease with which young children learn the local language, even if their parents speak it poorly or not at all. (Indeed, itinerant academics who take young children abroad for just a year are regularly amazed to hear them rattling away in the local language after a short time.) This is what naturally happens in the absence of deliberate attempts by the immigrant community to impede it, especially where these attempts include the provision of public education employing the community's language as a medium of instruction.

Let me sum up. The general theorem is that equality of opportunity plus cultural diversity is almost certain to bring about a different distribution of outcomes in different groups. Equal outcomes can be secured only by departing from equal opportunity so as to impose equal success rates for all groups. A culturally diverse society cannot be conceived as one in which everyone is trying equally hard to achieve the same goals. The prizes to be won may have a different value for different people, and people with different aspirations and priorities may not all be equally willing to make whatever sacrifices are needed in order to win them. Thus, even after all gratuitous barriers (including subtle ones) have been removed, it may well be that some ways of life and their associated values will lead to a relatively low level of occupational achievement, as conventionally measured. A liberal will have to say that that is the unavoidable implication of cultural diversity. There is no reason for saying it is an unfair outcome, so long as the criteria for employment are defensible.

It should be emphasized, however, that there is nothing in the general conception of liberalism that commits it to underwriting whatever economic inequalities a society may attach to different occupational positions. Even if groups had similar occupational profiles, this would be compatible with great inequalities within each group, arising from individuating characteristics such as natural talent, freedom from ill-health or disability, or the good luck of being in the right place at the right time. Egalitarian liberalism maintains that inequalities in income not arising from choices can be justified only indirectly. This can be done if it can be shown that such inequalities benefit everyone by making an economy work more efficiently. But the amount of inequality in incomes (after taxes and transfers) that could be justified by this is a great deal less than that found in most societies.

What should we say about inequalities flowing from choices rooted in culturally based preferences for certain ways of life against others? The implication of everything I have said so far is that it would be a mistake to regard these as a matter of good or bad luck. Many people, perhaps for reasons related to their culture, derive a satisfaction from their jobs that is entirely independent of the pay that they get for doing them.[139] Moreover, having the kind of upbringing and personality that leads people to place a very high value upon occupational success, in the conventional sense, is by no means obviously something to be envied by all others. It is quite possible that people whose priorities are elsewhere – with their family, their sports club, or their garden, for example – can live equally or more fulfilling lives than those driven to maximize achievement. But there is a material condition for that to be so in the form of a certain level of economic resources. Those for whom paid employment is not at the centre of their lives should still finish up with enough income to enable them to enjoy an acceptable standard of living and participate in the life of their society. If a society attenuated the inequalities created by the market in this way, it could be said to let people with different priorities and values pursue them without having to pay an excessive price in terms of material well-being.

# PART II

---

## Multiculturalism and Groups

# 4

## Theories of Group Rights

### 1. The Concept of a Group Right

In Part I, I looked at a variety of proposals for treating individuals in some special way in virtue of their membership in some culturally defined group. These rights were rights of individuals, not of groups. This is sometimes denied, and the denial has generated a good deal of gratuitous confusion in the literature. Thus, Bhikhu Parekh writes that 'being individual-centred many of our theories of equality come to grief when applied to groups, which call for a very different conception of equality'.[1] The examples that he gives are cases such as the religious slaughter exemption and the Sikh crash helmet exemption discussed in chapter 2. Now it is, of course, trivially true that a rule about wearing crash helmets that has an exemption for those Sikhs who choose to avail themselves of it by wearing a turban applies to all and only Sikhs. But it is a group right only in the uninteresting sense in which any rule (e.g. free entry to museums for students and pensioners) may be said to be a group right for all those covered by it: Sikhs enjoy the exemption individually, as do individual students and pensioners. Thus, as Jacob Levy has put it, since we are dealing with 'individually exercised negative liberties', these 'exemption rights are wholly immune to the criticism that "groups cannot be rights-bearers," for while they are group-differentiated they are not "group rights" in any meaningful sense'.[2]

The proposals for giving positive advantages to members of groups that were discussed in chapter 3 may seem to introduce group rights in a more interesting sense. If we think of a scheme guaranteeing a certain proportion of the places in a law school's annual intake to members of a certain group, we may be tempted to distinguish it from an exemption from a generally applicable law in the following way. An individual immunity can be fully exercised by each member of the group whose members are eligible to enjoy it, regardless of the actions of the other members of the group. Each Sikh, for example, is entitled to wear a turban on a motor cycle or carry a knife in public regardless of the number of other Sikhs who are doing so. To work a quota scheme, in contrast, entails reference to the collectivity of those qualified to benefit from its provisions. For the entitlement is predicated over the group of, say, American blacks as a whole.

Let me explain. Suppose that a law school reserves 20 per cent of its places each year for blacks. That does not provide any individual black with an entitlement to go to the law school. But it does guarantee that, regardless of their test scores in relation to the rest of the candidates, black students will make up 20 per cent of the intake. Whether or nor a given applicant's test score will be good enough to secure admission to the law school depends on the test scores of the other applicants eligible to enter within the quota. On the assumption that the law school takes account only of scores on the LSAT (the standard test for admission), it will establish separate cut-off points for black students and others. How high the cut-off point for black students will turn out to be in any year will depend only on the quality of the black applicants in that year. Preferential admissions do not have to take this form, however. Instead of assigning a quota, the law school could simply treat black candidates more favourably than others with similar test scores, either informally or by adding some predetermined amount (say fifty points) to their LSAT scores and admitting the candidates with the highest adjusted scores. This scheme would not make the prospects of any individual black candidate depend on the performance of other black candidates specifically. Rather, as in any competitive system of admissions, the prospects of each candidate would depend on the strength of the entire field of applicants.[3]

The essential point is that, whichever of these forms it takes, a preferential admissions programme is still one that confers its benefits on individuals (albeit on individuals in virtue of their membership in a group) rather than on a group as such. It might be said that it is in the interest of all blacks that there should be more black lawyers, either on the assumption that black lawyers will better understand and empathize with the problems of other blacks or on the assumption that the more black professionals there are the better it is for the status of blacks generally. Even if one or both of these assumptions is true, however, the gains to blacks in general accrue only as the by-product of a programme that is aimed at increasing the opportunities of individuals. There is still no corporate entity that receives special treatment, and hence still no question of 'group rights'.

It is sometimes suggested that the individualistic nature of liberalism precludes any policies that provide special benefits for people on the basis of their membership in some group. While this may be true of liberalism in some forms, it is certainly not true of the egalitarian liberalism that provides the premises for this book. According to this, any disadvantage for which the victim is not responsible establishes a prima facie claim to remedy or compensation. The implication is that special measures to help the disabled are fully justified – and indeed required by justice – as a way of compensating for disadvantage. There is, by the same token, no objection on the basis of egalitarian liberal principles to special measures for providing assistance to members of groups disadvantaged in other ways: by low income, poor quality housing, lack of a job (or a job that pays enough to live on), poor education, a high probability of being victims of physical violence, an unhealthy environment, and so on.

Policies targeted at those who suffer from these and other forms of deprivation are unquestionably justifiable and indeed morally necessary. Such policies are, however, universalistic in exactly the same sense as a national health service that covers everybody is universalistic: different people receive different treatment in accordance with their needs, but everybody with the same need receives the same treatment. Although we might say that all the members of the group consisting of people defined by a certain medical condition get special treatment, the group in question is defined by medical need and medical need alone. Similarly, policies aimed at helping those suffering from social and economic disadvantage offer special treatment to the group consisting of the disadvantaged.

Group-based policies can still run into problems, however, where the group is defined in a way that makes it either under-inclusive or over-inclusive. Thus, it is quite attractive as a way of targeting resources most efficiently to say: 'Let's put a load of money into improving conditions in the inner-city black ghettoes.' It is, indeed, true that these are the sites of the most geographically concentrated extreme and multiple deprivation: their inhabitants are, in the words of the title of a book by William Julius Wilson, 'the truly disadvantaged'.[4] But 'a growing number of poor Euro-Americans, who now greatly outnumber their Afro-American counterparts', exhibit all the social pathologies popularly associated with the ghetto.[5] Concentrating resources exclusively on the inner-city black ghettoes would thus be an under-inclusive policy because it would leave out others suffering from similar deprivations.

This is not to say that such a policy is to be condemned out of hand. Multiple deprivation in a dozen or so major cities is much easier to target than similar deprivation scattered around thousands of trailer parks. Tackling the problems of the ghetto would be a lot better than doing nothing at all: the best should not to allowed to be the enemy of the good. It would be a major move towards social justice, even if it created inequities. At the same time, however, it is doubtful that such an under-inclusive policy is good politics. It is bound to create resentment – which cannot be dismissed as unjustified – among others similarly placed who cannot see why they should be denied the same benefits. And it builds the policy on a perilously small constituency, which does not even punch its weight politically in accordance with its numbers. Universalistic policies that track individual deprivation are not only more equitable than group-based policies; they may well also be a good deal better able to attract and sustain political support, despite their greater total cost. For example, a federal programme that puts extra resources into every school that has any number of children in it who suffer from deprivation will benefit hundreds of thousands of schools all over the country. In contrast, only ghetto children attend ghetto schools, so extra resources for such schools will not directly benefit anybody outside the ghetto.

Over-inclusive policies also create problems. These are policies that offer benefits indiscriminately to all the members of a group that has the following property. its members are on the average deprived in relation to the average of the population as a whole, but some of its members are not deprived at all. Preferential admission and hiring policies based on race as a criterion for eligibility illustrate this kind of over-inclusiveness. Although it remains true that American blacks are on the average disadvantaged, there is now a flourishing black middle class, and it is their children who are the main beneficiaries of preferential admissions to the leading universities. This comes about because, within the universe of black applicants, they tend to have gained the highest test scores, to have attended the best schools, and to possess personal characteristics of a kind that make it look as if they will fit in easily. Yet it is surely plausible that these children should have to take their chances in the general competition for places.

Again, however, it may be argued that it would still be better to have an across-the-board system of race-based preferences than nothing. But these are not the only options. It would be possible to refine the system of preferential admissions by adding a cut-off point for eligibility defined in terms of parental income. Along those lines, Orlando Patterson has proposed that group-based preferential admissions should be phased out in two stages, each lasting five years, the first of which would eliminate from coverage children of well-to-do blacks and the second children of any black parents except poor ones.[6] This proposal is not without difficulties. Parental income would presumably have to be used as the measure of affluence or poverty, but it is not a very good surrogate for material deprivation because that is affected by so many other factors. Moreover, incomes fluctuate from year to year, yet it would be intolerable to pitch a child out of some place it had gained under an affirmative action programme the moment its parents' income increased, and disruptive to add late in the day children of parents whose income had declined. Entry into the programme would therefore have to take place on the strength of a given year's income, which might be atypical – and might indeed be deliberately manipulated by calculating parents so as to make it low in the critical year. Moreover, income, even if it were perfectly stable and a perfect surrogate for material deprivation, would still suffer from the difficulty that it is a continuous variable. Any cut-off point would therefore leave children on either side of it with unequal prospects despite a difference of only one dollar in their parents' incomes. Nevertheless, Patterson's proposal (perhaps with the lengths of the two phases extended somewhat) might still be preferable to either eliminating all preferences for black children or maintaining a system that in practice is chiefly advantageous to the children of professionals.

I am a good deal less keen on Patterson's further suggestion that, after affirmative action based on race (and sex) has been phased out, 'the nation should institute an affirmative action program for all American-born persons from poor families. This program should be indefinite, lasting as long as there is poverty in the midst of affluence.'[7] Instituting a programme open to all Americans and based entirely on income would enormously compound the problems that are already inherent in using income to establish eligibility within the group of black Americans. But there is a deeper objection, which would still stand if no weight were attached to practical problems. It would, I believe, be a thoroughly retrograde step to transform market-based inequalities into status inequalities, permanently creating an estate or caste of poor people with distinct rights and privileges. The effect would inevitably be to stigmatize the members of this group. Moreover, creating such a group would be a potent source of social and political division, splitting the potential constituency for redistributive policies down the middle. The applicants from posh private schools and public schools in the leafy suburbs would continue to get into selective colleges in virtue of their high test scores and strong academic records. The losers would be the marginal candidates whose parents were not quite poor enough to enable them to qualify for preferential admission. (I shall return to this point in the context of the politics of multiculturalism in chapter 8.)

It should be noticed that special treatment for the physically disabled and special treatment for the socially disadvantaged have in common that the beneficiaries are assumed to be people who want the same things as the rest of the population and simply lack the resources that would enable them to enjoy more of those things. If such policies succeed, moreover, they will tend to decrease social isolation and enable their beneficiaries to make the transition all the way into the mainstream society. This notion of an assimilationist virtuous circle is in sharp contrast with the rationale of the kind of group-based policies advocated by the theorists of multiculturalism.

For what they propose are group-based policies deliberately intended to perpetuate cultural differences indefinitely. Moreover, they do not make claims for the justice of such policies on the ground that they are needed to redress inequality of opportunity. Rather, the basis of the claim is that unequal uptake of opportunities, even equal opportunities, would still call for remedial action if it arose as a result of culturally based preferences. As I have argued, however, there is nothing unjust about the fact that different people will select different elements from the same choice set in accordance with their preferences. Thus, while egalitarian liberalism does not rule out special treatment for the members of certain groups, what it does rule out is precisely the kind of special treatment called for by the multiculturalists.

So far, the policies I have been discussing all count as policies that benefit individuals, albeit individuals whose eligibility depends upon membership in a group. In the rest of this chapter and in the next two, which comprise Part II of the book, we shall move on to consider policies that have groups as their subject-matter. The focus will be, in other words, on claims made by or on behalf of groups. Every liberal society allows some self-governing powers to communal groups (such as families) and corporate groups (such as churches), but each gives somewhat different answers to the question of the scope of those powers. Liberals find themselves exposed to conflicting pressures in relation to groups. Because of their fundamental commitment to the value of the individual, they cannot turn a blind eye to the potential that associations and communities have for abusing, oppressing and exploiting their members. Yet at the same time they recognize that much of every normal individual's well-being derives from membership in associations and communities. If the fulfilment of individuals depends on the flourishing of groups, it follows that groups must have rights of self-government. For a group that does not have the power to set its own course cannot be expected to have much life in it.

Is there anything to be said here except that we have two competing values that have to be weighed against one another on a case-by-case basis? Is it possible to discern a principled way of deciding what things groups should be free to do without external interference and where the limits to that freedom should be drawn? I shall have the temerity in this chapter to lay out and defend two principles that I believe can guide us in thinking about the appropriate scope of group freedom in a liberal society. I shall then in the following two chapters attempt to apply these principles – and in the process refine them – by working through their implications for two of the topics that seem to' me to create the greatest difficulties. Chapter 5 will be devoted to a variety of questions thrown up by the demands of religious groups for rights to self-government. Then in chapter 6 I shall ask what are the proper limits of self-government for one particular kind of group: families. I shall concentrate especially on the competing claims of parents and liberal states with respect to the education of children.

In the course of this discussion, I shall endeavour to respond to the criticisms of liberalism that are characteristically made by the partisans of multiculturalism. It is often argued that groups whose members do not subscribe to the tenets of liberal individualism are inevitably going to be put at a disadvantage in pursuing their collective ends in comparison with groups whose foundational commitments are congruent with liberal individualism. For groups of the former kind will be forced to amend their practices so as to bring them into line with the demands of liberal principles, whereas groups of the latter kind will run into no such problems. Thus, as in Part I, the charge to be addressed is that liberalism fails to live up to its promises. Its promise of equal treatment for groups is as hollow as its promise of equal treatment for individuals, because it does not offer equal treatment for liberal and non-liberal groups. Similarly, its promise of liberty is hollow because it does not respect the freedom of illiberal groups to arrange their internal affairs as their beliefs dictate.

My strategy in Part I was two-pronged. I argued that some criticisms of 'difference-blind' liberalism rested on misapprehensions about its premises, its implications, or both. Other criticisms should, I suggested, be rejected on the ground that the answers given by liberal principles were the right ones. My defence against the new line of attack just outlined will take the same twofold form. On one hand, I shall wish to deny that liberalism rests on the controversial premises sometimes attributed to it or has the expansively interventionist implications with which it is sometimes saddled by opponents. On the other hand, I shall insist that the concern of liberals for the well-being of individuals is quite rightly non-negotiable, from which it follows that there must be limits to the freedom of groups to do what they will with their members.

## 2.  Liberalism and Autonomy

Before putting forward my own ideas, later in this chapter, I shall explain what I think is wrong with a way of looking at the relation between liberalism and group rights that has gained a great deal of ground among political philosophers in recent years. A canonical statement of the thesis can be found in an article by William Galston entitled 'Two Concepts of Liberalism'. According to this, there are 'two quite different strands of liberal thought'. One is concerned with the promotion of the autonomy of the individual, and entails a 'commitment to sustained rational examination of self, others and social practices'. The other strand values 'diversity', understood as 'differences among individuals and groups over such matters as the nature of the good life, sources of moral authority, reason versus faith, and the like'.[8] An alternative formulation of what is essentially the same contrast suggests that 'the debate among liberals' is 'about whether autonomy or tolerance is the fundamental value within liberal theory'.[9] In this influential version of the antithesis, which is due to Will Kymlicka, 'autonomy' means roughly the same as Galston means by it: a psychological disposition that gives a high priority to Socratic questioning of traditional beliefs and customary ways of life. 'Tolerance' corresponds to Galston's 'diversity': what are to be tolerated by liberal states are the practices of groups whose way of life rests on the rejection of liberal ideas such as equality and liberty. To the extent that this account of what is at issue has imposed itself on anglophone political philosophy, it is hardly surprising that the resultant literature is confusing and confused. Given the choice between these two interpretations, the right answer is, I suggest, 'Neither of the above'. Let me explain in this section what is wrong with the first answer. Then, in the next two sections, I shall say what seems to me wrong with the second answer. The final section will be devoted to developing my own theory of group rights.

What, then, is to be said of the conception of liberalism that would put at its core the promotion of autonomy, understood as some kind of psychological disposition? Unquestionably, many liberals would be inclined to say that, other things being equal, a society is a better society the more widely diffused among its members is the disposition to ask if beliefs and practices can be justified. But it is a far cry from that to identifying liberalism with the demand that the state should take as its mission the inculcation of autonomy. John Stuart Mill is a good case in point. Clearly, Mill thought that it was good for people to reflect on their beliefs and to exercise some kind of self-conscious choice about their way of life. As he wrote in *On Liberty*:

> The mental and moral, like the muscular powers, are improved only by being used. The faculties are called into no exercise by doing a thing merely because others do it, no more than believing a thing only because others believe it.... He who lets the world, or his own portion of it, choose his plan of life for him, has no need of any other faculty than the ape-like one of imitation. He who chooses his plan for himself, employs all his faculties.... It is possible that he might be guided in some good path, and kept out of harm's way, without [exercising the faculties required by choice]. But what will be his comparative worth as a human being?[10]

At the same time, however, Mill was almost obsessively concerned in *On Liberty* with keeping the state out of any attempt to mould character – even into a form that he regarded as admirable. As a consequence, his view of the legitimate role of the state in relation to education was remarkably austere.

Far from laying on the state the duty of inculcating autonomy, Mill insisted that the state should stay out of the process of education entirely.

Its role should be restricted to requiring satisfactory performance in annual public examinations 'with a gradually extending range of subjects, so as to make the universal acquisition and what is more, retention, of a certain minimum of general knowledge, virtually compulsory'.[11] The fathers of children who failed would be (in a way congenial to the spirit of New Labour) 'subjected to a moderate fine'.[12] Above a certain basic level of attainment, Mill proposed that the state might offer certificates recording performance in voluntary examinations. But these too should be confined to 'facts and positive science exclusively', though these 'facts' might include 'the matter of fact that such and such an opinion is held, on such grounds, by such authors, or schools or churches'.[13] Moreover, Mill held that parents should be permitted to send their children to schools at which some specific religious belief was taught along with the rest of the curriculum.[14]

Despite all this, it has become routine among contemporary political philosophers to use the term 'Millian liberalism' to refer to the view that it is the job of the state to promote autonomy. Yet it is clearly a travesty of Mill's position to identify him with any such view of the role of the state.[15] This is not to say, of course, that Mill saw no connection between the development of an autonomous personality and the presence of liberal institutions. The cultivation of a disposition towards Socratic questioning would obviously be severely inhibited if those who engaged in it were liable to meet the fate of Socrates. Like Mill, contemporary liberals can, and do, regard it as an argument for liberalism that a liberal society makes individual autonomy possible. But that in no way commits them to the proposition that states should engage in the compulsory inculcation of autonomy – an expression whose strangeness calls attention to the peculiarity of the whole project.

It may be instructive to compare what we may call an 'ideal of autonomy' with the 'ideal of assimilation' discussed in the previous chapter. Let us recall, then, that Iris Young's 'ideal of diversity' was of a quite different nature from her 'ideal of assimilation'. Whereas her 'ideal of diversity' was actually a political programme designed to put the force of the state behind the perpetuation of group identities, her 'ideal of assimilation' was genuinely an ideal. It was simply a vision of society that might appeal to some people. The only connection between it and 'difference-blind' liberal institutions is that these institutions make the realization of the 'ideal of assimilation' possible. But that is all: they do not in themselves do anything to bring about a society in which the 'ideal of assimilation' is realized. For that to happen, uncountable numbers of individual decisions have to take a certain form, and if they do not do so the 'ideal of assimilation' will not be realized.

Along similar lines, let us define an 'ideal of autonomy' as a vision of a state of affairs in which all the members of a society devote a great deal of time and effort to such activities as questioning their basic beliefs and probing the rationale of the institutions and practices within which they live. No doubt this is a considerably more popular ideal than the 'ideal of assimilation' defined by Young, but the crucial point for the present purpose is that the relation of both ideals to liberal institutions is similar. These institutions provide the conditions under which autonomy can flourish but they do not do anything directly to bring about the 'ideal of autonomy'. In a liberal society, people who do not wish to devote themselves to Socratic questioning are perfectly free not to do so.

Young's 'ideal of diversity' necessarily conflicts with the 'ideal of assimilation' because its essence is to give different rights and privileges to individuals on the basis of their group identities. The public policies required for the pursuit of diversity or tolerance, as defined by Galston and Kymlicka, do not contradict an 'ideal of autonomy' logically in the same way. Nevertheless, there can be no doubt that their effects would tend to be inimical to the cultivation of personal autonomy. This is not accidental because, as we shall see, the object of political programmes designed to promote diversity or tolerance is precisely to insulate the members of illiberal groups from the danger of corrosion that illiberal values are liable to suffer from when exposed to the freedoms offered by a liberal society.

The analogy with the 'idea of assimilation' can be pressed further. I argued in the previous chapter that the case for liberal institutions can be made without invoking whatever tendency they may have to facilitate the realization of an 'ideal of assimilation'. I now want to say, in the same spirit, that no more does the case for liberalism have to rest on its congruence with an 'ideal of autonomy'. Although those who value this ideal will doubtless be led by this to support liberal institutions, their virtues can be established without recourse to any appeal to the value of autonomy. Even those who deprecate the ideal of autonomy can be given reasons for endorsing the kinds of individual rights that can be derived from liberal principles.

Andreas Føllesdal has put the point as follows:

> The concern for [the] individual's ability to change life plans does not stem from an assumption that this is a central interest of all individuals. . . . [Rather,] the interest in changing life plans is fundamental only in the following sense: we must recognize and regard as important the interest some have in changing religious views or cultural membership without government intervention. In conflicts, this interest must count for more than the interest others may have in using state power to enforce their world view.[16]

Thus, we might hold that ideally people would adhere unquestioningly to the prevailing beliefs of their community, while at the same time recognizing that in every generation a certain number are going to reject them. The question we would then have to ask is how those who suffer this fate should be treated. All that is needed to support the liberal position is to accept that it would be an unjust use of state power to inflict criminal penalties on them, and that it would be a legitimate use of state power to act so as to prevent them from being subjected to discrimination in the labour market, the housing market, and so on.

Similarly, Føllesdal suggests that the case for 'freedom of the press and freedom of speech...need not rely on a view that the autonomy of individuals is of intrinsic worth'.[17] The case can be made by arguing that suppressing these freedoms is liable to let corruption flourish unchallenged – and there is a vast amount of historical and comparative evidence to support this contention. More broadly, if we strip away its 'orientalist' trappings, there is still much to be said for the Victorian liberals' claim that any society lacking freedom of expression carries within it the seeds of its own decay. We can also say (as I did in chapter 2) that people should have the opportunity to transform their lives by exploring the spiritual, artistic and scientific heritage of the human race free of censorship. We do not have to posit a universal thirst for knowledge – or even wish that it were universal – to say that it is an oppressive and unjust use of state power to deny it to those who do seek it.

The defining feature of liberalism is, I maintain, the principles of equal freedom that underwrite basic liberal institutions: civic equality, freedom of speech and religion, non-discrimination, equal opportunity, and so on. These principles can be arrived at in a number of alternative ways. In the past, especially, God and Nature have been widely invoked to provide a foundation. In common with most contemporary egalitarian liberal philosophers, I disclaim any such grandiose designs. I suggest simply that liberal principles are the fairest way of adjudicating the disputes that inevitably arise as a result of conflicting interests and incompatible beliefs about the social conditions of the good life.[18] I have argued that appealing to fair treatment is sufficient to explain what is wrong with religious persecution and that appealing to equal opportunity is sufficient to explain why ignorance should not be forcibly imposed. However, if somebody were to insist that the line of argument seems to have built into it a certain preference for freedom over repression, I cannot say that I should feel the need to protest. It would, after all, be a little surprising if liberalism did not betray a bias towards liberty.

If I am right, the thesis that there are only the two varieties of liberalism defined by Galston and Kymlicka must be false, because it is possible to support standard 'difference-blind' liberal prescriptions without invoking the value of autonomy, while the whole point of the alternative form of liberalism that appeals to the values of diversity or tolerance is that it does not lead to these prescriptions. But this leaves us with the following question: is the first of the two versions of liberalism that Galston and Kymlicka claim to have identified really a conception of liberalism at all? The case against is straightforward. The 'ideal of autonomy' is, it may be said, a conception of the good life like any other, so the inculcation of autonomy by the state is as much of a violation of neutrality between conceptions of the good as would be the inculcation of, say, some specific religious doctrine. In reply it can be argued that the analogy is imprecise because autonomous people can have any substantive beliefs they like. What we mean by saying that people are autonomous is simply that whatever beliefs they do have will have been subject to reflection: their beliefs will not merely be those that were drummed into them by their parents, community and schools. I am inclined to think that this response is good enough to qualify autonomy-promoting liberalism as a bona fide form of liberalism. But it is not one that I myself wish to endorse, and it is my intention to ensure that the case I shall make against the active promotion of diversity by the state should not at any point rest on the claim that it is the duty of the state to promote autonomy.

## 3. Liberalism and Diversity

The partisans of diversity or tolerance are absolutely right to insist on the importance of freedom of association. They are in error, however, in suggesting that liberals are somehow inhibited by their principles from recognizing its value. It is true that liberal individualism has the implication that a group has no value over and above its value to its members (and to other people outside it), but this is quite compatible with a full recognition of the role played in our well-being by the communities and associations to which we belong.

It should be borne in mind that liberalism is, in the first instance, a doctrine about the way in which states should treat people. Over time, it has gradually come to be accepted that, in addition, states must impose certain standards on non-state organizations. It would, for example, make a mockery of the principle that equally qualified candidates should have equal access to jobs if firms in the private sector could flout it with impunity. Similarly, it would be absurd to hold that non-discrimination among passengers should be required only of municipally run bus companies, with the implication that privately owned companies would be perfectly free to order blacks to sit at the back of the bus. Interventions of this kind are essential to ensure that the principle of equal treatment is not rendered nugatory in central areas of people's lives such as employment, housing and travel. But that is far from entailing that every community and every association must operate within the constraints that it is appropriate to impose on a polity. There is no liberal principle to the effect that family decisions have to be taken by majority vote or that parents cannot censor their children's television viewing. Again, there is nothing to stop people from belonging to a church that vests ultimate authority in a Pope or Patriarch or is run auto-cratically by a charismatic preacher. Nor is there any liberal principle that forbids a church to instruct its members not to read certain books or watch certain films. The whole point of liberal institutions is to leave people with a great deal of discretion in their conduct, and one of the ways in which they can exercise that discretion is voluntarily to follow the orders issued by bodies whose authority they acknowledge.

It may be wondered what, in that case, all the fuss is about. What do the partisans of diversity or tolerance want that liberal principles are incapable of delivering? We can approach an answer to this question by observing that liberal principles limit the power of groups over their members. Thus, the condition on which churches can legitimately tell their members what to do is that those members are free to disobey without being liable to any penalty (in this world, anyway) except expulsion. In contrast, a church that could call on the Secular Arm (as the Inquisition called it) to punish heresy, apostasy or disobedience would clearly be out of bounds. Equally unac-ceptable, on liberal principles, would be a church whose members could without fear of legal sanctions inflict physical injuries on those who left it or disobeyed its rulings.

Similarly, while a liberal state can allow a good deal of discretion to parents in bringing up their children, that power must again be limited. Children need to be protected against parents who would inflict physical harm on them, even if this is prescribed by the parents' beliefs or customs. A familiar example is that of parents whose religious beliefs would lead them to withhold life-saving medical treatment from their children. Another well-publicized example is the practice, or more precisely set of practices, often referred to under the names of female circumcision or clitoridectomy but more comprehensively and accurately described as female genital mutilation. There is nothing specifically liberal about the view that the state should override the wishes of the parents in such cases. Any doctrine that gives the state the duty to prevent physical injury and death from being inflicted on its inhabitants will have the implication that the state should intervene. All that has to be said is that a liberal state is such a state.

If this is the liberal position, what do the critics think is wrong with it? I quoted in chapter 2 from an essay by Bhikhu Parekh on 'the narrowness of liberalism from Mill to Rawls'. How, we may ask, does this narrowness manifest itself? 'The liberal', says Parekh, ' "privatizes" non-liberal ways of life and denies them public recognition, status and support.'[19] Now to say that liberalism 'privatizes' non-liberal ways of life is simply to say that members of illiberal groups enjoy exactly the same rights as anybody else. If they so choose, they are perfectly free to participate with others in, say, the observance of a religious faith that is autocratic, misogynistic and bigoted. But the terms on which they can do so are just the same as those open to all their fellow citizens. The state does not lend any special weight to the norms of illiberal – or liberal – groups. This is, indeed, the essence of what it means to say that a society is a liberal society.

What of Parekh's alternative? If 'public recognition, status and support' are to amount to more than verbal gestures by politicians, they must consist of measures granting special legal immunities and powers to the leaders of illiberal groups that will enable them to control their members in ways that would otherwise violate the law. It requires little imagination to see how liberal rights for individuals are liable to be undermined by concessions whose intention and effect is to strengthen groups against their members. We may be reminded of Charles Taylor's complaint (discussed in the previous chapter) that 'difference-blind' liberalism is inhospitable to diversity because its principles cannot make room for policies aimed at thwarting 'those who might want to cut loose in the name of some individual goal of self-development'.[20] We may also, indeed, recall Parekh's own depiction of free speech as a benefit to writers and a cost to everybody else, and his proposed remedy, the suppression of non-respectful writings about religion.

I asked earlier if a theory that made it the primary task of the state to promote autonomy could properly be described as a liberal theory at all. Without great conviction, I suggested that it just might scrape in as one. When it comes to the alleged version of liberalism that makes diversity or tolerance central to it, however, the case seems to me completely clear. In the current context, 'diversity' and 'autonomy' refer to policies that would systematically enfeeble precisely those rights of individuals to protection against groups that liberal states ought to make it their business to guarantee. How can a theory that would gut liberal principles be a form of liberalism?

Galston gives the game away, I believe, by identifying his first version of liberal theory with 'Enlightenment liberalism' and his second version with 'Reformation liberalism'.[21] I have already, in chapter 1, pointed out that there is no such thing as a single 'Enlightenment project'; all I need add here is that it is especially bizarre to equate it with the notion that the state's main job is to inculcate (as against making possible) a disposition to autonomy. The assumption that there was a single 'Reformation project' is likewise suspect, and scrupulous historians today prefer to talk about 'the European Reformations' so as to emphasize that 'the reformation era' should be seen 'as a time of plural reform movements'.[22] Nevertheless, if there is one generalization that it is fairly safe to make, it is the one offered by a recent writer sympathetic to the reformers: 'toleration', he says, 'was not the long suit of the reformation'.[23]

The same author wisely cautions us that 'those living in contemporary pluralistic and secular societies easily forget how threatening the charge of unauthorized innovation was to the Reformers.'[24] Thus, he says,

Luther and Calvin ... aimed at, or found themselves committed to, a reformation limited to particular territories ... [whose] inhabitants, once reformation had been made official by their rulers, were expected to forswear 'popery' and subscribe to evangelical religion as a condition of residence.... A reformation in this manner, however limited and unsatisfactory, at least guaranteed some approximation to the inclusiveness of the Old Church and protected against disorderly (and even violent and millennialist) proceedings and sectarianism.[25]

Non-orthodox departures from 'popery' were just as much anathema as 'popery' itself. We shall see in the next chapter that Anabaptists were subjected to merciless persecution in Europe, which explains the presence of so many of their spiritual descendants in North America. In his *Defence of the Orthodox Faith*, Calvin 'declared that in cases of heresy the glory of God must be maintained regardless of all feelings of humanity', so justifying the burning at the stake of Servetus.[26] And Luther, it is worth bearing in mind, not only supported the imposition of orthodoxy among Christians but 'by the end of his life raged against the Jews and advised destruction of their homes, synagogues, and books as well as prohibition of Jewish civil rights'.[27]

Even where a degree of religious pluralism obtained, as in the well-known case of the Dutch Republic, it would be quite wrong to suppose that this came about as the consequence of a deliberately pursued policy of toleration. 'In the 1576 treaty uniting the provinces of Holland and Zeeland, William of Orange received the mandate to "maintain and preserve the exercise of the Reformed evangelical religion, causing to cease and desist the exercise of other religions which are contrary to the Gospel".' The 'unusual degree of religious liberty [that] developed in the Dutch Republic' came about simply as a result of 'the failure of church and state "to agree on new premises for unity, despite the best efforts of both"'.[28] Thus, we may conclude that, after almost a century and a half, contemporary historical scholarship supports Mill's assertion in *On Liberty* that 'those who first broke the yoke of what called itself the Universal Church, were in general as little willing to permit differences of religious opinion as that church itself'.[29]

It is true, of course, that the break-up of the Universal Church brought about religious diversity *between* states in Western Europe. But this was not regarded by anybody as a condition to be positively welcomed. The Roman Catholic Church still aspired to universality, while 'the reformers originally intended, and continued to intend, the reformation of the whole of Christendom'.[30] Thus, the Peace of Augsburg of 1555, which formalized a degree of religious pluralism between states 'was a provisional "public peace" constituted on political compromises that recognized, at least for the moment, the futility of forcing a religious settlement but still assumed the medieval vision of a *corpus Christianum*: one church and one empire. The peace ... was not a consequence of any sense of tolerance.'[31] In his quest for a model of a state that tolerated self-governing internally illiberal groups as anything other than a temporary second-best, Galston might more aptly have spoken of 'the Ottoman Empire project' than of 'the Reformation project'.

Suppose, however, that we were to imagine the principles laid down in the Peace of Augsburg applied not between states but within states. We would then indeed get an approximation to a policy of promoting group diversity by state action. To the principle that 'Where there is one ruler, there should be only one religion' would correspond the maxim 'Where there is one group, there should be only one set of beliefs and norms.'[32] And the provision of a 'right to emigration... for subjects unwilling to accept their prince's religion' would be endorsed for groups by most contemporary partisans of diversity and tolerance, who often emphasize the importance of a right of exit. They tend not to insist that people must really be able to exercise this right, however, and here too there is an analogy, since 'emigration required paying off one's debts to the prince, which could be economically impossible'.[33]

The point of all this is not simply that 'Reformation liberalism' is an oxymoron. The deeper point is that the policies advocated in its name are not liberal. If this is so, it is natural to ask why it should be thought by anybody that policies aimed at promoting diversity or tolerance (as they are defined by contemporary political philosophers) have any claim to count as implications of liberalism. The most important reason is that liberalism has in recent years been equated by many people with cultural relativism. I shall show in the next section how surprisingly pervasive this strange idea has become. In the remainder of the present section, I shall examine briefly three other lines of thought that crop up again and again among those who seek to argue that there is an authentic strain of liberalism devoted to the pursuit of diversity or tolerance.

The first argument runs as follows: 'The liberal is in theory committed to equal respect for persons. Since human beings are culturally embedded, respect for them entails respect for their cultures and ways of life.'[34] This particular formulation comes from Bhikhu Parekh, but the idea is common enough: it animates much of the rhetoric in James Tully's *Strange Multiplicity*, which I shall discuss in chapter 7.[35] The obvious problem with this argument is that illiberal cultures typically – I am tempted to say necessarily – are committed to violating the canons of equal respect. Equal respect for people cannot therefore entail respect for their cultures when these cultures systematically give priority to, say, the interests of men over the interests of women.

It does not follow, however, that groups whose norms contravene the canons of equal respect can legitimately be repressed by a liberal state. Freedom of association is, to repeat, a core liberal value, and it protects the freedom of groups whose norms mandate, among other things, the unequal treatment of men and women. The only condition on a group's being able to impose norms on its members is that the sanctions backing these norms must be restricted to ones that are consistent with liberal principles. What this means is primarily that, while membership of the group can be made contingent upon submission to these unequal norms, those who leave or are expelled may not be subjected to gratuitous losses. (I shall give this idea more specificity at the end of the chapter.) What I want to emphasize here is that the value underwriting the freedom of groups to operate in illiberal ways is not respect for their culture but rather an acknowledgement of the significance in people's lives of free association.

An example that I shall discuss at some length in the next chapter is that of Jewish and Muslim divorce law. Although this treats men and women unequally, it is beyond the scope of a liberal state to rewrite it, as long as the only reason for anybody's adhering to it is the wish to remain a member in good standing of a certain religious community. What a liberal state cannot do, however, is give the force of law to religious rules that contravene liberal principles of equal treatment. If we define 'group rights' so that they are 'self-government rights and means [for communities] to protect their religious and cultural practices', then we have to say, with Yael Tamir, that such rights are

> either dangerous or of little importance. They are dangerous if they can be turned inwards to restrict the rights and freedom of members; they are of little importance if they can only be bestowed upon groups which treat their members with equal concern and respect. Very few of the groups that demand group rights, if any, accord with this description.[36]

Indeed, Chandran Kukathas has made it clear that the usual reason for demanding group rights is precisely so as to violate the demands of equal concern and respect among the members of the group. 'If liberalism describes a nation-state governed by the principles of liberal justice, then the liberal state cannot condone deep cultural diversity. For many, the cultural rights it can offer are not worth having.'[37] Maybe this is so, but it does not follow that there is an alternative understanding of liberalism that would accommodate 'deep cultural diversity' by withdrawing standard liberal protections for individuals or putting the force of the state behind practices that violate basic liberal tenets of freedom and equality. The conclusion I would wish to draw is, rather, that liberalism cannot accommodate 'deep diversity' and that it is right not to do so.

A second argument purporting to establish a connection between liberalism and the promotion of diversity by the state may also be discussed in the form in which it is presented by Parekh. According to this, 'the liberal . . . argues [that] cultural diversity increases the range of available options'.[38]

Any liberal who did so argue would be mistaken. Parekh himself says a little later in the same article that 'cultures are not options', from which it obviously follows that the existence of a variety of different cultures does not 'increase our range of "options"'.[39] In fact, multiculturalism tends to restrict the range of options open to any given individual. 'Although seeking to "legitimize heterogeneity in British national culture"..., multicultural policies have paradoxically "created a space for separatist and fundamentalist movements which seek to impose uniformity and homogeneity on all their adherents."'[40] My only quarrel with that way of putting it is that I can see nothing paradoxical about the combination of heterogeneity between groups and homogeneity within them. If the state is going to lend its coercive powers to attempts to maintain the cultural distinctiveness of groups, it is hard to imagine how this can be done in any way that does not strengthen the hands of those within each group who wish to impose on its members uniform beliefs and standards of conduct.

A variant of Parekh's move that is sometimes made is to point to John Stuart Mill's enthusiasm for diversity in *On Liberty* and then draw the conclusion that, since Mill is an archetypical liberal, diversity must be a liberal value. Now it is quite true that, towards the end of chapter 3 of *On Liberty*, Mill argues that it is the 'remarkable diversity of character and culture' that 'has made the European family of nations an improving, instead of a stationary portion of mankind'.[41] Nevertheless, it has to be recalled that the title of this chapter is 'Of individuality, as one of the elements of well-being' – not 'Of diversity...'. Diversity is indeed valuable for Mill, but only in as far as it is an expression of individuality. As Mill puts it, in a passage of rather embarrassing floweriness:

> It is not by wearing down into uniformity all that is individual in themselves, but by cultivating it and calling it forth, within the limits imposed by the rights and interests of others, that human beings become a noble and beautiful object of contemplation; and as the works partake the character of those who do them, by the same process human life also becomes rich, diversified, and animating.[42]

It is surely apparent that Mill's praise for diversity cannot without grotesque distortion be brought to bear in support of, for example, Charles Taylor's so-called difference-friendly liberalism: the kind that is not 'neutral between those who value remaining true to the culture of our ancestors and those who might want to cut loose in the name of some individual goal of self-development'.[43] Throwing the force of the state behind the ancestral values may promote diversity between groups by preventing voluntary assimilation to some other set of values. But it can do so only by trampling on the individuality that was prized by Mill. 'As one would expect,' writes

Parekh, ' Millian liberalism cherishes not diversity *per se* but *liberal* diversity.'[44] So indeed, one *should* expect, provided that 'liberal diversity' is understood to mean simply whatever diversity is compatible with liberal institutions.

Parekh himself does not, it need hardly be said, understand 'liberal diversity' in this way: he follows Galston and Kymlicka in supposing that the only diversity permitted by Millian liberalism is that which is 'confined within the narrow limits of the individualist model of human excellence', which he equates with autonomy.[45] If 'the liberal way of life' and 'the autonomous way of life' are treated as synonymous, in the way that they are by Parekh, it is clear that we are once again being offered the false choice between autonomy and diversity.[46] Liberal ways of life should be defined simply as those ways of life, whatever they may be, that are not incompatible with the existence of liberal institutions. We can then point out – what Parekh's conceptual sleight of hand conceals – that liberal ways of life so understood do not have to value autonomy.

The third and last argument that I shall look at here invokes the public/private distinction. It has become virtually an orthodoxy, in particular among feminist critics of liberalism, that it is a doctrine uniquely attached to the protection of a 'private sphere'. This is then taken to mean that liberals are committed to withdrawing from public scrutiny and intervention what goes on within families. This claim is historically inaccurate to the point of perversity. It would be more correct to say that the condition of most societies that have existed in the world has been one in which the public sphere has concerned relations between households: in effect, the polity has been a league of households, represented by their heads. Within the household, its (male) head has had a more or less free hand over his wife (or wives), children, servants and, where they have existed, slaves. Thus, John Stuart Mill observed in *The Subjection of Women* that 'the man had anciently (but this was anterior to Christianity) the power of life and death over his wife. She could invoke no law against him; he was her sole tribunal and law.'[47] In ancient Rome, the father also had the power of life and death over his children. Now this is the separation of the public and private spheres with a vengeance. But it would be a travesty to suggest that it is a characteristically liberal idea. Quite the reverse: it is liberals who have been in the forefront of efforts to remove the legal disabilities of women, to make marital rape a punishable offence, to press for more active involvement by the police in incidents of domestic violence and for the prosecution of child-abusers, and to insist that parents should be legally obliged to provide for the education of their children.

Mill is exemplary here. So far from endorsing the notion that families belong to the 'private sphere', he argued that they constitute 'a case where ... [the sentiment of liberty] is altogether misplaced. A person should be free to do as he likes in his own concerns; but he ought not to be free to do as he likes in acting for another, under the pretext that the affairs of the other are his own affairs.'[48] Mill's strictures continue to have force. There is still an insidious tendency to assume that the interests of children are somehow subsumed under those of their parents. It is, however, conservatives touting so-called 'family values' who are typically guilty of this error – just as in Mill's day. Liberals are more typically concerned to protect children against parents by pressing for the prohibition of abuses such as corporal punishment, the genital mutilation of girls and parental coercion to marry. In this, liberals run up against objections from the more consistent enthusiasts for cultural diversity, as we shall see.

## 4.  Cultural Relativism and Toleration

A defining feature of liberalism is moral and religious toleration. Opinions to the effect that some forms of conduct (for example, homosexual relations between consenting adults) are sinful or unnatural may not be enforced by law: it is not the business of the law to regulate conduct as long as it does not violate the constraints imposed by a liberal state for the protection of individuals. This does not mean that liberals cannot themselves have definite views about the truth of some religious doctrines and the falsity of others, or more generally about the moral worth of actions that are legally permissible. They simply deny that the state can legitimately abridge the rights guaranteed by liberal principles in order to penalize beliefs or actions that they view with disapproval, and they wish to impose the same self-denying ordinance on non-liberals as well. Most liberals rightly also hold that the state should protect people from discrimination on the basis of such things as their religion or sexual orientation.

Liberal tolerance, as we have just seen, extends to the internal affairs of illiberal groups, provided that they stay within the framework of liberal laws. What is not up for grabs, however, is that framework itself. It is precisely this limit to toleration that is challenged by those who argue that there is a superior form of liberalism that gives the highest priority to 'diversity' or 'tolerance'. Thus, I am happy to agree with Chandran Kukathas that 'at the core of liberalism is the idea of toleration'.[49] But I dissent from his interpretation of that core idea. His proposal is that, in the name of liberal tolerance, the standard liberal safeguards for individuals against abuse by groups should be abandoned. I have said that freedom of association is an important liberal value. But Kukathas gives it such a central role that it displaces almost everything else: 'by seeing the right of association as fundamental, it gives considerable power to the group, denying others the right to intervene in its practices – whether in the name of liberalism or any other moral ideal.'[50]

I quoted Kukathas earlier as follows: 'If liberalism describes a nation-state governed by the principles of liberal justice, then the liberal state cannot condone deep cultural diversity. For many, the cultural rights it can offer are not worth having.'[51] My response was that this might be so, but all that followed was that liberalism was incompatible with some varieties of 'deep cultural diversity'. Kukathas's attitude is quite different. Would his view, he asks, 'run the risk of upholding injustice within minority communities?' His reply is as follows:

> if to do justice is to give each person his or her due, the answer...depends on what we think a person is due. The problem is that different cultural commun- ities have different conceptions of what individuals are due or entitled to, and in many cases, these conceptions will not value those freedoms and equalities which figure prominently in liberal conceptions of justice.[52]

As it stands, however, this does not state a problem – it merely sets forth a fact. It becomes a problem only if we assume that each community should be permitted to put into effect its own conception of justice. If we do that, the results are bound to be, as Kukathas says, that 'by liberal standards there may be injustice within some cultural communities: Freedom of worship may not be respected; women may have opportunities closed off to them; and the rights of individuals to express themselves may be severely restricted.'[53]

Kukathas has, I believe, performed a signal service by sharpening the issue between liberalism and the changeling that goes under the name of 'diversity' or 'tolerance' and is actually a form of moral relativism. As I mentioned in the previous section, it is sometimes suggested that liberalism is necessarily committed to moral relativism. Bhikhu Parekh, for example, maintains that liberals have 'epistemological grounds' for valuing 'cultural diversity and pluralism'.[54] And he makes it quite clear (if it were not clear enough from the context) that this means that liberals should support measures to ensure the perpetuation of ways of life that violate liberal principles. For he tells us that 'the liberal cannot consistently privilege and protect the liberal way of life'.[55] The view that this way of life 'alone is "true"' is, he says, 'one which the liberal cannot justify without incurring the changing [*sic* – perhaps 'charge'?] of circularity'.[56]

If a liberal is not somebody who believes that liberalism is true (with or without inverted commas), what is a liberal? The defining feature of a liberal is, I suggest, that it is someone who holds that there are certain rights against oppression, exploitation and injury to which every single human being is entitled to lay claim, and that appeals to 'cultural diversity' and pluralism under no circumstances trump the value of basic liberal rights. On this criterion, Kukathas is not a liberal – but no more is Kymlicka, despite his protestations to the contrary, as I shall show. Indeed, the dispute that has been carried on between them in a number of publications over the past decade bears some resemblance to the battle between Tweedledum and Tweedledee. Does this mean that there are not many liberals among the ranks of anglophone political philosophers? Not at all: a large proportion of those who do not write about multiculturalism are liberals. It means merely that there are not as many among those sympathetic to multiculturalism as these themselves like to claim.

Let us focus for now on Kukathas, who writes as follows:

> All societies to varying degrees, harbor a variety of religions, languages, ethnicities, and cultural practices and, so, a variety of moral ideals. The public realm . . . is a kind of settlement reflecting the need of people of different ways to develop some common standards by which to regulate their interaction – given that interaction is unavoidable.[57]

Revealingly, Kukathas suggests that a kind of 'moral commons' may emerge to provide norms that prevent conflict between groups, on analogy with the way in which 'rules of the commons have arisen and developed over time to deal with interaction between communities in areas where property rights do not exist and there may be conflicts over the use of common resources'.[58]

This is clearly a vision of society that owes a great deal to anarchist thinking. The story about the emergence, in the absence of any political authority, of a normative framework to regulate the use of common resources is one that anarchists like to tell, and Kukathas explicitly says that his suggestion is 'that the same process can account for how a public sphere emerges out of the interaction among groups or communities whose differences lie less in their conflicting interest in land-use than in their differing moral beliefs'.[59] Thus, the underlying assumption of 'toleration' is moral anarchy. There are no overarching norms by which groups and communities can be judged – or at any rate no such judgements can legitimately form a basis for the exercise of political authority.

A remarkably hardy fallacy is the idea that moral relativism can be invoked as a basis for religious and other forms of toleration. *Ex nihilo nihil fit*, and that goes for nihilism too. An equally fallacious variant is the suggestion that moral relativism underwrites the value of group diversity. John Gray, for example, writes that 'value pluralism' (which is in his vocabulary another name for moral relativism) implies 'that diversity is a good thing, [so] it follows that "the human world will be still richer in value if it contains not only liberal societies but also illiberal regimes that shelter worthwhile forms of life that would otherwise perish." '[60] In order to describe a way of life as worthwhile, however, we would have to have some universal criterion of value, which is precisely what the premise of the argument denies. (I shall take up this point at greater length in chapter 7.)

Diversity might, alternatively, be put forward as just such a universal value: with more diversity, it may be said, 'the human world will be ... richer in value'. But, as Daniel Weinstock has pertinently asked, 'richer for whom? ... It is only good to realize values if human beings can in some way or other benefit from them.'[61] Kukathas claims to accept the axiom of moral individualism: that all institutions must ultimately be judged by their effects on individual human beings.[62] But it seems overwhelmingly plausible that some groups will operate in ways that are severely inimical to the interests of at any rate some of their members. To the extent that they do, cultural diversity cannot be an unqualified good. In fact, once we follow the path opened up by that thought, we shall soon arrive at the conclusion that diversity is desirable to the degree, and only to the degree, that each of the diverse groups functions in a way that is well adapted to advance the welfare and secure the rights of its members. But that is precisely the liberal position.

A quite popular way of making a case for the unconditional value of diversity is to draw an analogy with the value of biodiversity. 'If we are prepared', Bhikhu Parekh argues, 'to preserve rare botanical and zoological species, even when we do not at present see their value, it makes no sense to destroy ways of life that do no obvious and identifiable harm to themselves or to others.'[63] There are so many things wrong with this that it is hard to know where to begin. Let me start by pointing out that many people (including me) would wish to say that the case for the preservation of species does not have to rest entirely on their presumptive value to human beings. We can take the view that the integrity of nature has a value in itself. It is hard to see, however, what value 'ways of life' can have independently of whatever advantages they bestow on individual human beings.

Even if we were to eschew the notion that species have a value independent of human interests, we would still have good reason for preserving species. So many useful products have been derived from unpromising-looking plants and bugs that it would obviously be imprudent to destroy others whose potential value is unknown. Moreover, even if we are primarily interested in the preservation of 'interesting' species – birds, reptiles, fish and, of course, mammals – the only way of ensuring their survival is to secure their entire habitat. 'If a "useless" species is lost from an area, other species that depend upon it will, likewise, be lost. Scientific understanding of ecosystems is too limited even to begin to list interdependencies among species, so it is impossible to predict which species will be included in the cascading effect of extinctions resulting from an initial extinction.'[64] I find it hard to see that much of this carries over to human ways of life. The probability that there are unsuspected virtues in torturing and killing political opponents, or in punishing women who complain of having been raped rather than pursuing the perpetrators, is sufficiently remote to be safely discounted.

Parekh talks about ways of life doing 'no obvious and identifiable harm to themselves and others'. But the notion of a way of life either harming or not harming *itself* does not seem to me to make much sense. A way of life might be conceived of as harming another, I suppose, if it interferes with its normal course. But whether that is to be deplored or welcomed depends, I suggest, on the nature of the way of life interfered with and the direction taken by the interference. What, at any rate, does make a lot of sense is the notion that a way of life might be harmful to some of those who participate in it. Ways of life that are compatible with liberal institutions are not threatened by those institutions. Therefore, the only ways of life that need to appeal to the value of cultural diversity are those that necessarily involve unjust inequalities or require powers of indoctrination and control incompatible with liberalism in order to maintain themselves. Since such cultures are unfair and oppressive to at least some of their members, it is hard to see why they should be kept alive artificially. Even in the case of species, there are a few that we feel sure enough about to wish for them not to exist. The appropriate comparison for some ways of life might perhaps be with small-pox. (Even smallpox, however, has been defended in the name of cultural diversity, as we shall see in chapter 7.)

One final argument that can be made for a regime of maximal tolerance is that it is conducive to peace. If the only rule governing relations between groups is that they shall not intervene in one another's affairs, it may be said, we have a formula for the elimination of conflict between groups. This is true as far as it goes, but it does not go very far. Peace at any price is a curious universal value when the price is measured in terms of the sacrifice of the liberties and even the lives of individual members of an oppressive group. If we are to judge institutions by their effects on individual human beings, it is hard to imagine how we could be led to endorse a regime within which the autonomy of groups is erected to the level of an overriding principle, when it leaves groups with the unfettered power to do terrible things to their members.

As Kukathas acknowledges, 'the image of the state as a settlement among different groups living under an arrangement of mutual toleration appears ...to present political society as a kind of international society.'[65] More precisely, it presents political society as corresponding to one particular image of it: 'International society, Michael Walzer has suggested, is essentially a maximally tolerant regime, and the doctrine of sovereignty is essentially a doctrine of toleration.'[66] Fortunately, major inroads have been made on the doctrine of sovereignty in the past fifty years, and the claim that a state's treatment of its own subjects is entirely its own affair is now appealed to only by states that have a lot to answer for (including, especially with respect to the death penalty, the United States). Nevertheless, Kukathas is right to draw attention to the parallel between Walzer's conception of international society and his own idea that it would be oppressive to subject communities within a state to principles of justice that they do not themselves accept.

Formally, the doctrine of sovereignty is a legal doctrine: it denies that states are subject to any superior authority. The legal impermeability of states is a corollary of this. But Walzer provides an argument in favour of legal impermeability that makes states morally impermeable as well. This is that there is a 'morally necessary assumption' of a 'fit' between government and community which is cancelled only in the event that the government pursues policies of genocide or enslavement against a part of the population.[67] Walzer is thus an upholder of the universal application within a country of the norms reflecting the shared values of the (presumptively unique) national community that inhabits the state territory. At the same time, he sets no limits on diversity between states. As long as they stop short of genocide and slavery, they cannot even be criticized by outsiders, let alone subjected to intervention to prevent oppression and injustice. For in Walzer's scheme of things 'oppression' and 'injustice' are cultural constructs. Walzer's approach, as his disciple David Miller has said, 'is radically pluralistic in nature. There are no universal laws of justice. Instead, we must see justice as the creation of a particular community at a particular time, and the account we give must be given from within such a community.'[68] As Walzer puts it, 'a given society is just if its substantive life is lived in a certain way – that is, in a way faithful to the shared understandings of its members.[69]

This is obviously cultural relativism, but of a curious kind that stops at the water's edge – a sort of philosophical analogue of the dictum that wogs begin at Calais. Kukathas accepts the premise of cultural relativism but asks, reasonably enough, why it should have to come in such large packages: why should not wogs begin next door?[70] Kymlicka occupies an intermediate position, which allows for cultural relativism to come in medium-sized packages. For him, wogs can begin at the Welsh or Scottish borders (or in the case of Canada at the borders of Nunavut and Quebec) rather than at Calais. In contrast to all of them, liberals are universalists: for them, there are no wogs, because everybody in the world is equally entitled to the protections afforded by liberal institutions, whether they actually enjoy them currently or not.

Walzer makes no bones about his cultural relativism. When addressing his fellow Americans, this entails that he should appeal to some interpretation of what he claims to be American values. To the extent that these are liberal, this makes him a liberal for domestic consumption. As he himself makes plain, however, he would regard it as inappropriate to criticize other societies on the basis of liberal values: each society's critics must start from its own values. A liberal is a liberal, not a chameleon, so Walzer is quite clearly not a liberal. But in that case neither is Kymlicka, and this is more interesting because he presents himself as one: indeed, the subtitle of his book *Multicultural Citizenship* is *A Liberal Theory of Minority Rights*. Yet he actually takes over Walzer's arguments 'against imposing liberalism on other countries' and adds that he thinks 'that virtually all of Walzer's points also argue against imposing liberalism on national minorities, although Walzer himself does not always make this connection'.[71] In fact, Walzer does not make the connection at all. His project is, as has been rightly said, 'the Romance of the Nation-State'.[72] In contrast, Kymlicka is equally spellbound by sub-state nationalities, and invests them in the same romantic spirit with a unique capacity to bring meaning to the lives of their members.

As between Walzer and Kymlicka, there can be no question that Kymlicka has the best of the argument. Walzer's approach simply makes national minorities disappear from view, unless the government engages in genocide against them or enslaves them. To see why this is a bad idea, we need only notice that it can underwrite the official conception of Israel as a Jewish state that happens to contain 20 per cent of 'Arab Israelis'. Kymlicka's approach would lead, in contrast, to the recognition of two nationalities, Jewish and Palestinian, within a single state, and to rights of self-government for Palestinians within the framework of the Israeli state. The third possibility is, of course, that Israel could be conceived of in civic terms, as a state of all its citizens. Currently, it is actually illegal for a political party even to espouse such a formula.[73] If a civic state is ruled out as beyond the present horizon of political possibility, the binational solution would manifestly be more equitable than the status quo, though it would still be subject to the strictures against ethnic nationalism set out in chapter 3.

There is no distinctive liberal theory of political boundaries at the level of principle. 'Good institutional design is more likely to be subverted than informed by grand architectural principles like the principle of national self-determination or the principle of nationality.'[74] What liberalism is about is how polities, however constituted, should be run. In particular, it is a theory about the constraints that should be imposed on the use of political power so as to avoid its being abused. All it has to say about boundaries is that they are better the more conducive they are to the creation and maintenance of a liberal political order within them. Whether that requires units that are large or small, heterogeneous or homogeneous, is a pragmatic question. There is not going to be any generally applicable answer. For example, secession or autonomy for a liberal group that would otherwise be subjected to rule by an illiberal state advances the cause of liberalism; secession or autonomy for an illiberal group that would otherwise be successfully ruled along liberal lines as part of a liberal state sets the cause of liberalism back.

The point of liberalism is that it is universalistic. It therefore necessarily conflicts with the claim that nations are the bearers of values that cannot, as a matter of principle, be overridden in the pursuit of liberal ends. Kymlicka, however, endorses exactly the same romantic nationalist premises as those set out by Walzer, and, not surprisingly, arrives at the same conclusions. That is to say, he holds (1) that national minorities should have self-government and (2) that self-governing national minorities should not be constrained by measures imposed by a liberal state to prevent violations of liberty and equality. These are simply Walzer's ideas about nation-states applied to sub-state nationalities. In this context, it is significant that Kymlicka actually makes use of an analogy between illiberal states and illiberal self-governing national minorities in support of his case. Thus, he says that it is 'obvious' that, 'if the illiberal group is another country', it would be wrong for liberals to 'impose their principles'.[75] But then, he says, the same principled non-intervention must by parity of reasoning be right if 'the Pueblo tribal council violates the rights of its members by limiting freedom of conscience, and by employing sexually discriminatory membership rules'.[76] In stark contrast to liberals who maintain that human rights should begin at home and then be extended internationally to the utmost extent feasible, Kymlicka clearly buys into the idea that human rights are a form of 'cultural imperialism'. No doubt he is correct to say that it would be inconsistent, as a matter of principle, to say one thing about states and another about national minorities within states.[77] But the only possible liberal answer is to reconcile the two cases by endorsing universalism for both – not, as Kymlicka does, by endorsing relativism for both.

The liberal position is clear. Nobody, anywhere in the world, should be denied liberal protections against injustice and oppression. However, in exactly the same way as liberals are pragmatic about what liberalism means in terms of boundaries, so here the move from principle to intervention has to be mediated by practical considerations. In both cases, the liberal end is clear enough, but it may be quite uncertain in some instances what are the best means to that end. At any rate, liberals are not so simple-minded as to imagine that the answer to all violations of liberal rights is to send in the Marines, or even a United Nations force. As in any just war theory, there must be some doctrine of 'proportionality'. Kymlicka gains an easy victory for the anti-interventionist position by observing that scarcely anybody would be in favour of the western powers invading Saudi Arabia so as to sort out the way in which it 'unjustly denies political rights to women or non-Muslims' – according to the liberal idea of justice.[78] There are many reasons for this, but their potency is surely illustrated by the deliberate decision to terminate Operation Desert Storm at a point that left the existing regime in

Iraq intact. Considerations such as these do not apply at all to the question of the powers that a liberal state should devolve on to some newly created self-governing entity; and they apply in only a very muted form to the question of revoking powers to violate liberal principles that may have already been devolved on to, say, self-governing Native American groups.

Pragmatic considerations may also, however, suggest in some circumstances that such powers should not be rescinded, and even that they should be extended. Suppose that, as a matter of practice, states are able to get away with gross violations of liberal rights. How does this affect the calculations of political leaders (whether popularly supported or not) who wish to violate liberal rights but are prevented from doing so as long as they hold power only in a subordinate polity? They have an obvious incentive to seek independence. If it is on the cards that they would succeed if they tried hard enough, anyone who (for whatever reason) is attached to the present state boundaries may well conclude that, if the illiberal outcome will occur anyway, it may as well be accommodated within the existing arrangements by allowing the sub-state to violate liberal norms. It may even be possible to present this as a way of moderating the illiberal outcome by suggesting that the existing state will still be able without provoking secession to set some limits to the extent to which liberal principles are violated, whereas an independent state will not be subject to any such safeguards. (All of this follows from the failure to achieve an international order in which states that violate human rights can effectively be made answerable, so it gives liberals a further reason for wishing international law to be liberalized.) However, compelling pragmatic reasons of this kind will rarely arise: Native American bands, for example, are not plausible candidates for sovereign statehood. In all other cases, self-governing sub-states should be required as the price of autonomy to operate within the constraints of liberal constitutionalism. It should not be permissible to have rules that restrict political power to men over a certain age, or to members of certain lineages, or rules that give women fewer legal rights (in relation to property, for example) than men.

It should be added that there is one difference between Walzer and Kymlicka, but it is of no real importance. Walzer, as we have seen, regards justice as constituted by each nation-state for itself according to the beliefs of its inhabitants. The government can be criticized for failure to live up to these, but only by insiders. (Thus, there are Saudi dissidents who complain that, despite its Islamic pretentions, the government fails to be sufficiently rigorous.) As far as outsiders are concerned, they cannot be 'connected critics', and have no *locus standi*. If they were to mount criticisms of another society, Walzer assumes, they would be doing no more than inappropriately applying their own local criteria. Kymlicka departs from this in thinking that liberals are entitled to hold the opinion that, say, Saudi Arabia violates liberal principles of justice. But he agrees with Walzer, as we have seen, in

holding that there is an overriding principle of non-intervention. The only
concrete implication of Kymlicka's philosophical difference with Walzer is
that liberals can, in his view, 'speak out against . . . injustice' and 'lend their
support' to reformers – if they have not been jailed or executed.[79] Talk is
cheap – at any rate if it is done at a safe enough distance away from an
oppressive regime. Liberals denounce the Taliban as repressive; Taliban
spokesmen return the compliment by branding the West as decadent. Critics
of illiberal policies in Singapore and Malaysia get lectured in turn on the
superiority of 'Asian values'. British television shows films exposing the
Saudi legal system, and the Saudis retaliate by financing Muslim groups in
Britain that denounce the country as degenerate. This is a game any number
can play, and they do.

Political philosophy is not about what we may think it would be nice for
people to do but what, at any rate in principle, they can be made to do. A
theory that has the implication that nationalities (whether they control a
state or a sub-state polity) have a fundamental right to violate liberal
principles is not a liberal theory of group rights. It is an illiberal theory
with a bit of liberal hand-wringing thrown in as an optional extra. Scholars
and politicians who denounce liberalism as a form of 'cultural imperialism'
are manifestly denying that liberalism is anything but a local prejudice: the
implication is that those who press for basic human rights in parts of the
world in which they are not established are on all fours with those who seek
to extend the death penalty for apostasy to Britain by calling for the murder
of Salman Rushdie. Kymlicka wishes to distinguish himself from them by
saying (as I understand him) that liberal principles have universal validity.
But his bottom line is exactly the same as that of the wholehearted cultural
relativists. For he agrees with them that it would be 'cultural imperialism' for
liberals to bring pressure to bear on regimes that violate human rights in an
attempt to increase the number of people in the world who enjoy their
protection.

It may at first sight appear that we are entitled to say on the strength of
liberalism's being true that liberal institutions are right for Canada and the
United States because they are right for everyone – right *tout court*. But the
trouble with this move is that we cannot then explain why liberalism's being
true does not underwrite the imposition (where feasible) of liberal institutions on non-liberal societies. We are thus reduced to saying that liberal
institutions are right in mainstream Canada and the United States because
liberalism is true *and* because most people in them are liberals. But then it is
clear that the truth of liberalism is not doing any work in the argument. All
we have is a special case of the general argument that the appropriate
institutions for any society are those that the members of that society believe
in. This is, of course, exactly what Walzer would say. Kymlicka's idea that
the liberal answer is *in some sense* the universally correct one is like one of

Wittgenstein's levers that looks as if it must serve some purpose but is not actually connected to anything.

Kukathas, in contrast to Kymlicka, believes that there should be one – extremely tolerant – constitutional and political order that applies to all alike. He is best known, in fact, for denying that there are (or should be) any cultural rights. One of the things that he means by this is that he does not support the delegation of state power to groups: whatever power they exercise over their members must be generated within a uniform set of libertarian rules. When we appreciate, however, the way in which these rules permit groups to harm their members with impunity, we may reasonably ask if there is any significant difference between what he advocates and what he rejects. Suppose, for example, that the law explicitly granted members of religious communities the right to kill apostates. Would this official connivance in murder be morally distinguishable from a state law making apostasy punishable by death?

If there is any distinction to be made, it seems to me that immunity for assassins acting to enforce group norms is even worse than direct state enforcement of those norms, because it leaves no room for the procedural safeguards that the law can provide. It is true that automatic immunity for religiously based murder is not simply equivalent to giving members of a community *carte blanche* to kill one another. If the perpetrators could be identified, they could in principle be open to criminal proceedings on the basis of the charge that the victim had not been guilty according to the group's norms. But proving beyond reasonable doubt that the assassins were not covered by the immunity law would be difficult – perhaps impossible if giving evidence in favour of the victim were liable to be regarded within the community as itself indicating a propensity towards backsliding. In contrast, if apostasy were a criminal offence, the burden of proof would lie upon those who wished to convict somebody of the offence. In practice, a much more common situation is one in which there is a law on the books prohibiting the infliction of physical harm (up to and including death) on anybody but it is enforced only selectively. This leaves it up to the police or the politicians who control them to decide which injuries or lynchings will not be investigated. In such a situation, the entire process of private 'justice' is beyond the reach of the law.

States, then, can give groups power over their members by omission as well as by commission, and there is nothing presumptively more benign about doing it by omission. Kukathas is quite open about the potential for harm to individuals that is inevitably created by the kind of polity he favours. For him, as we have seen, the job of the state is to mediate between groups, controlling spillover effects, but not to intervene in groups to protect their members. Group practices are to be tolerated as long as they do not 'directly harm the interests of the wider community'.[80] They may, he

concedes, be 'objectionable because they are morally intolerable in themselves or because they harm individuals in the groups which carry them
out'.[81] But objections grounded on moral intolerability or harm to individual members of groups should not, he says, be accepted as a reason for a
state to prohibit them: 'significant harms', he admits, 'can be inflicted (by the
dominant powers in the group) on the most vulnerable members of a
minority community – usually women, children and dissenters.'[82] Examples
that Kukathas gives in this context are clitoridectomy and the case of
'children who are denied blood transfusions in life-threatening circumstances'.[83] Other practices to be tolerated include ritual scarring, and ' "forcing" [women] into unequal marriages'.[84] I have no idea, incidentally, why
there are inverted commas around the word 'forcing' in this quotation.
Consider, for example, the case of 'an immigrant from rural Iraq [to the
United States, who] married his two daughters, aged 13 and 14, to two of his
friends, aged 28 and 34'.[85] Even if these children were not actually beaten
into submission, the term 'forced marriage' is surely not out of place here,
since it is hard to see what alternative they had to obedience.[86]

It may be recalled that in chapter 2 I analysed two alternative ways of
accommodating culturally prescribed acts that there were good reasons for
prohibiting. One was the rule-and-exemption approach: the activity would
be prohibited for most people, but those who could show that they had
specific reasons founded in religion or traditional culture for engaging in it
would be allowed to do so. The alternative approach was what I called the
libertarian one. According to this, if the reasons for having a law prohibiting
a certain kind of action were not sufficiently compelling to underwrite its
being imposed on everybody, the conclusion should be drawn that there was
no case for imposing it on anybody. In rejecting 'cultural rights', Kukathas is
not only denying that groups should be granted formal legal powers to
enforce their distinctive norms; he is also opting for the libertarian approach
over the rule-and-exemption approach. In effect, his argument is that there is
no need for 'cultural rights' in the form of special exemptions, because
virtually anything that members of a cultural minority might wish to do in
pursuit of their beliefs or norms would be legal for anybody to do under the
extremely permissive set of rules enforced by the state.

It is important to observe, however, that this is libertarianism with a
difference. The issues discussed in chapter 2 were ones in which, if the
libertarian solution were adopted, individuals would be free to do certain
things such as ride motorcycles without crash helmets or work on building
sites without hard hats. This is libertarianism as anti-paternalism: the state,
according to this view, has no business saving adults from themselves. It is
quite another matter to hold, as Kukathas does, that it is no business of the
state to save children from their parents. Here there is, as I have already
argued following Mill, no liberal principle that tells against state interven-

tion. What is miscalled liberty is actually in this case power: the power of parents to beat, mutilate and (by withholding life-saving medical treatment) kill their children.

It is worth emphasizing that the formally universalistic rights espoused by Kukathas actually create a host of particularistic powers. Thus, I take it that he does not advocate a regime under which any adult or adults could drag some passing girl off the street and subject her to genital mutilation without breaking the law. What he has in mind is that parents should be in effect authorized by the state to use physical force against their children to impose their wishes, even where what they want is (as he concedes it may be) injurious or even fatal. Similarly, it seems safe to assume that Kukathas would be opposed to legislation prohibiting parents from administering corporal punishment to their own children, but I would be surprised if he thought it should be legal for any adult to beat any child who was (in the view of the adult) misbehaving. Perhaps even more sharply than in the example I gave earlier, in which the state licensed group members to kill apostates, what is brought home by these cases is that, if the state turns a blind eye to private coercion, it is bringing about much the same results as would occur if it formally delegated legal decision-making power. By granting immunity to parents who do things to their own children that would be illegal if they did them to any other children, the state is handing over power to parents in a particularly brutal and uncontrolled way. Public tolerance is a formula for creating a lot of private hells.

I have focused so far on the powers that would be acquired by parents over their own children. How Kukathas imagines that these powers might articulate with those of ethnic, religious or cultural groups is, I must confess, obscure to me. Would 'a group' be able to claim immunity if 'it' carried out the mutilation of a young girl without the consent – or even over the opposition – of her parents? Or are all 'group' rights over children legally reducible to rights voluntarily transferred by parents? I shall argue in chapter 6 that, in a liberal society, the second alternative is the one that should be adhered to. The logic of Kukathas's position would suggest that there should be legal immunities for groups other than parents in relation to children. Let us, however, go against the grain of his argument, and assume that only parents and those authorized by them (religious authorities, school teachers, and so on) should be permitted to mutilate, beat or otherwise maltreat their children. Even then, the implications are striking.

Kukathas emphasizes that the wide latitude that he wishes to allow to parents will accommodate almost all the culturally prescribed practices that a state less committed to 'tolerance' might prohibit. But he is not so forthcoming on a further implication of a 'tolerant' regime: that whatever can be done for culturally prescribed reasons can be done for any reason whatsoever. Yet it is precisely the point of saying that there are 'no cultural rights' that the motive behind an action should be irrelevant to its legality. For the contrast with this libertarian approach is, let us recall, the rule-and-exemption approach, which would make cultural tradition or religious belief constitute a recognized excuse for certain people to do things that are illegal for everybody else.

Thus, as we have seen, Kukathas includes in the list of things that should not be prohibited what he calls 'ritual scarring'. By specifying that what is to be legal is *ritual* scarring, Kukathas suggests that what would be legalized would be the creation by parents (or their agents) of permanent scars (usually on the face) in accordance with some traditional practice which prescribes the way in which the markings are to be made. But if that were the only scarring that was to be legal, we would be back to 'cultural rights', that is to say rights that some people have and others do not depending on their culture. If we are not to have special exemptions of this kind, the rule must be that motive is irrelevant. The implication of this is that what is to be legal is – simply – scarring, so that parents could inflict scars on their children out of carelessness or malice and be as much beyond the reach of the law as those that did it in accordance with some tradition. It might be objected that ritual scarring and scarring for fun are 'not the same act', and that that is why the law should treat them differently. If we follow this line, however, it obviously leads us straight back to the rule-and-exemption approach and the regime of special 'cultural rights' that Kukathas rejects. Consider as another example female genital mutilation. Kukathas implies that this would be carried out in accordance with cultural norms, and no doubt if it were legal it would normally occur among those for whom it was a traditional practice. But in a 'tolerant' regime without special cultural rights, there would be no basis on which similar mutilation could be punished if it were carried out by parents as an act of pure sadism.

It should be borne in mind that the theory of tolerance put forward by Kukathas derives from a general view about the scope of permissible state action. Although Kukathas claims it as a virtue of the theory that a tolerant state (as he defines it) will be able to accommodate a great range of culturally prescribed practices, this is simply a fortunate by-product of limits that are to be set without regard to their impact on cultural minorities – or majorities. Therefore, if female genital mutilation is to be permitted on the ground that it does not affect others outside the group (in this case the family), we have to ask what other kinds of mutilation might be licensed by the application of the same criterion. 'The male equivalent of clitoridectomy would be the amputation of most of the penis. The male equivalent of infibulation would be "removal of the entire penis, its roots of soft tissue, and part of the scrotal skin." '[87] Would that be all right? And, more generally, if we want a rule that is not related to 'culture', how could we deny that any physical harm no worse than female genital mutilation might be immune to punishment? Cutting off an arm, for example, would scarcely be any worse, on any reasonable estimate of the gravity of the harm done.

As we have seen, Kukathas mentions, as an illustration of his thesis, that parents would be able to withhold blood transfusions from their children, when these were necessary to save life. I can see no reason why his example should be restricted in this way, and I feel confident that he would also accept, consistently with this, the right of Christian Scientists to withhold medical attention of any kind from their children. But, again, we must pay serious attention to the denial that there are any cultural rights. The naive reader of Kukathas may be inclined to think that what he has in mind is some sort of system under which parents who could prove a religiously based conscientious objection to blood transfusions or medical treatment would be permitted to violate a general rule that required parents to seek appropriate medical aid for their children. This would be a complete misapprehension of Kukathas's position. On his libertarian approach, it would be open to any parents to withhold vital medical treatment from their children, even if their motive was that they wanted to get rid of them and could do so legally by letting them die of a curable illness.

So far, I have confined myself to examples put forward by Kukathas himself or extensions of them. But what we need to ask about are the implications of his theory – not only those that he happens to mention himself. He does not, for example, say that a state bounded by the constraints he wishes to impose would be impotent to intervene in domestic violence. But this is plausibly one of the ways in which 'significant harm' might (as he concedes) be inflicted on 'vulnerable' people such as 'women, children and dissenters'. For domestic violence does not 'directly harm the interests of the wider community'.[88] Indeed, there are many cultures in which men are considered to have the right to beat their wives, so the recognition of such a right in law would have the added bonus of accommodating cultural diversity. Again, we could not say that the sexual abuse of children by other family members would 'directly harm the interests of the wider community'. And if we are prepared to allow parents to deny life-saving medical treatment to their children, why should they not be able to kill them? Restoring to parents the Roman father's power of life and death over his children would be quite compatible (as Rome itself proved over a long period) with peace between families. States that kill their own citizens do not thereby threaten other states, nor do fathers who kill their children threaten other families. Of course, the family members may feel insecure, as may the inhabitants of a state that kills a lot of its citizens. But if we are going to start worrying about that, where will it end?

This is, I believe, a question that deserves to be taken seriously. Suppose Kukathas were to draw the line at letting parents kill their children with impunity. Having once breached the principle that the state is there only to keep the peace between groups, what reason is there for stopping there? If we are to say that parents cannot kill their children without running foul of the law, why should they be permitted to withhold life-saving medical attention from them? Why not then go further, and prevent them from inflicting horrendous physical injuries on them? And then why not say that, in a contemporary western society, failing to ensure that one's child attends school regularly up to some statutory school-leaving age should be treated as criminal neglect? There is only one stopping point that makes any sense: the one that says that the interests of children should, as far as possible, be protected by the state from abuse by parents.

## 5.  Outline of a Theory of Group Rights

I have maintained that we should reject the widely accepted claim that we are faced with a choice between a form of liberalism that has at its core the fostering of autonomy (understood as a psychological disposition) and one that makes the central liberal value diversity or tolerance, as these are defined by Galston and Kymlicka. What this means is that liberals are free to object to the notion that the job of the state is to promote autonomy without thereby being committed to endorsing the promotion of diversity. Vice versa, we do not have to concede that the only possible reason for objecting to policies for the promotion of diversity is that they are incompatible with the promotion of autonomy. It would, nevertheless, be possible to opt for one of the alternatives, while recognizing that they do not exhaust the range of available positions. Clearly, anybody who chose to subscribe to the 'diversity' alternative would finish up by rejecting most if not all of the theses argued for in this book. Since my object is to encourage the reader to accept my theses, it will be easy to understand why I have devoted most of my critical remarks to this alternative.

I have argued that this so-called Reformation liberalism should not count as a variety of liberalism at all, because (whatever its proponents may claim) it fails to pay enough attention to the interests of individuals in being protected against groups to which they belong. I hope, however, that I have also pre-empted the response: 'In that case, so much the worse for liberalism.' It is not necessary to have an elaborate set of political principles, liberal or other, to appreciate what is wrong with the notion that groups should not be publicly accountable for what happens within them as long as it does not impinge on outsiders. A rudimentary sense of humanity is quite enough to prompt feelings of outrage, once the implications of this idea become apparent. Indeed, the only way in which such feelings can be kept in check is by adherence to an elaborate – and perverse – theory of the kind put forward by Kukathas.

Turning now to the alternative that makes the promotion of autonomy the core value of liberalism, I have accepted that this can be regarded as a genuine form of liberalism, in that the promotion of autonomy can arguably be distinguished from the inculcation of substantive beliefs. But I have also made it clear that I do not intend to rest my case against the 'politics of difference' on such controversial premises as these. Nevertheless, those who do accept them will tend to find themselves in agreement with most of the conclusions about public policy argued for in this book. More precisely, they are not likely to dissent from my criticisms of various 'multiculturalist' proposals. The one point on which they may part company is that of the state's role in relation to education, which I shall discuss in chapter 6. Yet even here the contrast is liable to be more in rationale than in policy implications, though there may be differences of emphasis.

This convergence does not, as critics may wish to suggest, show that there is no difference between the kind of liberal theory that I espouse and one that puts the state's duty to foster autonomy at the heart of liberalism. Rather, it reflects the way in which the theory of group rights that I shall develop in the remainder of this chapter attaches crucial significance to the voluntariness of group membership. For voluntariness has a number of conditions, which include the capacity of individual group members to make well-considered and well-informed choices from a range of realistically available options. And the public policies needed to ensure that group membership is voluntary overlap to a large extent (though not completely) with those that would be dictated by the promotion of autonomy.

I have suggested that my approach can accommodate much that would be supported by those who associate liberalism with fostering autonomy. More surprisingly, perhaps, it can also accommodate many of the concerns of those who stress the importance of diversity and tolerance. Daniel Weinstock has made the helpful proposal that we should distinguish

> between two types of theory of minority rights. A liberal theory of minority rights sets out to determine the manner and the extent to which a liberal regime can accommodate the groups within its midst, whereas a liberal theory of rights for liberal minorities does the same, but restricts its purview to liberal minorities, or to minorities whose internal modes of organization and belief systems already incline them towards liberal values.[89]

In these terms, what I am proposing is a liberal theory of minority rights. It is no part of liberalism, as I understand it, to insist that every group must conform to· liberal principles in its internal structure. It is a belief that liberalism is committed to this procrustean approach to groups that gives rise to the widely held view that we need some sort of escape-clause to accommodate diversity. Liberalism, it is thought, has to be tempered by some independent principle – call it 'toleration' if you will – so as to prevent its application from becoming unduly oppressive. All of this, however, rests on a deep misunderstanding of what liberalism is all about. Liberal principles themselves demand that groups should have the utmost freedom to handle their affairs in accordance with the wishes of their members.

The fundamental liberal position on group rights, which received its classic formulation in *On Liberty*, is that individuals should be free to associate together in any way they like, as long as they do not in doing so break laws designed to protect the rights and interests of those outside the group. There are only two provisos. The first is that all the participants should be adults of sound mind. The second is that their taking part in the activities of the group should come about as a result of their voluntary decision and they should be free to cease to take part whenever they want to. Provided these two conditions are met, there can be no doubt, for example, that people should be able to engage in relations of domination and submission that would clearly be insupportable in the absence of consent.[90] In practice, liberal states set some limits to what people can do to one another, even consensually. But qualms about excessive paternalism are likely to lead liberals to suggest that public policy should treat voluntary adult sado-masochism with a good deal of indulgence, perhaps prohibiting the infliction of bodily harm only when it is of a kind liable to lead to permanent injury.[91]

Those who are hostile to liberalism will be delighted to be able to say that its apotheosis is what they would no doubt describe as deviant sexual practices. But this would be a wilful misunderstanding. The question at issue here is not what relationships among human beings are the most valuable but what relationships are the most unproblematic. It is clear that communities (including that building block of larger communities, the family) play a more central role in most people's lives than clubs or more informal voluntary associations. Communities can do more good to their members, but by the same token they can do more harm to them.

What, then, of communities? Ian Shapiro has suggested that 'most liberals would say that all social relations should be redesigned to approximate the contractualist [i.e. voluntarist] ideal as much as possible'.[92] But this seems to me true only with qualifications. Undoubtedly, liberals wish to eliminate gratuitous barriers to exit from groups, because where exit is impeded this creates a presumption that the state needs to stand ready to intervene to protect the interests of individuals. Since liberals value freedom of association, they are naturally favourable to the creation of conditions in which association can flourish with the least possible public regulation. At the same time, however, they have no problems in recognizing that human beings are born into a number of communities – ethnic, cultural, religious, linguistic, and so on – as well as into families. Colin Bird rightly refers to those who

harp on 'the unchosen nature of our social identity' as purveyors of 'plati-
tudes', citing in evidence Daniel Bell's *Communitarianism and Its Critics* to
the following effect: 'I didn't choose to love my mother and father, to care
about the neighbourhood in which I grew up, to have special feelings for the
people of my country, and it is difficult to understand why anyone would
think that I have chosen those attachments, or that I ought to have done
so.'[93] It is not merely difficult to understand why anybody would suppose
that these attachments had or should have been originally chosen: it is
impossible. But has anybody ever expressed the contrary view? The response
of liberals to the involuntary nature of group membership is that, precisely
because this makes children vulnerable to abuse, they need protection. That
is, of course, the assumption on which I relied in criticizing Kukathas's
conception of 'tolerance'. Liberals also wish to insist – and this is where
Shapiro is right – that children must be brought up in a way that will
eventually enable them to leave behind the groups into which they were
born, if they so choose.

I am not suggesting that the availability of the exit option withdraws the
internal affairs of a group entirely from the possibility of public intervention.
Even if there are hostels for battered wives that provide a refuge from
abusive marriages, and a system of income support that removes the threat
of destitution, that is no reason for not making physical injury and marital
rape criminal offences. On the contrary, a woman is much more likely to
offer evidence for the prosecution if she has open to her a real chance of
leaving her husband. What we can say is this: if you remain in some
association that you have the power to leave, that establishes a presumption
that the perceived benefits of staying are greater than the benefits of the most
attractive alternative. How much that claim is worth depends on how valuable that alternative is. Where even the best alternative is very poor, your
choosing to stay does not entitle us to conclude that you are not suffering
from some kind of oppression, exploitation or injury. If, however, your
staying means that you are passing up at least one reasonably eligible
alternative, that is a much sounder basis for inferring that the association
is not treating you too badly. The inference may fail in a variety of ways: for
example, you may not be aware (or not clearly enough aware) of the alternatives, or you may be too inured to ill-treatment to recognize it, or you may
be held back from leaving by a sense of duty. Nevertheless, it is a legitimate
object of public policy to ensure as far as possible that members of associations have real exit options available to them. For this must surely reduce the
need for state intervention – which is only ever a second best – by giving
group members the chance to act themselves so as to avoid oppression,
exploitation and injury.

It is common to express the point just made by using the language of
costs. But we must be careful, if we are not to get the analysis wrong, to

characterize costs correctly. An obvious way of calculating the cost of exit is to compare the benefits of staying with those flowing from the most attractive alternative. But this will not give us the answer that is relevant in the current context. Suppose that membership in some association is immensely advantageous, and the next best alternative to it is far less advantageous. Then the cost of leaving, according to this way of counting, is very large. Nevertheless, as long as this alternative is not in itself excessively unattractive, the size of the loss is immaterial. We may be tempted to say that somebody who lives with a generous billionaire (in a state that does not have 'palimony') is 'bound by golden fetters'. From the present point of view, however, if that person has a well-paid job and a savings account, he or she is as free to leave as anybody else with an equally well-paid job and the same-sized savings account who derives only modest material advantages from living with somebody, or no material advantages at all.

The upshot of the discussion so far is that the picture of liberalism drawn by its critics is a travesty. Liberals are fully committed to freedom of association. This includes freedom of association for groups whose norms would be intolerable if they were backed by political power but are acceptable provided that membership in the group is voluntary. As Stuart White has said, 'with the freedom to associate comes the freedom to refuse association'.[94] The enthusiasts for 'diversity' are alert to the implications of this when the question is one of groups expelling and subsequently 'shunning' their members. But they tend to be less concerned when it is a matter of the individual member's ability to leave the group without incurring excessive costs. A liberal theory must balance these two forms of freedom to refuse association. It cannot, because of the importance of voluntariness, follow the 'diversity' school and slight the freedom of the individual to refuse association. But at the same time it must accept that the ability of groups to run their own affairs would be hopelessly compromised if they did not have the power to decide whom to admit and whom to exclude.

We need a way of adjudicating between these competing claims. What has to be added for this purpose to the analysis of voluntariness is a classification of costs of exit. I shall divide these into three kinds. First, there are those costs that the state cannot, in the nature of things, take any steps to prevent or ameliorate. Call these intrinsic costs. Second, there are costs that the state could try to do something about (even though its efforts might be clumsy and only slightly effective), but which come about as a result of people doing things that a liberal state should permit. Call these associative costs. This leaves us with a third category consisting of costs that the state both can and should do something about: if it cannot prevent them from occurring altogether, it should do whatever is possible at least to reduce their scale. For want of a more perspicuous term, call these external costs.

Let me illustrate this schema. Consider the case of members of the Roman Catholic Church who are excommunicated for (let us say) persistently publishing works of theology that the church authorities hold to be contrary to its tenets. The intrinsic costs that they suffer are those that are inherent in the fact of no longer being in the church. What these costs are will in each case depend on their beliefs. However, if you believe that Jesus gave St Peter the keys to heaven and that the current Pope has inherited them, this cost could be described as infinite. Nevertheless, it is not one that can be detached from the phenomenon of excommunication itself: it cannot be altered by the actions of states or anybody else. Of course, the state might decree that it is illegal for a church to excommunicate anybody. I shall assume, however, that the freedom to refuse association must extend in a liberal state as far as allowing any church to decide what beliefs must be professed as a condition of remaining a member in good standing. 'Why should, say, the Catholic Church be allowed to exclude Protestants and Buddhists from church membership?' The answer is, as White says, 'that the Catholic Church would quickly cease to be the *Catholic* Church if it could not exclude those with conflicting beliefs'.[95] Excommunication, with its inherent costs, must therefore be allowed to stand as a type of action that can legitimately be taken by a church.

Associative costs are those that arise as a result of decisions taken by group members that they are permitted to take by a liberal state. Thus, if members of the congregation break off social relations with you as a consequence of your expulsion, this is something that they are free to do. People in liberal societies cannot be prohibited from being narrow-minded and sectarian in this kind of way. Finally, for an example of a cost that is not legitimately imposed, let us recall the argument in chapter 2 in favour of a ban on religiously based job discrimination. Suppose that your employer is a devout – indeed fervent – Roman Catholic, and that he fires you as a consequence of your being excommunicated. This is a gratuitous loss which the employer has no right to impose on you, so it counts as an external cost. Even if the firm is owned and operated by the Roman Catholic Church, it should not be allowed to dismiss you unless it can show to the satisfaction of a court that the job is one that must for some reason be done by a member of the church. (We shall come across a parallel case in the next chapter involving a janitor employed in a gymnasium owned by the Mormon Church.)

We can conclude from this analysis that there are some things that group members should be allowed to do in relation to those who leave or are expelled, and other things that they should be prohibited from doing. But are we entitled to assume that membership of a group will necessarily be voluntary if its members resort only to actions that are permissible? We could close the gap by stipulating that the absence of external costs is to be the criterion of voluntariness. This would make it conceptually impossible that a group might be acting within its rights in imposing certain costs of exit and that at the same time these costs might be so grave as to undermine the voluntariness of membership. But I believe that we must leave open the possibility that a case might arise in which the costs imposed were legitimate but were nevertheless such as to make adherence to the group non-voluntary. If we follow this line, we shall have to accept that the two parts of the theory can in certain circumstances generate conflicting prescriptions: because the costs are legitimate, the law cannot prevent them from being imposed; but because they render membership non-voluntary, they open the group to public intervention.

This kind of problem should not be regarded as a fatal flaw in the theory. It quite often happens that there are morally valid considerations on both sides of an issue. We have already come across some examples. Thus, to go back to a case discussed in chapter 2, if Sikh religious beliefs entail that men carry a *kris* (or dirk), then prohibiting the carrying of knives in public is unquestionably an abridgement of freedom of religion for Sikhs. At the same time, though, there is an equally undeniable public order interest in not having one portion of the population carrying offensive weapons. We can disagree about which of these two values should prevail in this particular case, but it would not be sensible to deny that, whatever the outcome, something valuable will be lost.

Even where such cases occur, we are still ahead by having principles that produce a determinate answer most of the time. In the present case, I do not believe that situations will very often arise in which it will turn out to be necessary to make a choice between rival policy prescriptions generated by the two principles. Sometimes, the conflict is genuine enough but freedom to refuse association wins over the protection of individual interests simply because the situation is one in which not much can be done by the state to protect individual interests. Even if, therefore, we are inclined to say that the pressure exerted by the group is oppressive, we may conclude that there is nothing for it but to permit it to continue. Suppose, for example, your parents say that they will never speak to you again if you marry the person you wish to, because he or she has a different religion or ethnic identity. Even if we are inclined to regard this as amounting to coercion, and therefore in principle open to public intervention, the problem does not lend itself well to state-enforced remedial measures. Where, following a divorce, the custodial parent refuses the other parent reasonable access to their children, courts can intervene effectively and this can work because the only cooperation needed between the parents involves their passing the children to and fro at designated times and places. But it is hard to imagine that marrying outside the group would be made much easier if you could obtain a court order requiring your parents to invite you to tea once a month, under the supervision of a social worker to ensure that they talked to you. Informal intervention by friends, neighbours and relatives may help to bring about a reconciliation – though there will, unfortunately, also be instances in which it will reinforce the parents' intransigence.

In cases such as these, the conflict between the two operative principles – freedom not to associate and freedom from coercion – is not resolved. All we can say is that the conflict between them does not present an issue for public policy because there appears to be no practicable way of resolving the conflict in favour of the second principle. The first principle, which permits actions of certain kinds regardless of their consequences, therefore wins by default, as it were. There are other kinds of case, however, in which the aggregate effect of legitimate actions taken by a number of people amounts to coercion but in which the protection of the individual's interests can be achieved without infringing freedom not to associate. Let us assume, for the sake of argument, that the practice of 'shunning' the ex-members of a religious group ought to be acceptable in law, even where it has the following two features: first, it is instigated by the religious authorities, who expel any members of the congregation who fail to conform; and, second, a by-product of this systematic refusal to associate is a boycott that will seriously reduce the number of clients or customers of any ex-member who provides services or runs a business. It is surely plausible that the threat of a boycott renders involuntary the continued membership in the group of any member whose departure would lead to the imposition of such a cost. We thus have a case in which actions that are (we have assumed) legal nevertheless give rise to an outcome that makes the group's internal affairs subject to public scrutiny and regulation.

We could avoid this result by going back on our initial assumption that 'shunning' should be legal even when it includes a financially punitive boycott. But compelling the members of the group to maintain professional or business contacts with a renegade would be a quite serious invasion of the group's ability to conduct its own affairs. Fortunately, however, it would be possible in this case to obviate the financial loss to the ex-member without infringing the congregation's freedom not to associate. For we might suggest that, while they should be free to carry out their boycott without let or hindrance, this is not incompatible with requiring them to pay compensation to the victim. The form of compensation might be made to depend on the particular circumstances. Where the members of the group constitute only a minority within the area served by the victim's firm or practice, it might be appropriate to specify payment for a limited period so as to allow the victim time in which to recruit new customers or clients. But where the group is so dominant locally that a boycott is bound to drive the victim out of business, a more suitable form of compensation would be a sum of money sufficient to cover the victim's cost of relocating and getting re-established.

It cannot be denied, of course, that the right not to associate is 'burdened', as they say in American jurisprudence, by a requirement to pay compensation to those injured by it. But I see no reason for thinking that the liberal principle underwriting freedom not to associate has to be formulated so as to guarantee that its exercise should be costless. If this is correct, what we have here is a case in which – on the assumption that an organized boycott should be legal – legitimate actions can impose associative costs that are inconsistent with voluntary membership. Yet this creates a conflict between the two principles only as long as these costs are left to lie where they fall. Provided that the costs are shifted from the victim to the organization instigating the boycott, membership in the group can count as voluntary while at the same time the remaining members of the group can exercise their freedom not to associate with the ex-member.

There is another way in which state action can respect the right not to associate while protecting individual interests. To return to an earlier example, excommunication imposes an immense (if posthumous) cost on anybody who believes that outside the church there is no salvation; but nothing can be done about this cost because it is an intrinsic cost. Nor, I have suggested, can a liberal state legitimately intervene to prevent an ex-member from suffering associative costs, unless they threaten the ex-member's livelihood. Nevertheless, because there are such significant individual interests (tangible and intangible) riding on the decision to excommunicate somebody, states can legitimately intervene to protect those interests in any way that does not infringe the fundamental right of a church to define its own criteria for membership. An obvious way of achieving this is for the courts to be prepared to adjudicate challenges to the church's procedures or its fidelity to them in the case at hand. Thus, they could reasonably insist that a church's procedural rules should conform to the canons of natural justice, by allowing the accused to hear the case against, respond to it, call witnesses, and so on. Similarly, they could inquire into complaints that, even if the church's procedural rules were acceptable, it had violated them in some particular case. In practice, courts are extremely reluctant to intervene in the affairs of churches in this kind of way.[96] But they are prepared to do so in the case of decisions by schools to expel students and trade unions to expel members. The arguments for their reviewing expulsions from religious bodies are equally compelling, since there are significant interests at stake here too.

# 5

---

# Liberal States and Illiberal Religions

## I. The Claims of Free Association

In this chapter and the next, I shall ask how the liberal theory of group rights fares when it is put to work on several pressing and important issues. These constitute problems to which every state has to provide some answer. The conventional wisdom – which in this matter is shared alike by anti-liberals and liberals – holds that they pose especially difficult problems for liberalism. I shall take up in this chapter the question of the extent to which a liberal state should permit religious bodies to violate liberal precepts in their internal organization and in the rules that they impose on their adherents. The next chapter will focus primarily on the problems generated for a liberal conception of justice by the demands made by parents to restrict their children's education in line with their ethnocultural or religious norms.

Let me begin, then, by asking how the doctrine of free association bears upon religious bodies. Most of the discussion of this question in western societies has, for understandable reasons, been addressed to Christian churches – using that term in a generic sense to refer to religious denominations, sects, and so on. In what follows, I shall use 'church' in a completely generic sense, to include all religious bodies. I shall assume without argument that, if some religious bodies are to be treated differently from others, this cannot be in virtue of their doctrinal content *per se*. If any difference in the treatment of Christian, Jewish, Muslim, Hindu or Sikh religious bodies can be justified, this will have to arise from some feature of their practice or mode of organization that puts them into a different relationship with the principles laid out in the previous chapter.

The bearing of these principles on churches turns on the way in which we conceive of them. A way of putting this question that was much in vogue in the early years of the twentieth century was to ask whether a church was properly to be thought of as a kind of association or a kind of community. As the English pluralists construed the question, the answer given to it would determine whether a church should be seen as a creature of law, bound by its articles of association, or whether it should be seen as a self-subsistent organic body capable of autonomous doctrinal evolution.[1] The pluralists were right to regard a church as typically having the characteristics of a community. Most churches acquire the bulk of their members as a result of their being born into them. In this way they are similar to families and nations but unlike clubs. Moreover, churches commonly provide an important element in the identities of their members, in a way that clubs normally do not. The pluralists erred, however, in regarding these as reasons for leaving churches with the maximum freedom to conduct their own affairs without interference. According to them, the state should be construed as a 'community of communities'.[2] They deduced from this that the state 'must share sovereignty with all the self-governing sources of law within it'.[3] Hence, 'we should recognize [religious associations] as independent societies, and be willing to commit people to their care'.[4] On the premises adopted here, however, any exercise of political power must take place within liberal constraints. Therefore, if calling religious associations sovereign is appropriate, it must follow that they forfeit the right to conduct themselves in ways that violate the precepts of liberalism.

We find that in practice every liberal state permits the existence of a variety of religious bodies (Christian and other) that would, if they were exercising political power, comprehensively violate basic liberal principles of individual liberty and equal treatment. Few of them have an internal decision-making system that would pass muster in a body wielding state power: they are often hierarchically organized, with key decisions taken by officers who are not responsible to the congregation. Again, some churches presume to issue instructions to the faithful about books they must not read and films they must not watch. This kind of censorship would clearly violate liberal principles if it were practised by a state. Equality of the sexes is denied by churches that reserve the ministry to men. (I shall ask later in this chapter whether or not a liberal state should give churches a waiver of anti-discrimination laws in order to permit them to practise this form of discrimination.) There are a number of other ways in which religions may treat men and women unequally. Thus, some religions give men and women a very different status in relation to religious worship, with women relegated to the role of onlookers while men are the participants.

There may also be rules concerning marriage and divorce that place men and women in a strongly asymmetrical position. Thus, among Muslims, 'the form of divorce known as *talaq*, under which a husband may unilaterally repudiate his wife without showing cause, without the need to have recourse to any court or extraneous authority, and without any requirement of notification to his wife, is clearly discriminatory since it is not available to a wife.'[5] Traditional Muslim law, so far from allowing a woman to divorce her husband at will, does not have any provision for a woman to obtain a divorce at all without her husband's consent, which he has discretion to withhold for any reason.[6] Some Muslim courts in Britain have assumed the power to issue a divorce where the husband is deemed to be acting unreasonably or is construed as consenting by having taken the initiative in pursuing a civil divorce.[7] Orthodox Jewish law in Britain, however, continues to incorporate the feature that a husband may refuse to consent to a divorce and cannot be overruled by a rabbinical court, whereas a man can be granted a divorce without his wife's consent.[8] Here, innovation has occurred in the United States, where 'the head of the New York Beth Din (religious court)...claims to have unearthed an ancient Talmudic law allowing him to grant divorce without the husband's permission. He has [in 1999] divorced at least eight British women, bringing him and them into conflict with Beth Dins in [Britain], which consider the divorces invalid.'[9] Under the traditional rules, the man clearly has an enormous bargaining advantage, and some men do not scruple to use it to the full in order to obtain a lopsidedly advantageous settlement. For example, one American author 'tells the miserable story of an ultra-Orthodox, destitute mother-of-three whose family had paid her husband to give her the *get* [consent to divorce in Jewish law], leaving no money left to cater for the needs of the divorcée and her children. Her husband, on the other hand, had remarried and was lavishing attention and financial comfort on his new family, ignoring the old.'[10] Alternatively – or in addition – 'women may be induced to lose sight of the interests of their children by agreeing to custody or access arrangements which would otherwise never have seen the light of day'.[11]

Proposals periodically surface in England for the state to turn over legal powers to religious bodies so as to enable them to enforce their own system of family law. Thus, 'during the 1970s the Union of Muslim Organisations of UK and Eire (UMO) held a number of meetings which culminated in a formal resolution to seek official recognition of a separate system of Islamic family law, which would automatically be applicable to all British Muslims'.[12] These claims continue to be pressed. Similarly, during the passage of the Family Law Act (1996), the then Chief Rabbi, Lord Jakobovits, argued that it was anomalous for English law to recognize Jewish marriages with no further need of civil registration but not to put the force of law behind the decisions of Jewish ecclesiastical courts.[13] I cannot see why the concession permitting synagogues to be licensed for the performance of marriages recognized by the state should be taken as signifying anything except that the religious ceremony is to be treated as simultaneously satisfying the conditions of civil marriage.[14] If, however, it is an anomaly that the concession is combined with a legally uniform system of marriage, it is the concession that should go. (Since it is available only for certain faiths, it is in any case inequitable, so there is much to be said for getting rid of it anyway.) For the non-negotiable liberal position is that the state must not give legal recognition to laws governing divorce that are fundamentally pernicious from a liberal point of view. The state's giving legal effect to a manifestly unequal system of personal law administered by religious authorities is just as unacceptable as the state's enacting and administering an inequitable system of personal law itself.

From the point of view of a liberal state, adherence to the norms of Orthodox Judaism is voluntary. The lack of equity inherent in these norms is not, therefore, a basis on which the state can intervene. To say that adherence is voluntary is to say simply that the costs of leaving are limited to those that are intrinsic to the termination of membership and those that arise as a consequence of the exercise of their right of association by those who remain – which includes the right of dissociation. The possible size of these costs should not be belittled: 'in this context, voluntarism... does [not] imply that obedience to a religious law or tribunal is experienced as a "choice" by believers themselves rather than as an imperative.'[15] Nevertheless, we must count membership as voluntary as long as there are no illegitimate sanctions imposed on defectors.

In fact, there are signs of widespread resort to the exit option among those who are dissatisfied with the rules governing divorce: one woman who had been a victim of the present rules claimed 'on the basis of her own experience, that the rabbinate's attitude towards divorce is alienating women and their children, many of whom are marrying out'.[16] It may well be that this exodus will prompt internal efforts to make the rules governing divorce more equitable.[17] This is an incidental benefit arising from the exercise of the exit option. What is crucial, however, from a liberal point of view, is the existence of the option. For this entails that those who regard themselves as having been abused by the Orthodox regime have open the possibility of moving out into the wider (religious and secular) Jewish community or to lose their Jewish identity altogether. 'Judicial deference... does not deliver [dissidents] into the hands of tyrants or exile them into a moral vacuum – not in a society alive with religious groups and liberty to form new ones.'[18] I would add (what the author of that quotation, Nancy Rosenblum, omits) that turning one's back on religion in all its forms does not condemn one to a 'moral vacuum' either, even in the United States.

What has been said so far, however, should not be taken as giving religious bodies *carte blanche*. While they are free to impose their own rules on members, the condition of their being able to do this legitimately is that members who find these rules too burdensome should be free to leave. That freedom is compromised if those who leave are liable to suffer from costs over and above intrinsic and associational costs. The Church of Christ, for example, violated this requirement in relation to a woman who had 'resigned shortly before the church branded her publicly' by 'inform[ing] the congregation and four surrounding churches that [she] had been engaging in fornication'.[19] In response to her claim against the Church of Christ of 'an invasion of privacy and the intentional infliction of emotional distress', the Elders of the Church 'explained that "this process serves a dual purpose; it causes the transgressor to feel lonely and thus to desire repentance and a return to fellowship with the other members, and secondly, it ensures that the church and its remaining members continue to be pure and free from sin." '[20] The Oklahoma Supreme Court quite correctly 'emphasized that if a church treats harshly those who have fallen away, the religious exercise of individuals no longer convinced by a church's values will be inhibited'.[21] As the court put it, 'No real freedom to choose religion would exist in this land if under the shield of the First Amendment religious institutions could impose their will on the unwilling and claim immunity from secular judicature for their tortious acts.'[22]

According to the principles laid down in the previous chapter, then, adherents of Orthodox Judaism are deemed to belong to a voluntary association whose rules for the conduct of members (including those concerning divorce) are beyond the reach of the state, as long as they are not in violation of the ordinary law of the land. The conclusion that reform must come from within appears to be accepted by those campaigning for a change in the rules.[23] Just as a liberal state cannot rewrite the Orthodox Jewish rules, so it cannot punish husbands who refuse to grant their wives a divorce within those rules. In Israel, the state has given the rabbinate the power to order that a husband who unreasonably refuses consent may be imprisoned, though this power is used only very rarely.[24] This is, however, an illiberal remedy for a problem created by a fundamentally illiberal legal framework. For it is a by-product of the state's having resigned jurisdiction over marriage and divorce to religious authorities: 'All Israeli citizens...must have their marriage and divorce disputes settled by religious courts of their respective communities.'[25] The result is that 'in matters affecting their families, Israelis *must* function as Jews, Muslims, Druzes, etc.'[26] Thus, 'not only Jewish women, but also Moslem, Christian and Druze women are potentially subject to intra-group controls by their own group's traditions under Israel's accommodationist family law policy.'[27] This is the 'Ottoman Empire project' with a vengeance!

If English law similarly gave effect to the laws of religious communities, it might be reasonable to follow the Israeli precedent and provide for the imprisonment of recalcitrant husbands. For it would then be the state that, by handing over legal power to rabbinical courts, had created a situation in which a Jewish woman was unable to obtain a divorce without her husband's consent. Under current English law, however, all women have the ability to obtain a divorce on the same grounds, regardless of their religion. Thus, Roman Catholics are as free as anybody else to get divorced; the peculiarity of their position, which has nothing to do with the law, is that (unless they obtain an annulment from the Vatican as well) their divorce will not be recognized by their church. Similarly, Orthodox Jews and Muslims can obtain a civil divorce on the same terms as anybody else; and in a similar way, too, they have to go through a separate procedure, governed by different rules, if they want the divorce to be accepted as valid for religious purposes. Whether or not they choose to pursue the recognition of a civil divorce by some religious body is up to them.

A liberal state cannot criminalize behaviour that arises within a set of rules adherence to which is, in the relevant sense, voluntary. If it cannot itself inflict punishment on recalcitrant husbands, no more can it condone privately administered sanctions if they take a form that conflicts with generally applicable law. 'Maimonides is said to have advocated beating the unreasonable husband until he agrees to the divorce. . . . Some communities are said still to practice this form of compulsion.'[28] Clearly, if 'recalcitrant husbands are beaten up by gangs hired for the purpose', the gang members will have to be treated by a liberal state in the same way as anybody else who perpetrates an assault.[29]

In contrast, actions intended to put pressure on the miscreant that fall within the law present no problems from a liberal point of view. A good example is the practice of 'publicising the names of recalcitrant husbands in newspapers and on notice boards in Jewish communities'.[30] This is apparently common in the United States and is being introduced into England by 'Rabbi Pini Dunner of the Saatchi synagogue [, who] said he would post [on the internet] the names and addresses of men who would not give their estranged wives religious divorce. He would use the synagogue's website and noticeboard, and, if possible, Jewish newspapers.'[31] If the recalcitrant husband is still a member of the congregation, it seems quite appropriate that he should be liable to social disapproval on the part of his co-religionists for failing to make a certain move within the rules defined by that religion. What if the husband does not define himself as an Orthodox Jew, never attends services, and so on? In the nature of the case, it is far less likely that a policy of 'naming and shaming' will have much efficacy in such a case, especially if the husband (who may, of course, be divorced legally) does not live in the same area as his wife or ex-wife and has few Orthodox Jewish contacts. But it is still worth asking if such a policy, aimed at non-members, is objectionable in principle. Can we distinguish it from the case involving the Church of Christ?

I believe that we can distinguish between them in the following way. Once people have left the Church of Christ, what they do is no longer a matter of legitimate concern to the Church as a collectivity. Neither the hope that they will repent nor the fear that they will set a bad example are substantial enough considerations to justify the Church's publicizing among its congregation details of an ex-member's sexual conduct. In a liberal society, people must be free to go to hell in their own way, provided they stay within the law. In contrast, a man who has been an Orthodox Jew – even if only to the extent of having got married according to Orthodox Jewish rites – and is no longer one still has unfinished business with his wife's synagogue if he refuses her the *get*. (I assume that the wife is still an observant Orthodox Jew, since otherwise the problem presumably does not arise.) In this respect, and in this one respect only, the other members of his wife's congregation have a legitimate concern with his conduct, because it has severe repercussions for her religious status, and for that of any children that she subsequently has. If he wants to avoid embarrassment, all he has to do is give his wife the *get*. This is scarcely a burdensome undertaking. Moreover, since it can have no religious significance for him, the only possible motives he can have for withholding the *get* are malice or extortion.

Bargaining over the *get* can, as we have seen, give rise to highly inequitable divorce settlements. Can the civil courts play a role in redressing the balance? In Israel, the state courts have since 1992 adjusted settlements approved by rabbinical courts in the direction of greater equality between men and women. Ayelet Schachar has commented on this practice that, while it can attack 'extortion and blackmail', it cannot help with the case in which the 'husband refuses a *get* in order to avoid pain [ to himself, presumably – BB] or prevent [his wife] from marrying another man'.[32] Despite this, she regards a system with this provision that otherwise leaves the existing rules intact, and continues to endow religious courts with legally binding jurisdiction, as an ideal solution to the competing demands of equity and cultural integrity. Although Schachar's article is subtitled 'The Perils of Multicultural Accommodation', this suggests to me that she takes a rather frivolous view of those perils, which arise inevitably and inescapably once legal force is given to a fundamentally inequitable system of family law.

Since there is no such thing as civil marriage in Israel, it is impossible for Jews to obtain a legally valid divorce except through a religious court. In this situation, the state is underwriting Jewish law, so the involvement of the state's courts in the terms of the divorce is scarcely surprising. But in countries such as Britain and the United States, in which religious personal law has no legal significance, it would seem at first sight that courts should take no cognizance of its existence. However, the state has legitimate interests in the outcomes of civil divorce, and these extend to ensuring that they are not subverted by the power that Jewish religious law gives to men. It seems clear, for example, that there is a public interest in protecting the interests of children. I quoted earlier the claim that 'women may be induced to lose sight of the interests of their children by agreeing to custody or access arrangements which would otherwise never have seen the light of day'.[33] If bargaining over the *get* leads to an agreement on custody and access of this kind, it is essential that courts should be able to set it aside. Similarly, there is a public interest in adequate maintenance arrangements for children, and courts should once again be able to insist that these are made, if necessary overriding any agreement made by the parties.

More broadly, it may be said that 'the *get* has the effect ... of subverting the secular legal system, particularly its attempts to equalise the bargaining positions of husbands and wives in the context of divorce proceedings'.[34] Courts in England and in New York State have intervened on an *ad hoc* basis to provide equitable relief for women who have been induced to make highly disadvantageous financial settlements in order to obtain the *get*.[35] In Ontario, the legislature has systematized such intervention; it has

> made a provision empowering divorce courts within the jurisdiction to 'set aside all or part of a separation agreement or settlement, if the court is satisfied that the removal by one spouse of barriers that would prevent the other spouse's remarriage within that spouse's faith [i.e. cooperation in the execution of the *get*] was a consideration in the making of the agreement or settlement.'[36]

What such a measure can do is reduce the incentive to withhold the *get* for purposes of extortion. But it can still have no efficacy in the face of a man who wishes to withhold the *get* out of spite or malice. Within a liberal society, the only remedy available is social pressure of a legally permissible kind, and this may very well be ineffective. The only adequate solution is a change in the religious rules themselves. But that, if the analysis presented here is correct, can come about only by an internal process of reform.

## 2. An Alternative Approach

Before moving on, I want to pause for a brief defence of the position taken here against the one put forward by Will Kymlicka in *Multicultural Citizenship*. According to him, liberal principles entail that 'non-liberal minorities' are precluded by liberal principles from imposing 'internal restrictions which limit the right of individuals within the group to revise their conceptions of the good'.[37] Clearly, a group cannot literally prevent people from changing their minds about the truth or value of its constitutive beliefs or norms, though it can attach consequences to the expression of such a change of mind and whatever conduct flows from it. The question is what a group may legitimately do to those whom it defines as heretics or apostates.

If a group were exercising political power, Kymlicka would certainly be quite correct in saying that it should be constrained from 'prohibiting apostasy and proselytization'.[38] In that context, it would be accurate to describe the rights to change one's religion or expose oneself to rival propagandists as 'civil liberties'.[39] It is quite clear, though, that Kymlicka is not thinking (or at any rate not thinking mainly) of legal sanctions imposed by a minority sub-state. Outside that context, however, talk about 'civil liberties' seems out of place, since the concept of civil liberties applies to the rights that people have as members of a political order. At the most, we might describe the rights against churches proposed by Kymlicka as analogies of civil rights. But then we have to ask: is the analogy close enough?

What, precisely, would it mean for (say) the Roman Catholic Church to prohibit apostasy and proselytization? It could enjoin its adherents to remain faithful to its tenets and to show the door to visiting Mormons. But it is hard to see how its right to do that could reasonably be impugned, since those who do not wish to accept such injunctions are free to leave the church. If it meant that the church could invoke the law to punish rebels or renegades, that would obviously be inconsistent with liberal principles. So, equally obviously, would the law's turning a blind eye to the beating or killing of apostates either by the church itself or at the instigation of the church. These, however, do not seem to be the kinds of thing Kymlicka has in mind.

Jacob Levy has suggested that the prohibition of apostasy may be intended to mean that 'the person who openly rejects the faith [must] continue to be welcomed as a member of it'.[40] Yet this, as I have argued, would be a completely improper demand, because it would fundamentally violate freedom of association. Nonetheless, Levy's conjecture is supported by what Kymlicka goes on to say, which suggests that it should, as far as is humanly possible, be rendered costless to change one's mind in matters of religion – and if that means that apostates cannot be ejected, so be it. Crucial to the analysis of group rights proposed here, however, is the distinction between costs that an individual excluded from a group has to bear and those for which legal relief can be sought.

To illustrate the importance of distinguishing between the two kinds of costs, let me take up a case discussed by Kymlicka. This involved a community of Hutterites in Canada. Hutterites, like the Amish, are spiritual descendants of the Anabaptists. Unlike the Amish, who have a system of private property, the Hutterites 'live in large agricultural communities, called colonies, within which there is no private property. Two lifelong members of a Hutterite colony [in Canada] were expelled for apostasy. They demanded their share of the colony's assets, which they had helped create with their years of labour.'[41] Their complaint was that they could leave only at the cost of 'abandoning everything, even the clothes on their backs'.[42] The Hutterite response, which was accepted by the Canadian Supreme Court, was 'that freedom of religion protects a congregation's ability to live in accordance with its religious doctrine even if this limits individual freedom'.[43] The claim to compensation by the expellees was denied by the Court on this basis.

Kymlicka thinks that the Hutterite response should have been rejected altogether by the Court, and I understand him (on the lines suggested by Levy) to mean that the Hutterites should not have been free to expel the apostates. But the Court was quite correct to regard it as a necessary implication of the principle of freedom of association that the community should have been able to expel those whom the authorities within it deemed to be heretics. Where the Court erred was in drawing the conclusion that the ex-members' claim to some sort of pension from the Hutterites should also fail. The analysis that I would propose for this case is like that which I set out in the previous chapter for the hypothetical case of a religious body that organized a boycott directed against ex-members as an aspect of 'shunning'. The Hutterite community's right to expel heretics is quite compatible with the community's having to make payments to those whom it expels (or those who leave of their own accord) so as to ensure that they are not destitute. That is the price that the Hutterites have to pay for qualifying as a voluntary association, and it is by no means an excessive price.

Levy takes Kymlicka to be saying that what is incompatible with liberal principles is 'a high cost on abandoning one's religion at will'.[44] How could this cost be rendered negligible? Levy speculates that

> the rule [sought by Kymlicka] may be that a religion cannot be so central or dominant a part of a person's life that abandoning it imposes high costs; that is clearly a rule for which one could articulate a defense, though it would require a standard for measuring the size of the costs. But it would hardly be a *liberal* standard.[45]

This is putting it mildly! There are some costs of exit that are the legitimate concern of a state and others that are not. It is surely not the job of a state to go around telling people that they cannot regard, say, excommunication from the Roman Catholic Church as having more significance in their lives than being thrown out of a fairly congenial darts club. The main impulse behind the creation of the Spanish Inquisition was, as I mentioned in chapter 2, the suspicion that those who had converted to Christianity to save their lives were less than wholly enthusiastic about their new faith. To implement

Levy's rule (or more precisely the rule he thinks may be required by Kymlicka's view about costs of exit) would call for a body with the same all-embracing powers as the Spanish Inquisition but dedicated to roughly the opposite end. Its task would be to search the inner recesses of people's minds to make sure that they were sufficiently lukewarm about religion. But state-enforced Laodiceanism is surely no more acceptable to a liberal than compulsory enthusiasm for one particular faith.[46]

## 3.  The Limits of Toleration

I conclude from the discussion of Kymlicka that his theory of group rights is vitiated by his failure to draw crucial distinctions between the different kinds of cost to which those who leave a religious body are liable. I shall therefore continue to explore in the rest of this chapter the implications of the theory developed so far, which turns on the legitimacy of some costs and the illegitimacy of others.

Let us begin by reviewing what has already been established. The central point is that voluntary associations do not have to have internal rules satisfying the demands that liberal principles make on political bodies. There is, of course, nothing in this that applies only to churches. Other kinds of organization are often not run democratically, and there is no objection to this provided that membership is voluntary. Nobody, for example, is offered the opportunity to vote for the leaders of Greenpeace or determine its policies. All that happens is that the people who run it decide what it will do, and everybody else decides whether to send it money or not. Again, many organizations (including most clubs) have rules that members are expected to obey and impose penalties on those who break them. Here, too, as long as people are free to leave such organizations any time that they find the rules unduly onerous, it is hard to see why the law should intervene, even if the rules would violate liberal norms in a political body. Churches, admittedly, play a larger role in the lives of their members than that played typically by cause groups or clubs. But that difference does not undermine the case for bringing churches under the rubric of free association, on condition that they do not add gratuitous sanctions to the intrinsic and associational costs of exit.

It may be said, reasonably enough, that I have so far tackled only relatively easy cases. What do liberal principles tell us about cases, not until now discussed, in which a church acts in a way that would normally be illegal? Even among those who extol the value of 'diversity' or 'tolerance', there is a sense that there must be some limits to what can be done in the name of freedom of association. This is illustrated by the case of a fundamentalist Christian university, the Bob Jones University. Its trustees 'once claimed, no doubt sincerely, that it was against the tenets of their religion to admit black students. When the government threatened to rescind its tax-exempt status if it barred blacks, Bob Jones changed its admissions policy, admitting blacks but forbidding interracial dating and marriage among its student body.'[47] This prohibition in turn led the Internal Revenue Service to withdraw its tax exempt status 'on grounds that Bob Jones university practiced racial discrimination and was therefore disqualified as a charitable institution, even though its discriminatory policy...was based on a sincere religious belief that the Bible forbids miscegenation'.[48] On appeal to the Supreme Court, the decision of the IRS was upheld. The argument that carried the day was 'that overcoming racial discrimination in education is a compelling government interest, sufficient to override a religiously run university's claim to free exercise of religion'.[49] Significantly, even William Galston, despite his enthusiasm for 'diversity', endorses the decision of the Supreme Court in this case.[50] A fortiori, he must therefore support the denial of tax-exempt status to a university that actually excludes black students.

Consider, again, Nancy Rosenblum's book *Membership and Morals*. This is so extraordinarily keen on maintaining freedom of association for even the most unpromising groups that readers may occasionally wonder if their legs are being pulled. Even she, however, takes the view that the decision of the American Supreme Court in the case of *Corporation of Presiding Bishop of the Church of Jesus Christ of Latter-Day Saints* v. *Amos* 'concedes too much' to the Church.[51] Amos had worked for sixteen years as a janitor in a gymnasium open to the public that was owned by the Mormon Church. He was 'fired for not complying with the eligibility test for attendance at Mormon temples (the standards involved church attendance, tithing, and abstinence from coffee, tea, alcohol and tobacco)'.[52] This was clearly a case of job discrimination based on religious affiliation, which is in general illegal in the United States. However, the same federal civil rights law that makes religious discrimination illegal 'makes an exception for religious organizations. Prior to 1972, the exemption covered only religious activities of those organizations; it was then expanded to cover all activities.'[53] But can that exemption include the operation of a gymnasium?

> The district court found the Deseret Gymnasium indistinguishable from any other health club operated for profit, and the janitor's job similar to jobs in those facilities.... Nothing in the church's operation of the gym was 'even tangentially related to any conceivable religious belief or ritual of the Mormon church or church administration.'[54]

The Supreme Court did not accept the District Court's view that the exemption from anti-discrimination law would be impermissibly broad if it were taken to cover the requirement that a janitor in a gymnasium must be a member of the Mormon church in good standing. 'All the justices united behind the rationale that it would be an interference with the autonomy of religious organizations for the government to decide which non-profit activities are religious and which are not.'[55] As Justice Brennan wrote, concurring with the Court's decision, 'ideally, religious organizations should be able to discriminate only with respect to religious activities, [but] while a church may regard the conduct of certain functions as integral to its mission, a court may disagree.'[56] The conclusion he drew from this would have warmed the heart of the English pluralists: unless all the activities of churches – however apparently remote from their doctrinal core these might be – were exempt from anti-discrimination legislation, 'the [religious] community's process of self-definition would be shaped in part by the prospects of litigation'.[57]

As we shall see in the next section, this extravagant all-or-nothing position with regard to religiously based claims came back to haunt Brennan and his allies. What is important here, however, is to notice that the effect of the decision was to give religious bodies extremely broad scope for exercising job discrimination – so broad that it might be thought to threaten religious liberty itself. For, as Rosenblum has said, 'there is no sharper deviation from liberalism than coercing belief by conditioning vital secular benefits on declarations of faith'.[58] As she points out 'the Deseret Gymnasium employee's liberty (which includes the right *not* to believe) was clearly burdened by the church's exemption from federal law, as was the religious liberty of other non-Mormon, potential employees'.[59]

The claims made by religious bodies for exemptions to generally applicable laws are a corporate equivalent of the claims for exemptions made by individuals that were discussed in chapter 2. I argued there that claims for exemptions by individuals based on religious beliefs were subject to a pincer movement. In most cases, one of two things could be said: that the end pursued by the law was sufficiently important to underwrite the conclusion that there should be no exemptions, or that the argument for exemptions was so powerful that it overthrew the case for having a law at all. I believe that, for the most part, exemptions for religious bodies will fall to the same pincer movement. But there is one major exemption that must escape.

Employment discrimination based on religion is illegal in the United States and in Northern Ireland. (I argued in chapter 2 that it should be illegal in the whole of the United Kingdom.) In a jurisdiction that prohibits religious discrimination, there must surely be an exemption to allow churches to apply religious criteria for ordination, at the least. In some instances, where religion and ethnicity are intertwined, the right of a religious body to impose a membership requirement for appointment to sacerdotal office must also entail a waiver of any prohibition on ethnically based discrimination. A constitutive element in Orthodox Jewish religious belief is the definition of a Jew, and it would seem absurd to maintain that being counted on the prevalent criteria as a Jew cannot legitimately be made a necessary condition of becoming a Rabbi. The English courts have found Jews to be an ethnic group for the purposes of the law against discrimination. Without a waiver, therefore, restriction of employment as a Rabbi to Jews would constitute racial discrimination. Yet there would surely be something crazy about a prosecution on this basis.

It seems uncontroversial that discrimination based on religion should be permitted when it comes to a church's choice of candidates for the priesthood or its equivalent, and that this permission should not be rescinded in cases where the adherents of the religion have been held to constitute an ethnic group. This still leaves open the possibility that the right of churches to engage in what would otherwise be illegal discrimination should stop there. This would entail, in particular, that a church would not be able to restrict the ministry to men: doing so would be invalidated as discrimination on the basis of sex. Ian Shapiro has suggested – as a step short of declaring sex discrimination illegal – that the precedent given by the Bob Jones case might be extended. Thus, tax-exempt status might be denied to churches 'in which some offices are reserved for men, persons of a particular race, or any other group defined in a morally arbitrary way'.[60] Shapiro deduces this proposal from egalitarian liberal principles. It is therefore incumbent upon me to explain why I think he is wrong. I should make it clear that I am not in favour of giving churches specially advantageous tax treatment at all; but I do wish to claim that the case of a church that restricts the priesthood to men can be distinguished from the Bob Jones University case. If churches are to get favourable treatment at all, their doing so should not be contingent upon their abandoning their position on the necessary qualifications for holding religious office.

This necessarily commits me to rejecting the stronger claim that a religious body should be prohibited from acting on its own doctrines about the criteria for somebody's being a candidate for the ministry. I am not aware of any political philosopher who has argued for that. However, Cass Sunstein has maintained that it is incoherent to subscribe to what he calls 'the asymmetry thesis', the asymmetry in question being that between on one hand applying ordinary laws to religious institutions (even when these create special burdens for them) and on the other hand exempting them from antidiscrimination law in the employment of officials. 'There is no plausible rationale', he writes 'for the view, embodied in the practice of many liberal cultures, that it is unproblematic to apply ordinary civil and criminal law to religious institutions, but that it is problematic to apply, to those institutions, laws forbidding sex discrimination.'[61]

## 4.  In Defence of 'Asymmetry'

I want to argue in favour of a thesis that bears some resemblance to Sunstein's 'asymmetry thesis'. A good deal of ground will have to be cleared, however, before I can get to the point of stating the version that I propose to defend, let alone actually making the case for it. For there is much to take issue with in Sunstein's own statement of the 'asymmetry thesis'. Consider, for a start, the assertion that there is 'a view, embodied in the practice of many liberal cultures, that it is unproblematic to apply ordinary civil and criminal law to religious institutions'. It is not altogether clear how we are supposed to be able to tell that a practice embodies the view that the absence of something is unproblematic. The best evidence, however, would seem to be that the thing in question does not find a place in the practice. If this is the correct interpretation of Sunstein's claim (and I cannot think of any plausible alternative) then it is simply false.

In chapter 2, I discussed quite a number of exemptions from ordinary laws for religious believers. The examples were for the most part drawn from English law. Federal and State law in the United States provides similar exemptions. The world's two officially 'multicultural' societies, Canada and Australia, are at least as generous in providing religiously based exemptions from ordinary laws. I doubt that it would be possible to find a large number of other countries with liberal cultures that have substantial religious minorities and do not accommodate them in the ways with which we are by now familiar. In any case, Sunstein himself focuses entirely on the United States in his discussion of the 'asymmetry thesis', which suggests that he has in mind countries such as those I have listed.

A possible move that Sunstein could have made would have been to rule out examples such as these, on the ground that they involve exemptions for individuals, whereas he formulates his thesis in terms of 'religious institutions'. But this move is not open to him. He says that he leaves the term 'deliberately vague'.[62] But his argument depends crucially on a contrast between an individual exemption denied and a corporate exemption accepted. Unless both of these cases involve 'religious institutions', the argument collapses. The *Smith* case, which is the first one, is a claim for an individual exemption, based on religious belief, to a generally applicable anti-drug law.[63] The second case is a Supreme Court ruling that the *Smith* decision 'did not undermine previous holdings that there was an exception [i.e. exemption] for ministers from the general sex discrimination law'.[64] This is a question of the right of a church as a corporate entity to act in a way that would generally be illegal.

Sunstein's claim that the 'asymmetry thesis' is 'embodied' in the practice of the United States turns on the interpretation of the *Smith* case. As the leading American case on individual exemptions based on religion, it is worth some attention anyway to complement the discussion of English law in chapter 2. We should begin our discussion by noticing the tortuous way in which the Supreme Court insinuated itself into the case. 'Respondents Alfred Smith and Galen Black (hereafter respondents) were fired from their jobs with a private drug rehabilitation organization [in Oregon] because they ingested peyote for sacramental purposes at a ceremony of the Native American Church, of which both are members.'[65] They were denied unemployment compensation on the ground that they had lost their jobs as a result of 'misconduct'. The Court held that *if* the use of peyote in a religious ritual was illegal *then* Smith and Black could legitimately be denied unemployment compensation, reasoning that 'if a State has prohibited through its criminal laws certain kinds of religiously motivated conduct without violating the First Amendment, it certainly follows that it may impose the lesser burden of denying unemployment compensation benefits to persons who engage in that conduct'.[66] This ruling opened the way to the Court's taking cognizance of the question of the legality of the conduct itself. The Oregon Supreme Court held that

> respondents' religiously inspired use of peyote fell within the prohibition of the Oregon statute, which 'makes no exception for the sacramental use of the drug.'. . . It then considered whether the prohibition was valid under the Free Exercise Clause [of the United States Constitution] and concluded that it was not. The court therefore reaffirmed its previous ruling that the State could not deny unemployment benefits to respondents for having engaged in that practice.[67]

The US Supreme Court reversed the decision of the Oregon Supreme Court, on the ground that the law's not allowing a religious exception to the prohibition of peyote was consistent with the 'free exercise' clause.[68]

Our chief concern here is the claim for a religiously based exemption to anti-drug legislation, derived from the constitutional guarantee of 'free exercise of religion'. While I am sympathetic to the Court's reasoning on that issue, I want in passing to remark on the monstrous nature of the Court's decision on the question about unemployment compensation from which the case arose in the first place. The first miscarriage of justice here was that Smith and Black had not been prosecuted for the ceremonial use of peyote, and it appeared in the case that nobody had ever been prosecuted for this in Oregon. It is true that an employer can fire somebody for misconduct on the job without having to prove the misconduct in court; it is then open to the dismissed employee to challenge the employer's claim of misconduct before an industrial appeals tribunal or some equivalent body. But an employer should not be permitted to take account of other forms of 'misconduct' unless they have been legally established to have occurred. Even if Smith and Black had been found guilty, however, this should still not in itself have been an adequate basis for saying that they could be denied unemployment compensation because they had been dismissed for 'misconduct'. Why should a shop-assistant convicted for speeding be liable to lose unemployment benefit if his employer fires him after reading about the case in the newspaper? The Supreme Court did not accept as valid the ground on which Smith and Black were actually denied unemployment compensation, which was that ingesting peyote constituted 'work-related misconduct' in people employed in a drug-rehabilitation programme.[69] Yet misconduct related to an employee's suitability to do the job is surely the only sort that should count as a legitimate reason for firing him.

We can now move on to the main question: does the constitutional right to practise your religion entail that you must be given an exemption to a general law which prohibits the ingestion of (among other drugs) peyote, on the ground that the use of peyote forms a part of your religious ritual? Several State courts had preceded the Oregon court in deciding that it did.[70] But the position taken by the Supreme Court was that, provided a law is not overtly discriminatory (by singling out a particular religion or all religions for adverse treatment), the United States Constitution does not require it to be invalidated or limited in its scope simply because it has a disproportionate impact on some religious believers. This is broadly in line with the position that I took in chapter 2 to the effect that justice (in the form of equal treatment) and freedom of religion do not require exemptions from generally applicable laws simply on the basis of their having a differential effect on people according to their beliefs, norms, compulsions or preferences.

At the same time, I emphasized in chapter 2 that this left open the possibility that a legislature might quite properly decide to make an exemption, and I actually argued for a continuation of the hard hat exemption for turban-wearing Sikhs in Britain, at least to include those already employed in the construction industry. Similarly, Justice Scalia, writing for the Court in *Smith*, pointed out that

> a society that believes in the negative protection accorded to religious belief [in the form of a constitutional prohibition of overtly discriminatory laws] can be expected to be solicitous of its value in its legislation as well. It is therefore not surprising that a number of States have made an exception to their drug laws for sacramental peyote use.... But to say that a nondiscriminatory religious-practice exemption is permitted, or even that it is desirable, is not to say that it is constitutionally required, and that the appropriate occasions for its creation can be discerned by the courts.

Courts should not try to run 'a system in which each conscience is a law unto itself or in which judges weigh the importance of all laws against the centrality of all religious beliefs'.[71] Making these trade-offs was, Scalia suggested, the job of legislatures.

Thus, the issue was not whether it was a good idea or not to have an exemption for the ceremonial use of peyote but whether or not courts should mandate such an exemption where a legislature had not written one into the law. This point is widely misunderstood. For example, Stephen Macedo has written that 'we may...sometimes consider claims for accommodations or exceptions or even adjustments in public policies based on comprehensive [e.g. religious] grounds'.[72] Macedo's discussion of the point makes it clear that he has in mind political rather than judicial decisions. Thus, he says: 'We must listen to dissenters, engage them in political conversation, and indeed encourage them to state their objections publicly. We cannot guarantee that we will do more.'[73] In all of this, he is simply spelling out Scalia's view that the political forum, rather than the courtroom, is the right place for arguing about exemptions. Despite this, Macedo asks (citing *Smith*) if the willingness to 'consider claims for accommodations' must 'open the sort of Pandora's box of religious complaints that Justice Scalia and others have warned against'.[74]

The point is, however, that Justice Scalia's warning was directed purely at the *judicial* creation of exemptions. To this end, he did indeed offer what was described as a 'parade of horribles' – a list of issues in which judges would have to 'balance against the importance of general laws the significance of religious practice' if they once accepted that it was their job to do this. These included

> compulsory military service...payment of taxes...health and safety regulations such as manslaughter and child neglect laws...compulsory vaccination laws...drug laws...and traffic laws...social welfare legislation such as minimum wage laws, child labor laws, environmental protection laws, and laws providing for equality of opportunity for the races.[75]

But what was 'horrible to contemplate' about the list was that judges should perform the weighing.[76] Justice Scalia's proposed solution – 'leaving accommodation to the political process' – was exactly what is advocated by Macedo.[77]

In the event, the Congress did not avail itself of Justice Scalia's invitation to legislate whatever religiously based exemptions it saw fit to enact, though a number of States joined those that had already legalized the sacramental use of peyote. (What the Congress did instead was take the easy way out by passing the so-called Religious Freedom Restoration Act in 1996, which the Court invalidated a year later as an illegitimate attempt to tell it how to do its own business.) But there are still already a large number of federal and – far more numerous – State and local exemptions in existence that arise out of successful lobbying by religious organizations. Thus, to anticipate my discussion of the Amish later in this chapter, almost all of the many exemptions from generally applicable laws that Amish communities have acquired over the years have been won in legislatures and government agencies as a result of remarkably sophisticated and effective political campaigns. Only a few exemptions have been obtained in the courts, at any level of jurisdiction. The same is true of exemptions for members of other religious groups. Despite this, the writings of American legal and political theorists focus almost entirely on the constitutionally based exemptions that have been granted, and the larger number that might have been granted but have not been. Needless to say, this produces a highly misleading picture of the actual legal situation. Only thus can we account for Sunstein's suggestion that the ordinary law of the land applies strictly to 'religious institutions' without any exceptions other than a waiver of the anti-discrimination law for churches.

If we equate court decisions overruling legislatures with the current practice in countries with 'liberal cultures', we come up with even more bizarre results when we move outside the United States. In England, the courts do not have the ability to overrule parliament, so the position might be described as *Smith*-plus. Yet, as we have seen, there is a plethora of religiously based exemptions arising from legislation. The incorporation of European law into English law will predictably make little difference to the situation. The doctrine that governments are allowed a 'margin of appreciation' in balancing religious claims against the demands of amenity and public order has led to the British government's prevailing in the European courts when challenged on grounds of religious freedom. English courts will presumably follow the lead that those courts have given when they assume the task of applying European law.

Leaving all that aside, however, there still remains a more accurately formulated question that we can ask. This is: notwithstanding *Smith*, should the Supreme Court hold that the constitutional guarantee of 'free exercise' of religion gives churches immunity to prosecution under anti-discrimination law if they appoint only men to the ministry? I have already quoted Sunstein as saying that the Supreme Court has considered the question of sex discrimination by churches in the light of *Smith* and 'held, without much explanation, that *Smith* did not undermine previous holdings that there was an exception [i.e. exemption] for ministers from the general sex discrimination law'.[78] Sunstein takes this as some sort of incoherence in the Court's position – as showing that 'some exemptions are necessary'.[79] On the assumption that 'necessary' here means 'constitutionally necessary', the Court's dictum shows nothing of the kind. For the Court's position is that it is open to legislatures to create exemptions from general laws if they so choose, and the exemption from sex discrimination law for religious bodies is covered by the provisions of the law on discrimination itself.

It is true that the specific exemption for religious bodies already mentioned extends only as far as discrimination on the basis of religion.[80] But the wording of the legislation permits discrimination 'where religion, sex, or national origin is "a bona fide occupational qualification reasonably necessary to the normal operation of that particular business or enterprise"'.[81] It may be recalled that Ian Shapiro dismissed any qualification involving (among other things) sex as a 'morally arbitrary' basis on which to choose ministers. That means it is irrelevant. But how can it be irrelevant if the people concerned believe it to be of the essence? If you believe that the sacraments have efficacy only if administered by a man, you can scarcely regard the sex of the person administering them as irrelevant. What could be said on this point by traditionalist adherents of the Roman Catholic Church could also be said by members of all the Orthodox Christian churches, as well as Muslims, Orthodox Jews, Hindus and Sikhs. For they could all claim that, according to their beliefs, the valid performance of the sacerdotal function requires it to be performed by a man.

There is an obvious argument based on liberal principles to the effect that freedom of religious worship for individuals, which is an undeniably liberal value, can be achieved only if people are free to attach themselves to churches with a variety of doctrines. (It should be noticed that this is not an argument from the value of diversity but from the value of individual choice.) These different doctrines will, in the nature of the case, include ideas about the appropriate structure of authority within the church, the beliefs and behaviour expected of members of the church, and so on. Thus, for example, let us suppose that some church bases its claims to legitimacy on apostolic succession. Those who believe that this is the only valid basis of religious authority would be denied the opportunity to worship God in the way they think He ordained – by accepting the authority of the current successor of St Peter – if the church were obliged to reconstitute itself so that it was run on Congregationalist lines. Equally, those who accept the validity of a certain source of religious authority (for example, the Pope) would be prevented from worshipping in accordance with their beliefs if the right of that authority to determine the criteria for ordination were overridden by the law.

This, finally, brings us to the 'asymmetry thesis'. As stated by Sunstein, this presupposes that liberal democratic societies do not permit exemptions from ordinary laws for 'religious institutions', while allowing them to discriminate in employment on the basis of (among other things) sex. The thesis itself then maintains that liberal democratic societies can consistently do both at the same time. In this form, the 'asymmetry thesis' is of no interest because it rests on a false account of the facts. The only way in which life can be breathed into it is to restate it as a constitutional doctrine according to which it is consistent to say (1) that *Smith* was rightly decided and (2) that nevertheless the 'free exercise of religion' clause of the US Constitution would require churches to be given a waiver from a law prohibiting discrimination in employment even if no provision permitting one were written into the law itself. If this is taken to be the 'asymmetry thesis', it is not incoherent and is indeed correct.

I am not primarily concerned in this book with American (or other) constitutional issues. However, the case for 'asymmetry' turns on a particular aspect of free association, so discussing it will help to refine the liberal theory of free association set out in the previous chapter. Let me take up the two elements of this revised 'asymmetry thesis' in turn. I argued in chapter 2 that, although prudent and enlightened public policy might in some instances involve granting an exemption for individuals from some general law in order to accommodate their religious beliefs, this was not something required by justice. The decision in the *Smith* case ran parallel to this. Similarly, I do not believe that churches as collectivities can properly demand special treatment as a matter of justice, though this does not rule out the possibility that a political decision might under some circumstances be made in their favour. The extension of *Smith* to churches as organizations is thus, I wish to maintain, in general defensible.

Sebastian Poulter has discussed a number of cases in which a religious body in England has wanted to build a church, temple or mosque on a site deemed unsuitable by the local planning authority for any such construction because of its adverse effect on road safety and amenity. Although some appeals against these decisions succeeded, none of the decisions suggested that religious bodies could demand to have normal planning criteria set aside simply on the ground that their activities would be impeded by decisions based on those criteria.[82] The European Commission of Human Rights took the same line. Thus, it upheld refusal of permission in a case involving a very large Hindu development in the Green Belt in Hertfordshire. It was satisfied that the decision to refuse permission 'had been reached on proper planning grounds and not on any objections to the religious aspects of the activities of ISKCON [The International Society for Krishna Consciousness]'.[83] This is clearly in line with the *Smith* doctrine that governments may not single out religious bodies for adverse treatment but are not obliged to give them especially favourable treatment. A large supermarket generating the same amount of round-the-clock traffic as the Hindu complex would have been an equal blight on a small village.[84] That the cause of the disruption would instead have been the activities of a religious body was not an adequate reason for making the inhabitants of the village put up with it.

If this is the implication of *Smith* for churches as collective entities, is Sunstein right in claiming that there cannot, consistently with it, be a constitutional right for them to engage in employment discrimination? I believe that he is wrong because, as one US court put it in a civil case, ' "who will preach from the pulpit of a church and who will occupy the parsonage" is a purely ecclesiastical question'.[85] For a court to intervene in such a matter would be to come down on one side and against another in a purely internal dispute within a church. Consider the position of a woman who wants to be ordained as a minister in a Christian church. She could do so, if she went through the procedures necessary to qualify, by joining a church that already admits women to the ministry. She will ask a court to intervene on her behalf only if she is not prepared to do that but insists on becoming a minister in a church whose own authoritative rules do not permit women to the ministry. But this puts her in a paradoxical position. She claims (say) to be a Roman Catholic, which entails acceptance of papal authority. Yet at the same time she is asking a court to overrule the Pope's decision about women priests.

It would be perfectly coherent for a woman with the ambition to become a priest to wish (as many Roman Catholics do) that the Pope would change his mind.[86] It would also be possible while remaining a Roman Catholic to hope that the existing system for making decisions might be used to change that system so as to make it less dictatorial.[87] But to want either the decisions or the decision-making system to be changed by a secular authority is simply to want what Henry the Eighth achieved several centuries ago: the substitution of secular for religious authority. It is surely not to be wondered at if the courts would decline to reproduce the work of the Reformation in the guise of enforcing a law against employment discrimination. Those who despair of the prospects of reform from within the Roman Catholic Church, and are attracted by the idea that its rules might be rewritten by the state, always have the option of joining the Anglican Church.

## 5.  The Amish and the State

Sooner or later, all political theorists who address the rights of illiberal communities to run their own affairs without interference feel called upon to say something about the Old Order Amish in North America. This is not surprising, because Amish communities have made exceptionally sweeping demands to be permitted to contravene ordinary laws, claiming that their entire way of life has religious significance and thus falls within the scope of the guarantee of 'free exercise of religion'. Although much discussion of the Amish focuses entirely on their educational practices, I shall postpone my own treatment of those practices until the next chapter. I shall devote this section to setting out some basic information about the history, beliefs and practices of the Amish, and the ways in which these have brought them into conflict with the state. This is worth doing because, in the absence of some understanding of such matters, it is easy to make comments about them that are ill-founded, as I shall illustrate. In the next section, which concludes the chapter, I shall ask how far Amish communities meet the conditions for counting as voluntary associations.

To begin with history, the Amish are like the Hutterites in being spiritual descendants of the Anabaptists. A third group with the same origins are the Mennonites, who are less uniform in beliefs and practices but generally speaking less distinct from the mainstream society. Indeed, Mennonite churches offer a refuge for those brought up as Amish who 'decide not to be baptized and do not join the church. ... [These] frequently live nearby and join more progressive churches, often conservative Mennonite groups, which share the Amish community's historical roots.'[88] The defining belief of the Anabaptists (literally 'rebaptizers') has from the outset been that baptism 'was only meaningful and valid after adults made a voluntary confession of faith'.[89] Anabaptists date back to the early sixteenth century, when they emerged in Switzerland, the Netherlands and southern Germany. Their beliefs led to ferocious persecution by the civil authorities. 'The first martyr was drowned in 1527. Over the next few decades, thousands of Anabaptists burned at the stake, drowned in rivers, starved in prisons, or lost their heads to the executioner's sword.'[90] This experience has continued to shape their descendants' attitudes to the state. Amish still read the *Martyr's Mirror*: 'filled with etchings of torture, this large book in its many editions portrays the persecution of nonresistant Christians in the sixteenth and seventeenth centuries by the governments of their day. ... Thus, the story of martyrdom rooted in their history greatly affects the Amish view of the state even today.'[91]

I pointed out in the previous chapter that Galston's notion of 'Reformation liberalism' is an oxymoron. 'Although both [Luther and Calvin] modified the medieval concept of the *Corpus Christianum* (the union – or partnership – of church and state), neither of them supported the modern view of the separation of church and state.'[92] No more did the Anabaptists. For their view of the appropriate degree of separation was – and remains – much more radical than is implied simply in the idea that the state should not enforce subscription to any religion and should (within the limits of the ordinary law of the land) leave churches to organize themselves as they choose. Thus, a still influential treatise written by Hans Schnell in 1575 maintained that

> the kingdom of this world and the kingdom of Christ were not only distinct realms, they were antithetical – separated by a great chasm. He said that 'neither can have part of communion with the other.' The kingdom of this world is based on vengeance; the kingdom of Christ is based on love. The magistrate who, as an agent of the wordly government, metes out vengeance puts himself outside Christ's kingdom.[93]

The Amish 'came to North America in two waves – in the mid-1700s and again in the first half of the 1800s. The "Old Order" label evolved in the latter part of the nineteenth century. At the turn of the twentieth century, the Old Order Amish numbered about 5,000. Now scattered across twenty-two states and into Ontario, they exceed 130,000 children and adults.'[94] This enormous rate of expansion, which owes almost nothing in this century to new recruits, has potential significance for public policy. Stephen Macedo says that 'the Amish case [*Wisconsin* v. *Yoder*, discussed below] was, in a way, politically easy, since being Amish is not a growth industry: the Amish pose no threat to the wider liberal society.'[95] It would scarcely be possible to be more mistaken. The Amish are reproducing at a rate close to the limits of human fertility. It is true that about 20 per cent in each generation opt out of being baptized and leave the community.[96] Even with this degree of attrition, however, the rate at which Amish numbers grow is remarkably high. In fact, the current doubling rate, extrapolated through the twenty-first century, would leave them at the end of it with a population in North America somewhere around that of Norway today, with incalculable consequences for the governability of many local jurisdictions.

The Amish accept the legitimacy of the state on essentially Augustinian lines. While holding themselves aloof from its operations, they do not seek to impede them. Thus, while refusing to serve in either combatant or non-combatant roles in the armed forces during the Second World War, they did not join the minority who were jailed for refusing any service whatever, but enrolled in the 'Civilian Peace Service' programme, under which they performed 'work of national importance'.[97] In a similar spirit, the Amish accept the obligation to pay taxes, and they do not worry about what those taxes get spent on.

> Most Amish would agree that 'when a tax is paid, it is no longer our money, and it is not our responsibility to dictate how it is to be used.' Similarly, the Christian should not tell the government when it may not use the sword. This virtual abnegation of political responsibility has been labeled a 'strategy of withdrawal.'[98]

In line with this strategy, Amish refuse to accept jury duty. They also tend to take little part in electoral politics, though there is some variation in this from one community to another.[99]

A further, and important, aspect of this 'strategy of withdrawal' is a 'taboo of lawsuits', which can be derived directly from the Anabaptist forebears of the Amish, who were 'unalterably opposed to instituting suits at law'.[100] This has come under pressure as 'Amish people have become entrepreneurs in a variety of businesses', and some 'buy types of insurance in which it is assumed that the insurance company will sue to recover damages'.[101] Nevertheless, the norm is apparently still adhered to, in that 'disputes in which both parties are members of Amish congregations may not be submitted to the courts. For these they have their own time-honored *Prozess*, or congregational court.'[102] 'If the church community takes a position [in relation to an internal conflict], any member resisting it risks being excommunicated and shunned. Other members are forbidden to socialize, eat, or do business with the violator in the hope that he or she will repent and conform to the church's *Ordnung*.'[103] Moreover, although the traditional prohibition on resort to law concerns only civil law suits, in practice the Amish have a pronounced tendency to avoid bringing the criminal law into their affairs as well. Thus, 'cases of statutory rape and incest . . . usually . . . are dealt with according to accepted Amish church discipline and do not come to the attention of the courts'.[104] Similarly, 'law enforcement officers are rarely called upon to intervene' when 'Amish youth who have not yet joined the church' engage in illegal activities such as 'consumption of alcoholic beverages, disturbing the peace, and vandalism'.[105] Again, some kind of internal Amish discipline is presumably brought to bear.

The Amish account for a quite large proportion of all the religiously based exemptions to generally applicable laws that are to be found in the United States, and most of these (as I have mentioned) arise from political victories rather than favourable decisions by courts. The Amish have prevailed at all levels of government. They have been particularly successful with State legislatures, winning exemptions from State-mandated requirements involving, among other things, education, certification of midwives and vaccination. At county level, too, Amish (especially in their heartland of Lancaster County, Pennsylvania) have extracted many waivers of local regulations, including those involved in land-use planning, those requiring cess-pits to meet certain minimum standards and those controlling the stabling of horses in built-up areas. The Amish have also won concessions from administrative agencies at all levels of government. For example, 'a rule of the Federal Occupational Safety and Health Administration (OSHA) requiring workers to wear hard hats in construction and carpentry jobs conflicted with the Amish requirement that men wear broad-brimmed hats. Amish lobbying convinced OSHA to grant Amish workers an exemption from the regulation.'[106]

The reference to 'Amish lobbying' draws attention to the point that, unworldly as the Amish may wish to be in certain respects, this does not mean that they are politically naive. We are thus told that

> while separation from the world is the ideal, a well-developed but generally unpublicized network of relationships has developed with non-Amish individuals and groups who willingly use legal services and political action to protect the Amish. For their own reasons, these outsiders have provided additional layers to the protective social cocoon around the Amish and other conservative groups.[107]

For other conservative religious groups, the Amish function as the legal equivalent of a miner's canary: if they can escape the clutches of the law by invoking religion so as to, say, allow the manure on their fields to run off into other people's drinking water, other religious groups with slightly less outrageous demands can breathe easy.

The Amish have created a central body, the National Steering Committee, which

> negotiates special relationships that protect the Amish from unacceptable national, state, and local regulations. The efforts of this committee are virtually identical to those of lawyers and politicians in some of America's toughest urban and bureaucratic environments. Amish lay lawyers in effect do everything we might expect of professional lawyers – lobbying, negotiating settlements, inventing and successfully selling unique legal loopholes, and advocating other members' cases before official bodies.[108]

What they do not do is argue in court or accept fees. But this is taken care of by outsiders, whose work is coordinated by a parallel non-Amish body which calls itself 'The National Committee for Amish Religious Freedom'.[109]

This body engages not only in lobbying and legal action but also in publicity aimed at advancing the claim that any law or regulation that in any way impedes the (selectively) traditional way of life of the Amish violates the religious liberty guaranteed by the US Constitution – whether the courts agree or not. Indeed, the book *The Amish and the State* from which I have been quoting may be seen as part of this propaganda exercise, dedicated as it is to wrapping up every Amish demand in the cloak of religious freedom.[110] Thus, the editor, in his introductory essay, prefaces a list of exemptions won by the Amish by saying that, in their absence, laws would have 'threatened the prerogative of some minorities to exercise their religion freely as safeguarded in the First Amendment to the Bill of Rights'.[111] But that simply presupposes – what is obviously open to controversy – that the First Amendment does proscribe (say) sanitary regulations that the Amish find it expensive or inconvenient to comply with (as, no doubt, do others).

State and local officials always have too much to do, so sheer obduracy will tend to produce results, simply because giving in to Amish demands is much less time-consuming than resisting them. The well-established willingness of Amish Elders to go to jail if they do not get what they want intensifies the pressure on politicians, bureaucrats and elected district attorneys or sheriffs, who fear unfavourable public reactions if they hold out. All this, of course, takes place against a generally well-disposed public opinion brought about by skilful propaganda, normally sympathetic media coverage and the desire of the public to delude themselves about the true character of the Amish: 'Amish society is protected by the tendency of outsiders to project their own values and dreams onto Amish behavior and philosophy. Such misperceptions provide a buffer of tolerance for unconventional Amish behavior because outsiders tend to romanticize the Amish as models of American virtues.'[112] There is, for example, a widespread perception that Amish farming practices are exceptionally 'green', whereas they are in fact exceptionally unsound environmentally.[113] Similarly, many outsiders imagine that the Amish are committed to asceticism.[114] This merely betrays a lack of imagination: wealthy people lived in plenty of comfort before there were cars or mains electricity, and so do those Amish today who can afford to do so.

In sharp contrast with their success with legislators, county planning boards, environmental agencies and bureaucrats, the Amish have on the whole got short shrift from the courts. The argument that the 'free exercise of religion' demands many and various concessions to the Amish has played well with the public and with their elected representatives, but it has cut little ice with the judiciary. The misleading impression to the contrary given by almost all political theorists who discuss the Amish arises from one simple cause: the tendency to focus almost exclusively on one case, that of *Wisconsin* v. *Yoder*. This is the great exception, and at the time the decision was handed down in 1972 it was hailed as a triumph for the notion that the way of life of a whole religious community could be insulated from the state under the rubric of the 'free exercise of religion'.

In reaching its decision, the Supreme Court held that 'the traditional way of life of the Amish is not a matter of personal preference, but one of deep religious conviction, shared by an organized group and intimately related to everyday living', and apparently took the view that its practices could claim protection *en bloc*.[115] However, '*Yoder* represents the greatest length to which the Supreme Court [has] ever gone in upholding religious liberty', as one enthusiast has written, 'not only in the practical result of the decision (freeing the Amish of the legal obligation to send their children to high school), but also in the breadth of the Court's reasoning in coming to that decision. . . . But . . . Supreme Court decisions after *Yoder* never again maintained this degree of protection.'[116] What is significant here is that the 'many ramifications that the decision would have for the religious liberty of others' have not been followed up – especially by the US Supreme Court.[117] More typical of its dealings with the Amish was the case of *US* v. *Lee*, in which the Court refused to accept that the First Amendment bestowed on Amish employers and employees a right to opt out of paying social security contributions.[118'] As we shall see in the next section, the Amish succeeded with the Congress where they had failed with the Court.

Similarly, the Amish have not been wholly without success in the State courts, though again most of their gains at State level have been won through legislative and administrative concessions. But the implication of the decision in *Smith* is that most of the concessions won in the State courts before it was handed down are now open to challenge. They can be saved, however, if State courts are prepared to maintain that the language of the State constitution is more sweeping than that of the US Bill of Rights and thus makes *Smith* irrelevant. This was the line taken by the Supreme Court of Minnesota, in the course of upholding the claim made by some Amish that displaying reflective triangles on the backs of their horse-drawn buggies violated their rights to the free exercise of religion. These cases (one decided before *Smith* and the other after it) illustrate the breadth of the demands that Amish and their sympathizers are prepared to make in the name of religious liberty.

I can best explain the significance of these decisions by going back for a moment to Sunstein's critique of the 'asymmetry thesis'. His preferred alternative would require courts to engage in a 'balancing' of interests in deciding cases involving claims to freedom of religion: an 'appropriate test' might be one that 'depends on both the strength and nature of the state's interest and on the extent of the adverse effect on religion'.[119] This would differ from the current position of the Supreme Court in two ways. In contrast to *Smith*, it would require the state to demonstrate a 'compelling interest' before it could impose general legislation on religious believers or organizations, if that legislation had the effect of burdening their 'free exercise of religion'. But, equally, it would depart from many other cases, including *Amos* (the case of the janitor in the Mormon-run gym), in necessitating judicial determination as to the centrality of a certain kind of activity to a religion.

As we have seen, Justice Brennan wrote in his concurring opinion in the *Amos* case that it was too dangerous for courts to attempt to make any determination of the centrality of any activity because 'while a church may regard the conduct of certain functions as integral to its mission, a court may disagree'.[120] The minority in *Smith*, which included Justice Brennan, continued to adhere to this position formally, and eschewed the word 'centrality'. However, it was clear that what they very much wanted to emphasize was the central role played by the ingestion of peyote among adherents of the Native American Church in virtue of its sacramental status. They therefore talked about its prohibition's being a 'significant burden' or having a 'severe impact'. As Justice Scalia pointed out in his own opinion, these were simply 'centrality' under another name.[121] This was what I had in mind when I said earlier that the extreme deference to religious believers developed in previous cases by the Court had come back in *Smith* to haunt those like Brennan who were generally sympathetic to religiously based claims for exemptions to generally applicable laws. Having insisted that courts could not make judgements of centrality, they were in no position to differentiate the issue in *Smith* from that in *Amos* by saying that the ingestion of peyote was far more important to members of the Native American Church than the religious status of the janitor in a Mormon gymnasium was to the Mormon Church.

The other half of Sunstein's proposal is that the state should have to demonstrate a 'compelling interest' in regulating conduct of a certain kind if doing so would have an 'adverse effect on religion'.[122] What the minority in *Smith* wanted was to apply a test that included the 'compelling interest' requirement. This test had been developed in a number of cases involving claims to unemployment benefit by people who had resigned from or been dismissed from jobs that they claimed violated their religious convictions. In the leading case of *Sherbert* v. *Verner*, the Court elaborated an 'analysis under which (1) the claimant has to show a sincerely held religious belief (2) burdened by the government's action, (3) which the government cannot prove is justified by a compelling state interest, (4) or which, even if justified by a compelling state interest, cannot be regulated by a less burdensome alternative'.[123] It was this 'compelling interest/least restrictive alternative' test that the minority on the Supreme Court wished to use in the *Smith* case.

Justice Scalia, writing for the Court, argued that exemptions from the ordinary law could not reasonably be granted on the basis of *Sherbert* unless the 'centrality' test was employed to balance it. If courts were going to second-guess the importance of the interest served by a law and the means chosen by the legislature to promote that interest, they could not avoid second-guessing the importance of the prohibited act to the religious believer. As Scalia wrote,

> dispensing with a 'centrality' inquiry is utterly unworkable. It would require, for example, the same degree of 'compelling state interest' to impede the practice of throwing rice at church weddings as to impede the practice of getting married in church. There is no way out of the difficulty that, if general laws are to be subjected to a 'religious practice' exception, both the importance of the law at issue and the centrality of the practice at issue must reasonably be considered.[124]

The force of Scalia's argument can be illustrated by expanding his own example. Let us suppose that somebody could convince a court of a sincere belief that no marriage in a church is complete without the throwing of rice. Then the state would have to prove that the prohibition on throwing rice furthered a 'compelling interest'. On the assumption that the interest served was the avoidance of refuse in the streets, this might be hard to do; and, even if that hurdle were cleared successfully, it would still be necessary to show that there was no less restrictive alternative. It is easy to imagine that a court could invent some elaborate scheme according to which those with appropriate religious convictions could obtain a special licence allowing them to throw rice on condition that they undertook to sweep it up afterwards and take it away. That this would divert the time and effort of local authority staff from more pressing duties would not be the concern of the court.

This may sound far-fetched, but I do not believe that it is any more absurd than the case which arose in Minnesota as a result of a refusal by some members of an Amish community to display the red and orange reflective triangle that was required by law to be fixed to the backs of slow-moving vehicles (SMVs). Rejection of this law is by no means a majority Amish position. 'Most Amish . . . see the SMV requirement as a safety feature they are willing to accept for the welfare of the larger community.'[125] Opposition was concentrated in one sub-group of Amish, the Swartzentrubers, who broke away from the main body of Amish in 1913 because they believed that other Amish were insufficiently rigorous in shunning those who left the community after baptism.[126] Even among them, only some refused to use SMV symbols. Those who did object maintained that they were 'worldly symbols', that they were 'too "loud" or bright in color' and that 'using them would mean trusting in the symbols of man rather than in the protection of God'.[127] (Those encountering an Amish vehicle without a reflective triangle had no alternative to putting their trust in the protection of God as well.)

Gideon Hershberger was one of those who refused to pay fines for violating the law and 'was sentenced to jail for seven days'.[128] Overruling the lower courts, the Minnesota Supreme Court held that the SMV requirement 'infringe[d] on the rights guaranteed by the free exercise clause of the First Amendment to the United States Constitution'.[129] This case, *Hershberger I*, was decided in 1989, a year before *Smith*.[130] The Court therefore applied 'the compelling interest/least restrictive alternative' test to conclude that, because the requirement 'burden[ed] the exercise of Amish religious beliefs', those Amish who objected to it could outline the back of their buggies in silver reflective tape and hang a red lantern behind them.[131]

While challenging the right of the legislature to determine the best means to promote road safety, the Minnesota Supreme Court at the same time followed the *Sherbert* test, which meant that it made no effort to probe the centrality to Amish life of the requirement that buggies should display reflective triangles. On the contrary, the Court quoted from another insurance benefits case, *Thomas*, in which the US Supreme Court held that 'religious beliefs need not be acceptable, logical, consistent or comprehensible to others in order to merit First Amendment protection'.[132] Thomas worked in a steel factory, and, as a Jehovah's Witness, distinguished between making steel some of which he knew would be used in gun turrets for tanks and working on the gun turrets themselves. 'We see, therefore,' the *Thomas* decision read, 'that Thomas drew a line, and it is not for us to say that the line he drew was an unreasonable one.'[133]

The Minnesota Supreme Court, like the American Supreme Court minority in *Smith*, regarded it as unproblematic to apply the rulings in insurance benefit cases to violations of criminal law. However, there are three significant differences. First, there is nothing illegal about quitting a job that calls for working on your Sabbath (as in *Sherbert*), or working on armaments (as in *Thomas*). The only issue that arises is eligibility for unemployment benefits. Accepting that 'good cause' can be constituted for this purpose by sincere belief is a very different matter from accepting that somebody has a strong prima facie case on the basis of sincere belief to have the criminal law annulled in as far as it applies to him. A second difference was pointed out by Justice Scalia in *Smith*. 'The statutory conditions [in *Sherbert* and *Thomas*] provided that a person was not eligible for unemployment benefits if, "without good cause," he had quit work or refused available work. The "good cause" standard created a mechanism for individualized exemptions.'[134] Thus, 'the Sherbert test...was developed in a context that lent itself to individualized government assessment of the particular circumstances behind an applicant's unemployment.'[135] In other words, whereas the uniform application of an SMV law entails punishing anybody who does not display the prescribed symbol, the uniform application of a law that explicitly permits exemptions for 'good cause' actually demands that different people who do the same thing (i.e. leave the same job) must be treated differently if one of them had 'good cause' and the other did not.

The third point is related to this. In citing *Thomas* as its authority, the Minnesota Supreme Court was clearly treating refusal to display a reflective triangle as a case of individual conscientious objection. But it is questionable that the two can be assimilated in this way. It is true that, in terms of the distinction drawn in chapter 2, the demand to be dispensed from the reflective triangle requirement is an individual rather than a group demand. At the same time, however, the only reason for supposing that reflective triangles could conceivably fall foul of the guarantee of free exercise of religion is that the whole way of life of an Amish community is somehow protected, because driving buggies rather than cars is indissolubly linked to religious practice. But this seems to invite an inquiry into the extent to which reflective triangles on the backs of those buggies are really a threat to the Amish way of life. And here it is surely to the point that most Amish, and many even among the Swartzentrubers, did not find them unacceptable. Thomas's claim was, quite rightly, not undermined by the willingness of some other Jehovah's Witnesses to work on making armaments, even though they would have agreed with him in refusing to join the armed services. But Hershberger had a particular view about what was entailed in being a member of an Amish community. However sincere he may have been in his belief, that should not have been enough to let him endanger the lives of other road-users. Sincerity is not enough: Hitler and Pol Pot were probably sincere.

In the event, the US Supreme Court vacated the judgement in *Hershberger* in the light of *Smith*. The Minnesota Supreme Court reconsidered the case, and held (in *Hershberger II*) that the 'compelling interest/least restrictive alternative' test could be resuscitated on the basis of the Minnesota Constitution.[136] While it is true that this document contains some wording about 'freedom of conscience' that does not appear in the US Bill of Rights, it is clear that the logic of *Smith* (and the actual text in places of Scalia's opinion) would lead to the conclusion that freedom of conscience does not underwrite the violation of generally applicable laws.[137] Shifting to the Minnesota Constitution was, in effect, a device for refusing to accept the validity of *Smith*.

The upshot is that, in Minnesota, anybody with a sincere belief can have any law specially tailored to fit, unless the state can satisfy the 'compelling interest/least restrictive alternative' test. But that, judging by the Minnesota Supreme Court's performance in the *Hershberger* cases, is going to be virtually impossible to meet. Thus, the State's claim, which was upheld in the district court, was that what makes the reflective red and orange triangle uniquely effective as a warning sign is that 'it is almost universally the same in design and recognition throughout the United States' and 'is included in most Driver's Training Manuals so it is easily recognizable in all areas by all users of our highways'. The point, therefore, is not simply that it is visible, but that its significance will be known to motorists, whereas 'reflectorized tape would only confuse other drivers on the highway'.[138]

The Court sneeringly (by the use of sneer quotes) dismissed this argument as resting on the evidence of 'experts', and added that the only other evidence consisted of 'anecdotal claims' by residents in the area occupied by the Amish 'of dangers associated with encounters involving Amish vehicles on the highway'.[139] The Minnesota Supreme Court apparently took the view that expertise and the personal experience of those involved could be disregarded, and that it was free to substitute its own guess that silver reflective tape outlining the shape supplemented by a red lantern would be decoded at night in rain or fog by car drivers as a buggy in the few seconds they would have in which to react if they were not to collide with it.[140]

Expert testimony (especially when it reinforces common sense) and the personal experience of those who have had close calls would seem to be exactly what legislation about road safety should be based on. If this was not sufficient to persuade the court, what more would have been needed to shake the Court's arrogant faith in its own judgements about the requirements of road safety? Presumably, the contrast with 'anecdotal' evidence is statistical evidence. But the problem with demanding this as a condition of acting is that, even if the Court is tragically wrong in its judgement, it will take many years before there have been enough accidents involving on the one hand buggies with reflective red and orange triangles and on the other hand buggies with silver tape and lanterns before it would be possible to establish – at, say, the 5 per cent confidence level – that there is no satisfactory alternative to reflective triangles. Legislators are right to act on the balance of probabilities where road safety is at stake. Justice Scalia's argument in *Smith* that courts are not equipped to discern the occasions for exemptions to general laws could scarcely be better supported than by this saga of judicial tomfoolery in Minnesota.

## 6.  Are Amish Communities Voluntary Associations?

In this final section, I shall try to determine the status of Amish communities – with the proviso that I shall defer until the next chapter any consideration of the bearing of Amish educational practices on this issue. Leaving aside that (admittedly large) question, I want to ask where Amish communities stand in relation to the theory of group rights laid out in the previous chapter. Can their authoritarian mode of governance and their illiberal internal rules be protected from public intervention on the ground that Amish communities should be counted as voluntary associations? Or should they be regarded as possessing the attributes of a sort of sub-state polity, and therefore subject to the liberal constraints that all sub-state polities should have to observe?

Whatever we wish to say eventually about the voluntariness of membership in an Amish community, what is at any rate clear is that their status is not to be assimilated directly to that of a politically organized Native American tribe such as the Pueblo Indians. For these are, as Jacob Levy puts it, 'a self-governing, semisovereign nation', which enjoys devolved powers to tax and spend, make and administer criminal law and put state authority behind a system of personal law.[141] In contrast, whatever authority the decisions of Amish bodies possess arises not from the exercise of devolved state power but from the way in which submission to their decisions is the condition of continuing membership in the community. The question in their case is simply how far that submission may be said to be voluntary.

It is not simply that the Amish are not as a matter of fact politically organized bodies deploying state power that has been devolved upon them. As we have seen, their foundational beliefs would prevent them from assuming such power if it were offered to them. Lack of appreciation of this point has led some political philosophers astray. For example, Allen Buchanan 'seems to suggest that the Amish and Mennonites be given the power to keep pornography and other "cultural influences that threaten to undermine the community's values" out of the areas near their settlements'.[142] But, as Levy points out, 'seeking to control and direct the power of the criminal law would be unthinkable'.[143] Again, Levy observes that it is 'ambiguous at best and mistaken at worst' for Buchanan to treat 'the "government of a territorially concentrated community such as the Amish or Mennonites" as analogous to Indian tribal governments'. For, as he says, 'the relevant religious authorities would be extremely resistant to seeing themselves as force-wielding governments'.[144] Whether or not their resistance is justifiable is, of course, precisely the question that has to be answered. But we must begin from an understanding of the way in which the Amish themselves see the position.

It is instructive to contrast the Amish with the example that Levy gave of a community that quite unequivocally exercises devolved state power, the Pueblo Indians. The principle that a liberal state should not permit sub-state polities to behave in ways that violate basic liberal tenets has not been accepted by the federal courts. These have declined to accept jurisdiction in a case brought by some Pueblo Indians who had become Protestant Christians and complained that, as a result, they had been denied access to 'communal resources and functions'.[145] It appears to be common ground among those who have commented on this case that, if the federal courts had accepted jurisdiction and held the First Amendment to apply to the government of the Pueblo Indians, the conduct complained of would have been held to be in violation of the constitutional guarantee of freedom of religion. Will Kymlicka, for example, says that Christian converts were denied housing benefits that were made available to adherents of the traditional religion by the tribal government of the Pueblo Indians.[146] This is a clear case of state discrimination based on religious affiliation that would be thrown out by a court on the basis of the Bill of Rights in any other context.

Assuming this to be so, Iris Young cannot be correct in saying that, 'as members of a tribe [American Indians] have specific political, legal, and collective rights, and as U.S. citizens they have all the civil and political rights of other citizens'.[147] For the Pueblo Indians can enjoy the constitutional guarantee of freedom of religion only by giving up the special rights that flow from their Pueblo Indian citizenship. In contrast with this, the Amish have only the status of ordinary American citizens and are thus the beneficiaries of the rights guaranteed by the Constitution. Indeed, as we saw in the previous section, it is precisely by appealing to the constitutional guarantee of the 'free exercise of religion' that the Amish have won waivers of laws held to 'burden' that exercise.

If it is an error to assimilate Amish communities to sub-state polities, it is equally an error to assimilate the Pueblo Indians to the Amish. This error is committed by Chandran Kukathas, who writes about 'the ostracizing of, and denial of resources to, those apostates who had thus violated Pueblo religious norms'.[148] This makes the case sound like one of a church whose members cut off contact with those who leave it and refuse to let them benefit from its scheme for supplying groceries to poor parishioners. What this leaves out of account is that the Pueblo Indians are 'citizen[s] of a particular kind of self-governing polity' and that it was the actions of this polity that damaged the Christian converts.[149]

To be a Pueblo Indian is to have a legal status that is the equivalent to citizenship in a state. On the principles laid out here, it is clear that a state, or (as in this instance) a sub-state with delegated powers, cannot consistently with liberal principles operate a religious test for the enjoyment of the benefits of membership. If the Pueblo Indians want to constitute themselves as a religiously defined community, there is nothing to prevent them from doing so. What they cannot do without violating liberal precepts is run a sub-state that is religiously exclusive. They could give up their special political rights as members of a self-governing group, and erect communities like those of the Amish that do not depend upon any special political powers. A Pueblo Indian would then simply have the civil status of an ordinary American citizen, and could invoke the rights that American citizens have to live in a community with a religious test for membership, as the Amish do. If, alternatively, the Pueblo Indians want to retain their special political status, they should be required to observe the constraints on the use of political power that are imposed by liberal justice. They should thus have to accept that the exercise of political power cannot legitimately be used to foster religious discrimination. The Pueblo sub-state, whose membership is ascribed on the basis of Pueblo ethnicity, would have to be religiously neutral, leaving religion with the private status that it normally has in liberal societies.

What I have just said, however, assumes what still has to be settled: is it true that there is nothing about the way in which the Amish run their affairs that violates liberal norms? Are they really to be regarded as a voluntary association, and therefore as rightfully enjoying the immunities to which voluntary associations are entitled? I quoted Levy to the effect that Amish elders would resist 'seeing themselves as force-wielding governments'. But is their resistance to seeing themselves in this way self-deluding or is it well founded? What is at stake here is the ability of the Amish to differentiate themselves in the relevant respect from the Pueblo Indians. As we have seen, Amish communities have their own system of adjudication and impose penalties on their members in accordance with it. They look in this respect very much like polities. The only way in which they can avoid being treated as polities, and hence subject to liberal constraints, is by maintaining that submission to their edicts is voluntary, in the sense that anybody who does not wish to accept them is free to depart. How plausible is this claim?

The Amish, as a distinct branch within the Swiss Anabaptist movement, 'emerged as a separate group in 1693 when Jacob Ammann, an elder of the church sought to revitalise it'.[150] Among his other reforms, 'Ammann advocated shunning excommunicated members. This issue drove the decisive wedge between Ammann and other Anabaptist leaders.'[151] The shunning of those expelled from the congregation must have been a potent force in keeping Ammann's followers together. No doubt it goes a long way towards explaining why there are today more than one hundred and thirty thousand Amish in North America while Anabaptists in Europe have gone the way of the Cathars and the Albigensians. But is it a force so potent as to undermine the claim that the Amish are a community within which membership is voluntary?

'In many states,' Kent Greenawalt has pointed out, 'organizing a boycott of someone's business and encouraging wives or husbands to refrain from contact with their spouses are civil wrongs.'[152] As we have seen, 'shunning' means that 'other members [of the Amish community] are forbidden to socialize, eat, or do business with the violator' of the church's *Ordnung*.[153] The legality of shunning arose in a case involving a sister church, the Reformed Mennonite Church. Here, the Supreme Court of Maryland took the view that 'the shunning practice of [the] church and the conduct of individuals may be an excessive interference within areas of "paramount" state concern, i.e. the maintenance of marriage and family relationship, alienation of affection, and the tortious interference with a business relationship'.[154] The case was brought by Robert Bear, who

> claimed that he had been excommunicated from the reformed Mennonite Church for criticizing its teaching and practices and that church officials had ordered all church members, including his own family, to shun him. Church officials argued that [,] even if all Bear's claims that he was shunned were true, the free exercise clause provided a complete defense.[155]

The implication of *Smith*, however, is that, if an act of some kind is illegal in general, the mere fact that somebody performs an act of that kind in pursuit of religion does not protect it.

Greenawalt, who believes that *Smith* was wrongly decided, maintains that religiously motivated shunning should be given a special exemption from laws prohibiting boycotting and alienation of affection. 'The effects of shunning can be devastating in the lives of some few individuals. But shunning involves encouraging people to behave in a way that is legally permitted for each individual. It, thus, differs from physical assault, slander, and many other torts that are wrong even if committed by an isolated individual.'[156] If this is a good argument at all, though, it is a good argument across the board. Just as the anti-paternalistic argument for allowing Sikhs not to wear crash helmets cannot be confined to them, so Greenawalt's argument does not lead to the implication that there should be an exemption for religiously motivated shunning. Rather, it suggests that, in a liberal society, there is no place for laws prohibiting the organization of a boycott or making it illegal to encourage a wife to have nothing to do with her husband (or vice versa).

In as far as shunning entails absence of association with family and neighbours, then, it should be legal for the Amish because it should be legal for anybody. And a refusal to buy from somebody who has been excommunicated should be legal too, with the proviso that the victim should be able to claim compensation for loss of earnings. However, anti-discrimination legislation in the USA rightly prevents shops, restaurants and hotels from discriminating against potential customers on the basis of, among other things, religion. Similarly, employers should not be able to fire employees because they fail to meet a test of religious conformity, unless passing this religious test is demonstrably related to ability to do the job satisfactorily. It is hard to see that membership of the Amish church is any more essential to employment as an operative in (say) a jam-making plant owned by Amish than it is to employment as a janitor in a gymnasium run by Mormons.

Suppose, however, that these discriminatory practices were ruled out. It would still be true that members of an Amish community would find it well nigh impossible to remain after being excommunicated or after having announced that they no longer wished to be a member of the church. Assuming this to be so, do the costs of being driven out of an Amish community – after, perhaps, having lived in it for fifty or sixty years – undermine the status of Amish communities as voluntary associations? The intrinsic and associational costs do not count in this context. What about the extrinsic costs of exit? These vary according to the situation of the person concerned. Unlike the Hutterites, the Amish have a regime based on private property. The owner of a farm may be able to do very well by selling up: farms in the Amish heartland of Lancaster County, Pennsylvania sell for over a million dollars.[157] One Amish family, excommunicated for buying a second-hand car, retaliated by selling its farm for a commercial and residential development, which the Amish and their political allies had great difficulty in getting scaled back.[158] (Just in case anybody might make the mistake of feeling sorry for the Amish, it should be added that they have opposed zoning rules limiting development – common in other agricultural areas of Pennsylvania – because they are keen to maximize the value of their property.[159] On similar grounds, they have refused to donate or sell rights to develop their land.[160]) However, by no means all Amish own farms, and the proportion of those who do so is decreasing as a result of rapid population growth.[161] What is the position of Amish who are employees or self-employed but do not own farms or businesses?

People in this position may, I suppose, be able to accumulate some personal savings. But it is unlikely that these would be sufficiently large to enable somebody who left the community at retirement age to live on the interest. What every other employee in the United States can count on is a social security pension, contributed to over his or her working life by both employee and employer. However, the Amish have won the right to withdraw from the social security system, for the self-employed in 1965 and then also for those employed by other Amish in 1988. As long as they remain in the community, it can be said that they 'have little need for Social Security. . . . Since elderly Amish generally live with or adjacent to one of their married children, the larger extended family, the church, and supplemental income provide ample economic security. The disabled and widowed are also cared for by family and community.'[162] This is all very well; but none of it, of course, is available to anyone who leaves or is expelled.

Precisely this point was raised in a memorandum produced by the Department of Health, Education and Welfare (HEW) in 1964 that opposed the provision of a legislative opt-out for the Amish. It 'questioned what would happen to individuals who left the Amish church after they had opted out of social security, a possibility heightened by the Amish practice of shunning those who are excommunicated.'[163] (As it stands this sentence does not make any sense, but presumably the thought lurking somewhere in the author's mind was that the possibility of destitution is increased by shunning.) It is true that those who leave can reverse their opt-out – a choice not available to those who remain, for whom it is irreversible. But even the vociferous supporter of the status quo who wrote the chapter on social security in *The Amish and the State*, Peter Ferrera, concedes that 'those who leave the Amish well into their working years have lost many years of coverage, which significantly reduces their benefits'.[164] Moreover, since the opt-out also applies to Medicare, the federal system of health cover for the elderly, they are liable to be thrown on to the tender mercies of the facilities that America provides for the 'medically indigent'.

Against this, the best that Ferrera can offer is the thought that 'few leave the Amish community at this point' – which is scarcely surprising, given the prohibitive economic costs of doing so – and that 'any that do would have fairly exercised their freedom to enter and to leave the Amish faith and would validly bear the consequences of such decisions.'[165] This, however, simply begs the question, which is precisely whether or not a successful lobbying campaign by Amish leaders to pull their followers out of social security does leave ordinary Amish with 'freedom to leave' in a strong enough sense to make it plausible to say that remaining within the community is really the exercise of a free choice.[166]

Recall that, although each member of an Amish community 'must individually file to receive the exemption, which applies to Social Security and Medicare', there is in fact no choice about whether or not to exercise the option.[167] Anyone who declined to opt out would be excommunicated. Under these circumstances, it seems hollow to say 'You made the choice, so you must accept the consequences.' Of course, we can push it further back and say 'You made the choice to be baptized as a member of the Amish community.' But slavery, let us bear in mind, cannot on Millian principles be justified by original consent. Consent to enter a community on terms that make it inordinately costly to leave after a certain period cannot be valid, for essentially the same reason.

I am leaving on one side in this chapter the questions raised by the very limited education that Amish children are permitted. However, the issues that arise in the context of education are curiously foreshadowed in the final move made by Ferrera to defend the opt-out from social security. 'The government should not paternalistically deny [the Amish] the freedom to make such choices, particularly since that would deny the vast majority of the Amish the freedom to exercise their permanent choice of an exemption.'[168] This presents the question as one of siding with the majority or siding with the minority, the suggestion being that the interests of the majority should prevail. However, there is an alternative way of looking at it, which is the one that I wish to press – here and in the case of education. This is that the right of Amish communities to operate a system of law on an authoritarian and fundamentally illiberal basis depends on membership's being voluntary.

My conclusion is, then, that – quite apart from anything we may wish to say about the implications of Amish educational practices – Amish communities do not as currently constituted satisfy the conditions for voluntary membership. The simplest way of meeting these conditions would be to rescind the opt-out from social security. A less satisfactory alternative would be a legally enforceable undertaking by all Amish communities to provide those who leave (either of their own accord or because they are expelled) with a lump sum payment. This would have to be calculated so as to yield an annuity equivalent to the pension to which somebody with the same employment record (whether as an employee or self-employed) would have been entitled under the social security system. It is hard to see, however, that this would be much more acceptable to the Amish politicians than the termination of the opt-out from social security would be. Congress should therefore reverse its decision to allow the Amish to opt out of social security and Medicare. The alternative is that Amish communities should be forced to reproduce internally all the features constitutive of a liberal democratic state, which is tantamount to saying that they should cease to exist.

# 6

## The Public Stake in the Arts and Education

### 1. The Limits of Laissez-Faire

Liberal institutions are remarkably successful in accommodating cultural diversity. There is a tendency to overlook the extent of this success because it does not make news. Even people who ought to know better, such as television news presenters, sometimes complain that almost all news is bad news. But how could it be otherwise? A plane crash is news; a lot of planes that arrive without incident at their destinations are not. Two countries that are at war are news; all the other thousands of pairs of countries that are not at war are not. There is nothing wrong with this, but unless we self-consciously correct for selection bias we are liable to finish up believing that air travel is much less safe than it is and war much more pervasive than it is. In the same way, by focusing our attention on cases in which a uniform system of liberal laws gives rise to protests, we are liable to overlook the immensely larger number of cases in which there are no complaints.

Within the framework of a general system of law that applies to all alike, people worship in different ways, do some things and refrain from others in accordance with their religious beliefs, associate with some (and not others) in pursuit of distinctive cultural activities, and so on. Many forms of cultural diversity are catered for by the market so unobtrusively that we are inclined to overlook the extent and importance of the phenomenon. Wherever there is an effective demand for some kind of cuisine or entertainment (for example, popular Indian films) that appeals especially to the members of some ethnocultural group, there is an excellent chance that somebody will spot the possibility of making money by meeting the demand.

In the absence of special reasons for public subsidy or provision, liberals will be in favour of leaving to the market the determination of what goods and services are to be supplied and in what quantities. If the point is to satisfy demand, markets have the advantage of leaving people free to decide for themselves how they want their fair share of their society's resources to be spent. This does not mean that people are constrained to use that share only on private consumption, whether their own or anybody else's. They are entirely free to contribute to collective projects, either altruistically or in return for participation in the benefits of the project.

Markets, however, respond to effective demand, that is to say, demand backed by willingness to pay. Willingness to pay for something, in turn, depends on how much one wants it and what one would have to give up in order to get it. The market will satisfy the frivolous desires of somebody with a hundred thousand pounds a year before it will satisfy even the urgent necessities of somebody on the minimum state benefit. Although, therefore, it is true that liberals, in virtue of their concern with the liberty of individuals, are favourably disposed towards markets, egalitarian liberals (as against some other kinds) hold that the way in which goods and services are allocated by markets is fair only if the distribution of income and wealth is fair. For egalitarian liberals the market is a very poor mechanism for bringing about the 'fair shares' of income that are called for by a theory of egalitarian justice. John Stuart Mill is, quite rightly, denounced by anti-egalitarian liberals as the keeper of the liberal economic flame who treasonously gave away the dirty little secret of laissez-faire. For he pointed out that it is possible to gain most of the advantages of the institution of the market without having to accept it as the final arbiter of the distribution of income and wealth. The more that people are left to pursue their ends (individually or in concert with others) through the market, the more important it is to get the distribution of income right, so that opportunities for people to pursue their ends in this way are spread throughout the society.

It is instructive to contrast the egalitarian liberal approach that I have just outlined with that put forward by Michael Walzer in his book *Spheres of Justice*.[1] For liberals, the presumption is that things should be allocated through the market unless there is some good reason for providing them publicly. In contrast, Walzer's presumption is that public provision should be the norm, with the market picking up the residue. Walzer's prescriptions are oppressive, impracticable and misleading. The theory is oppressive because it stipulates that each of a number of goods and services is to be distributed in conformity with the 'shared understandings' of the members of the society about the 'social meaning' of different goods. It thus 'assume[s] a consensus of evaluations within fields', as the Dutch sociologist Veit Bader has commented.[2] This assumption is contrary to fact. There is controversy even among the members of the cultural majority in relation to most items (as a number of Walzer's own examples illustrate), and cultural minorities will (almost by definition) have other 'understandings' in many cases. Hence, as Bader says, theories such as Walzer's in practice 'only register the interpretations and evaluations of the dominant elites'.[3]

Walzer's proposal is impracticable because his claim that it can deliver what he calls 'complex equality' rests on the assumption that it is possible to block exchanges between money and anything other than consumer goods. This is a fantasy. In every society that has a generalized medium of value – money – those with a lot of it have always been able to deploy it to obtain power, privilege and status. There is no way of limiting inequality in those respects unless the disparity of income and wealth is kept within limits as well. Finally, Walzer misleads by suggesting that, in a society reconstructed along the lines advocated by him, differences in income would manifest themselves only in differential access to luxury goods such as fancy audio equipment or luxury yachts. Yet he has no proposal for taking the distribution of groceries – or even housing – out of the sphere of money. It is therefore entirely wrong to say that, as long as each 'sphere' is autonomous, the distribution of income is of no great importance and does not raise issues of justice. On the contrary, how much money people have determines such fundamental matters as their ability to obtain a nutritious diet or live in decent housing.

Clearly, any attempt to implement Walzer's idea that goods should be distributed in the light of their 'social meanings' would be bad for cultural minorities, since the false consensus presupposed by the whole approach would leave cultural minorities out in the cold. Let us lay this on one side and take the most favourable case, in which special resources are made available with the object of enabling members of cultural minorities to pursue common interests derived from their shared culture. This relatively benign scenario still runs into the fundamental objection that provision in kind aimed at cultural minorities is bound to be a highly inefficient way of meeting consumer demand, in comparison with the alternative of dividing up the money among the members of the minority community and letting them spend it on what they choose. If they get the money instead of the cultural activities, they can then decide for themselves how important those activities are to them. If they would rather spend the money on improving the quality of groceries that they buy, that should be their business.

Specific public provision is an inefficient way of meeting consumer demand for two reasons. The first is that it would be an amazing fluke if the amount and kind of provision exactly matched what would occur if the beneficiaries had divided the money that went on it among themselves to spend as they chose. And, second, there is inevitably a deadweight loss associated with the procedure for allocating funding. There have to be committees to decide who gets the money and administrators to arrange for its disbursement. In addition, organizations hoping to receive funding may well find it worth spending money on consultants and lobbyists to improve their chances of success.

Why, in that case, is state financing for minority cultural activities a staple of the multiculturalist programme? One answer is that earmarked money generates rents which can be appropriated by cultural entrepreneurs. This is, of course, simply a redescription of the phenomenon that I have just described. Some cultural entrepreneurs will be content to live off the income that can be derived from writing grant applications for organizations, lobbying on their behalf, and administering programmatic grants. Others with greater ambitions will court visibility and build up an organizational nucleus as a way of launching themselves into a wider sphere as ethnocultural politicians. Either way, the point is that there are direct beneficiaries of the multicultural pork-barrel.

A less cynical answer rests on the assumption that the redistribution of income is a lost cause in most liberal democracies. Since cultural minorities tend to be less well off economically than most of the population, pumping public money into minority cultural programmes is at any rate a way of transferring some resources to ethnocultural minority groups. However, this despair about the potentiality of a redistributive political agenda is to some extent a self-fulfilling prophecy if the energies that might have gone into promoting it are instead dissipated in struggles between the representatives of different groups over the division of a rather small multicultural cake. (I shall return to this point in chapter 8.) It is also worth emphasizing that the only people who finish up with income that they can actually spend on such things as food, clothing and housing are the cultural entrepreneurs who solicit and administer the grants and, of course, the people who actually receive them. The mass of the minority group get whatever it is that the people with the grants produce; but it may well be that its value to them is only a few pennies in the pound.

If we are looking for a principled rationale of public provision or public subsidy, there is only one way in which to go. We have to challenge the assumption that, if the distribution of income is right, there is no reason for overriding the allocation of goods and services thrown up by market choices. If people were in a position in which they could make the trade-off for themselves, they might give up only a trivial amount, measured in terms of groceries, to ensure the existence of some cultural manifestation. But that need not be regarded as a decisive objection to funding it at some level much higher than would be warranted on the willingness-to-pay criterion, as long as there is some reason for believing that it is undervalued by that criterion. What might this reason be?

Almost all art – taking the term in a descriptive rather than an evaluative sense – falls into one of two categories. If it is produced by professionals for a market, there is no more reason in general for subsidizing it than there is for subsidizing any other goods or services whose rationale is to satisfy consumer demand. If it is produced by amateurs for their own satisfaction, there is no more reason in general for subsidizing it than there is for subsidizing any other hobby. The only possible rationale for subsidization is that there are some artistic endeavours that are of very high quality and need public support either to continue at all or to be accessible to more than a privileged elite. The obvious examples are grand opera, symphonic music and non-commercial theatre, which is why they are subsidized by every state that has a serious policy of public support for the arts. These are all, of course, examples of performance of already existing works. What about the creation of new works? Novelists who are any good (and a lot who are not) seem to be able to make a living – in some cases a very good one – from sales, and the same is true of painters. Composers and playwrights can be supported to some extent by commissions and royalties from publicly supported symphony orchestras and theatre companies. In addition, there are the elite universities and foundations that have taken over the patronage role played in earlier times by bishops and nobles. If these institutions are left to provide the time and facilities necessary for the production of (say) political philosophy, it is hard to see any good reason for not leaving them to fill the remaining gaps in the arts. (If it is said that there is no necessary connection between being good at composing music or writing poetry and being good at teaching, the obvious reply is that there is no necessary connection in the case of political philosophy either.)

The implication is that there is no case for public subsidization of minority cultural activities as such. If Robert Hughes is correct in claiming that 'most of the "art" that results from [multicultural] programs is affirmative, prolix kitsch', then most of it has no value beyond that established for it by the market.[4] If some is of high quality and for some reason cannot recoup its cost, there is then a case for subsidizing it, but the case rests on quality and not on cultural minority status. The alternative is to spread the money around, as the National Endowment for the Arts does in the United States and the Arts Council is increasingly doing in Britain, so that it goes on (to quote an NEA brochure) 'Hmong needlework, coastal sea-grass basketry and woodcraft, Pacific Island canoe building and Appalachian banjo-playing'.[5] This widens the constituency of the NEA, but at the cost, as Hughes complains, of opting for 'the easy task of "supporting ethnicity and gender differences in the arts" instead of the hard one of looking for real excellence'.[6]

The terms of this objection presuppose, of course, that it makes sense to talk about 'real excellence' as something that is more than a matter of opinion. But the rationale of public support for the arts depends upon the truth of that presupposition. If it is merely a matter of opinion that Beethoven is better than banjo-playing, then it is a mere matter of opinion that either is better than the monetary equivalent in groceries. And in that case there is no case for earmarking funds at all: let people spend the money on Beethoven, banjo-playing or groceries as they choose. On the same lines, if we say that the object of arts funding should be to spread the money among cultural groups in accordance with some implicit or explicit quota system, this undermines the rationale of having special arts funding at all. If we once withdraw from the position that the only criterion for funding should be excellence, why not really spread the money around by spreading it around the entire target population in the form of cash?

## 2.   Can Liberalism Cope with Children?

Education could be treated by the state in exactly the same way as groceries. Nobody is required to buy any particular quantity or type of produce, and the prices that people pay are set by supply and demand. Over much of history this has in fact been the normal way in which education has been treated. The situation in Britain when Mill published *On Liberty* was precisely of this kind: there were charities offering free education, but there were also charities offering free groceries – in both cases, of low quality. The point is that the state did not intervene. The parents (more precisely, given the current legal position, the father) had complete discretion with respect to the education of children: 'instead of his being required to make any exertion or sacrifice for securing education to the child, it is left to his choice to accept it or not when it is provided gratis!'[7]

Enthusiasts for parental rights over children's education nowadays tend to be in favour of voucher systems, but it is worth noticing how far this leaves them from the position described by Mill. Vouchers are proposed as an alternative to publicly funded schools, whether these are publicly or privately run. But the proposal still assumes that there should be public funding for education: it is concerned only with the modality of that funding. Moreover, the background against which the proposal is made is normally the assumption that the state can and will make it compulsory for children to acquire a certain amount of education. If the paradigm of laissez-faire is the state's relation to groceries, these contemporary libertarians have already sold the pass by countenancing compulsory education and taxation to pay for it, in the form of earmarked funds that can be spent by parents only on approved educational purposes.

What, then, is the public stake in education that can justify the state's overriding the decisions of parents, or of ethnocultural or religious communities, about the amount and kind of formal education that children are to receive? There is an oft-repeated notion that 'liberalism has always had special difficulties dealing with children and education. Liberals are always happier talking about adults, precisely because it is they who can most easily be envisioned as possessing autonomy and giving consent. But adults die, to be replaced by the children they bear.'[8] Thomas Hobbes notoriously once said that his theory of political obligation applied to 'men . . . as if even now sprung out of the earth . . . like mushrooms'.[9] Critics have since suggested that the only significant difference between Hobbes and later theorists who have placed normative weight on consent is that Hobbes let the cat out of the bag whereas his successors have tried to carry on regardless, ignoring the squirming and mewing. Thus, Susan Okin has said that liberal political theorists (among others) 'take mature, independent human beings as the subjects of their theories without any mention of how they got that way'.[10] Constant repetition, however, does not render an opinion true, and this one is false.

Every society has rules specifying the age at which people acquire different rights, such as the right to sign contracts, the right to drive, the right to vote, the right to marry, the right to buy cigarettes or alcohol, and so on. Although these ages are different in different societies, the age at which any given right is acquired is normally the same for everybody within any one legal system. (At most, there may be one age for males and another age for females.) It could be argued that this uniformity is absurd, because it is apparent that individuals mature at different rates. But the obvious response to that is that making case-by-case determinations about the readiness of each individual to assume each right would be impossibly burdensome. Even if it were feasible, it would still be objectionable on liberal grounds because it would put too much discretionary power in the hands of the officials charged with taking the decisions. The upshot is that there has to be a uniform system which sets standard minimum ages for the exercise of rights on the basis of an estimate of the age at which most of the population will be able to make prudent use of the right. (The same goes for duties, such as serving on a jury or in the armed forces.)

Why should it be imagined that liberals are bound to encounter difficulties in coming to terms with these familiar features of every society? That the enjoyment of liberal rights is age-dependent is in no way a derogation from liberal principles. Rather, it is an application of them. In regard to children, liberals have two primary concerns. The first derives from the basic liberal presumption that adults are (unless certifiably incompetent) capable of managing their own affairs in a way that will protect their interests. This presumption is going to be satisfied only if children are brought up in such a way that they actually will, when they become adults, have acquired the necessary capacities. A liberal society cannot be indifferent, therefore, to the way in which children are raised and educated, because its legal, political and economic system can function well only if its members are fit to exercise the responsibilities with which they are entrusted as legal, political and economic agents. But liberals are not concerned exclusively with childhood as a preparation for adulthood. Their other primary concern stems from the obvious fact that children are not in a position to protect their own interests. As infants they are totally dependent upon adults. This dependency lessens as they become older, but they remain vulnerable to neglect and abuse. Liberals see a crucial role for the state here as a protector – as far as lies within its power – of the basic interests of children.

Liberalism of this kind is to be distinguished sharply from the libertarian perversion of it discussed in chapter 4, according to which parents should be able to deny their children education or medical care, inflict grievous physical injuries on them, force them into marriages against their will, and so on. Quite often, parental rights are justified as a natural extension of the liberty of the individual. Thus, Charles Fried has argued that 'the right to form one's child's values, one's child's life plan and the right to lavish attention on that child are extensions of the basic right not to be interfered with in doing these things for oneself.'[11] In effect, having brought the child into existence, the parents own it: 'the sense of possession of oneself . . . extends to possession of one's function. And this extends naturally to reproduction.'[12] As we saw in chapter 4, Mill had a short way with this kind of purulent nonsense, saying that 'the sentiment of liberty' is 'altogether misplaced' in the relations of parents to children. 'A person should be as free to do as he likes in his own concerns; but he ought not to be free to do as he likes in acting for another, under the pretext that the affairs of the other are his own affairs.'[13]

The same kind of move is quite often made by illegitimately extending the rights of parents so that they subsume the interests of their children. In the United States, needless to say, these abuses are given constitutional underpinnings. A recent example is the bizarre suggestion that the parents' right to free speech ought to be taken to entail their right to control the content of all communications received by their children, whether at home or at school. 'Interpreting the First Amendment right to free speech' in this way 'requires that judges evaluate educational regulations "in terms of their impacts on parents," rather than on children'.[14] As Amy Gutmann remarks, 'the needs, interests, and rights of children fade from the picture, as the free speech rights of parents are converted into authority over other people insofar as it affects their children's education.'[15]

More commonly, the parents' freedom of religion is deployed as a cloak for the exertion of power over their children. Thus, in the *Yoder* case, the Supreme Court held that the adult members of a community of Old Order Amish could legitimately stop their children from going to school after the age of fourteen, two years earlier than was required by the State of

Wisconsin. The basis of this decision was a finding by the majority 'that enforcement of the State's requirement of compulsory formal education after the eighth grade would gravely endanger if not destroy the free exercise of respondents' [the parents'] religious beliefs'.[16] As Richard Arneson and Ian Shapiro point out in a critique of the decision, however, there is something of a mismatch between the rationale, which concerns parents, and the content of the decision, which concerns children.

> The free exercise interests in question were the interests of the Amish parents in practicing their religion in their traditional way. But the state's expressed interest concerned the education of Amish children. On the face of it, there was a gap between the rights claimed by the parents, having to do with their practice of religion, and the claims of the state having to do with *the children's* education.[17]

In asking how much of a say parents should have in their children's education, we must take it as axiomatic that the interests of the parents and those of the children are distinguishable, and potentially conflicting. The authority of parents over children must be seen as a devolved power, whose scope is limited by the legitimate claims of those over whom the power is exercised.[18] Mill unhesitatingly drew this conclusion. 'The State', he wrote, 'is bound to maintain a vigilant control over [the] exercise of any power which it allows [anyone] to possess over others.' And he singled out 'family relations' as a sphere within which 'this obligation' on the part of the state was 'almost entirely disregarded'.[19] This could not be said now, but it is clear that it still remains true that 'many of the convictions to which people find themselves drawn in thinking about the authority of parents over children reflect the archaic idea that the child is the chattel of the parent (which once went hand-in-hand with the patriarchal idea that the wife is the chattel of the husband)'.[20] If we are going to repudiate the notion that, by bringing children into the world, the parents acquire powers of life and death over them, we had better give it up all the way and accept that the rights of parents derive from positive law and social convention. We are then left with the question of the criteria on which we should judge the laws and institutions that prevail within any given society.

Just as democracy is the worst form of government except for all the others, so parents (whether natural or adoptive) are, for all their faults, better than any yet-discovered alternative for raising children. Certainly, the record of state-run institutions is generally depressing, whether assessed in terms of the educational qualifications of their products, their attachment to the labour force, their chances of keeping out of the hands of the police, their mental health or their ability to sustain personal (including family) relationships. This suggests that parents have to be really quite bad at the job before their children would be better off in the care of a local authority. The implication is the one stated by Arneson and Shapiro: 'Having made an initial assignment [of responsibility to parents], society does better to leave well enough alone for the most part, trusting parents whose competence and motivation have not been impugned by gross and readily verifiable tests to carry out their parental obligations as they see fit.'[21] But this still means that sexual and physical abuse must create a liability to prosecution and it must still open up the possibility of removing the children from the abusive parents. A state can (as some have done) make the use of corporal punishment by parents illegal. Neglect can also be a justification for intervention: leaving children without supervision, failing to feed them properly and not looking after their health are obvious examples.

It is worth noticing immediately that the ultimate responsibility of the society for the welfare of children may entail the state's overruling the religious convictions of parents. Thus, while adult Jehovah's Witnesses are perfectly free to refuse blood transfusions for themselves, they cannot insist that their children should be denied a blood transfusion if they need it. If it comes to it, their children can be made temporary wards of court so as to take them out of the parents' control. Adults may eschew all medical treatment for themselves, even where this will predictably lead to preventable death, but they may not condemn their children to death on the basis of their own religious beliefs. In 1996, for example, 'the father of a nine-year-old girl who died after being denied life-saving insulin injections was ... jailed for $2\frac{1}{2}$ years' and the mother was given a suspended sentence.[22] The parents, who were members of the Zion Ethiopian Church, were found 'criminally at fault for ignoring medical advice on "religious or cultural grounds"'.[23] In line with Mill's dictum, people are free to act as they see fit in their own affairs, even if it is foreseeable that they will come to harm by so doing, but that licence does not extend to taking decisions for others that will have predictably harmful results.

This is the liberal approach, as I understand it. Let it be noted that it permits diversity, in that it leaves parents with a good deal of freedom of action. Within the limits I have laid out, parents are free to raise children according to their own conceptions of the good life, or simply their own desires. 'If I fancy putting my child in the Little League, or in the church choir, I generally may do so.'[24] But although the position set out here is compatible with diversity, its rationale does not lie in any tendency to foster diversity any more than it lies in any tendency to foster autonomy. (Again, however, it is important that it is compatible with autonomy.) Rather, its justification is that it assigns rights and responsibilities in a way that provides liberty where that is appropriate while at the same time attempting to limit the abuse of power.

In the rest of this chapter, I shall ask what are the implications of this approach for the division of authority over the education of children. It is often suggested that, in the absence of a consensus about the right answer to this question, turning responsibility over to the parents is 'a default position' that somehow avoids controversy. But, as Amy Gutmann has pointed out, 'no conception – including that of exclusive (or nearly exclusive) parental rights over schooling – can claim a social consensus.'[25] That conception would be uncontroversial only if nobody was concerned about the education of children except their parents. But the only people of whom this is true are those in favour of absolute parental power. Liberals, in particular, are committed to the belief that the education of the next generation is a matter in which all citizens have a legitimate interest.

If individual parents should not have exclusive control over the education of their children, it is equally objectionable to confine the power to take decisions about the public educational system to the parents of school-age children. Schools should no more be conceived of as catering to the wishes of parents collectively than they should be conceived of as serving parents individually. This basic precept is violated by the British government's legislation allowing for local voting on the abolition of selective secondary schools within the state system but limiting the right to vote to parents of children who would be directly affected by the change. If there is to be this kind of 'local option' about the organization of the school system, all registered voters within the area should be entitled to take part in the decision. The alternative is, in effect, to assume that the only people with a stake in the public education system are the parents of children currently in it. But then why should anybody else be required to contribute to the expense of running it? 'No taxation without representation' is as good a slogan now in Britain as it was two and a half centuries ago in America.

The notion that 'he who pays the piper calls the tune' can explain why, if there is a publicly funded and publicly run school system, all citizens should have a right to a say in the way that system is organized and a say in the question of what goes on in those schools. Even where the schools are not publicly run, their costs may be met publicly (in part or in whole) either by transmitting funds directly to churches or other organizations that run them or indirectly by giving educational vouchers to parents. Either way, the principle that he who pays the piper calls the tune will still imply that the state should be able to set standards and monitor the performance of schools to ensure that these standards are met. It would be superficial, however, to think that the legitimacy of state control over education flows from state financing of schools. For the rationale of having state funding in the first place must be that there is a legitimate public concern for the education of all children, and not only those whose education is supported financially by the state. Otherwise, why should the state get into the business at all? It follows that what goes on in private schools not in receipt of public funding is just as much a matter of legitimate public concern as what goes on in those that are. By the same token, 'home schooling' should be subject to vigilant scrutiny by some designated public authority.

No doubt, it is in the nature of the case that what is taught in the schools and how it is taught will be most closely regulated in the case of state-run schools. Schools that are independent but publicly supported financially are also easier to control than completely private schools, because continued funding can be made contingent upon compliance with norms laid down by public authorities, whereas other schools can be brought to heel only through the much cruder instrument of a threat to close them down if they fail to comply. I wish to insist, however, that all this is of relatively minor significance. The important question is what, according to liberal principles, can be demanded of anybody who undertakes the education of children, regardless of who does it or pays for it. That is the question on which I shall focus here.

## 3.  The Locus of Decision-Making

Assuming that there is a public stake in education, there can be no doubt that the state is one party that is involved in decisions about the education of children. ('The state' may, of course, operate for this purpose at a variety of levels and through a number of different agencies.) What about the area of decision-making that this leaves over? Who should exercise this authority over the education of children? In practice, western polities recognize only one legitimate source of authority other than their own, and that is the authority of parents. This statement is legally accurate for all contemporary western countries, to the best of my knowledge. However, it is sociologically naive, by which I mean that in many cases the parents may have no real choice about the form to be taken by their children's education if they wish to remain members in good standing (or perhaps at all) of their community, whether it be defined in terms of ethnicity, language, religion or in some instances social class.

Clearest are the pressures on parents exerted by religious communities. We begin here from the point that one of the rights assigned to parents is that of raising their children in their own religious faith (or absence of it). In a liberal society, it must be open for a child to repudiate this upbringing later, but it is assumed without question that parents are at liberty to enrol their children in their own faith and subject them to its teachings. The rationale for this is to be found in the 'strategy of privatization' for dealing with religious diversity. If the state is to avoid taking sides in matters of religion, it obviously cannot prescribe any particular regime of religious worship and instruction or prescribe the inculcation of atheism. This means that it must turn the decisions over to somebody else. The only plausible way of doing this that is compatible with neutrality is to assign the decision to the parents.

There is surely a strong presumption that, if parents are to have any say in their children's education, it will have to be legally permissible for them to send their children to religiously based schools. When I introduced the 'strategy of privatization' in chapter 2, I mentioned that one possible version is for the state to fund on equal terms religious schools as well as secular ones. Alternatively, religious schools can be funded privately by some combination of fees charged to parents and contributions from the sponsoring religious body. This still leaves it open to the state to impose conditions not only on the quality and content of private education but also on the amount of money that can be spent on pupils. Although I am not aware of any state that does this, I believe that it is essential to the maintenance of even rough equality of opportunity to make it illegal for any private school to spend more per head on its students than the average amount spent by the state system, unless the school can show that it has disproportionate numbers of children with special physical, psychological or educational needs.[26] Although any such measure would no doubt be attacked by saying that it infringes parental freedom, it would do nothing to restrict the ability of parents to determine the kind of education their children receive. Its only effect would be to prevent already advantaged parents from buying unfair educational advantages for their children. (In a similar way, stringent limits on inheritance of wealth are required to limit the intergenerational transmission of inequality.)

The implication of all this is that in a liberal society parents will have the opportunity – on more or less favourable financial terms – of reinforcing the religious upbringing of their children by sending them to a religious school. But it must be recognized that the parents are not the only people with a stake in the decision. For example, the hierarchy of the Roman Catholic Church and the more committed lay members of the church have an interest in ensuring its cultural reproduction. This is an interest that is separable from the interest that parents may have in the way in which their children are educated. As Sanford Levinson has said:

> The cultural rights at issue are ultimately held, if at all, by a group for whom a particular individual is, at best, merely a synecdoche. Education is initiation into a preexisting, collective, way of life, and it is those who are already committed to that way who are most insistent that it be protected against the inevitable death that comes with the failure of renewal through proper initiation.[27]

The result of this is that Roman Catholic parents are put under great pressure to send their children to a church-run school. This will be felt most intensely by parents living where there is a high concentration of Roman Catholics – and this is where there is most likely to be a parochial school, of course. One particular function of Roman Catholic schools is to enforce the undertaking that Roman Catholics who marry outside the faith are urged (they used to be required) to obtain from their spouse to the effect that the children of the marriage will be raised as Roman Catholics. The parents might prefer simply to go through the motions so as to achieve a *modus vivendi*, but they can be locked in willy-nilly if they succumb to pressure to send the children to a church-run school.

Formally, then, it is the parents who choose the school, in the sense that they are the only people with the legal right to make the decision. There is no 'group right' recognized in law that enables religious (or other) groups to decide what schools should be attended by children born to members of the group. At the same time, though, the parents may be mere cyphers, putting a legal rubber stamp on a decision that they have no choice in making as long as they wish to remain in the group. Provided that the costs of expulsion or voluntary exit are limited to those that are legitimate in a liberal society, there is nothing to prevent an approved choice of school from being a condition of continued good standing in a group. What has been said about Roman Catholic schools could equally well be said about Orthodox Jewish schools in areas in which large numbers of Orthodox Jews are concentrated, and may become true of Muslim schools in Britain if their numbers increase.

The same analysis carries through to the case of the Amish. As we saw in the previous chapter, it is central to the Amish belief system that they do not seek – and positively refuse – the exercise of state power. No more do they wish to direct the exercise of state power by others. I mentioned in chapter 5 Allen Buchanan's proposal that Amish and cognate religious groups should be granted the legal authority to keep pornography and other deleterious cultural influences away from their settlements. A similar misunderstanding of the Amish attitude to the state underlies Amy Gutmann's suggestion that the most fruitful way of thinking about the issues raised by *Yoder* would be to ask: 'To what degree, if any, should the Old Order Amish community be treated as a separate nation within a nation and, therefore, be granted its own educational jurisdiction?'[28] The Amish do not want educational juris-diction, except in the negative sense that they want to be excused from the application of mandatory requirements that would interfere with their con-trol over the content of education and the number of years over which formal schooling extends. They are also concerned that the timetable for lessons should be constructed so as to allow children to help with seasonal farm work and take part in communal religious ceremonies.

The Amish are, thus, content to leave the choice of school to the individual parents, in the sense that they do not wish to employ the force of the state to compel attendance at Amish schools. But that choice by parents is, of course, inevitably exercised under conditions that guarantee the 'right' result. In practice, no doubt, any Amish parents who aspired to something better for their children than a one-room schoolhouse with an unqualified teacher educating them 'for farm and domestic work' would pack up and leave.[29] But if they stayed and sought to enrol their children in the local high school they would unquestionably be censured and, if they remained obdurate, excommunicated. As with the opt-out from the social security system discussed in the previous chapter, the decision to opt out of high school education is taken by individuals: there is no legal provision for the option to be exercised by the community as a whole on behalf of the parents. Thus, the Amish are no exception to the generalization that decisions about education in contemporary western societies are shared without remainder between states and parents.

In the *Smith* case, which I discussed in the previous chapter, the Court described *Yoder* as a case which turned on 'the right of parents . . . to direct the education of their children'.[30] This description has been queried by Kent Greenawalt, who says that 'many readers, including [him]self, have been inclined to think that . . . this . . . creat[ed] a novel account of previous religion cases'.[31] But legally (as distinct from sociologically), this account of the rationale of *Yoder* seems impossible to fault. The majority opinion in that case emphasized that 'it is the parents who are subject to prosecution here for failing to cause their children to attend school'.[32] No rights were attributed to the Amish community as a whole. On the contrary, the Court said that 'this case involves the fundamental interest of parents, as contrasted with that of the State, to guide the religious future and education of their children'.[33]

What Greenawalt is really concerned with here is a different question from that of the locus of educational decision-making established by *Yoder*. What concerns him is, rather, whether the scope of *Yoder* should be taken to extend beyond parents who are, like the Amish, members of an integral religious community – a community that, among other things, provides employment within it for those who stay on as adults – or whether we should deduce from the Court's reasoning in *Yoder* that it 'would not sustain a claim by individual parents, even one sincerely religious, if the claim is unconnected to membership in a religious group'.[34] This is a question that I shall address in the last section of this chapter. Regardless of the answer, however, it still remains true that *Yoder* attributed rights to individual parents and not to Amish communities.

All this, however, simply brings to the fore the disjunction between a legal and a sociological analysis. The official Amish doctrine has been laid out in the following terms: 'In the eyes of the Amish, children do not belong to the state. They belong first to God, then to the parents, and then to the church through their parents.'[35] Even leaving aside the repellent vocabulary of ownership, this is highly misleading. As we saw in the previous chapter, the Amish are prepared to make extravagant claims against the state based on the sanctity of conscience. At the same time, though, they have no time for the claims of the individual conscience against the religious community. Their draconian way with dissenters is enough evidence of that. 'Rooted in the Anabaptist tradition, baptism symbolizes the ultimate pledge to surrender one's life to the community of faith.'[36] Hence, children's belonging first to God amounts to their belonging first to the community, because only the community as a collectivity (in practice, its elders) has authority to interpret the Word of God. Again, to say that children belong secondly to the parents is an ideological obfuscation of the reality. Unless the parents raise their children in a way approved by the community (which includes sending them to the community school), they will soon cease to be members of it. Although it is the parents who sign up to exercise the right to keep their children out of school after the eighth grade, we may say – rather more appositely than in the case of most of the biblical tags with which the Amish lard their petitions and declarations – 'The voice is Jacob's voice, but the hands are the hands of Esau.'[37]

If the state and the parents must somehow partition between them decisions about the education of children, we have to ask how far the preferences of parents for the education (or non-education) of their children should be accommodated by the state. This is, as I have been at pains to argue, not simply a matter of what is taught in schools that are run or financed by the state, but one of the public stake in education at large. The answer falls into two parts. First, the public has a legitimate interest in the education of children because citizens are concerned with the future of their society; and the future of their society, including its economic prosperity, its social stability and even its continued existence as a distinctive entity, depends on the way in which those who are now children turn out. More controversially, perhaps, I wish to maintain that there is also a public stake in education in the form of a paternalistic concern for the best interests of the children themselves – considered both as children and as future adults. The state is conceived of here as a guardian of children's interests, if necessary in opposition to the parents' view of those interests. It can be urged, with some plausibility, that the societal concern for children's education may well lead to many of the same prescriptions as the paternalistic concern. I would not dispute this. But saying that it is possible to kill two birds with one stone presupposes that there are two different birds. In any case, I shall show that there is a less than perfect harmony between the means to the one objective and the means to the other.

I have said that the paternalistic stake in education may be more controversial than the societal one. State paternalism in relation to adults is generally looked on with disfavour, because it violates the liberal presumption that adults who are not certifiably of unsound mind should take their own decisions and abide by the consequences. In practice, there are a great many matters, especially involving health and safety, in which regulation is far better than the alternative of simply requiring information to be given, since we would have to devote our whole lives to trying to understand the information about the risks and benefits of alternative consumer goods, pharmaceutical products, and so on. Even after exhaustive study of the data, most of us would still do a very poor job of processing it to reach a decision, because very few people are any good at drawing valid statistical inferences. Be that as it may, there is no liberal case for even a presumption against state paternalism in the case of children. Just because they are immature, children cannot be left to decide everything for themselves: that is simply not an option. Unless, therefore, the parents are to be left with absolute discretion, the state must be prepared to step in to protect their interests. Mill, it may be noted, ascribed just such a back-up role to the state. It was, he said 'one of the most sacred duties of the parents (or, as law and usage now stand, the father), after summoning a human being into the world, to give to that being an education fitting him to perform his part well in life towards others and towards himself'.[38] But if the parent failed to discharge this obligation, he added, it was the job of the state to see that it was fulfilled.

Shelley Burtt has accused liberals of being inconsistent in that they prescribe a much more activist role for the state in relation to education than in relation to other aspects of children's welfare. Thus, where education is concerned, liberal states typically require parents either to send their children to a school licensed by it or to prove that their child is receiving an adequate education at home. 'By contrast', Burtt says,

> in cases concerning the emotional and physical welfare of individual children, a presumption in favour of parental autonomy severely curtails state interference in the parent-child relationship. While it is not impossible under a presumption of parental autonomy to take the steps necessary to remove children from abusive parents before they get very badly hurt . . . the state must await proof of a complete breakdown in family relations in order to justify any restraint on parental autonomy. But since the proof of irremediable family breakdown is usually the actual injury of the child, the theory requires one to await [before intervening] the very maltreatment one would wish to prevent.[39]

There are good reasons for activism in relation to education and also for reluctance to act in the case of general nurture. Both the activism and the reluctance flow from the same liberal concerns: the need to protect children against abuse and neglect while at the same time keeping state action from being unduly obtrusive or repressive. Balancing the two considerations gives rise quite reasonably to different measures in different contexts. Thus, one reason for distinguishing between education and general nurture is that states can be a good deal more confident about their comparative advantage in the case of education. A quite mediocre state school does a better job than most parents could do. 'Home schooling', however good in other respects, is bound to be weak in developing the ability to cope with treatment as an equal among others and in fostering the realization that others do not share the beliefs and norms in which one has been raised. I have already suggested, however, that parents would have to be well below the average to be less effective at general nurture than even a relatively well-run state institution.

There is another reason for the state's reluctance to intervene in child-rearing outside the sphere of education. This invokes – validly, for once – the public/private distinction. In essence, the contrast that Burtt draws is between a focus on process and a focus on outcome. There is a sound basis for this. In the case of education, it is easy to verify whether or not a child is attending a school. Moreover, even if the parents maintain that the child is being adequately educated without attending a school, there are ways of testing their claim that do not require the process to be monitored. All that is necessary is that the child should present itself at some specified time and place to be tested. But there would be no way of checking up on other aspects of child-rearing short of equipping every room in every house with a television camera connected to some central surveillance unit, as in *Nineteen Eighty-Four*. It is therefore unavoidable that state action has to be initiated on the basis of reports by neighbours, midwives, doctors and schoolteachers who suspect abuse.

The defining feature of paternalistic concern with education is that its concern is purely with the interests of the child. But what are those interests? I shall take up three possible answers to that question. The first answer is that each child has an interest in attaining whatever competences are required for it to be able to function successfully in the world into which it is going to grow up. I shall analyse this idea in the next section and show the difficulties to which such an apparently simple notion of functional capacity gives rise. A second, more ambitious, objective that a state might pursue on behalf of children is knowledge and appreciation for its own sake – or, more precisely, for the sake of living well. I shall take this up in section 5 along with a third idea, already introduced in chapter 4. According to this, the central task of the state is to ensure that everyone becomes 'autonomous'. Section 6 is devoted to non-paternalistic interests in education – those interests that other members of a society have in what children are taught and the way in which they are taught it. Then, in section 7, I shall discuss the notion of multicultural education. Section 8, the final section, pulls all these strands together by asking what is the role for parental discretion left by the public stake in education.

## 4.  Functional Education

I shall define functional education as education designed to ensure, as far as possible, that its recipients will grow up able to make a living by working at some legally permissible occupation, engage in commercial transactions without being exploited as a result of ignorance or incompetence, deal effectively with public officials, know enough about the law to be able to stay within it (if they choose to) and possess (or have the means of gaining) enough knowledge of hygiene and public health to be able to practise effective contraception and to raise children properly. The key to all of these capacities is the acquisition of literacy, which is why the proportion of literate adults in a society is such an important indicator of what is often nowadays called 'human development'. Given that, in societies with less than universal literacy, the task of looking after children normally devolves almost exclusively on females (though often not primarily the mother), this last point makes it especially important that the achievement of literacy should not be neglected among girls, even in societies that deny them equal legal rights and occupational opportunities. (Of course, women with educa-tion are liable to demand these other rights and opportunities, and it is precisely because they understand this that the religious and political authorities in such societies resist international pressures for the education of girls.)

Basic education of the kind that I have described is manifestly in the interests of the recipients, so states have a clear paternalistic duty to ensure that all children receive such an education, whether their parents wish it or not. But there is also a strong collective interest in making sure that, as far as possible, future members of the society will have the functional capacities created by basic education. For we all gain if those with whom we share common institutions have learned how to be legally competent and economically self-supporting. There is also clearly a social as well as a paternalistic concern that the education received by the rising generation should fit them to be good parents. Where the abuse and neglect of children is at issue, an ounce of prevention is worth a ton of subsequent intervention – especially because, as I have argued, states are not well equipped to intervene promptly enough to avert harm.

These are capacities that are useful both to the possessor and to the rest of society. But there are some other functions that are valuable to others but much less to their possessor. Thus, in a liberal democracy, it matters a lot that the bulk of the citizens should make a good job of voting in elections.

This entails, ideally, that they should know enough to be able to detect lies and fallacies, and that they should be immune to the rhetoric of demagogues. More demandingly, we might say that a good use of the vote is one that advances what the voter sees as the common interest or the cause of justice, rather than his or her narrow individual interests. From the point of view of the individual's interests, however, all that is needed is the ability to cast a self-interested vote, which may often be done by supporting some sectional or ethnocultural block to which the voter belongs. More radically, it may be said that, taking only the interest of the individual voter into account, it is not really worth bothering to vote in an election at all, since the likelihood of one vote's making a difference is negligible. The case for civic education must lie in social rather than paternalistic concerns. The same is even more clearly true if the notion of 'civic education' is extended to include the inculcation of sentiments that will have a tendency, if the occasion arises, to foster a spirit of sacrifice for the collective interest.

Conversely, if we focus on what it is in the interest of an individual child to receive in the way of functional education, we may find that there is a conflict between this and the education with which it would be advantageous to provide that child, taking account only of the interests of the other members of the society. One way in which this gap can open up is that the acquisition of educational qualifications may be collectively self-defeating. The problem arises because, in the competition for desirable jobs, what matters is not how highly qualified you are but how highly qualified you are in comparison with the other applicants. The consequence is liable to be credentialism: the socially wasteful inflation of the level of qualifications required in order to get a job. A first approximation to the phenomenon is illustrated by the story of two hikers in the woods who suddenly encounter a hostile grizzly bear. One quickly changes into running shoes. 'That's silly – you can't run faster than a bear', says the other. 'No, but I can run faster than you', replies the first as he takes off. That, however, is only a first approximation, because the kind of competition between the two hikers is more benign than that represented by the job market. It is merely a zero-sum game: one of the hikers will get caught by the bear anyway, and the competition simply establishes which one it is to be. A closer analogy would have the two hikers committing enormous amounts of time and effort to training for the sole purpose of outrunning one another, even though at the end they will still have established only which one gets caught by the bear. The point about credentialism is not simply that there are more qualified applicants for jobs than there are jobs but that the qualifications of the applicants are higher than are needed to do the job competently.

This comes about as a result of rational action on both sides. When I left school, only 5 per cent of my age cohort went on to university. As a consequence, many jobs in both the public and private sectors that now demand a degree as the price of entry were filled by school-leavers. It would be very hard to maintain that the civil service or the banks, for example, have become more effective institutions in the past half century. The point is that, in order to obtain employees of a calibre equivalent to that of the top 25 per cent of school-leavers then, it is now necessary to take only graduates, because over 30 per cent of each age cohort go into tertiary education. Conversely, those who wish to obtain a job of a certain kind have no alternative but to acquire whatever level of qualification is currently required for eligibility, whether this is really needed to do the job or not.

We have here a game that has an equilibrium, but it occurs where the qualifications required for a certain job become so high that all the gains from that job are wiped out by the cost *to the individual* of acquiring the qualifications needed to get it. If the state provides free or subsidized education, and perhaps also contributes to maintenance costs, that may be an exceedingly inefficient equilibrium. It seems fairly clear here that state paternalism conceived individualistically is collectively self-defeating, and that the collective interest in not wasting resources should win. Observe, however, that where (as in the European Union) the relevant labour market is wider than that of the country, what will be required to restrain credentialism is joint action by states.

We can see another way in which there may be a divergence between individual and social interest in functional education by asking this question: If we say that every child should be educated so as to be able to function in the world that it is going to grow up in, how are we to say what that 'world' will be? When it grows up, the child will, within limits, be able to make decisions of its own about the life it is going to lead and where it is going to lead it. But the range of options open to it will themselves depend on the nature of its education. Consider the case of a child growing up in a desperately impoverished country. Within that country, there may well be so few openings for trained professionals that, if we took its boundaries as our horizon, we would have to say that it was of doubtful value (at any rate from a purely economic viewpoint) to be well educated. But if we include in the child's future prospects the possibility of emigrating to a wealthier country, we may well reach a different conclusion. This clearly opens up the prospect of a conflict between individual interest and collective interest. If a state spends a lot of money producing trained doctors or engineers and most of them then emigrate, it is getting a very poor return on its own investment, unless it is satisfied with whatever foreign currency flows in as remittances from emigrants to those who have remained behind. Moreover, the state is facilitating the export of the most intelligent and highly motivated members of the next generation, who might have done the most for improving things at home if they had been constrained to stay by lack of education.

An analogous conflict between individual and social interest can occur at a sub-state level. The representatives of a group defined by a certain minority language (which may not be the first language of most of its members) may press for that language to be taught in the schools as a major compulsory subject, even though this is bound to compete for time with other subjects (including other languages) that would better equip the products of the school system for the job market. An example is the case of Welsh, discussed in chapter 3. It is true that there is an advantage in knowing Welsh in as far as this is a requirement for many public sector (and some other) jobs in Wales. But this is – at any rate outside the relatively sparsely populated Welsh-speaking area – an advantage that is an entirely artificial creation. The point can therefore be reformulated by saying that the policy which creates an artificial career interest in knowing Welsh has the effect of closing off opportunities that might otherwise have been open to children growing up in Wales. This deliberate limiting of capacities to function effectively outside a child's community of birth recalls Charles Taylor's claim that there is a version of liberalism that will underwrite policies designed to forestall attempts to 'cut loose from the ancestral culture'. The way in which this works in Quebec (as I can attest from personal experience) is that in the past thirty years competence in English among some highly educated francophones has declined to the point at which it is possible to go right through the system, finishing up with a PhD and a postdoctoral fellowship in anglophone political philosophy, without enough fluency in English to take part in an international conference on the subject or have any chance of obtaining an academic job in the rest of Canada, or indeed the rest of North America.

Bilingual/bicultural classes or schools for Hispanic children in the United States raise a number of issues that go to the heart of the question of what schools are for. These issues are so complex and so important that I shall devote the rest of this section to them. The most basic question is: what are bilingual/bicultural programmes supposed to achieve? The answer that tends to be given by educational bureaucrats is that they are, in effect, remedial. The long-term objective is that children from Spanish-speaking households should become fluent in English and be 'mainstreamed' into an environment in which instruction is in English. Meanwhile, it is maintained, instruction in Spanish will facilitate the transition, while the elements of Hispanic culture in the curriculum will lead children to feel comfortable at school, and therefore do better academically.

Although there may be a sound basis in educational theory for all this (experts disagree), there is little doubt that it is not the way in which things have worked out in the United States. 'Integrated bilingual programs working with the goal of mainstreaming children as quickly as possible are not unimaginable; they are simply seldom tried because they, with some truth, are perceived to be expensive and to require administrative innovation. True bilingual-bicultural programs that expose all children to different languages and cultures have similar restrictions.'[40] Jennifer Hochschild and Nathan Scovronick have made the general point that 'too often, [policies that create separate categories of students] have permitted the creation of second class education, thus neither helping their intended beneficiaries nor promoting pluralist interaction'.[41] In practice, bilingual/bicultural programmes tend to be highly segregated. This would probably occur to a degree as a result of free choice, simply because not many non-Hispanic children (or their parents) would find such a programme attractive. In addition, however, school administrators have a financial incentive to get Hispanic children (and not others) into these programmes because the federal government reimburses local school boards only for 'limited English-proficient' students in bilingual classes.[42]

In some instances, parents whose children go to public schools are given no option: 'since 1989, the New York State Education Department has ruled that all [school] students who test under the fortieth percentile on an English proficiency test must be enrolled in bilingual programs.'[43] This creation of a captive clientele for bilingual/bicultural programs was challenged unsuccessfully in a court case in 1994 by 'a coalition of parents in New York City, most of them Hispanic', who complained that their children were (in their words) 'imprisoned' in bilingual programmes.[44] The basis for this complaint was the poor results achieved by bilingual/bicultural education.

> In a study commissioned by New York City schools chancellor Ramon Cortines in 1994 that compared outcomes for non-English-proficient schoolchildren who entered either bilingual or ESL [English as a Second Language] programs in kindergarten, it was found that 79 percent of the ESL students versus only 51 percent of the bilingual students passed English proficiency tests within three years.[45]

It might have been hoped that lower proficiency in English would be offset by greater command of regular academic subjects, but in fact children exposed to bilingual education tend to 'test more poorly in other subjects as well'.[46] Thus, 'the end result can be segregated education that reinforces rather than eliminates inequities in educational opportunities.... Becoming a "bi-illiterate" is hardly better than having the same lack of ability in one language.'[47]

A cynic might imagine that bilingual/bicultural education was a device invented by politicians and administrators to segregate Hispanic students and give them low-quality education, thus pandering to the preferences of Anglo parents. On the contrary, it came about and is sustained by successful lobbying (from the federal level down) by Hispanic community leaders and by victories in cases fought by them to compel school boards to provide bilingual/bicultural education. 'In New York State', for example, 'the Hispanic advocacy group ASPIRA won a court-imposed consent decree in 1974 mandating bilingual education in every New York school district.'[48] In order to explain this, we need to bear in mind that there is more than one way of understanding the purpose of bilingual/bicultural education. Rather than conceiving of it as one possible mode of transition, to be compared for efficacy with ESL or 'immersion' (of either the old-fashioned 'cold turkey' kind or sophisticated recently developed programmes), it may be seen instead as a way of fostering Hispanic identity. From this point of view, it is not a failure if instruction is segregated, follows a distinctive curriculum, continues in Spanish all the way through school and includes many children who would be perfectly capable linguistically of being 'mainstreamed'.[49] On the contrary, these features of the programme are what show it to be working. Even if it is true that 'many children entering bilingual programs are more proficient in English than in their putative "native" language and lose their fluency after years of "transitional" instruction', this is not an objection if the purpose of the programme is not taken to be transitional.[50] What happens to these children may be seen, rather, as a way of restoring members of the ethnically defined community to their 'roots' in their language and culture, and thereby stabilizing their identity as Hispanics.

The key to all this is, again, the question: if education should prepare children to get by in the world they will grow up into, how is that world to be defined? A lot turns on whether the answer is a state, an area wider than a state defined by a legal right to live and work within it (e.g. the European Union) or any country that it may prove possible to emigrate to. As we have now seen, the relevant world may also be defined in terms of membership in an ethnocultural group. But what precisely is the nature of the group membership which is to be affirmed and reinforced by bilingual/bicultural education? The answer to this is far from obvious because, while 'Hispanic' (or 'Spanish surname') is a census category which also has legal significance in relation to affirmative action programmes and some school desegregation cases, it does not refer to a social reality except to the degree that these uses of the concept have created one. The reality is that there are different groups distinguished by, among other things, the way in which the members (or their ancestors) became United States residents, their expectations about their movements in the future and the viability of the group as a self-sufficient economic unit.

Will Kymlicka emphasizes the importance of making such distinctions. However, what he has to say about the different groups illustrates rather clearly the inadequacy of the apparatus that he brings to bear on these questions. Many Mexicans were involuntarily incorporated into the United States as a result of conquest. 'The Treaty of Guadalupe Hidalgo, ending the

Mexican-American war, annexed Texas, Arizona, New Mexico, Colorado, and California to the United States. Mexican citizens residing in the territory were granted U.S. citizenship.'[51] Their descendants therefore constitute, according to Kymlicka, a national minority, since national minorities are defined by him as coming about by 'the incorporation of previously self-governing, territorially concentrated cultures into a larger state'.[52] This should mean that the descendants of these involuntarily incorporated groups will want to maintain separate institutions, and Kymlicka does indeed assume that the 'demands of Spanish-speaking national minorities' are quite different from those of 'Hispanic immigrants who come to the United States with the intention to stay and become citizens', who are 'committed to learning English and participating in the mainstream society'.[53]

The assumption is factually false, but we need not be surprised at this because the underlying theory is false. That one's ancestors were involuntarily incorporated in a state does not in itself make any case for separate institutions. It may just as well lead to a demand for integration on equal terms with other citizens. (That has characteristically been the demand of American blacks, whose ancestors were in a different way involuntarily incorporated.) As early as 1930, advocacy organizations were taking school districts to court, especially in Texas, on the ground 'that Mexican-American students were being denied equal protection of the law under the U.S. Constitution by being placed in segregated facilities'.[54] This makes sense because, unless they are to be confined to menial jobs, Mexican-American children need to be prepared linguistically and academically to compete for jobs in the mainstream economy.

We may contrast this instructively with the position of Cubans in Miami. Driven by his theory, according to which everything turns on the original intentions of immigrants, Kymlicka has to say that the crucial feature of 'the Cuban refugees living in Miami' is that they 'see themselves as exiles. When they arrived in the United States, they assumed that their return to Cuba was imminent', and this 'explains why they have not had the incentive to integrate'.[55] However, had the Cuban refugees spread themselves randomly around the United States, they would have been forced to assimilate, at least to the extent of learning English, regardless of their expectations. What really made the difference was 'the occupational status of the first immigrants, the large government commitment to resettlement aid, and the ability to establish a thriving enclave within which solely Spanish-speaking persons are not at an employment disadvantage'.[56] It should be an embarrassment to Kymlicka that the Cubans in Miami actually satisfy all his criteria for a national minority, with their own economic, social, political and educational institutions. Even so, the range of occupations for which people of Cuban origin who speak only Spanish are not at a disadvantage is still truncated, in comparison with the range open to those fluent in English. Despite the attachment of the first generation to Spanish, the world to which the second generation want access is wider – and probably few of them see their future in a post-Castro Cuba. 'The proportion of second-generation Cuban Americans who speak English primarily is estimated to be as high as two-thirds.'[57] Here we have a phenomenon that is incomprehensible within Kymlicka's framework, even though the history of the world has been full of it: a self-sufficient national minority whose members choose to assimilate linguistically to a larger society.

What Kymlicka says about a third group, Puerto Ricans, is totally baffling, in that he identifies them as one of two 'Spanish-speaking national minorities', the other being the Mexican-Americans (Chicanos) already discussed. On the basis of this, he again distinguishes their 'demands' from those of ordinary immigrants.[58] But Puerto Ricans are not a national minority either in Puerto Rico or in the continental United States. Puerto Rico is a self-governing commonwealth. Although its residents are US citizens and can travel freely to the USA, they do not have a vote in American elections.[59] Their position is similar to that of members of the British Commonwealth (and before that the British Empire) until the 1970s, when for the first time the hitherto undifferentiated category of 'British subject' was modified so as to distinguish those with the 'right of abode' in the United Kingdom from others. Thus, if Puerto Ricans living in Puerto Rico are a national minority in relation to the United States, so were Canadians living in Canada in relation to the United Kingdom until the last quarter century. Both suppositions are equally absurd.

But if Puerto Ricans are not a national minority in Puerto Rico, they are no more a national minority in the United States: they are in effect immigrants from another country. It is true that they come in as US citizens, and this differentiates them from most other immigrants. But the same was true of immigrants from the British Commonwealth in the 1950s and 1960s. Kymlicka would not presumably wish to say that, in virtue of this, immigrants to Britain from the Caribbean or the Indian subcontinent were really national minorities. He has therefore no more reason for describing immigrants from Puerto Rico as constituting a national minority. It would clearly subvert Kymlicka's distinction between immigrants and national minorities to say that an immigrant (or the descendant of an immigrant) turns into a member of a national minority by acquiring citizenship, either by naturalization or by birth. But in that case it should make no difference if an immigrant has citizenship from the outset.

If Puerto Ricans are to be counted as immigrants to the United States, they constitute another anomaly within Kymlicka's scheme, since they are not a national minority and yet they (or at any rate the more successful of their advocacy groups) wish to maintain their original language and culture.

The explanation of this is the considerable mobility between Puerto Rico and the United States. 'More than other Hispanics, Puerto Ricans aspire to return to their native land, where fluency in Spanish and knowledge of Puerto Rican culture is important.... Thus, bilingual-bicultural education is highly prized among Puerto Ricans.'[60] Indeed, 'the Puerto Rican Legal Defense and Education Fund...never argued for desegregation.' Rather, 'bilingualism was the organization's primary goal from the beginning'.[61]

What is the world for which young Puerto Ricans living and going to school in the United States should be prepared? If it is Puerto Rico, bilingual/bicultural education has some obvious attractions, even if it does not on average produce a very high level of academic attainment in regular school subjects. If it is the United States, bilingual/bicultural education has to be assessed as a way of creating competence in English and other school subjects. Judged by this standard it appears to do poorly. It is tempting to say that the answer to the question about the appropriate world should turn on a forecast of the choices that Puerto Rican children growing up in the USA will make as adults. But what choices people make depends on the options open to them, and the form taken by education itself opens up some options while closing others. Fluency in English and competitive academic attainments make the United States more attractive; the lack of them makes Puerto Rico more attractive. To the extent that bilingual/bicultural education brings about the second state of affairs, the flow to Puerto Rico will be higher than it would otherwise have been. But that would be a circular basis on which to argue for its continuation.

The easy way out is, of course, to say that education should prepare children of Puerto Rican descent so that they can thrive in either the United States or Puerto Rico. That is easy to say but hard to do. It is, after all, what bilingual/bicultural education is supposed to be doing already. In the end, anyone who advocates state paternalism in relation to functional education has to take a view about where the best interests of the children lie. What Puerto Rican children are conspicuously short of are academic qualifications in any language. 'In New York, only 16 percent of Puerto Rican students earned academic high school diplomas, qualifying them for admission to college.... The situation was much the same for Puerto Ricans in Boston and Chicago.'[62] If non-segregated classes conducted in English are (as appears to be the case) the best way of improving academic results, state paternalism demands an end to bilingual/bicultural education. This is, of course, consistent with saying that courses in Spanish language and literature ought to be available in all schools – and for all students. Apart from any other considerations, this would seem to be no more than a reasonable accommodation to the fact that the United States shares a continent with several hundred million people whose first language is Spanish.

## 5. Education for Living

So far, I have focused on education in its functional aspect: as a means to getting a job, dealing with the bureaucracy, and so on. I now want to take up a broader paternalistic interest in education. What I have in mind is simply that education is a good thing in itself, or, more precisely, that it provides people with the opportunity to live better lives. Understanding the world around us and being able to appreciate the finest creations of the human mind and spirit are, quite straightforwardly, benefits. And they are benefits that parents should not be permitted to withhold from their children. If we accept that the state has a legitimate interest in the education of children, it would be crass to limit that interest so that it extends no further than functional education, leaving education for life to the whims of parents.

It need hardly be said that there is a large overlap between the requirements of functional education and those of cultural education. 'Learning to read enables a child to fill in job applications and to read *Emma*. Becoming fluent in French qualifies a child for a wider range of occupational positions than otherwise, but also adds to the range of jokes, movies, and books she can enjoy and potential marital partners she can realistically consider.'[63] There is, however, an important difference between the significance of education conceived of as a way of improving job prospects and education as an end in itself. Conceived of in the first way, education beyond a certain minimum level is competitive: the more of it that other people have in comparison with you, the worse that is for you. Conceived of in the second way, however, education is if anything complementary: so far from one person's trained ability impoverishing the prospects of others, it is likely to enrich them. As a consequence of this, it may seem that adding this cultural dimension to the paternalistic objectives of education will mean that we need not worry about the collectively self-defeating tendencies of education when it is viewed as a means to getting a job. But this is not altogether so because a significant component in job-related education is vocational, and this does little to cultivate either the intellect or the spirit. Much of it would not be undertaken for any reason except the hope that it will be a means to getting a better job. To the extent that the vocational qualifications that are needed to obtain a certain job are greater than those needed to perform it adequately, there is still a deadweight loss created by credentialism.

The notion that the primary purpose of education is knowledge, critical capacity and aesthetic appreciation as ends in themselves obtains little support from politicians. In Britain, for example, Conservative and Labour governments are indistinguishable in their adherence to the values of Gradgrind, treating as 'frills' the studies that in a civilized society would be regarded as the core of a good education. Still, we might expect philosophers to insist that every child should, as an end in itself, be taught to acquire an ability to think logically and critically, and to obtain an understanding of the sciences, a broad knowledge of history and an appreciation of literature and the arts. In fact, however, it is noteworthy that American philosophers who have written on the subject feel constrained to come up with the instrumental justification that democracy requires well-educated citizens. Thus, for example, Martha Nussbaum quotes Alexander Meiklejohn with approval to the effect that 'people do need novels and dramas and paintings and poems, "because they will be called upon to vote"'.[64] This is bathetic. We can argue till the cows come home about the number of poems that somebody needs to have read in order to cast a vote intelligently. (The answer 'None' is not without plausibility.) What is far less open to dispute is that somebody who has never cracked open a book of poetry is not well educated. This strange mode of argument flows, I suspect, from American philosophers' violent antipathy to state paternalism and its extension to the case of children, where the classic Millian reasons for opposing it are completely irrelevant.

We can see the same forces at work in an article by Amy Gutmann that is specifically addressed to the issue of paternalistically motivated educational objectives. She says that what children have a right to 'will depend upon what is adequate for living a full life in their society – for being capable of choosing among available conceptions of the good and of participating intelligently in democratic politics if they so choose'.[65] Surely, there is more to a full life than choosing among the conceptions of the good and participating in democratic politics! Indeed, it is hard to imagine that a life centred around these two activities would be found satisfactory by many human beings. For what it is worth, I have to confess that I spend very little time on either – unless writing this book counts towards the latter. Yet Gutmann is completely explicit in holding that the legitimate paternalistic concerns of the state do not extend to any demand for a broad education in the arts, humanities and sciences.

> The priority of children's rights to education over parental rights of religion [or, presumably, any other objectives parents might have – BB] only justifies state regulation of private and public education to the extent that such regulation provides the best guarantee to all children of an education adequate to full and equal citizenship. Once a liberal state insures that every child is so educated, it has no further rights of paternalistic agency over children with regard to education.[66]

The clue to this curious view is that, although the ostensible subject is paternalism, education for citizenship is not a paternalistic objective. Thus, Gutmann does not recognize as legitimate *any* genuinely paternalistic objectives that a state might have in relation to children's education, and in this she is representative of contemporary American political philosophers. John Rawls has lent his weight to her position, writing in *Political Liberalism*: 'Society's concern with [children's] education lies in their role as future citizens.'[67]

Gutmann has criticized John Dewey's assertion of state paternalism, which runs as follows: 'what the best and wisest parent wants for his own child, that must the community want for all of its children.'[68] She points out that, 'if democracy includes the right of citizens to deliberate collectively about how to educate future citizens', they should have a right to decide on something other than this 'moral ideal of education'.[69] It is undeniable that democracy entails the right of people collectively to behave unwisely, just as liberty entails the right of people individually to behave unwisely. But if that were the last word that political philosophy could offer, a book about education (or any other substantive question) would be very short. What political philosophers can do in addition is make arguments about what courses of action would not be unwise. As Gutmann says, Dewey was putting forward a 'moral ideal': when he said that a community 'must' want the best for its children, he meant that this was what, morally speaking, it should want. There is no reason for supposing that Dewey, of all people, wished to be understood as saying that a community that did not pursue the best should be overruled by Platonic Guardians drawn from the ranks of the country's philosophers.

In fact, Gutmann's *Democratic Education* is quite long, so it can be deduced that she does not content herself with saying that in a democracy education should be whatever a majority says it should be. She does have a view about the objects to which education should be directed in a democratic society, which is explained as follows:

> As citizens, we aspire to a set of educational practices and authorities of which the following can be said: these are the practices and authorities to which we, acting collectively as a society, have consciously agreed. It follows that a society that supports conscious social reproduction must educate all educable children to be collectively capable of collectively shaping their society.[70]

I have to confess that the argument here goes too quickly for me. The 'must' here seems to be intended, unlike Dewey's, to denote a logical rather than a moral necessity. But I simply do not see how it follows from our being 'committed to arriving at an agreement on our educational aims' that the content of the agreement has to take the form postulated by Gutmann.[71] She deduces from it 'that "political education" – the cultivation of the virtues, knowledge and skills necessary for participation – has moral primacy over other purposes of public education in a democratic society.'[72] But I cannot

see why it has to. Why should not the upshot of democratic deliberation
equally well be to endorse Dewey's claim that the community should pursue
what the best and wisest parents would want for their children? The implication will then be, if I am right about what that is, that children should get an
education that will equip them for practical success and enable'them to live
fulfilling lives by introducing them to the arts, the humanities and the
sciences.

It will have been noticed that, in the general statement of the content of
state-mandated education, Gutmann included the capability of 'choosing
among conceptions of the good'. The explanation is that she believes this to
be one of the preconditions of democratic citizenship. This claim, however,
seems to me (to anticipate the next section) highly implausible. If it is a goal
of education at all, it is a paternalistic one: Gutmann is, it seems to me,
trying to smuggle it in as part and parcel of the 'civic education' objective.
From a strictly paternalistic point of view, there is much to be said for the
view that education should be 'autonomy-facilitating', to use a term introduced by Harry Brighouse. This is to be distinguished from the idea, rejected
in chapter 4, that any form of liberalism that rejects 'diversity' as the
objective of state action must ascribe to states the duty of promoting
autonomy. As Brighouse argues, an education that facilitates autonomy
'does not try to *ensure* that students employ autonomy in their lives, any
more than Latin classes are aimed at ensuring that students employ Latin in
their lives. Rather it aims to *enable* them to live autonomously should they
wish to'.[73] Brighouse (who is British, though he is based at an American
university) is an unabashed paternalist: the 'argument starts with the obligation which adults have towards prospective adults, to provide them with
certain kinds of opportunity to live well'.[74] The attraction of this is that it
puts the emphasis not on instilling a certain kind of motivation but simply
on providing a certain kind of capacity. Indeed, it is hard to see how
education for living, as I understand it, would not create a capacity for
autonomy as a by-product, simply because exposure to the highest achievements of the human spirit must include some appreciation of logical and
scientific thinking and a realization that on all the great issues there are a
variety of views that have been held by intelligent and learned people.
Moreover, as Martha Nussbaum has pointed out, education must be more
than the passive absorption of material.[75] You do not know something
unless you can think about it, and that requires a certain capacity to think
for yourself.

Unfortunately, it is not so clear that an education geared to either fostering or facilitating autonomy must have as a by-product a solid exposure to
the humanities and the sciences. On an all-too-common conception of
autonomy, what it calls for is encouraging children to express the way they
feel about a thing, whether or not these feelings have any adequate ground-

ing in reality. The rigorous study of a text or the painstaking mastery of a body of scientific theory is liable to be seen as crimping spontaneity, which is confused with autonomy. Some teachers even believe that correcting children's spelling or grammar is wrong because it is too repressive. This witless pedagogy is epitomized in a recent book whose author 'draws a sharp distinction between understanding and "mere knowledge". "There should be less time defining words like 'nationalism' and more time discussing what the world would be like if there were no countries." '[76] What this proposal comes to is that children should be denied the opportunity of learning about an important phenomenon in a way that might foster analytical thinking. Instead, they should be encouraged to engage in ill-informed 'discussion' of a poorly focused question. James Traub asks in a review: 'But doesn't this encourage students in a false sense of competence, promoting the kind of vacuous self-assurance that so besets us now?'[77] What marks out well-educated people is their capacity to recognize when they do not have an adequate basis for having a view on a topic. The notion that it is possible to possess 'understanding' without its having a foundation in knowledge subverts this basic aim of education.

## 6.   Societal Interests in Education

Up to this point, I have been focusing on what schools should teach in as far as they are concerned to promote the best interests of their pupils. It is now time to look at education from the perspective of the society within which the schools are situated. I need not enlarge on the point that there are societal as well as paternalistic state interests in functional education. Similarly, there is a strong societal as well as paternalistic interest in having the schools play an active role in reducing the number of teenage pregnancies and preventing the spread of AIDS and other sexually transmitted diseases. Amy Gutmann quotes the head of the New Orleans child abuse unit as saying: 'With teen-age mothers the problem is primarily in the area of physical abuse and neglect. They don't have parenting skills, they don't have resources and they don't know how to obtain resources.'[78] These are such vital societal interests that parents should not be allowed to withdraw their children from this part of the curriculum on the basis of religious or cultural objections. Nor should individual schools or school districts be able to opt out. The interests at stake are far too important to leave decisions about what is to be taught to the likes of those in charge of Community School District 24 in New York City, who have prevented instruction about AIDS and 'essentially banned sex education by forbidding teachers to use the words abortion, masturbation, homosexuality or condom'.[79]

I want now to pick up again the questions raised in section 4 about bilingual/bicultural education and ask how they appear when they are looked at from the point of view of the society in which the education takes place. From this perspective, there is no doubt that so-called bilingual education should be condemned if it fails to produce universal literacy and fluency in English, and that bicultural education should be rejected if it is intended – or works out in practice – as a distinctive curriculum taken virtually exclusively by Hispanic children. One obvious reason for this is that everybody has an interest in the rising generation's being educated so as to be able to get a job, and the range of jobs in the United States (outside Miami) open to those who are not fluent and literate in English is very limited indeed. Similarly, employers are more likely to offer jobs to applicants who have studied the standard curriculum than those who have pursued some special ethnically orientated course of studies.

There is a further reason for saying that there is a broad societal interest in having integrated instruction in English in a common curriculum. This is political. A single state may contain more than one linguistic community because it has been put together in a way that cuts across a historic linguistic frontier (or more than one), or because autochthonous communities have been overrun but not assimilated. In all such cases, forcible imposition of a single language as the only legitimate public means of communication would clearly be oppressive as well as a violation of international covenants. Certain group rights must therefore be accepted: the different linguistic communities have a valid claim to conduct their collective life in their own language. However, what must be acknowledged is that this kind of arrangement takes its toll on the functioning of a democratic regime.

If some linguistic group forms a small minority, it is liable simply to be excluded from the majority discourse and hence marginalized. Even where all linguistic groups count, as in Switzerland, Belgium and Canada, the linguistic communities tend to carry on parallel conversations confined largely to their own members. The disruptive potential of this is currently illustrated by Belgium and Canada. Even if these survive as single countries, the price is that the state is hollowed out as all tasks of government that can be devolved are lost to it. Thus, Quebec has already succeeded in opting out of institutions (such as social insurance) that are otherwise Canada-wide, and blocks any moves towards greater centralization of such matters as tertiary education and the environment that might well be enacted by the rest of Canada in the absence of Quebec.[80] Switzerland has always had a weak federal government which operates by consensus. Real political life occurs at cantonal level, and it is significant that the great majority of cantons are either French-speaking or German-speaking, so that political discourse takes place in one language. In Belgium, 'almost every major institution ... is either split into Flemish and francophone versions or consists of a loose confederation of the two groups. ... As a result, there is no pressure, and no arena, for arranging compromises except in the central institutions of government, and particularly in the cabinet.'[81]

In some respects, Belgium functions like a microcosm of the European Union, which is commonly accused of suffering from a 'democratic deficit'. The charge is certainly sustainable if the model of a democratic polity is taken to be one in which there is a single comprehensive realm of discourse giving rise to a unified 'public opinion' – unified not in the sense that everybody thinks the same but in the sense that everybody is aware of what the others think and takes it into account. This model seems to me largely inapplicable to the European Union, now and for the foreseeable future. For even if the trend within the countries of the European Union towards ever more widespread knowledge of English continues until it is universal, most people will still read newspapers and watch television in their native language. There will therefore continue to be parallel national discourses, and governments will continue to be expected to pursue within the European Union policies arrived at through national politics.

As all these examples suggest, political communities are bound to be linguistic communities, because politics is (in some sense) linguistically constructed. We can negotiate across language barriers but we cannot deliberate together about the way in which our common life is to be conducted unless we share a language. Where historic communities based on language exist already, there is no satisfactory alternative to recognizing them as political communities as well, at any rate where they occupy geographically compact areas. (The redivision of Indian states along linguistic lines since Independence is a further example of the inexorable pressures at work.) However, it is clear that countries forming a single linguistic community have powerful reasons for trying to prevent the development of distinct linguistic communities within their territory.

The conflict between the two models of democratic politics – as elite brokering of interests defined within linguistic communities and as a single realm of discourse – was played out in the American Supreme Court in the case of *Katzenbach* v. *Morgan*. The issue in this case was whether or not the Congress could enact a law providing 'that no one who completes sixth grade in an "American-flag" school may be denied the right to vote because he or she is not literate in English'.[82] Kent Greenawalt has commented that the effect of the federal law was to afford 'many Puerto Ricans a right to vote in New York despite the state's requirement of English literacy'.[83] The Court held that Congress could legitimately impose on New York State the right of those not literate in English to vote, because it could have had a factual basis for maintaining that this was necessary for the 'equal protection of the laws' to be extended to all citizens. Thus, Justice Brennan wrote for the Court, one of the 'possible factual conclusions by Congress' was that 'voters might be adequately informed by Spanish-language newspapers, radio and television'.[84] This gives the impression that the media simply supply 'information', which each voter processes atomistically in order to arrive at decisions about politics. But all news is a mix of fact, interpretation and evaluation; and news value is relative to the concerns of the consumers. In practice, therefore, to say that a flow of news in Spanish can be adequate to enable people to vote in the United States is to endorse the 'parallel discourse' model as an appropriate one.

To sum up so far: except where each linguistic group maintains an entire economy and polity within a state (as in Belgium, Switzerland and Canada), the maintenance of linguistic diversity is a recipe for condemning successive generations to dead-end jobs (or unemployment) and for denying them the ability to take part in public affairs except as voting-fodder for a politics of sectional interest. The rest of the society has a legitimate direct interest – not only a paternalistic one – in avoiding such an outcome. For it has a legitimate interest in all its citizens having the capacity to be economically productive and being equipped to take part in its national politics as participants in a single national discourse. Democratic states that still have an open future have every reason for pursuing the course that leads to a linguistically homogeneous polity. The educational system is crucial to this, and fluency in the prevalent language of the polity and economy can legitimately be demanded of all children, whether they attend publicly run schools, privately run schools, or no schools at all.

Are there any other demands that can legitimately be made in the interest of ensuring that the next generation will be able to play its part in sustaining a democratic political system? Contrary to most American political philosophers who have written on this topic, I am inclined to believe that, if a state could ensure that all children had an education that was sound from a paternalistic point of view, it would have done all it needed to do or should do. Thus, if we want an electorate that is resistant to lies and fallacies, and has both the disposition and the capacity to vote reflectively, we are not asking for anything that a good education will not provide without having to go out of its way to do so. Similarly, if we want citizens to be able to participate effectively in politics, what they need are skills that a good education will automatically provide: the ability to acquire and manipulate information and the ability to present an argument lucidly, both on paper and orally. These are abilities that any child of normal intelligence can be taught, but they require systematic instruction and even a certain amount of drill, as the formidable articulateness of the typical product of a French *lycée* attests.

I do not therefore believe that anything special need be done to accommodate 'political education' of the kind that is advocated by Amy Gutmann. If I am right, it can be accomplished as a by-product of an education for living well. I am doubtful, however, that the converse is true. That is to say, 'political education' is not, in my judgement, likely to satisfy the paternalistic criteria that I put forward in the previous two sections. Gutmann tells us 'that "political education" – the cultivation of the virtues, knowledge, and skills necessary for political participation – has moral primacy over other purposes of public education in a democratic society'.[85] An implication that she draws is that 'inequalities in the distribution of educational goods can be justified if, but only if, they do not deprive any child of the ability to participate effectively in the democratic process.'[86] Even functional education above the minimum is not called for: schools are not to be criticized if they 'fail to give equally talented children an equal chance to earn the same income or to pursue professional occupations', but only if they 'fail to give all (educable) children an education adequate to take advantage of their political status as citizens'.[87]

What 'political education' requires was not spelt out in the first edition of Gutmann's *Democratic Education*. In the Epilogue to the second edition, however, she specifies a 'civic minimum' which is long on preaching and just as short as one might have feared on education for living:

> what democratic education identifies as a good civil education [consists of] teaching not only the 3R's but also religious toleration and nondiscrimination, racial and gender nondiscrimination, respect for individual rights and legitimate laws, the ability to articulate and the courage to stand up for one's publicly defensible convictions, the ability to deliberate with others and therefore to be open-minded about politically relevant issues, and the ability to evaluate the performance of officeholders.[88]

Of course, achieving these aims could (however implausibly) be held to entail an entire education in the humanities and sciences, as Nussbaum urges that it does. But the reference to the 3Rs, in conjunction with the indifference to equality of educational opportunity expressed earlier, would make this a strained interpretation.

In addition, we may observe that Gutmann believes political education of the kind she advocates to be actually in a state of tension with academic achievement. For it requires, according to her, that schools themselves practise participatory democracy: 'even when student participation threatens to produce some degree of disorder within schools,' she writes, 'it may be defended on democratic grounds for cultivating political skills and social commitments.'[89] My bet is, however, that adults who have been well educated along the lines I have sketched will, when it comes to the crunch, be far more politically effective than those who attended disorderly schools at which large amounts of time were devoted to 'student participation'. Sidney Webb once said that he did not mind what happened at a committee meeting as long as he got to write the minutes. Which kind of school is more likely to produce the person who writes the minutes? Which kind of school is more likely to produce people who can marshal facts and arguments articulately in a public meeting? I fear that 'participatory' schools are liable to create the kind of 'vacuous self-assurance' criticized by James Traub, at the expense of the hard skills actually needed for effective participation in politics.

There are, of course, many other possible objectives of 'political educa-tion' besides fitting people to play an effective role in democratic politics. One of the greatest attractions of mass education to rulers from the nine-teenth century onward has been that it can be turned into an instrument of state propaganda. From their tenderest years, children can be indoctrinated in schools with historical myths glorifying the nation and vilifying other nations; they can be told stories about heroic feats of self-sacrifice for the nation and encouraged to emulate them; and they can be imbued with beliefs about the uniquely wonderful political system that they live under and the god-like qualities of their rulers. Non-democratic regimes in countries devel-oped enough to have centrally controlled mass education systems are the most virulent exponents: fascists, communists and nationalists, if they agree on nothing else, have happily concurred in pursuing this kind of 'political education' with great enthusiasm. But the same phenomenon, albeit in a more tempered form, is not unknown in democratic countries.

'In the first decades of this century ... many citizens saw immigration as a frightening challenge to democracy, and demanded that the schools be transformed in order to "Americanize" these future citizens.'[90] In this con-text, it should be borne in mind that, in the period between the 1880s and the 1920s, the United States took in immigrants from a far wider range of countries (most of which had no traditions of individual liberty or represent-ative government) than Canada, Australia or New Zealand, which until as late as the 1960s drew most immigrants from (in different proportions) England, Scotland and Ireland. Even today, there is a widespread view that the reproduction of the polity is a prime task of the schools. In one survey, 'seventy percent [of respondents] were willing to teach outright that "democracy is the best form of government"'.[91] Among American political philosophers, too, we find the same emphasis on the reproduction of the polity, though what is to be reproduced differs from one theorist to another, depending on what the essence of the polity is taken to be. For Amy Gutmann, the focus is on fitting future citizens for political participa-tion, as we have seen. It may be recalled from chapter 4 that William Galston envisions the United States as a society in which the value of diversity is pursued by public policy. However, to offset the centrifugal forces that this is liable to unleash, he lays on the schools a heavy burden of instilling patriotic sentiments and loyalty to the country's political insti-tutions. Thus, the schools are to inculcate 'courage', defined as 'the willingness to fight and even die on behalf of one's country', and 'the developed capacity to understand, to accept, and to act on the core principles of one's society'.[92]

There are two objections to 'political education' of this kind, one principled and the other pragmatic. The principled one has been well expressed by Harry Brighouse. Liberal democracy, unlike other forms of government, depends for its legitimacy on consent. But the quality of that consent is compromised if it is simply manufactured by the state through the school system. Galston, as Brighouse points out, is quite explicit that the liberal democratic criteria of legitimacy cannot be met and that the schools must fill the gap with propaganda:

> few individuals will come to embrace the core commitments of liberal society through a process of rational inquiry. If children are to be brought to accept these commitments as valid and binding, the method must be a pedagogy that is far more rhetorical than rational. For example, rigorous historical research will almost certainly vindicate complex 'revisionist' accounts of key figures in American history. Civic education, however, requires a nobler, moralizing history: a pantheon of heroes who confer legitimacy on central institutions and are worthy of emulation.[93]

Thus, as Brighouse says, 'not only do Galston's civic educators aim to inculcate an unacceptably deferential citizenship, but their method involves systematically misleading future citizens, erecting serious barriers to the critical and informed consent to which liberal legitimacy aspires'.[94]

Galston's case for perpetrating improving myths of the Washington-and-the-cherry-tree variety is that there is no alternative if liberal democracy is to survive: 'it is unrealistic to believe that more than a few adult citizens of liberal societies will ever move beyond the kind of civic commitment engendered by such a pedagogy.'[95] If this were true, it would be hard to see why liberal democracy should be regarded as worth defending anyway, since its justification surely presupposes that elitist conceptions such as Galston's are false. Fortunately, however, I can see little reason for believing that the capacities of ordinary citizens are as limited as Galston alleges. The advantages of living in a country that has established liberty under law and in which the government is ultimately responsible to the people are not recondite. Anybody who reads a newspaper or watches the news on television has ample opportunities to appreciate these advantages by seeing what life is like in countries that do not enjoy these benefits.

There is a second, more pragmatic, argument against giving the schools in a liberal democracy the job of engaging in overt political indoctrination. This is simply that it politicizes education in an unwholesome and potentially even destructive way. I have emphasized throughout this chapter that there is a large public stake in education. But unless that stake is carefully delimited, conflicts about the future direction of the society that should be fought out within and between political parties are liable to tear apart the schools – and, indeed, the universities. If it is once accepted that the teaching of history can be manipulated for ulterior political ends, what has been created is in fact a zero-sum game that any number can play. The Pollyanna version of history favoured by Galston is open to a complete *bouleversement*, for example, leaving a conservative blowhard like Peter Salins complaining that Columbus and his men are described as having been guilty of genocide – though he admits that they did kill a lot of people and their diseases killed many more. According to him, this

> multicultural revisionism of the schools also deprecates the U.S. Constitution, as well as America's political and civic leaders, westward expansion, technological progress, foreign policy, and military engagements.... Schoolchildren are taught that Andrew Jackson caused the Cherokee Trail of Tears and that Washington was just a rich slave owner.[96]

The trouble with this, according to Salins, is that 'it robs our children – indeed an entire impressionable next generation of Americans – of their most precious birthright: a justifiable pride in the American Idea and the generally enlightened and idealistic trajectory of America's domestic and foreign policies.'[97] At the end of this road lie the Oakland and New York State history wars, the first of which left the schools without textbooks for a year.[98]

There are, I suggest, five ways of bringing the politicization of the curriculum under control. First, it is essential for all parties to accept that truth should be the controlling value, one that trumps whatever desirable objectives people may have in proposing that children should be taught one thing rather than another. This still leaves room for arguments about selection and emphasis, but the range of dispute can be limited by adherence to the ground rule that it is never an adequate reason for teaching something that belief in it would have desirable consequences. A second strategy is to provide a good education, in the sense defined in the previous section. To the extent that their education encourages children to read widely and critically, it makes less difference what is in the list of set texts in literature courses or what the history textbook says. This should make it less worth fighting to the death over every novel in the list or every line in the textbook. A third strategy is to cultivate a certain scepticism about the depth of the effects of schools on political attitudes: 'Were Americans better patriots when Lincoln and Washington were on the school walls instead of Martin Luther King Jr., and Cesar Chavez, and if they were, was it for that reason?'[99] It could be argued that it is a different matter where an authoritarian regime endeavours to ensure that the schools, the mass media and the books that people are allowed to read all tell the same story; but the failure of Soviet Communism to impress itself over a period of seventy years suggests the limits even of this kind of concerted effort. A fourth strategy is to cast doubt upon the tight connection sometimes assumed between historical beliefs and self-esteem. Is the self-esteem of black children or Native American children really so fragile that it depends on their not being permitted to know that most of the slaves brought to America were obtained from African slavers or that the American Constitution owes about as much to the Algonquin Club as it does to the Iroquois Federation?[100] Finally, the link between self-esteem generated through the curriculum and learning should also be regarded as highly suspect, and this ought again to make the stakes less high. Thus, as Glazer points out, 'the experience of Jews and Asians [of earlier generations] is devastating counter-evidence to the argument that a curriculum designed to enhance self-esteem is essential for learning'.[101] In the words of Jeff Spinner, 'teachers should encourage students to believe that they are capable of doing well in school, but distorting history is not a good way of doing this'.[102]

I would not for a moment wish to suggest that, even if all of these strategies for lowering the stakes were followed, there would not still be plenty of room for dispute about the content of the school curriculum. But it is perfectly reasonable that there should be disagreements, and that these will have to be resolved ultimately by a body that has (directly or indirectly) some kind of democratic legitimacy. What matters is that the discussion leading up to that decision should be constrained by shared presuppositions and mutually accepted ground rules, so as to keep it within the bounds of civility. The five proposals I have put forward are intended to contribute to the achievement of that end.

## 7. Multicultural Education

One of the issues that would still be left open by the defusing moves that I have recommended is the question – or set of questions – going under the name of 'multicultural education'. The feature of the curriculum whose merits I intend to assess under this heading is the one singled out by Nathan Glazer in his recent book *We Are All Multiculturalists Now*. In explaining in what sense he wishes to maintain the thesis contained in the title of the book, Glazer writes: 'When I say multiculturalism has won and that "we are all multiculturalists now," I mean that we all now accept a greater degree of attention to minorities and women and their role in American history and social studies and literature classes in schools.'[103] It may seem perverse that I have got this far in a book about multiculturalism without once mentioning the sense of the term that has assumed such an important role in both the public and the academic debate, especially in the United States. Glazer, indeed, argues that the word 'multiculturalism' should be reserved exclusively for advocacy of the specific feature of the curriculum singled out by him. The reason he advances for this proposal is that all other policies advanced under the name of 'multiculturalism' have other descriptions, such as affirmative action or ethnic group representation, and should not therefore be included in the scope of 'multiculturalism'.[104] This, however, seems to me a poor argument, on a par with saying that we do not need the word 'tree' because we already have the words 'oak', 'pine', and so on; more exactly, it is like saying that the word 'tree' should be reserved exclusively for some species that does not yet have a name of its own.

Even though the policies advocated by multiculturalists are diverse and in some cases incompatible with one another, they have in common that they in one way or another politicize group identities. Glazer objects that some of the groups proposed for special treatment by the advocates of multiculturalism are not defined by distinctive cultural attributes.[105] This is true, and I have elaborated on precisely this point in chapter 3. (I shall return to it again in chapter 8.) No doubt it is bound to give rise to a suspicion that some multiculturalist policies are based on a false premise. But nothing is gained conceptually by running together criticism and definition. I believe, therefore, that it is better to conceive of multiculturalism broadly, as I have done in this book.

In defence of my neglect of multiculturalism in the sense defined by Glazer, let me point out that this book is billed as a critique of multiculturalism. Truth in advertising therefore demands that I focus mainly on those aspects of multiculturalism that seem to me misguided. I can see no reason for criticizing the general idea of multiculturalism understood in the way proposed by Glazer. 'In its most benign and well-intended form, multicultural education...seeks to expose all students to the wide range of cultural heritages represented in the school, district, state, or nation', write Jennifer Hochschild and Nathan Scovronick. 'It is an attempt to redefine American culture away from that of the culturally dominant Anglo-Saxon Protestant majority, and to enrich it.'[106] This is not to say that such an objective is totally non-controversial. Despite the title of his book, even Glazer has to admit that 'we are not *all* multiculturalists'.[107] Nevertheless, in a number of opinion surveys, 'between half and three-quarters of Americans endorsed teaching "the diverse cultural traditions of the different population groups in America" even when that implies "decreas[ing] the amount of information on traditional subjects in...U.S. history"'.[108] The opportunity cost is, in any case, not very great: in the 1970s, my son managed to graduate from a quite well-regarded Chicago high school without knowing much about the history of America (or anywhere else for that matter); and university teachers of history have confirmed my impression that there never has been within living memory a lot of scope for children to learn substantially less history in American high schools than they were learning already.

It seems to me that there are two lines along which the case for multi-cultural education can be made. One is to present it as a special case of the general principle that all public services should operate in a way that is responsive to their clientele. The museum of city history should reflect the diversity of the city's composition, and not devote its coverage disproportionally to the achievements and contributions of the majority ethnic group. Those who run the municipal public library should be sensitive to the demands of all of its potential users; and, if this entails recruiting staff according to ethnocultural criteria, it can be justified as a case in which the introduction of such criteria is necessary to the effective conduct of the enterprise. At the same time, however, it is important that this should be seen as a way of expanding options rather than as an excuse for closing them off. It is quite wrong for public authorities to act on the assumption that members of cultural minorities are interested only in 'their' culture. 'Les Black quotes one young black South Londoner saying he would much rather be reading Shakespeare, but all he can find in his youth centre's library are books about Rastafarianism.'[109] As we shall see, those who stock the youth centre library, and apparently believe that young blacks should have access only to books about Rastafarianism, have their counterparts in the schools.

The argument that public services should be offered on a non-discriminatory basis is one that can be used to make the case for a multi-cultural curriculum in schools run or subsidized by the state. But it cannot be extended to other schools. Nevertheless, there is a case for multicultural education that makes it legitimate to demand that all children should be exposed to it. This is simply that children should not be taught what is false. The reason for telling children about the iniquities of slavery and westward expansion is that they really were iniquitous. Conversely, the sort of tri-umphalist Eurocentric history that marginalized the sufferings and wrongs of the blacks and the Native Americans was a lie, and that is why it was wrong to teach it. To the extent that multicultural education is a matter of setting the record straight, how could it be controversial? One answer is that not everybody wants the record set straight. Galston, as we have seen, believes that the historical truth would be too disturbing and wants it distorted so as to send an appropriately upbeat message. There is, however, another possible answer. We can best approach it by observing that Galston's proposal rests on a certain presupposition. He does not wish to deny that there is a truth about the past that is in principle accessible; he simply does not think that it is appropriate for transmission to schoolchildren. But there are other people who deny that there is an objective truth at all. This way of thinking tends to lead to a kind of collective solipsism: each group, it is suggested, can constitute a self-contained universe of discourse all on its own. A good example is provided by 'Afrocentrists, who ... seek to ban or require certain books and to restructure school curricula and pedagogical methods in accordance with their understanding of an African-based epistemology and value system. In addition, they sometimes seek to limit attendance at Afrocentric schools to African American children.'[110]

Even if attendance is not formally limited to African-American children, it can be safely predicted that any school teaching an 'Afrocentric' curriculum of the kind described will in fact be attended exclusively, or almost exclusively, by them. The goal of segregation is explicit among 'proponents of gender-based schools or schools based on sexual orientation, who argue for boys-only, girls-only, or gay-and-lesbian-only public schools, with corresponding changes in curriculum, pedagogy, and staffing'.[111] What is implicit in this demand is what was explicit in the demand for 'Afrocentric' education: that each group should be taught a distinctive curriculum. We can see that this is central by asking why otherwise single-sex schools or schools admitting only those with a certain sexual orientation should require 'corresponding changes in curriculum, pedagogy, and staffing'. What would make for this 'correspondence'? Clearly, it has to be assumed that, once we have assembled a group of school children who share a certain characteristic – sexual identity or sexual orientation in the present case – we somehow have a mandate for teaching them a unique curriculum, which is to be taught in a special way by (presumably) teachers who share the characteristic on the basis of which the children have been brought together.

Such proposals are bound to be controversial. In fact, they should be rejected. Liberal democracy is indissolubly connected with modernism – as against postmodernism – in one crucial respect: it depends on a general belief that there is such a thing as truth, as against my truth or your truth. If the only thing that can be said is that what people believe is a function of (for example) their race, gender or sexual orientation, there is nothing worth discussing. Yet democratic politics rests on the assumption that it is possible to give reasons for taking one course of action or another that are good or bad reasons – not just my reasons or your reasons. There is no way in which decisions taken by a majority can be accepted by the minority unless both sides occupy a common universe, in at least this minimal sense. George Orwell explored imaginatively in *Nineteen Eighty-Four* the possibility of a society in which the notion of the objectivity of truth had disappeared. The point was that such a society could not be anything but a dictatorship. For only by the exertion of absolute power could a set of common (if constantly changing) beliefs be established. Fortunately, the experiment of trying to combine participatory decision-making with postmodern epistemology has so far been confined to a few English departments in the United States. The failure of the experiment in these particular cases is, perhaps, no great loss. But the experience illustrates in microcosm the importance of a common belief in the proposition that truth is not simply whatever the winning coalition defines it as.

In my discussion of Galston, I said that we should not teach things in schools simply on the ground that belief in them would have desirable consequences. I realize that an extension of this dictum may be turned against me here: it is not a proof of the falsity of postmodern epistemology that it would be destructive of liberal democracy if it came to be generally believed. I also said, however, that it would be worth spreading myths if they were necessary to safeguard liberal democracy, though I qualified that by saying that I doubted if liberal democracy had much of a future if it had to depend on myth. Here too, I doubt if it would do me much good to say that radical perspectivism should be denied, even if it is true, in order to save liberal democracy. But I have seen no convincing argument for its truth. It is undeniable that there are unresolved disagreements about history and about the current state of society. But we shall never find out how close it is possible to get to agreement if the whole enterprise is written off in advance. In the absence of any knock-down argument to the contrary, everybody who is persuaded that liberal democracy is preferable to other forms of government has an excellent reason for embracing the faith of the Enlightenment that we can, by cooperative effort, approach the truth ever more closely.

There is another reason for objecting to multiculturalism in its separatist form. This focuses not on its premises but on its consequences. There is, quite simply, little chance for a society to operate in a way that serves the long-run interests of any of its members if it is divided up into mutually exclusive groups who have not only gone to different schools but have followed different curricula in them. This objection not only applies to 'Afrocentric' schools or to schools intended to teach different curricula to boys and girls, with each group perhaps subdivided further according to sexual orientation. It also applies to 'proponents of cultural maintenance in bilingual education programs, who seek to ensure that English language learners be taught in their native language and be helped to retain the social and cultural practices that they bring from their community of origin'.[112] These, like Afrocentric programmes, are *de facto* if not *de jure* segregated in that children from outside the group are very unlikely to join them. The rationale is different: it does not depend on the claim that Puerto Ricans, say, have unique access to truths necessarily denied to others. But the effect is the same: separate schools (or at least classrooms) and separate curricula. As Hochschild and Scovronick argue, the result of satisfying all these (and other) demands based on the notion of group rights is that 'the idea of a common culture is sacrificed, the benefits of inclusion to all sides become secondary, and individual or small group goals triumph at the cost of collective ones'.[113]

To sum up, then, the term 'multicultural education' covers two educational policies that are diametrically opposed in their presuppositions and implications.[114] The first is that children should have a common curriculum, regardless of 'race' or ethnicity, gender, sexual orientation, religious belief or any other characteristics. This curriculum should be multicultural in the sense that it should be inclusive, paying due attention to both the past and the present situation of all these groups. The second policy rejects the whole notion of a common curriculum. Beyond a certain point, it is quite likely that the proliferation of schools with separate clienteles and different curricula will become self-reinforcing, as more and more groups break away from the 'mainstream' schools in self-defence. 'The "regular children," the "normal students" then live in a small, gated community of default within the school or school district, surrounded by those defined as different for some reason or another.'[115] Hochschild and Scovronick are concerned with the threat to the system of public education in the United States that is represented by this prospect of proliferating special programmes. It is clear, however, that the same proliferation would have equally malign effects on the society and the polity if it occurred through the growth of privately run and privately financed schools. No doubt, however, long before that had happened the pressure for the introduction of school vouchers would have meant that these private schools would in fact be publicly financed. The only way of averting this development is for the public stake in a common curriculum to be better understood.

## 8.  Parental Rights In Education

If multicultural education is pursued in the right spirit, it is the antithesis of an education designed to foster narrowness and bigotry. It can form an integral part of what I have called education for living, since the point of that is to expose children to the widest possible range of the arts, the humanities and the sciences. There are, however, parents who want at any price to prevent their children from enjoying a broad education. If their children attend the public schools, these parents demand the right to pull them out of the classroom while certain subjects are being taught. They may alternatively withdraw their children from the public school system so as to impose stringent limits on what they may learn. One way in which parents can pursue this aim is to send their children to a private school that is committed to instilling a certain world-view or set of religious doctrines in its pupils and denying them access to any competing ideas. Another way is to teach the children at home, employing only textbooks that reinforce their own beliefs.

What has been said so far in this chapter about the public stake in education provides reasons for resisting all these demands, since there are both paternalistic and societal interests in saving children from ignorance and bigotry. There is, however, a further line of argument pointing in the same direction. I can explain the point at issue conveniently by returning to Chandran Kukathas's theory, which I discussed in chapter 4. Kukathas, it will be recalled, assigns a very limited role to the state. According to him, its job is to prevent conflict between groups, but not to intervene in their internal affairs to protect their individual members. He is therefore quite prepared to say that the state should stand by and let parents mutilate their children with impunity and that they should not be liable to any punishment for causing the death of a child by failing to seek or authorize lifesaving medical treatment. It is therefore quite natural that he should occupy the most extreme 'parentalist' position on the spectrum of views about the rights of parents in relation to their children's education. Kukathas's thesis emerges starkly in what he has to say about the education of gypsy children.

British law contains a special provision which has the effect of permitting the children of gypsies to go to school for only half as many days as other children. Even this minimal requirement is not enforced because there is no nationwide system for checking on school attendance, and local authorities do not see it as their business to chase up truancy among people who move in and out of the area without notice. Hence, as Kukathas puts it,

> because gypsy custom does not value schooling, the parents believing that they can educate a child satisfactorily through informal instruction in the ways of their culture, only a minority of children receive any formal primary education. Their freedom to associate and live by their own ways, however, would, by my argument, make this permissible.'[116]

My contention is that this claim runs up against another part of Kukathas's theory of rights. When challenged to defend the liberal credentials of his theory, he invariably appeals to his thesis that members must always be free to leave a group if it is to escape external regulation of its affairs. Provided this condition holds, he suggests, group members must be assumed to consent to their treatment if they choose to stay. An obvious limitation on the scope of this proviso is that it does nothing to protect the interests of children who are too young to leave home. This is already a very serious objection. Let us leave it aside, however, and focus on those who are old enough to leave their family and the community within which they were brought up. What is required before we can say that young adults have an opportunity to leave? 'The theory advanced here . . . is a liberal theory inasmuch as it does not sanction the forcible induction into or imprisoning of any individual in a cultural community.'[117] If the possibility of exit were to be understood as no more than the absence of locked doors or chains, its value as a safeguard against oppression and exploitation would be extremely scant. If it is to mean a real possibility of living outside the group, however, we cannot neglect the significance of education.

If the world for which education had to prepare gypsy children was a traditional gypsy way of life and nothing else, the answer given by Kukathas would be hard to gainsay. But it is not. Kukathas quotes Sebastian Poulter as saying 'that because "at present many gypsy children are being denied the sort of education which would fit them to make a rational choice of lifestyle as adults" there may be reason to convict the parents under the Education Act and override "this particularly harmful aspect of gypsy tradition and culture"'. He replies that 'there is no more reason to insist that gypsy parents offer their children a "rational choice" of lifestyle through public education than there is to require that other parents offer their children the opportunity to become gypsies'.[118] This is just plain silly. The education (or rather non-education) of a gypsy child fits it for nothing except to be a gypsy, whereas a conventional education opens up a potentially limitless range of occupations and ways of life. Indeed, the average sixteen-year-old school-leaver could, I have little doubt, quickly learn everything there is to know about occupations such as selling sprigs of heather in the street and breaking up cars for scrap. The lack of opportunity to become a gypsy does not arise from lack of appropriate educational qualifications but from the fact that gypsies are an ethnic group, so there is no way in which non-gypsies can simply decide to become gypsies. What it is possible to become by choice is a New Age Traveller, and a standard education appears to present no impediment to that.

If Kukathas were to take seriously the notion that closed groups should make available opportunities for exit to their members, consistency would require him to accept that gypsy children should receive a regular education. But there is also a powerful societal interest in ensuring that all children obtain an education that will enable them to hold down a job in the mainstream economy, understand the law and deal effectively with the central and local bureaucracy. The major occupation of gypsies in England is breaking up old cars. As Poulter concedes, this is done in a way that gives rise to legitimate objections from people living anywhere near the sites at which this is done: 'Fires are often lit to burn the upholstery and tyres of cars that are being scrapped and this creates an unpleasant stench over a wide area.'[119] No doubt burning rubber and the plastic materials of which car seats are constructed also creates a significant health hazard. There is an obvious case for prohibiting this practice, but Poulter maintains that 'it is clearly in the public interest that one of the mainstays of the gypsy economy is retained and encouraged rather than that the bulk of them are left to rely on social security'.[120] Why should it be accepted that these are the only alternatives? In the nature of the case, breaking up old cars cannot be a very long-standing 'traditional' occupation, since there have been sizeable numbers of old cars in Britain only in the past forty years or so. There are many communities in England and Wales whose economic mainstay has been coal mining for three or four times as long as that, but nobody has ever suggested that the members of those communities should expect to depend on social security in perpetuity after the mines have closed. Even if the ex-miners themselves are ill-prepared for alternative occupations, it is assumed that the next generation will become as capable of gaining employment as the rest of the population. 'A great deal of paternalism is embedded in the assumption that while "we" can survive change and innovation and endure the tensions created by modernity, "they" cannot; that "we" can repeatedly reinvent ourselves, our culture, our tradition, while "they" must adhere to known cultural patterns.'[121]

It might be held that to take a course of action that would rule out this mainstay of the gypsy economy in its current form would be an illegitimate interference in a minority culture. However, there is no requirement that minority cultures should be accommodated if there are sound environmental reasons to the contrary. Thus, all the rights bestowed on cultural minorities by the International Covenant on Civil and Political Rights are hedged around with the proviso that they are subject to 'restrictions...which are provided by law, are necessary to protect national security, public order, public health or morals, or the rights and freedoms of others, and are consistent with other rights in the Covenant'.[122] As a last-ditch defence of illiteracy, it might be argued that the Convention on the Rights of the Child declares that a child belonging to a cultural minority 'shall not be denied the right...to enjoy his or her own culture', and that illiteracy is an integral part of gypsy culture.[123] But even Poulter maintains that this cannot be used to confer immunity on 'the traditional practice of gypsies not to educate their children', because it conflicts with 'the unequivocally expressed right of all children to education' contained in that Convention and other international human rights documents.[124] Since those who have not been educated up to the minimum standard are essentially unemployable in the contemporary British economy, there is an overwhelming case for ensuring that the next generation of gypsies is not put in the position accepted fatalistically by Poulter in which the only alternatives are breaking up old cars and relying on social security.

Let us recall the central contention of Kukathas, which is that there are 'no cultural rights'. Appearances to the contrary, therefore, Kukathas is not proposing that there should be a special exemption from normal educational requirements for gypsy children. Rather, the implication is that the position should revert to that which obtained when Mill wrote *On Liberty*: it should be entirely at the discretion of the parents whether their children receive any education at all. I hope that the analysis developed so far in this chapter shows why no such unconditional right of parents over their children's education can be sustained. In the rest of this section, therefore, I shall focus on claims that fall under the rule-and-exception rubric rather than those deriving from an overall libertarian position such as that of Kukathas.

The communities whose claims to a special exemption from general educational requirements have found most favour with political theorists are those of the Amish. Even political theorists who are by no means uncritical supporters of multiculturalism have endorsed *Yoder*, following essentially the rationale of that decision: that, if the kind of makeshift schooling provided by the Amish suffices as preparation for participation in the Amish way of life, it must be counted as adequate. In arriving at its decision, the Court maintained for precisely this reason that the State of Wisconsin had no 'compelling interest' in requiring any more education than was already being provided. That was to take for granted the crucial assumption that the world for which Amish children needed to be prepared by their education was circumscribed by the Amish community. Yet 20 per cent of young Amish decide to quit the community before the ceremony of baptism that makes them liable to be 'shunned' for the rest of their lives if they defect thereafter. At the very least, it is surely clear that this reasoning simply ignores the interests of this minority in being prepared for life outside the Amish community. Nevertheless, the Court's line of thought has been echoed by both Stephen Macedo and Jeff Spinner. The former has suggested that the number of young Amish who leave each year is insufficient to trigger any concern for their preparation: 'If the defection rate were higher, of course, we would probably insist that Amish children be fully prepared for life in the wider society.'[125] On similar lines, Spinner says that 'if it became apparent that the Amish were not preparing their children for the lives they wanted to pursue – if the number of young adults leaving the community for mainstream society increased from a trickle to a stream – then the *Yoder* decision would have to be revisited.'[126]

I would regard 20 per cent of each age cohort as more a stream than a trickle. Accepting for a moment, however, that 20 per cent is below the threshold, let us imagine that the figure rose to 30 or 40 per cent. What I have so far quoted Macedo and Spinner as saying would appear to commit them to the proposition that this would be a reason for requiring the Amish to provide their children with an education designed to enable them to function effectively outside the community. Despite this, they also say that an increase would show there to be no need for a change in the educational status quo, because we could then deduce that it must be giving young Amish a real choice already. Thus, Macedo maintains that even the current defection rate entitles us to conclude that 'there appears to be a real, if constrained, "exit option" from the Amish community, and that should at least soften our anxieties about the Amish high school exemption.'[127] The obvious implication is that, if even more of each cohort left, we could safely set aside our anxieties altogether. Similarly, Spinner writes that 'the steady number of Amish that leave the Amish community shows that many believe that they have the ability to survive outside the Amish community'.[128] This, again, suggests that an increase in the defection rate would actually undermine the case for holding that the current system of Amish education is inadequate to prepare those who leave the community for life outside it.

In Joseph Heller's novel *Catch-22*, the eponymous catch was, it may be remembered, that it was possible to be excused from flying any more missions if you could prove that you were insane, but the desire not to fly any more missions was evidence that you were sane. Generations of young Amish are similarly caught by a variant propounded by Macedo and Spinner: if not many leave, that shows that they do not need a better education; if a large number leave, that also shows that they do not need a better education. Even more wonderfully, according to Macedo and Spinner, the present rate of defection has the property that it is too small to lead to the conclusion that those who leave should be better prepared for life outside the community and *at the same time* large enough to justify the conclusion that those who stay are not constrained to do so by lack of preparation for life outside the community.

This is absurd. No valid inferences can be drawn from facts about the proportion of each age cohort actually opting to leave. For the key issue is the voluntariness of membership of Amish communities, and that is not a question of numbers. It turns on a judgement about the extent to which it is possible to leave without incurring costs over and above those that necessarily flow from ceasing to live in the community in which one has been born and raised. If we take the view that the very limited kind of education received by Amish children puts those who leave at a severe social and economic disadvantage, then we may deduce the level of desperation that there must be from the fact that one-fifth of each cohort leave. If more left, we could deduce more desperation; if fewer left, we could deduce that the level of desperation must be lower. What we cannot say anything about on the basis of the numbers is the size of the barrier to exit.

Let us suppose that we came across an Amish community that nobody ever chose to leave. Macedo and Spinner would presumably conclude that the obstacles facing those who might wish to leave must be insurmountable. But we are not entitled to draw any such conclusion: the reason could simply be that belonging to this community is extremely attractive. What if it turned out that there were as a matter of fact quite severe impediments but that, even if there were not, nobody would leave anyway? If this could somehow be established, would it have the implication that it was unnecessary to insist that the impediments be removed? The answer is that membership in the group would still be non-voluntary, and this would make the authority that it exercised over its members illegitimate. If you are locked in a room, you are not free to leave it; and this is equally true whether you want to leave it or not. What matters is having the opportunity to leave. Like freedom, opportunity is (as I argued in chapter 2) not a desire-dependent concept. If nobody wants to leave the community, that is fine. But the only condition upon which a community should be able to exert as much control over its members' lives as the Amish do is that the option of exit should be genuinely open. Because of the high intrinsic and associational costs of leaving an Amish community, this is still of only limited value as a safeguard against abuse. But it is something that a liberal state can insist on, and it should do so.

The hypothetical case just posed draws attention to the distinctiveness of the argument from the prerequisites of voluntary membership. For it is not implausible that, if nobody ever left the community, the societal interest in education would be very attenuated. This is because the Amish are economically self-sufficient and take little part in public life except where the interests of their community are directly involved.[129] The state's paternalistic interest in what I have called education for living is not so easily disposed of. Nevertheless, if better and more extensive education would not result in anybody's choosing to leave the community, it could be said that the education received by Amish children now is education for living the lives they are going to live. This was, as we have seen, the reasoning of the Supreme Court in *Yoder*. Although it was unsatisfactory given the facts of the actual case, it might be thought to come into its own in this hypothetical case. Even if we were to accept that this was so, however, there would still remain the public stake in education constituted by the requirements of voluntary membership. And this is adequate in itself to underwrite the reversal of *Yoder*.

It is important to emphasize that the issue is not one of knowledge of alternatives. Both William Galston and Shelley Burtt suggest that, provided children are aware that alternative ways of life exist, that is sufficient to generate the conclusion that they are not unduly constrained by the education foisted on them by their parents. Thus, Galston writes that 'the basic features of liberal society make it virtually impossible for parents to seal their children off from knowledge of other ways of life'.[130] And Burtt claims that 'we can assume, given the high rates of defection from the Amish community, that even their "unworldly" teenagers become aware, very powerfully, of the life outside their closed community'.[131] Of course they are aware of it: indeed, some have recently imported it to the Amish heartland in Pennsylvania in the form of a drug ring. If you have been educated by the Amish, your job opportunities are very limited and you are restricted to the enjoyment of the most primitive forms of mainstream culture, that is to say comic books, network television and not too demanding films. You may still find this prospect more attractive than the Amish way of life, but that does nothing to mitigate the disabling effects of Amish education, both on your ability to earn a living and your ability to live well.

Burtt appears to take the view that the only significant aspect of a broad education in the sciences and humanities is that it reinforces 'the dominant secular culture'. As long as children are aware of this by seeing 'a tempting display of electronic games' in the 'windows of the local toy store' or 'hearing about the high school prom from the girl next door', they have, apparently, no need of this education.[132] 'Precisely because of the robust pluralism of our culture [illustrated by these phenomena], then, we would do better to encourage a parental environment filled with consistent, not conflicting, messages.'[133] Yet it is utterly crass to reduce the opportunity to become acquainted with the greatest achievements of the human mind and spirit to nothing but reinforcement of 'the dominant secular culture'. To the extent, indeed, that that culture promotes consumption as the highest value, what I have called education for living may plausibly be regarded as something of an antidote. It would be absurd to deny that there are certain basic prerequisites, in the form of time and money, for the pursuit of knowledge, the enjoyment of literature and the appreciation of the arts. But these are within the reach of most people, and once they are in place they make possible the attainment of goods that have no essential relation to the categories of getting and spending. There is no need to be priggish about all this: what I have called education for living does not preclude a relish for electronic games or dances; what it does do (if it works) is put them into perspective.

Unfortunately, it is just that sense of perspective that antagonizes the most fanatical American fundamentalist Christians. A much-discussed court case that illustrates the extravagant lengths to which some parents are prepared to go in order to limit their children's education is that of *Mozert* v. *Hawkins*.[134] This case arose when 'a group of fundamentalist Christian parents claimed a right to exempt their children from the basic reading curriculum of the Hawkins County, Tennessee, school system.... The parents objected to exposing their children to any idea that conflicted with their religious beliefs as based on the literal word of the Bible.'[135] Among the items to which they objected were 'a short story describing a Catholic settlement on the grounds that it teaches Catholicism' and 'a reading exercise picturing a boy making toast while a girl reads to him ("Pat reads to Jim. Jim cooks. The big book helps Jim. Jim has fun.")'[136] They claimed this ' "denigrates the differences between the sexes" that the Bible endorses'.[137] The *Mozert* parents also complained about 'an excerpt from Anne Frank's *Diary of a Young Girl* because Anne Frank writes in a letter to a friend that nonorthodox belief in God may be better than no belief at all' and 'a text that describes a central idea of the Renaissance as being "a belief in the dignity and worth of human beings" because that belief is incompatible with their faith'.[138]

Judge Lively, who wrote the opinion rejecting the claims of the *Mozert* parents, pointed out the fallacy upon which the claims rested: 'Exposure to something does not constitute teaching, indoctrination, or opposition of the thing exposed.'[139] Indeed, the ability to distinguish between a story about Roman Catholics and the advocacy of Roman Catholicism is one of the things an education should provide. The Tennessee schools had clearly failed the *Mozert* parents in this regard, and these parents were intent on transmitting the same lack of comprehension to their children. If the *Mozert* parents had deformed their children's bodies by restricting their ability to move freely, nobody (with the possible exception of Chandran Kukathas) would have any doubt that some public agency had a duty to intervene so as to protect the children from abuse. In exactly the same way, parents should not be able to get away with cramping their minds in the way that the *Mozert* parents wished.

The *Mozert* case settled only one point concerning parental rights over education. What it decided was that parents could not pick and choose what their children would be exposed to within the curriculum of a publicly run and publicly funded school. However, it was specifically noted, in an opinion concurring with the *Mozert* decision, that 'the children [more accurately, the parents] may resort to Christian schools or home schooling'.[140] And in fact a number of the children concerned in the case were taken out of the public schools and taught instead in 'Christian schools', presumably in a way sufficiently mind-numbing to satisfy even the exigent demands of the *Mozert* parents. Some others were subjected to 'home schooling', which enabled the parents to avoid the chance of even the smallest gap opening up between what the children were told at home and what they learned at school.[141]

Spinner is thus quite wrong to imagine that the *Mozert* case established that 'parents do not have the right to control the education of their children completely'.[142] On the contrary, the whole point of the concurring opinion from which I have just quoted was to emphasize the limited scope of the decision by calling attention to the right of the parents to withdraw their children from the public school system in pursuit of their educational goals. Gutmann's discussion of *Mozert* in the Epilogue to the second edition of *Democratic Education* is similarly misleading. In this, she argues against Galston's claim that the decision 'failed to recognize a constitutional right of the Mozert parents – based on their right of free exercise of religion – to exempt their children from the mandated reading curriculum of the public school that they attended'.[143] Against him, she maintains that 'the right to free exercise of religion does not entail the right of parents to near-exclusive or comprehensive authority over their children's schooling'.[144] But that absolute right is not denied if all she is prepared to say is that 'courts should not overturn the decisions of public school boards on matters of reasonable curricular requirements'.[145] What would have to be said (and is conspicuously not said by Gutmann) is that courts have to be equally willing to reject the claim that the 'right of free exercise of religion' underwrites the power of parents such as the Mozerts to make up for their failure to achieve their ends within the public school system by withdrawing their children from it and sending them to a 'Christian school' or educating them at home. For permitting this would be precisely to accept 'the right of parents to near-exclusive or comprehensive authority over their children's schooling'.

The impression that this omission is no slip of the pen is supported by Gutmann's treatment of the teaching of creationism in schools. The section of her book entitled 'Teaching Creationism and Civics' opens by saying that 'democratic communities should have a broad range of authority over education'.[146] However, the only question that she raises in this context is: 'May a school board mandate balanced treatment of creationism along with evolution within high-school biology classes?'[147] And it is quite clear that she does not intend this to be a question about high-school classes in all schools, since she identifies it with the question of what should be taught in the public schools.[148] It is worrying enough that Gutmann does not raise the crucial question: may a school board (or some other state agency) mandate the teaching of evolution in all schools? What is even more alarming is the rationale of her conclusion that the Constitution prohibits the teaching of creationism in the public schools. This is that either teaching solely creationism or even teaching it alongside evolution would amount to an 'establishment of religion', prohibited by the First Amendment. But in the nature of the case this can be an argument that applies only to what goes on in the public schools.

Gutmann does consider a reason for prohibiting the teaching of creationism that is not limited in its scope to public schools. This is that creationism is false. While she concedes that 'the scientific case against creationism is straightforward', she immediately qualifies this by saying that 'the democratic case is complex'.[149] (It turns out to be the argument from establishment.) As a consequence, she says, 'we cannot conclude that, having determined that the evidence favors evolutionary theory over creationism, "we will know what belongs in the classroom and what does not." '[150] Why not? I argued earlier that the possibility of democratic government depends upon shared criteria of rational discourse. Following a line of thought like this, Stephen Holmes has suggested that 'the [Supreme] Court's prohibition against creationist tampering with textbooks' might be seen as necessary to 'protect "reason" itself, rather than merely individual freedoms. How could the scientific method, in a minimal sense of the examination of embarrassing facts and the hearing of rival viewpoints, be overriden [sic] without undermining an essential element of democratic government itself?'[151] Holmes asks: 'if the Court must protect the conditions of democratic government, can it be oblivious toward truth inculcated in public schools?'[152] I fail to see how, if the conditions of democratic government are at stake, Holmes's conclusion should be restricted to public schools.

It is quite true, as the creationists like to say, that nobody was around when life began.[153] But if that makes evolution 'theory, not fact', the same may be said for the existence of Abraham Lincoln – and, a fortiori, Jesus – since nobody now alive was around when they are thought to have lived. It is, of course, logically possible that God created the universe ten minutes ago, complete with background radiation, fossils, written records and the memories encoded in our brains. But there is no reason for believing it to be so. The point is not simply that creationism is false. It is, rather, that there is no way of arguing for it that does not violate the most elementary canons of rational thought. It is not my concern here to ask if Holmes is right to conclude from this that the Supreme Court should prohibit creationism in the schools on the ground that teaching it undermines the conditions of mutually intelligible public discourse. What I do wish to claim is that the educational authorities of a state can quite properly take the view that creationism is too intellectually corrupting to be taught in any school, whether public or private.

An analysis by Albert Menendez of fundamentalist Christian textbooks offers an eye-opening picture of the kind of thing that goes on in their 'fast-growing private school constituency', and in 'home schooling' that is based on these textbooks.[154] Sticking with evolution for a moment, let us see what *Biology for Christian Schools*, the textbook put out by Bob Jones University, has to say. 'A major portion [of the book] consists of a refutation of the evolutionary process and a defense of Biblical Creationism. The author admits that this is a difficult and dangerous area. "Because Satan has used evolutionary theory effectively against Christians, they should know what they believe concerning this theory." '[155] The active role attributed to Satan here is scarcely surprising, since students are also told that 'Satan is in control of the physical world around us'.[156] They are also told, among other things, that 'the earth is not billions or even millions of years old' and that 'the genetic basis of biological evolution is statistically impossible'.[157] In literary studies, the *bête noire* of the *Mozert* parents, the Bible is again the touchstone. Students are warned: 'A reader must be careful not to allow the ideas presented in a literary work to determine his beliefs or be the basis of his perception of truth; all ideas should be tested in the light of God's word.'[158] Predictably, the only form of criticism of English or American authors that is contained in 'Christian' textbooks consists of assessments of the degree to which each author expressed the Word of God. Needless to say, scarcely any major figure in the past few centuries emerges with much credit; the only writers who receive approval are ones that (thankfully) nobody else has ever heard of.[159] History is treated in the same way. Thus, 'the United Nations is denounced as "unbiblical"'.[160] This is because 'its aim of eventual one-world government goes directly against the plans of God, Who dispersed the nations at the tower of Babel when they sought to unify (Genesis 11: 6–8).'[161]

It is impossible to convey in a handful of quotations the mind-destroying qualities of these textbooks. I do not think, however, that anybody who reads Menendez's book with an open mind will be in much doubt that young adults whose education had been drawn from 'Christian' textbooks would know less that is true and believe more that is false than an average well-educated and well-read northern European from the early eighteenth century. What is completely undeniable is that the products of 'Christian' education would have a far more impoverished appreciation of western literature than a well-educated person three centuries ago would have had. Of all the books available to such a person, the only book (apart from the Bible, of course) that the recipients of a 'Christian' education will have come across is probably *Pilgrim's Progress*; and of almost all subsequent authors they will know only that they were unreliable exponents of evangelical Protestantism. If there is any public stake in education, it must surely extend far enough to save children from this travesty.

I am not an expert on the American Constitution. It may be that the 'free exercise of religion' would be held to prevent States from closing down 'Christian' schools that teach from the books quoted here. A case which gutted Ohio's 'minimum standards for the operation of schools' might suggest this, since the decision 'found unreasonable' such unobjectionable standards as those 'requiring a determined amount of instruction in areas that do not lend themselves to the teaching of religious principles'.[162] However, the Supreme Court does not appear to have passed on such a case, and the *Smith* decision provides some encouragement for the hope that the current Court would rein in the more extravagant interpretations of the scope of 'free exercise' that have been favoured by its predecessors. If the American Constitution really does get in the way of sensible action by public authorities in relation to private education, that is too bad, but it does not in any way alter the conclusions to be drawn about the public stake in the education of all children. Other countries have no more reason for following the United States on schools than they have for following it on guns.

# PART III

---

## Multiculturalism, Universalism and Egalitarianism

# 7

## The Abuse of 'Culture'

### 1. 'It's a Part of My Culture'

Multiculturalists tend to be intellectual magpies, picking up attractive ideas and incorporating them into their theories without worrying too much about how they might fit together. In this chapter, I shall look at three claims about culture that are drawn upon by theorists of multiculturalism. The first is that it is some sort of defence of a practice to say that it forms an element in the culture of the group whose practice it is. I show in the rest of this section how surprisingly pervasive is this assumption – it can scarcely be dignified by being described as an argument. In response to the obvious objection that all we have so far is an anthropological observation, we get the claim that to justify a practice it is not necessary to demonstrate that it satisfies some universalistic criterion of value. All we need say – and, indeed, all we can say – is that, simply in virtue of forming part of the group's culture, it is essential to its well-being. I shall devote the second section to this idea.

Both of these appeals to culture depend (the first implicitly, the second explicitly) upon the notion that there is no common standard by which cultures, and the practices embedded in them, can be evaluated. This is logically incompatible with a third claim, which is that cultures are of equal value, or at any rate should be presumed or affirmed to be of equal value. Yet this inconsistency between cultural incommensurability and cultural equality does not prevent some theorists of multiculturalism from embracing both of them. In section 3, I shall take up in turn the presumption and the affirmation of equal value. I shall then in section 4 take up the contention that standard liberal rights cannot be defended except by invoking the notion that cultures are equally valuable. I shall argue that, so far from this being true, the idea that liberal rights have to rest on public acceptance of the equal value of cultures is actually a threat to those rights. The last two sections, 'The Limits of Conventionalism' and 'The Limits of Universalism', form a pair. The question that runs through both is: under what conditions is an appeal to local norms an adequate defence of their legal imposition?

Let us begin, then, with the assumption that the appeal to 'culture' constitutes some sort of justification in and of itself. In order to appreciate its peculiarity, let us think for a moment about the way in which people usually defend their actions when challenged to do so. Suppose you are asked to justify some action that you have performed. Your response will normally be to explain why you did it by calling attention to features of the action that made it the right thing to do in the circumstances. An outside observer may choose to say that you are appealing to your culture, in the rather banal sense that you have made use of your stock of ideas about what makes actions right or wrong, that you almost certainly share them with some other people, and that you were quite probably brought up with at least some of them. But this outside observation – by, perhaps, a visiting anthropologist – has no bearing on the logical structure of your defence of your action. What you are saying is that your action was right for such-and-such reasons. Since you have offered reasons, the person who challenged you to justify yourself can argue with you about whether they are good reasons or not. You can attempt to rebut his objections, of course, but what you cannot do without changing the subject is fall back on the claim that doing the action was part of your culture. There is nothing to prevent you from saying it, but when you do so you have ceased to engage in moral discourse and switched to the perspective of the anthropologist.

How could anybody seriously imagine that citing the mere fact of a tradition or custom could ever function as a self-contained justificatory move? Even as an explanation, it runs into problems because it comes close to tautology.[1] But as a justification it does not even seem to be the right kind of thing to do the job. Nevertheless, precisely this naked appeal to the fact of 'culture' as a justification is widespread and remarkably durable. Here is an example dating back to 1835, when Maori from the North Island of New Zealand invaded the Chatham Islands, five hundred miles to the east. This area was occupied by the Moriori people of the same original stock, who had become separated perhaps a millennium before and adopted a simple and peaceful way of living. The nine hundred Maori invaders, armed with guns, clubs and axes, 'attacked en masse. Over the course of the next few days they killed hundreds of Moriori, cooked and ate many of the bodies, and enslaved all the others, killing most of them too over the next few years as it suited their whim.'[2] One of the Maori 'explained, "We took possession ... in accordance with our customs and we caught all the people. Not one escaped. Some ran away from us, these we killed, and others we killed but what of that? It was in accordance with our custom." "[3]

This story illustrates, incidentally, what is wrong with the popular idea that a world in which each group adhered to its own norms would be bound to be a peaceful one. For the outcome would depend on whether the norms were peaceful or warlike. What made the encounter between the Moriori and the Maori so fateful was that it was a meeting between pacific norms and norms that underwrote warfare, slavery and extermination. Once they were all on shore,

> groups of Maori began to walk through Moriori settlements announcing that the Moriori were now their slaves, and killing those who objected. An organized resistance by the Moriori could still have defeated the Maori, who were outnumbered two to one. However, the Moriori had a tradition of resolving disputes peacefully. They decided in a council meeting not to fight back but to offer peace, friendship and a division of resources. Before the Moriori could deliver that offer, the Maori attacked en masse.[4]

The genocidal slaughter just described ensued.

Nowadays, indiscriminate slaughter is defended as 'part of our culture' not so much when the victims are fellow human beings (that is usually thought to need some other defence, however inadequate) but when the victims are other mammals. Consider, for example, the Canadian sealers.

> The London-based International Fund for Animal Welfare (IFAW) claims that seals are skinned alive on the ice after their penises [sold as aphrodisiacs] are removed. It also contends that baby seals continue to be killed, even though this practice was banned. The public relations kit being prepared by the sealers' association contains no images of seals, but it does contain a video featuring a sealer and his wife defending their way of life. 'My family has gone sealing for generations,' says Will Alyward of Newfoundland. 'It's a vital part of our culture.'[5]

Notice that the reporter falls into the trap of describing as a 'defence' what is nothing more than the mere statement of a fact. If somebody says 'We've been doing this for a long time', the right response may be 'Well, in that case it's high time you stopped doing it.'

Whales also suffer from the 'rights of minority cultures'. Thus, the Chukchi people of Russia's far north have been exempted for the past ten years from the international ban on whaling on the basis of 'the right to hunt whales when it is deemed a traditional part of their culture and diet'.[6] Their 'distant relatives across the Bering Straits in the United States, the Makah Indian tribe of Washington state' also demanded the right 'to kill five grey whales a year as part of their "cultural renaissance"'.[7] They succeeded in being granted by the International Whaling Commission 'permission in 1997 to catch 20 whales over five years', which presumably generates four-fifths of a cultural renaissance in the average year.[8]

We can appreciate how deep-seated is the 'cultural' defence by noticing that even those who would like to rescind the whaling exemptions already made and deny any new ones apparently accept that the 'cultural' case would be valid if its premises held. The response of Masha Vorontsova, a zoologist working for IFAW, to the Chukchi claim was as follows: 'Grey whales are not even an important part of the Chukchi diet and it's ridiculous to talk about a cultural need to kill them.'[9] On similar lines, Lennie Lonsdale of the (American) Environmental Investigation Agency is reported as having said of the corresponding Makah claim: 'There's no need for the Makah to kill whales because for decades they have done without whale meat in their diet.'[10] But the point is that *nobody* 'needs' to kill whales, whether or not this is 'part of their culture' or a customary part of their diet.

*Moby-Dick* reminds us how far whaling used to be the economic – and it would scarcely be too much to say the cultural – lifeblood of a number of towns in New England. When the whale population fell to the point at which whaling became uneconomic, the economy and the associated culture that had been based on whaling had to change. Today, there are powerful reasons, both conservationist and humanitarian, for a ban on whaling. The implication is that the remaining economies and cultures that involve whaling will have to adapt in the same way. It is worth noting, incidentally, that the 'cultural' defence of whaling cannot be confined to aboriginal peoples. If it is admitted at all, it allows the Norwegians to say that their traditional culture includes catching whales and the Japanese to say that their traditional culture includes eating them. Both of these claims are undeniably true.

Perhaps the most vigorous defender of aboriginal claims based on the appeal to 'culture' is James Tully. In his book *Strange Multiplicity*, he strongly commends the waiving of general rules for aboriginal peoples wherever the application of those rules would be incompatible with their being able to enjoy their culture in an unchanged form. According to him, the possibility of making exceptions under these conditions shows that it is possible to allocate rights 'so they do not discriminate against citizens' identity-related differences that can be shown to be worthy of protection'.[11] The casual reader might take Tully to be inviting some inquiry into the worth of the practice in question such as might be undertaken in relation to any practice: we would ask what there was to be said for it and what there was to be said against it. This, however, would be wholly contrary to Tully's intentions, because it would presuppose some criteria of worth external to the culture in which the practice is embedded. What Tully has in mind is a criterion internal to the culture: according to this, the worth of a practice is measured by its centrality to the culture.

Let me illustrate Tully's approach by taking up his discussion of a case that closely parallels those just discussed. This involved an appeal by a band of Native Americans against a fishing ban imposed in the interests of conservation. Tully tells us that the decision in their favour, which he applauds, turned on the finding 'that fishing a specific body of coastal water is constitutive of the cultural identity of the Aboriginal Musqueam nation'.[12] It is a necessary truth that, if fishing a certain body of water was part of Musqueam culture, a prohibition on fishing that body of water would have entailed some change in the culture. But this does not in itself make the change a threat to their 'cultural identity', unless we simply define 'cultural identity' so that it is destroyed by any change in the culture. That would be no more sensible than it would be to define 'personal identity' so that it was destroyed by any change in circumstances: moving house, taking a new job, getting married, and so on. To put it another way, if we make it a tautology that any change in a culture destroys the identity of that culture, then it is not an objection to change that it destroys cultural identity.

How might 'cultural identity' be defined so that it would be a serious count against a change in the way of life of a group that it would destroy its cultural identity? Suppose that the members of the group no longer recognized one another as the bearers of a common culture that was in some degree distinctive. That would surely mean that they had lost their cultural identity. Another possibility, which we might also describe as the loss of cultural identity, is that the authority of the group's norms might disappear, without their being replaced by another set of norms. This would reduce the group to the condition of a Hobbesian 'war of all against all'. If the ban on fishing was really needed to conserve fish stocks, the Musqueam may have won only a limited reprieve. Suppose that in a few years time there simply are no more fish. Will this result in the inability of the Musqueam to recognize one another as the bearers of a common culture? Or will their normative structure disintegrate, so that they descend into a 'war of all against all'? Perhaps so, but it seems unlikely. At the least, a lot more would have to be said to make it plausible than making the observation that fishing a certain stretch of water is a traditional practice.

The idea that aboriginal cultures are extraordinarily fragile is profoundly patronizing. Charles Taylor insists (as we shall see later) that we must recognize in all human beings an equal capacity for culture. I endorse that proposition, and simply wish to add that we should also attribute to all human beings an equal capacity for cultural adaptation. Of course, just as an equal human capacity for culture does not entail equal cultural achievement, so an equal human capacity for cultural adaptation does not entail that all cultures are equally well equipped to cope with change. But we can at least reject the idea that the elements in a way of life are so rigidly locked together that no part can change without causing the whole to disintegrate.[13] The attraction of this idea for many theorists stems from the belief that substantive conclusions can be drawn from the tautology that a change is a change, I conjecture.

Especially interesting for the light it throws on Tully's thinking is the account he offers of the much-discussed case of *Thomas* v. *Norris*. Thomas was by birth a member of the Salish Indian band, which occupies a reservation in north-western Canada. He had grown up off the reservation and continued to live off it. He had little knowledge of Salish culture and no interest in it. Despite all this, he was kidnapped by members of the band and forced to undergo the tribal initiation ritual. He successfully sued the perpetrators for assault, battery and false imprisonment. Tully approves of the court's decision in favour of Thomas, but only on the basis of an account of its rationale that makes the court's decision turn on the finding

> 'that the Spirit Dance, and more specifically the involuntary aspect of it, was not a central feature of the Salish way of life.' Therefore, 'the group claim to involuntarily initiate participants into the Spirit Dance could not override' the individual members' 'rights to be protected from assault, battery and false imprisonment.'[14]

We are given to understand by Tully that the crucial issue was the degree to which the initiation rite was a central feature of Salish culture. This implies that, had the court found that the initiation rite was central to the culture, Thomas would have lost his case, and rightly so.

For the present purpose, it does not matter whether the reasoning of the court is accurately represented by Tully or not. What is significant is that it is on the basis of this interpretation of what was at issue that he approves of the court's decision. And it is this kind of reasoning that he suggests ought to be deployed in all such cases. This is, he says, because it 'take[s] ... cultural differences into account'. The alternative approach, which Tully decries, is liberal constitutionalism, which applies notions of rights 'without taking these cultural differences into account'.[15] On this liberal approach – which Tully regards as crass and culturally insensitive – assault, battery and false imprisonment would be punishable offences regardless of the purposes that they might be held to serve.

It is an implication of the liberal position that any culture whose survival (in its existing form) depends upon recourse to assault, battery and false imprisonment is going to have to change. As Ian Shapiro has observed, 'some of the worst of what often (misleadingly) gets labeled interethnic violence is actually intraethnic violence that results when different parties seek to mobilize support in the same ethnic group'.[16] Commonly, the preliminary to taking on other groups is to eliminate 'disloyal elements' within the group, that is to say those who are opposed to bellicosity. Similarly, the beneficiaries of traditional (or pseudo-traditional) structures of authority are always liable to resort to violence against dissidents if they think they can get away with it. The job of a liberal state is to ensure, as far as possible, that they do not get away with it.

The theme of this section could be summed up in the slogan: '*Culture is no excuse*'. If there are sound reasons against doing something, these cannot be trumped by saying – even if it is true – that doing it is a part of your culture. The fact that you (or your ancestors) have been doing something for a long time does nothing in itself to justify your continuing to do it. In 1997 the British government proposed to set up a commission to regulate the routes of the annual 'marches' carried out by the Orange Order in Northern Ireland, so as to ensure that, as far as possible, these marches would go down streets where they would be welcome. The official response of the Order was: 'There is nothing in this legislation for us and we reject totally the thinking that allows our faith, tradition and culture to be treated with such contempt.'[17] Television interviews elicited briefer statements on the lines of 'We've always marched', as if that demonstrably created an unconditional right to march through areas occupied by Roman Catholics to celebrate the defeats of their ancestors by the ancestors of the Protestants.

The Ulster Protestants could, admittedly, have claimed with perfect accuracy that it was part of their culture to monopolize political power in the province, and to reinforce this symbolically by playing the national anthem on every possible occasion, making lavish use of the royal title and insignia (no other police force in the UK is 'royal', for example), and 'marching'. The Ku Klux Klan, like the Orange Order, could equally well claim to be an integral part of the local culture. If slave-owners in the South had had access to the currently fashionable vocabulary, they would doubtless have explained that their culture was inextricably linked with the 'peculiar institution' and would have complained that abolitionists failed to accord them 'recognition'. But this simply illustrates that the appeal to 'culture' establishes nothing. Some cultures are admirable, others are vile. Reasons for doing things that can be advanced within the former will tend to be good, and reasons that can be advanced within the latter will tend to be bad. But in neither case is something's being part of the culture itself a reason for doing anything.

## 2.  Up the Creek in the Black Canoe

Even if we accept that the naked appeal to 'culture' cannot possibly do duty as a justification for anything, we may still feel that something must have been left out. Surely there must be arguments in favour of sticking to traditional ways of behaving? There is, indeed, one such argument which is fine as far as it goes; but it does not go very far in aiding the multiculturalist cause, because it simply supports conservatism. Acting in ways that you have become used to has obvious advantages. Among a group, it keeps the costs of coordinating behaviour to a minimum: each person knows what to expect from others and what are the expectations of others. This is especially important in relation to informal norms (as against laws and public policies), because shifting from one set of societal norms to another is difficult. In the absence of some compelling reason for doing things differently, we go on doing them in the same way as we have in the past because it is less trouble to do that than to do anything else: 'cultures are conservative in the sense that institutions represent inertia.'[18]

In contrast, self-conscious traditionalism, as Jürgen Habermas has remarked, 'is itself a thoroughly modern movement of renewal'.[19] Its position is that the culture of each group is in some sense uniquely suited to it. Those who belong to the culture will never thrive unless they remain true to it and ensure that any developments that do occur maintain the purity of its spirit. This kind of ideological traditionalism also naturally gives rise to the idea of 'cultural renewal', understood as a deliberate attempt to revert to customary ways of acting that have fallen into desuetude. (Sometimes the traditions have really been lost, and then some invention will quite likely be passed off as a discovery.) There is an instructive contrast here with unselfconscious traditionalism, which is simply a force tending to reproduce, more or less faithfully, whatever exists. In the absence of deliberate attempts to freeze the status quo, some degree of cultural drift is bound to occur. Once the culture has changed, unselfconscious traditionalists will tend to perpetuate the modification, along with the rest of the culture. They will have no reason for wishing to engineer a cultural counter-revolution; on the contrary, any such deliberate change in the current set of practices would lose the advantage of spontaneous coordination that makes conservatism attractive.

We can see, then, that unselfconscious traditionalism offers only modest support for the appeal to culture as a justification for continuing to do what you are doing now, and none at all for invoking culture as a basis for making deliberate efforts to revert to what you (or your ancestors) used to do. This is because (to use a word of which multiculturalist theorists are fond) it does not 'valorize' culture. A change imposed from the outside, such as ceasing to fish a certain stretch of coastal water to conserve fish stocks, is disadvantageous from this point of view in as far as it has a disruptive effect on traditional practices around which social coordination has coalesced. But it has no deeper significance than that. As long as the disruptive effect is not too drastic, it can be regarded as a temporary inconvenience, and compared in those terms with the advantages (to these people and to others) that can be anticipated from the change.

If we want more potent medicine, we have to switch to self-conscious traditionalism. This certainly produces the desired results, but only those with strong stomachs will be able to keep it down. It 'valorizes' the concept of culture with a vengeance. The idea of culture upon which it rests was, in the words of Dennis Wrong,

> originally an expression of German nationalism and was deployed against the universalism of the French Enlightenment. The gist . . . was that . . . different people developed their own unique ways of life that could only arbitrarily be measured against a common standard. . . . Culture was identified with *Volks-geist*, or the spirit of the people, meaning their total way of life, especially the underlying ethos or mentality.[20]

The further twist that gives this idea of culture such potency is the idea, put about by writers such as Herder, that each *Volk* has a *Geist* that is uniquely suited to it: Germans, for example, should sternly resist cultural imports, which can only contaminate the purity of their ancestral culture. French ideas are good for the French, and German ideas are good for the Germans, but neither will prosper if they borrow from the other.[21] But why should the mere biological fact of German ancestry somehow make a human being incapable of living well except as a participant in German culture? The obvious answer is that Germans are a biologically distinct people, and that German culture is inherently suited to inborn German traits. Thus, as we saw in chapter 1, 'the thinkers of the Counter-Enlightenment . . . claimed that there was no universal human nature, and that human beings were not just contingently linked to their native cultures'.[22]

It is not hard to see how the German nationalist conception of culture provided fertile ground for the development of racial explanations of the course of history. But these racial theorists did not simply give romantic nationalism an explicitly physiological, pseudo-scientific cast: they also dropped its notion that cultures are incommensurable. Arthur Gobineau, one of the founders of modern racism, had no qualms about ranking races and their associated cultures: the title of his book, *The Inequality of Human Races*, says it all.[23] The Nazis, needless to say, took over this aspect of racialist thinking. Thus, it is incontrovertible, as Wrong says, that 'there was a direct temporal filiation between the German concept of culture and Nazi racial ideology'.[24] But it should be borne in mind that the notion of a biological basis to cultural differences can in principle be detached from the claim that some races and cultures are superior to others. There is no conceptual problem in holding to the idea that differences between cultures have a basis in physiological differences between human groups and at the same time maintaining that cultures are incommensurable.

As Todd Gitlin has pointed out, the rise of multiculturalism has been accompanied in some quarters by a revival of the idea that biology is fate, giving rise necessarily to differences in traits between groups.

> Many exponents of identity politics are fundamentalists – in the language of the academy, 'essentialists' – and the belief in essential group differences swerves toward a belief in superiority. In the hardest version of identity thinking, women are naturally cooperative, Africans naturally inventive and so on. These pure capacities were once muscled into submission by Western masculine force – so the argument goes – then suppressed by rigged institutions, and now need liberating.[25]

Even those who are officially opposed to racism are still liable to assume that biology is fate: 'The anti-racist celebrates Chicano identity and stands up for the particular rights of the Chicano, but these rights are available only to a person who was born to be a Chicano.'[26] An example that we came across in the previous chapter is the tendency to assign children with Hispanic surnames to Spanish-speaking classes even if they are more fluent in English than in Spanish. Cultural identity is, thus, attributed to people on the basis of descent. Gitlin has pointed out the irony of this idea's having been taken over by those who think of themselves as being on the political left. For it denies what has always before been the core belief of the left (whether in its liberal or socialist forms), the idea that there is a common emancipatory project equally available to the whole of humanity and equally valuable for all.

> Between Left and Right there has taken place a curious reversal. Throughout the nineteenth and twentieth centuries, the Left believed in a common human condition, the Right in fundamental differences among classes, nations, races. The Left wanted collective acts of renewal, the Right endorsed primordial ties of tradition and community against all disruptions.... Today it is the Right that speaks a language of commonalities. Its rhetoric of global markets and global freedoms has something of the old universalist ring. To be on the Left, meanwhile, is to doubt that one can speak of humanity at all.[27]

The doubt that one can speak of humanity at all surfaces in a rather bizarre fashion in James Tully's book *Strange Multiplicity*, which I have already mentioned. The whole book is constructed around the conceit that the claims of 'cultural recognition' can be represented by a large sculpture of a black canoe occupied by various animals from the mythology of 'the Haida nation of *Haida Gwaii* (the Queen Charlotte Islands) off the northwest coast of Great Turtle Island (North America)'.[28] This is for the most part harmless enough (if rather tedious), but in the last few pages of the book

Tully deploys the canoe sculpture to show what he thinks is wrong with contemporary liberal constitutionalism.

> Imagine the large father grizzly bear at the bow of the canoe addressing the other passengers. . . . He claims that the ways of the bear clan are superior to all the others in their civility or efficiency. Alternatively, he may claim that they are not bear ways at all, but universal ways that the bears, being at a higher stage, are able to discern. Or he confidently asserts that his articulation of the association comprehends and sublimates the constitutional ways of the others in a higher synthesis. The other passengers would accept these ways if they too were reasonable, if they would think through the following thought experiment, or if they would only speak in the language of constitutionalism he uses.[29]

Why are we inclined to agree immediately that this would be, as Tully claims, an 'injustice'? Simply because these creatures on the canoe belong to different species! We could imagine the raven, who sits at the helm, responding: 'It's all very well for you to say that everybody should live in caves and hibernate, but that wouldn't suit ravens at all. In fact, so much of our behaviour is hard-wired into us that the whole idea of deliberating about alternative ways of life is absurd.' (Of course, a raven capable of saying all that might be capable of anything, but let that pass.)

'If we now view ourselves as members of the black canoe', as Tully invites us to do, what carries over?[30] The answer is: precisely nothing. There is nothing intrinsically absurd in any of the argumentative strategies that Tully attributes to the mythological bear, once we substitute a human being for the bear. It is quite legitimate to hope that eventually a common standard of reasonableness will prevail over a certain range of ethical questions, in a way similar to that in which acknowledgement of the soundness of the physical sciences has diffused through the world. As Thomas Nagel has said, this is not, as critics of a largely imaginary 'Enlightenment project' such as Alasdair MacIntyre suggest, a matter of 'sweeping the boards and starting over with a few moral axioms "which would be found undeniable by all rational persons"'. Rather, 'there are no axioms, only questions that aim to be as widely comprehensible as possible, and answers of increasing sophistication that attract a wide range of agreement and disagreement, followed by further questions. The aim is to construct gradually a point of view that all reasonable persons can be asked to share.'[31]

The idea that there is one way to live that is best for bears, ravens and all other creatures is, obviously, absurd. But precisely because human beings are virtually identical as they come from the hand of nature – at any rate at the level of groups – there is nothing straightforwardly absurd about the idea that there is a single best way for human beings to live, allowing whatever adjustments are necessary for different physical environments. Disagreements will in fact arise because there are bound to be differences of opinion about what is the best way to live – what, for example, is the true religion, if any – and there is no known method of resolving such disagreements. But it is consistent with that to hold that the human situation is sufficiently uniform to make it possible to say that there are quite a number of things that every society ought to achieve if it is to provide a tolerably good life for all its members. Moreover, the very fact of irresolvable disagreement over the nature of the good life, once we get beyond the basics, is itself a premise in the argument for liberal institutions. For, in the face of these disagreements, what we need is a fair way of adjudicating between the conflicting demands that they give rise to. This is what liberalism offers. But saying that is to make a universalistic claim.

I am not suggesting that Tully literally believes that different cultural groups (such as Native American bands) actually are different species, or that cultural differences have a genetic basis. Nevertheless, the analogy is made to carry a good deal of argumentative weight. The heavy-handed irony at the expense of the grizzly bear's support for constitutional liberalism continues over several more pages after the passage I have quoted. Yet unless the analogy holds up in certain crucial (and highly disputable) respects, nothing follows from our agreeing that constitutional liberalism would be inappropriate to mediate relations between bears, ravens and all the other creatures on the canoe. It is not therefore surprising that Tully is among those who suggest that the case for saving species from extinction can somehow be carried over to provide support for the deliberate preservation of cultural diversity.[32]

The idea that people can flourish only within their ancestral culture accounts for the main features of romantic nationalism as it developed in the nineteenth century. Thus, nationalists have typically mistrusted the cities as hotbeds of cultural (and, according to taste, racial) hybridization. Even though nationalist intellectuals have normally come from the cities themselves (where else would they come from?), they have held up the peasantry as the repository of the soul of the people because peasants are presumed to have preserved intact the ancient folkways. Similarly, the quiddity of the ancestral culture is assumed to be contained in the ancient language, which nationalists painstakingly set about learning (and, to a greater or lesser degree, making up). This set of ideas explains how the term 'renaissance', instead of summoning up an image of the extraordinary creativity that was the European renaissance, is now associated with a reversion to the practice of killing a few whales each year. Similarly, it explains how the 'worth' of a practice is supposedly established simply by pointing to its 'centrality' to the culture in which it plays a role.

Why should we believe the premises from which these conclusions follow? Groups of human beings are not like the different species on board the black canoe, each genetically programmed to perform some distinctive behavioural repertoire. The fact that you or your ancestors have done something in the past is not in itself a good reason for going on doing it regardless of whether or not it was a good idea then, is a good idea now, or will ever be a good idea in the future. There are certain advantages to cultural inertia, especially where informal norms coordinate the actions of many people, but these are far from being sufficient to underwrite the key ideas underlying romantic nationalism.

## 3.   The Equal Value of Cultures

According to the doctrine of romantic nationalism, each culture constitutes a self-contained moral universe. For each of us, the horizons of our thought are set by the boundaries of our culture. Typically, romantic nationalists draw from this the conclusion that cultures are incommensurable, because there is no transcultural standpoint from which they could be compared. Strictly speaking, this assertion is self-refuting, for it is not a theorem of any particular culture – unless that culture has already been profoundly modified by widespread adherence to the doctrine of romantic nationalism. Since this kind of sophisticated historicism is relatively rare, we can be sure that most people have never had any qualms about using the criteria furnished by their own culture as a basis on which to reach judgements about the comparative worth of other cultures. The assertion that cultures are incommensurable is in fact a transcultural claim rooted in universalistic philosophical thinking. Moreover, it is so far from conforming to the maxim that cultures can be criticized only from within that it condemns virtually every culture's image of itself as a valid source of criteria for judging other cultures.

My business here is not, however, with problems internal to the notion of incommensurability. Whatever its pedigree, I believe that it should be rejected, and I shall give my reasons for this in section 6 of the present chapter. What I want to take up here is the idea that cultures are of equal value – or, at the very least should be affirmed to be of equal value or presumed to be of equal value. It should be apparent that this idea is logically incompatible with the idea that cultures are incommensurable. As Peter Jones has put it: 'Equal recognition . . . requires us to bring a common standard of value to all cultures and to believe that, whatever the appropriate standard is, cultures will perform equally when judged against it.'[33] In contrast to this, the claim of incommensurability constitutes an explicit denial of the possibility of making the sort of comparative judgement that the claim of cultural equality embodies.[34]

In response to Wittgenstein's gnomic utterance in the *Tractatus*, 'Whereof one cannot speak thereof one must be silent', Frank Ramsey offered the splendid comment: 'What we can't say we can't say and we can't whistle it either.' This admonition is as often as not ignored by contemporary proponents of incommensurability. Thus, for example, John Gray takes the standard Counter-Enlightenment line made familiar by de Maistre that 'the philosophical anthropology of the Enlightenment' was defective, urging against it 'that human identities are always local affairs, precipitates of particular forms of common life, never tokens of the universal type of generic humanity'. Thus, 'there is no impartial or universal standpoint from which the claims of all particular cultures can be rationally assessed. Any standpoint we adopt is that of a particular form of life and of the historic practices that constitute it; it is the expression of a human identity that is historically specific, not of one that is universally and generically human.' This is, Gray says, an expression of 'the central thesis of value-pluralism, which is that of the constitutive uncombinability and incommensurability of values'.[35] On this 'pluralist view', he says, 'neither liberal rights nor the democratic project has any special status'.[36] At the same time, however, Gray tells us that 'if value-pluralism is true the range of forms of genuine human flourishing is considerably larger than can be accommodated within liberal forms of life'.[37] But if value-incommensurability is true, we can't say any of that, and we can't whistle it either. For it involves making precisely the kinds of comparison that the thesis of incommensurability rules out in principle. Gray correctly claims that 'value-pluralism cannot mandate liberalism', because we cannot say that liberal societies are better than others. But we also cannot say, as Gray does, that non-liberal societies 'do as well *or better*'.[38]

Not surprisingly, Charles Taylor's approach is a good deal more subtle than this. Unlike Gray, he does not suggest that incommensurability actually entails the judgement that a lot of extremely different cultures all must conduce to human flourishing. But he still tries to whistle a tune about the equal value of cultures while at the same time continuing to sing the old song about incommensurability. As an avowed disciple of Herder, Taylor naturally has recourse to the doctrine of incommensurability when it suits his purpose, and we shall see later in this chapter that much of what he says in his essay on 'The Politics of Recognition' depends crucially on an appeal to the incommensurability of cultures.[39] Yet he also in that essay evinces a considerable sympathy for the notion that cultures can be said to have equal value.

Taylor intimates that we shall be able to appreciate the inherent attractiveness of the idea that all cultures have equal value if we follow through the following train of reasoning. The first step in the argument asks us to agree 'that all humans are equally worthy of respect'. According to Taylor, our intuitions – backed by a line of philosophical thought reaching back to Kant – tell us that 'what is picked out as of worth here is a *universal human potential*, a capacity that all humans share'. The next move is to say that the basis of the politics of difference is 'the potential for forming and defining one's own identity, as an individual, and also as a culture. This potentiality must be respected equally in everyone.'[40] This still does not get us to the claim of cultural equality. Getting there requires us to take a further step and 'accord equal respect to actually evolved cultures'.[41] But why should we take this step?

Undoubtedly, the claim that all *human beings* are entitled to equal respect is an assertion of fundamental equality that lies at the heart of egalitarian liberalism. But what Taylor has in mind is something quite different: that 'even to entertain [the] possibility' that some cultures might be 'less valuable than others' is 'to deny human equality'.[42] Ultimately, Taylor rejects this demand and falls back on something weaker: a 'presumption' of equal value.[43] Even on the basis of this, though, Taylor still manages to make extraordinarily heavy weather of a remark that he attributes to Saul Bellow (while admitting that he has no basis for doing so) to the effect that 'When the Zulus produce a Tolstoy we will read him.'[44] Contrary to Taylor, how-ever, I suggest that this cannot reasonably be objected to on the basis of anything less than the strong claim of cultural equality. Indeed, leaving aside mere abuse (Bellow's remark is said to show 'the depths of ethnocentricity'), what Taylor has to say in the way of argument on this point is remarkably feeble.

Taylor makes two points against Bellow. One is that he is 'assuming that [the Zulus'] contribution is yet to be made (*when* the Zulus produce a Tolstoy ... )'.[45] However, Taylor does not himself offer any candidates for the role of a Zulu Tolstoy. It is hard to see why Bellow should be faulted for thinking that there has not yet been one if (as we must assume) Taylor, driven by his commitment to the presumption of cultural equality, has searched in vain. Taylor's other complaint is that Bellow makes 'the implicit assumption that excellence has to take forms familiar to us: the Zulus should produce a *Tolstoy*'.[46] But why should we read into Bellow's remark any assumption about what Zulus may or may not have achieved outside the sphere of novel-writing? If I were to say that the Irish have not produced a Hobbes (or even a Locke), do I fail some test of cultural sensitivity if I fail to add immediately that there have, of course, been a number of admirable Irish playwrights?

Since Bellow's remark is apocryphal, let me fill in the context in which it undoubtedly occurred – if it did occur. We have to imagine somebody saying to Bellow that he ought to read novels by Africans simply *qua* Africans, or perhaps (and this would avoid the impression given by the use of the plural that Bellow suffers from delusions of grandeur *à la* Thatcher) the context was the preparation of the reading list for a course on the novel. Either way, the contrast is between my telling you that you ought to read Latin American novelists in pursuit of some supposed duty to regulate your reading habits by geographical quotas and my telling you that you ought not to neglect such excellent writers as Gabriel Garcia Màrquez or Mario Vargas Llosa.

Taylor offers the less than blinding insight that 'to approach, say, a raga with the presumptions of value implicit in the well-tempered clavier would be forever to miss the point'.[47] But anyone who approached the music of, say, Harrison Birtwistle with these presumptions would be a great deal more baffled than they would ever be by any raga. In fact, there can surely never have been any civilization in the history of the world that has been as culturally omnivorous as that of the West in the past century or so. No other culture has ever ranged so far in time and space in search of ideas and artefacts or made such serious efforts to understand the contexts in which they were produced. Compared to almost any previous peoples that have ever existed, we are all historicists now. In the end, however, as even Taylor is driven to admit, we must speak as we find. In the words of Robert Hughes: 'we know that one of the realest experiences in cultural life is that of inequalities between books and musical performances and paintings and other works of art.'[48] Generalizing from this, it is clear that some societies have created more valuable ideas and artefacts than others. In the same way, we are bound to judge that some cultures (in the anthropological sense of 'culture') are better than others: more just, more free, more enlightened, and generally better adapted to human flourishing.

In the rest of this section, I shall move on from Taylor's 'presumption' that all cultures have equal value to the alternative, and stronger, demand that the cultures of different groups must be publicly affirmed as being of equal value. In a number of slightly variant formulations, this idea turns up repeatedly in the work of those who support the 'politics of difference'. Thus, Iris Young writes: 'Groups cannot be socially equal unless their specific experience, culture, and social contributions are publicly affirmed and recognized.'[49] And Tully argues that 'one of liberalism's primary goods' is 'individual self respect'. But, he goes on,

> the social basis of this threshold sense of self respect is that others recognise the value of one's activities and goals.... Since what a person says and does and the plans he or she formulates and revises are partly characterised by his or her cultural identity, the condition of self respect is met only in a society in which the cultures of all members are recognised and affirmed by others, both by those who do and those who do not share these cultures.[50]

Tully claims that 'some liberals now see the error of their ways'.[51] But the context suggests that he has in mind Will Kymlicka as the chief exhibit, and I challenged Kymlicka's liberal credentials in chapter 4. Tully also maintains that John Rawls, because he makes self-respect one of the 'primary goods' whose distribution is the concern of social justice, is thereby committed, even if he does not realize it, to endorsing Tully's programme for the public recognition and affirmation of all cultures.[52] This claim, however, rests on a multiple misapprehension of the nature of Rawls's theory of justice. It is quite true that, in *A Theory of Justice*, Rawls says that a person's self-respect requires that 'the activities that are rational for him are publicly affirmed by others'. Taken in isolation, this certainly sounds like what Tully is demanding. But the sentence reads as a whole as follows: 'It normally suffices [to ensure self-respect] that for each person there is some association (one or more) to which he belongs and within which the activities that are rational for him are publicly affirmed by others.'[53] Thus, the 'public' whose 'affirmation' Rawls regards as sufficient can be as limited as the members of the same sect, communal group, and so on. As Daniel Weinstock puts it, 'though their ends might not be admired or affirmed by all other citizens... nonetheless [people] can come into association with a sub-class of citizens with whom they are sufficiently in tune for their ends to get affirmed within this more limited community.'[54] We can see, therefore, that Rawls is actually saying the exact opposite of what Tully wants him to say, in that Tully insists on the need for 'a society in which the cultures of all members are recognised and affirmed by others, *both by those who do and those who do not share those cultures*'.[55]

In fact, contrary to Tully's claim, Rawls does not describe self-respect as one of those 'primary goods' whose distribution forms the subject-matter of a theory of social justice. What he does say, which is quite a different matter, is that among the 'primary goods' are 'the social bases of self-respect'. These are the equal civil and political rights that cash out the concept of equal citizenship and in addition whatever material resources are required to enable people to take advantage of those rights. Egalitarian liberals are undeniably committed to all this, but it has no connection with the notion that a whole society must be orchestrated so as to confer on each person an equal share of the good opinion of others, regardless of what those others really think about their beliefs or conduct. Rawls maintains, indeed, that a society instantiating his two principles of justice would have done all that was necessary to ensure the appropriate distribution of the 'social bases of self-respect'.[56] It can be, and has been, argued that Rawls's principle for the distribution of economic resources, the difference principle, may under some circumstances be compatible with a degree of inequality that would undermine the promise of 'the social bases of self-respect' for all. The difference principle says that the worst off should be as well off as possible. It thus sets no limits to permissible inequality, yet it is plausible that, beyond a certain point, material inequality subverts the equal status of citizens. That, however, is an intramural argument among egalitarian liberals, who share the premise that justice – in relation to self-respect as much as anything else – concerns the distribution of rights and resources.

There are two objections to the demand for equal recognition of all cultures. One is simply that it shifts into the realm of public control matters that should be left to individual judgement. The notion that everybody should be entitled to an equal ration of 'recognition' cannot be accepted by those who attach any value to individual liberty. In a liberal society, common legal status as a citizen should, ideally, be translated into equal treatment in everyday transactions. Shop assistants should treat all customers alike, whether they are black or white, male or female; conversely, customers should treat all shop assistants alike. Who sits and who stands on a crowded bus should depend on age or disability but not on ascribed characteristics. And so on. As Nancy Rosenblum has remarked, this kind of equal treatment

> always required self-discipline, but the discipline involved in treating people similarly was modest. For one thing, men and women could see its utility; uniform and simple forms of civility greased the wheels of democratic society, facilitating social mobility. More important, it was not morally onerous because it was not supposed to reflect our *real* sentiments about whether individuals or groups warrant our respect, or whether we think they have grounds for respecting themselves.[57]

In contrast, as Rosenblum says, 'the politics of recognition...looks for specific attestations of appreciation, or deference'.[58] Thus, the differentiated treatment of others according to their group membership that was characteristic of hierarchical societies re-emerges in a new form: 'The recognition claimed is not for social class or status, to be sure, but for defining elements of personal identity, for past or present suffering, or for group merits and accomplishments – the worth of one's culture.'[59]

The illiberal implications of the proposal to make 'recognition' a moral imperative are brought out very clearly by Iris Young. Thus, the central plank in Young's platform (and her own claim to originality) is the need to displace what she calls the 'distributive paradigm' of social justice.[60] 'Injustice should be defined primarily in terms of oppression and domination. The scope of justice . . . is not limited to distribution, but includes all social processes that support or undermine oppression, including culture.'[61] As the 'most general' of the 'nondistributive issues', culture 'includes the symbols, images, meanings, habitual comportments, stories and so on through which people express their experience and communicate with one another'.[62] What this means is, as we saw in chapter 1, that nothing less than a 'cultural revolution' is required to bring about justice. As Young puts it, 'no aspect of everyday life would be exempt from reflection and potential criticism –

language, jokes, styles of advertising, dating practices, dress, norms of child-rearing, and countless other supposedly mundane and trivial elements of behavior and comportment'.[63] Moreover, it is not simply a question of 'reflection and potential criticism'. For Young also tells us that 'no social practices or activities should be excluded as improper subjects for public discussion, expression, or *collective choice*'.[64] Thus, as Robert Fullinwider has commented, 'these "private choices" ought to be subject to political intervention and modification'.[65]

The second objection to the demand of equal recognition of all cultures is that, although a lot of damage could be done by an attempt to implement Young's 'cultural revolution', it could not actually be achieved. This is because the proposal is logically incoherent. The inescapable problem is that cultures have propositional content. It is an inevitable aspect of any culture that it will include ideas to the effect that some beliefs are true and some false, and that some things are right and others wrong. The demand for cultural equality runs into conceptual problems of a kind that are not inherent in the demand that we should find equal value (or any value at all) in every cultural artefact such as a painting. This is, indeed, an absurdly inappropriate demand. But the reason is simply that, unless discriminations are made, ascribing value to something ceases to have any point. It is true that a state could decide to treat all paintings *as if* they were of equal value, and buy them indiscriminately by the square foot. The Dutch government did for a time have exactly such a policy, but it still could not overcome the problem that people would insist on making discriminations. Even when this abundance of 'art' was offered free of charge to schools and hospitals, almost all of it was rejected, leaving the government with the upkeep of large air-conditioned warehouses full of paintings that it literally could not give away.[66]

As we saw in chapter 3, Young's notion of treating all groups equally would amount to a generalization of the Dutch scheme, in accordance with the Dodo's dictum: 'Everybody has won, and *all* must have prizes.' Even if this demand is (as I argued) misguided, it is at least logically coherent. We can imagine a possible world in which the state of affairs called for had been realized: it would be one in which public policies had brought it about that all groups had equal overall success rates. As we can now appreciate, Young herself sees this proposal as merely one element in the pursuit of equal respect for all group cultures. But this demand for 'recognition' all round raises problems about its intelligibility, as well as its feasibility and its desirability.

Thus, suppose we were to 'recognize and affirm' the culture of the *Mozert* parents so as to prop up their self-esteem. That entails that we affirm the value of their views (and those of the wider community of 'born again' Southern Baptists) about the sinfulness of homosexuality. But then how do we simultaneously affirm the value of a gay lifestyle? As Fullinwider has asked:

> Why, for example, should I respect the Southern Baptist who believes I am damned for not practicing his brand of religion? Why should I respect his belief? And why should he reciprocally respect my contempt for his benighted superstition? Why should Young respect fellow citizens in virtue of rather than in spite of their misogyny? In any society of size there are bound to exist groups loathsome and contemptible from our particular points of view. An ideal that calls for each of us to respect all others in virtue of their differences is otherworldly.[67]

I wish to add that it is not simply psychologically unattainable but logically impossible. We cannot simultaneously affirm everybody's culture. Peter Jones has put the point succinctly: 'People are allowed to believe in the worth of their own culture, including the beliefs and values that it embodies, yet they are also required to believe that others' cultures, embodying different and conflicting beliefs and values, are of no less worth. How can we expect people to embrace that absurdity?'[68] Only, it seems fair to surmise, with a great deal of encouragement from the Politically Correct Thought Police.

## 4. Does Equal Treatment Require Equal Value?

Iris Young, as we have seen, wishes to displace what she calls 'the distributive paradigm' from its central position by restricting the scope of the concept of distributive justice to the distribution of 'wealth, income and other material goods'.[69] The concept of distributive justice should not be regarded as relevant to 'the distribution of such nonmaterial goods as power, opportunity, or self-respect'.[70] I agree that self-respect is not an appropriate subject of distributive justice, but that is simply because self-respect (as against the 'social bases of self-respect') is not an appropriate subject of collective action. But if Young is correct about other 'nonmaterial goods', virtually every argument made in this book has been invalid. For I have throughout identified liberalism with a set of principles that lead to a demand for equal rights and equal opportunities.

Fortunately, however, Young's arguments are remarkably weak. Thus, she says that Rawls and others conceive of justice as being concerned with the distribution of rights. 'But what does distributing a right mean? One may talk about having a right to a distributive share of material things, resources, or income. But in such cases it is the good that is distributed, not the right.'[71] This is simply not so. The subject of distributive justice here is the distribution of rights to income and property. If there is something wrong with the notion that we can talk about a distribution of rights, then property rights are vulnerable too. 'Rights', Young tells us, 'are relationships, not things; they are institutionally defined rules specifying what people can do in relation to one another.'[72] Quite so; and this applies to property rights as much as to any other rights. To say that 'rights are not fruitfully conceived as possessions' is incoherent.[73] For possession is a source of rights in exactly the same sense as ownership is. Both are equally creatures of law. All of social, political and economic life is relational in some sense or other. But that does not mean that there is anything mistaken in saying that people 'have rights'. Indeed, Young is unable to avoid falling into that way of talking herself: what other locution could she employ?

We are still left with the question: what is supposed to be wrong with the notion of rights being equal or unequal? Why should we not say, for example, that all citizens have an equal right to vote if every citizen has one vote and that they do not have an equal right to vote if either some citizens do not have the right to vote or some citizens have more than one vote? The only objection that Young has to make is based on the unargued presumption that we can talk about distribution only where there is some fixed amount of 'stuff' to be divided up. To avoid any accusation of slighting Young's argument on this point, I reproduce it in full.

> What can it mean to distribute rights that do not refer to resources or things, like the right of free speech, or the right of trial by jury? We can conceive of a society in which some persons are granted these rights while others are not, but this does not mean that some people have a certain 'amount' or 'portion' of a good while others have less. Altering the situation so that everyone has these rights, moreover, would not entail that the formerly privileged group gives over some of its right of free speech or trial by jury to the rest of society's members, on analogy with a redistribution of income.[74]

But why must all references to a distribution as equal or unequal have to manifest that particular feature of a distribution of income? Clearly, Young is committing here the fallacy of *petitio principii*: she assumes her conclusion, that the distribution of income is the paradigm of distributive justice, as the premise in her argument for that conclusion. I can see nothing in what she says that should deter us from continuing in the belief that it makes perfectly good sense to say that there is either an equal or an unequal right to free speech or a jury trial, depending on whether everybody has it on the same terms or not.

'Talk of distributing opportunities involves a similar confusion.'[75] This turns out to be only too true in that Young simply makes all the same points about opportunity that she has made about rights, and they are equally misguided. The only novelty is a different version of the same *petitio*. Thus, Young says, quite reasonably, that 'male children and female children, working-class children and middle-class children, Black children and white children often do not have equally enabling educational opportunities even when an equivalent amount of resources has been devoted to their education.'[76] But she draws the following curious conclusion from it: 'This does not show that distribution is irrelevant to educational opportunity, only that opportunity has a wider scope than distribution.'[77] Obviously, it shows this if we have already assumed to begin with that 'distribution' can refer only to the distribution of (economic) resources – yet this is precisely the point that the argument is supposed to be establishing! If we do not make that assumption, we shall simply wish to draw the conclusion that there is more to equal educational opportunity than financially equal inputs. We have no difficulty in recognizing that enabling a deaf or blind child to have the same chance of achievement as a child with normal hearing and sight is bound to require more resources. The same must be true of children with specific learning problems such as dyslexia or attention deficit disorder. It is surely reasonable to extend this line of thought to children who simply come to school from homes that provide them with fewer of the skills that make for educational success.

What is Young's alternative to the 'distributive paradigm'? It is the idea that liberal rights are of little significance in the absence of an 'affirmation' of a way of life that they protect. Thus, in her discussion of homosexuality, Young perpetuates the standard anti-liberal myth (disposed of in chapter 4) that liberalism is obsessed with a 'private sphere', suggesting that 'the typical liberal approach to sexuality... tolerates any behaviour as long as it is kept private'.[78] The standard liberal view is, it is true, that homosexual sex should be legal if it occurs between consenting adults in private; but that simply puts homosexual sex on exactly the same footing as heterosexual sex, which is likewise legal if it occurs between consenting adults in private. There is, indeed, nothing in liberal principles that says public sex should be illegal – that is a matter of 'the way we do things here', an idea whose scope I shall discuss below. What liberal principles say is that the rules about public sex, whatever they are, should not discriminate. Similarly, the age of consent should be the same for homosexual as for heterosexual sex. Beyond that, however, there is no liberal principle calling for the public concealment of homosexual identity. On the contrary, just as liberals have insisted that public displays of interracial affection should be permitted, regardless of the outrage that they may cause in some quarters, so they insist that public displays of homosexual and heterosexual affection should be treated equally by the law.

For Young, however, legal rights that would give homosexuality and heterosexuality equal standing in law are 'merely civil rights'.[79] What 'most gay and lesbian liberation advocates seek' is not these but 'the affirmation of gay men and lesbians as social groups with specific experiences and perspectives'.[80] There is nothing to prevent anybody who wishes to engage in 'affirmation' from doing so: the framework of liberal laws will certainly place no barriers in the way, provided that the usual requirements of public order are adhered to. But why should anybody who does not wish to join in have to do so? As liberals, we can demand equal treatment, including the extension of anti-discrimination legislation to cover discrimination based on sexual orientation and the revision of rules about pensions, benefits, rights of next of kin, and so on. But we cannot say that public officials should be obliged to make announcements in their official capacity about the equal value of a homosexual way of life. Nor can we try to prevent those who believe homosexuality to be sinful or immoral, or who believe a homosexual way of life to be inferior to a heterosexual one, from saying so in public and seeking to win others over to their way of thinking.

Those who demand public 'recognition' of a gay lifestyle help themselves freely to the word 'homophobia' to describe disapproval or disparagement of homosexuality. Since a phobia is, by definition, an irrational fear (and one whose irrationality is normally recognized by the victim of the phobia), this way of talking creates a whole analysis of the phenomenon without any need for recourse to argument. If disapproval of homosexuality is psychologically akin to the irrational fear of spiders, the remedy is inevitably some kind of therapy. And for those who are not obliging enough to sign up for it, it had better be administered through every available public channel. However, we must presumably count adherence to one of the monotheistic religions as rational – certainly multiculturalists can scarcely afford to deny this, committed as they are to 'equal respect'. Then we must concede that Jews, Muslims and Christians all have scriptural authority for the condemnation of homosexuality. What this suggests is that the need is not for therapy but rather for persuasive arguments about the interpretation of sacred texts in the light of subsequent knowledge or changes in circumstances.[81]

Young plays up the importance of 'affirmation' at the expense of liberal rights but still appears to accept the need for them. Yet she does not explain exactly how we are to justify these rights without resorting to the 'distributive paradigm' which would enable us to appeal to a principle of equal treatment. The question of the relation between 'affirmation' and rights receives more attention in the work of Nancy Fraser, whose overall approach has some similarities to that of Young. Thus, in her article 'From Redistribution to Recognition? Dilemmas of Justice in a "Post-Socialist" Age', she says that there are two ends of the 'conceptual spectrum'. One is distribution, understood à la Young as concerned only with material goods, and the other is 'recognition'. Homosexuality, according to

Fraser, can be interpreted as 'approximately the ideal type' of a 'cultural-valuational' issue.[82]

> Thus, any structural injustices [the] members [of the group] suffer will be traceable ultimately to the cultural-valuational structure. The root of the injustice, as well as its core, will be cultural misrecognition, while any attendant economic injustices will derive ultimately from that cultural root. At bottom, then, the remedy required to redress the injustice will be cultural recognition, as opposed to political-economic redistribution.[83]

Clearly, what this crude dichotomy squeezes out is the possibility that the answer is 'neither of the above': the possibility that the injustice suffered by homosexuals is the lack of equal legal rights – rights that no doubt have financial implications but are not captured by the category of 'political-economic redistribution'. Autocracy, repression and persecution are not reducible to economic inequality, but no more are they perspicuously classified as 'cultural misrecognition'. We already have a perfectly good vocabulary for describing various ways in which the distribution of rights and powers can take obnoxious forms.

It follows from Fraser's premises that the position of homosexuals can improve only as a result of what Young would call a 'cultural revolution'. Thus, she says,

> overcoming homophobia and heterosexism requires changing the cultural valuations (as well as their legal and practical expressions) that privilege heterosexuality, deny equal respect to gays and lesbians, and refuse to recognize homosexuality as a legitimate way of being sexual. It is to revalue a despised sexuality, to accord positive recognition to gay and lesbian sexual specificity.[84]

As in much literature of this kind, Fraser moves on after saying this to other matters, leaving us to speculate about the precise forms that she would imagine this 'recognition' to take, the political means that she thinks would be needed to bring it about, and the way in which she thinks a legislative majority could be put together (in the United States, for example) to implement these measures. However, there is no need to pursue these questions, because the basic objection to the thesis is that it gets everything back to front. More liberal attitudes to homosexuality (and similarly to abortion) have followed permissive legislation rather than preceding it. Those who deprecate such liberal attitudes have been shrewder sociologists than the theorists of 'recognition'. Their understanding that liberal reforms were likely to cause changes of opinion in a liberal direction has fuelled their opposition to the reforms that have occurred, and it continues to animate their opposition to further reform. What Fraser relegates to parentheses –

the establishment of complete legal equality for homosexuals – is the only thing that is within the scope of legitimate political intervention. Fortunately, evidence from even the imperfect moves towards legal equality that have occurred already indicates that it is enough to eliminate over time the stigmatization of homosexuality.

Fraser's ideas are bad politics as well as bad sociology. One obvious respect in which this is so is that, if legal reform had to wait on the conversion of most of the population to a belief in the 'equal validity' (as it is often put) of a homosexual and heterosexual way of life, it might have to wait much longer than if the case for equal rights were pressed on the basis of the requirements of equitable treatment. Moreover, to the extent that Fraser envisages, like Young, some sort of state-sponsored 'affirmation' campaign (and it is difficult to see what else she is talking about), it is impossible to see where sufficient political support for this would come from unless two conditions were met. First, a majority of the population would already have to have been converted to upholding 'equal value'; and, second, not too many of them would have to have principled reservations about the legitimacy of a campaign by the state to promote 'equal value'. Clearly, it is not very likely that both of these conditions will be fulfilled together. But it may be observed that, provided the first condition is met, no campaign will be needed. For its objectives will already have been achieved.

It is easy to see that the strategy supported by Young and Fraser is unwise, as a sheer matter of practical politics. Thus, in Britain there was a campaign in 1998 to make the age of consent the same for homosexual and heterosexual relations. The cause received a setback when those campaigning for reform, not content to present the issue as one of elementary equity, insisted that it should be seen as an aspect of the public affirmation of the equal worth of a homosexual lifestyle. (In the event, the homosexual age of consent was lowered, but not all the way to sixteen, the age of consent for heterosexual relations.) Again, in the United States, where in some of the States sodomy is still on the statute books as a serious criminal offence, the Christian Right (aided and abetted by Republican politicians, some sincere and some opportunistic) has been able to make headway in opposing the enactment of equal rights for homosexuals by capitalizing on their opponents' claim that the whole point of equal rights is to make a public affirmation of homosexuality. Thus, *The Weekly Standard*, a conservative American magazine founded in 1995 by Rupert Murdoch, called 'in one article in late 1996, for the "reaffirmation by states of a sodomy law" that would imprison gay men for private sex as a counterstrike against the threat of same-sex marriage'.[85]

By raising the stakes, Young and Fraser and those who think like them put at risk the survival of the liberal rights that have already been won and even more their extension so as to complete the movement towards legal equality. If 'merely civil rights' are disparaged as worthless in the absence of a 'cultural revolution', they are liable to be swept away by a cultural counter-revolution. In the United States especially, it is clear that cultural conservatism is a far more potent force politically than the cultural radicalism espoused by Young and Fraser. Writing in October 1998, William Sullivan pointed out that

> the issues that are driving the Republican base this fall have little to do with economics or politics or national security. They are issues of morals: infidelity and honesty, abortion, family cohesion and homosexual legitimacy.... The new moralism...is an orthodoxy, to put it bluntly, of cultural and moral revolution: a wholesale assault on the beliefs and practices of an entire post-1960s settlement. And, if recent polls hold out, it could be on the verge of coming to power in November.[86]

It turned out, fortunately, that the Republicans did not gain seats but actually lost a few. Even so, they still retained control of both Houses of Congress; and, especially in the House of Representatives, the culture warriors rallied their forces, giving rise to the spectacle half a year later of a majority of the House of Representatives committing themselves to the proposition that violence in schools has nothing to do with the availability of guns but everything to do with the availability of abortion and the lack of a copy of the Ten Commandments pasted to the walls of every classroom.

The problem that all this presents for Young and her allies is that they have no principled way of objecting to this politicization of culture because, let us recall, 'no social practices or activities should be excluded as improper subjects for public discussion, expression or collective choice'.[87] They can object to the direction taken by the collective choice of an electoral majority, but they have no way of impugning the right of the majority to give legal effect to its own version of a 'cultural revolution'. Liberals, in contrast, can argue that the politicization of culture is a gross infringement of individual liberty, whether it takes the form advocated by Young and Fraser or that advocated by *The Weekly Standard* and pursued by the Republicans in Congress.

The failure of the Equal Rights Amendment was an earlier example of the way in which the politicization of cultural issues endangers liberal rights. The text of the Amendment could scarcely be a more straightforward application of egalitarian liberal principles: 'Equality of rights under the law shall not be denied or abridged by the United States or by any State on account of sex.' But precisely this feature of it led to its being disparaged by adherents of the point of view represented by Young and Fraser. 'Particularly for younger feminists, many of whom had been politically socialized in the movements of the New Left and had a skeptical view of the political utility of liberal political rhetorics of "law" and "rights", the ERA was a merely symbolic effort.'[88] By the time they rallied round the ERA, ten years after its enactment by Congress in 1972, it 'had become "too controversial" ', becoming 'a condensation point for unresolved anxieties in the political culture, anxieties having to do with sexual roles, gender identities, family life, and quality of life issues that do not admit of easy translation into rubrics "equality" and "rights" '.[89] This transformation of the issue was at least as much the work of the supporters of the ERA as it was the work of its opponents. While it was the opponents of the ERA who in the end benefited politically, those who supported it from the New Left position also insisted that support for the ERA was inextricably bound up with certain ideas about the value of alternative 'lifestyles'. Both sides, therefore, conspired to bury the case for the ERA that rested on considerations of elementary equity.

The fundamental error made by Young and Fraser, from which their sociological and political mistakes flow, is the rejection of the liberal contention that it makes sense to talk about equal rights, and that the case for equal rights can be made on the basis of an appeal to justice. It is not necessary first to establish the equal value of whatever activity is to be protected by the right in question. To make the point, let us think about the equal liberty of religious worship. Because religions have incompatible propositional content, it would be absurd to suggest that they had to be publicly affirmed to be equally valuable. But the case for giving different faiths the same rights does not depend on any such absurd claim: it can be derived from a principle of fair treatment. In the same way, the whole point of the liberal case for equal rights for homosexuals is that it quite explicitly leaves each person free to form a view about the relative value of heterosexual and homosexual ways of life.

Andrew Sullivan has recently written in the *New York Times* that he finds 'hard to figure out' his 'liberal friends who support every gay rights measure they have ever heard of but do anything to avoid going into a gay bar with me'.[90] Would he find it equally hard to figure out friends who enthusiastically support freedom of worship but would do anything to avoid attending a Roman Catholic mass with him? If not, why not? Perhaps his friends dislike equally the institutionalized 'gay scene' and the Roman Catholic Church. That does not make them hypocrites in not calling for their suppression. Similarly, the support for the principle embodied in the Equal Rights Amendment should not be made to turn on having a positive attitude towards a distinctive 'women's culture' which (as I quoted Iris Young in chapter 3) 'draw[s] on images of Amazonian grandeur, recover[s] and revalue[s] traditional women's arts, like quilting and weaving, or invent[s] new rituals based on medieval witchcraft'.[91]

My conclusion is, then, that we should totally reject the notion that the only way in which the case for equal rights for homosexuals can be made is to establish first the equal worthiness of homosexual and heterosexual life-styles. Making such comparisons is not, it seems to me, a thing that we would ever have any practical reason for wishing to do unless we had already bought into this theory. (Whatever is the route by which people become homosexual or heterosexual, it is implausible to suppose that many do it by totting up the pros and cons first.) What would be the measures by which the two were to be compared? It might be said that heterosexuals have the advantage in that a society without them would not last long. Conversely, it could be said that the arts (and the church) would be sadly depleted without gays. No doubt many more items could be put into both columns, but I have no idea how the ultimate reckoning might be made. My point is not, of course, that we need to try harder. Rather, it is that the whole ridiculous exercise is unnecessary.

## 5.   The Limits of Conventionalism

Nobody has any doubts about the adequacy in many circumstances of 'This is the way we do things here' as a justification for the legal imposition of some norm. If we go to live in a foreign country, we naturally expect that things will be done differently, and we take it for granted that we will have to conform to local customs. Some differences will have arisen as a result of historical accident, while others will reflect different priorities – for example, between pedestrian safety and saving time for motorists. It is the mark of the unsophisticated traveller to criticize foreign ways of doing things simply on the ground that they are different from those that are familiar at home.

Cultural relativists seek to capitalize on this reluctance to appear naive, and suggest that liberal universalists are guilty of extrapolating their national prejudices to the rest of the world. Yet there seem to be some local practices, such as torturing and killing political opponents, that are not susceptible of defence by saying 'This is the way we do things here.' In this and the next section, I shall seek to give 'This is the way we do things here' a good run for its money, but I shall also be concerned to establish its limits as a justification for giving legal effect to local norms. In the course of making this argument, I shall explicitly put the case for the liberal univers-alism whose validity I have so far assumed.

Let me begin by returning to Charles Taylor's essay on 'The Politics of Recognition'. Here, he discusses the move constituted by saying 'This is the way we do things here', but in my view illustrates not its proper use but its abuse. His example is the cultural conflict brought about by the Iranian *fatwa* calling for the death of Salman Rushdie. According to the cultural presuppositions underlying the *fatwa*, Rushdie deserves to die as an apostate and a blasphemer, and anybody who killed him outside the law would be meritorious. In contrast, liberal norms entail that, while cocking a snook at the Koran may be an offence against good taste, it is not an offence of which the law should take cognizance, and that anyone who killed Rushdie would deserve to be treated as a common murderer.

Taylor tells us that problems of this kind arise with increasing frequency because 'all societies are becoming increasingly multicultural'.[92] What this implies is that a problem does not occur until representatives of different cultures occupy the same geographical space, and as a consequence make conflicting demands on the same polity. The cause of this increased heterogeneity is that societies are increasingly 'open to multinational migration' so that they have 'members [who] live the life of a diaspora, whose center is elsewhere'.[93] Taylor explains that 'in these circumstances, there is something awkward about replying simply "This is how we do things here,"' when the imposition of one of the conflicting norms is challenged by the adherents of different norms.[94] What this clearly means is that, in other circumstances (defined as conditions of cultural homogeneity), there would be nothing awkward in facing down external critics by 'replying simply, "This is how we do things here"'. In a liberal society, there would be nothing awkward in imposing the liberal norm and protecting Rushdie from death threats; but in another society there would (if the local norms were sufficiently supportive) be nothing awkward in executing him.

We need not be surprised at Taylor's taking this position. It is precisely what we should anticipate from a disciple of Herder. If cultures are incommensurable, conflict between them is best avoided by arranging matters so that to each culture there corresponds one state, and each state minds its own business. The doctrine of romantic nationalism has no principled way of dealing with cultural heterogeneity. To avoid the 'awkwardness' that it engenders, many romantic nationalists have been prepared to go to what might seem disproportionate lengths, including forcible assimilation and, wherever they can identify a cultural minority with an ethnic group, 'ethnic cleansing' or genocide. Subscribers to romantic nationalism who would not endorse such drastic steps still typically wish to prevent cultural heterogeneity from coming about in the first place by standing against the forces to which Taylor correctly ascribes it, that is to say by restricting immigration as far as possible and denying citizenship to immigrants and their descendants in perpetuity.

If each culture constitutes a self-contained moral universe, it appears to follow that there is no room for any approach to cultural conflict that aspires to transcend the limits of any one culture. Among those who start from the premises but are uncomfortable with the conclusion, a popular move is to reaffirm the rejection of a universally valid morality (such as a doctrine of universal human rights) but at the same time to postulate a truth about the relative value of different cultures that is not a truth within any particular culture. One historically important version of this approach is the thesis that, if groups bearing conflicting cultures fight it out, there is some reason for supposing that the group gaining the victory will be culturally superior. The argument can appeal to pseudo-religion, giving rise to Hegel's glorification of nationalist warfare and to the American invocation of 'manifest destiny'. Alternatively, it can appeal to pseudo-science in the form of Social Darwinism: 'survival of the fittest' is then treated as a group phenomenon, so that the 'fittest' cultures are those whose bearers can prevail. This argument was popular, especially in the last quarter of the nineteenth century, as a justification of European and American imperialism.[95]

A variant on this kind of justification by results is calculated to be attractive to (in Matthew Arnold's terms) Philistines rather than Barbarians. In *Culture and Anarchy*, Arnold poked fun at the spokesmen for the Victorian middle class who claimed that English prosperity proved the superiority of English culture.[96] In the 1930s the same move was made by some defenders of the Soviet Union who adduced the productive superiority of its centrally planned economy as an overall justification of the 'new civilization'. Today (or at any rate yesterday) the argument has shifted to yet another terrain and is deployed to show that a concern for human rights must be a local western prejudice, because some countries in Asia have had high rates of economic growth while trampling on human rights. John Gray, for example, argues that countries such as China 'may be regarded as the most radical empirical falsification of the Enlightenment project hitherto and so of traditional liberalism, since they are examples of successful adoption of Western technologies by flourishing non-Occidental cultures that remain deeply resistant to Western values', in as far as they do not possess 'the Western apparatus of democratic institutions, *or* a Western-style civil society in which "human rights" are accorded privileged status'.[97]

It should be apparent that either version of this kind of claim, so far from avoiding any appeal to substantive universalistic values, actually presupposes the truth of some very strong universalistic ideas. If 'the survival of the fittest' is anything except the tautology that what survives is what survives, it must mean that whatever survives is necessarily better in some other way than what does not. But there is no reason for thinking this. The expression 'the survival of the fittest' was, in fact, not Darwin's but Herbert Spencer's, and Darwin was always scrupulous about avoiding the equation of evolution with improvement. If the level of hard radiation on the earth rose greatly, cockroaches would have a much better chance of survival than mammals, because they are immune to high levels of radiation, but this would not prove their superiority in any interesting sense to the life forms that had become extinct. In the application to human societies, the thesis that survival is an indicator of value presupposes that we already have criteria for comparing the value of different cultures. The proposition is then that the culture of a society that defeats another in war is generally more valuable than that of the society that it has defeated. It is hard to imagine any remotely plausible criteria for the value of a culture on which that would be true. History is replete with examples of societies that have reached a high pitch of civilization being defeated by others that were no good at anything except fighting.

Similarly, the proposition that a culture must be valuable if it is that of a society with a high rate of economic growth requires some universalistic criteria of value before it can get any purchase. We are then asked to believe that whatever it takes for a society to have a high rate of economic growth must be associated with valuable cultural attributes. But why should anyone believe that? It has now been established that a government can – for a few years, anyway – create the conditions for a high rate of economic growth by adopting most or all of the following measures: providing nothing in the way of an economic 'safety net' for those without incomes, whether this lack is due to sickness or injury, old age, or unemployment; banning trade unions and putting the police (and if necessary the army) at the disposal of employers; doing nothing to require employers to protect the health and safety of their workers; placing no restrictions on the use of child labour; selling off or using up natural resources that are either non-renewable or can regenerate themselves only over a long period of time; taking no measures to prevent air, water and soil pollution, even when the pollution assumes life-threatening proportions; and borrowing large sums of money from gullible foreign investors.

This shows more than anything else what a misleading measure of economic performance is a conventional index of growth in the gross national product. Even where a better measure would still show some gain, however, the case for the universal validity of human rights claims would remain unaffected. If the case for liberal institutions somehow derived from the idea that there was some necessary connection between respect for them and economic prosperity, as Gray imagines, it would indeed be undermined by the possibility of achieving prosperity while trampling on human rights. But it is nonsense to suppose that the case for universal human rights has ever been, or is now, of that kind. As I shall seek to show in the next section, the argument is simply that human rights are what all human beings need in order to live minimally decent lives.

I need hardly say that Taylor has no truck with either of these egregious attempts to escape from cultural particularism. Nevertheless, he still faces the problem to which they were addressed. The answer that he himself proposes is to urge the value of compromise as a response to cultural conflict. But what is the source of this value? From the inside, as it were, most cultures do not attach a value to compromise with other cultures. This may be conceded for most cultures, but it may be said nevertheless that liberalism is an exception. But is it? Liberalism is, indeed, culturally 'thinner' than other normative systems – a feature for which it is, of course, often criticized by anti-liberals. But a liberal cannot coherently believe that liberal principles should themselves be compromised to accommodate the demands of anti-liberals. There is, indeed, a remarkably pervasive view that liberalism is to be equated with moral relativism, but I hope that I scotched that once and for all in chapter 4.

Taylor exhibits what appears to be genuine regret that the case of Rushdie does not lend itself to compromise: 'in the nature of things, compromise is close to impossible here – one either forbids murder or allows it.'[98] This seems to me to show a sad lack of imagination. There would have been nothing to prevent the British government from proposing to the Iranian authorities some compromise solution. For example, it might have been possible to reach a deal according to which the British government would undertake to transport Rushdie to some neutral venue and an expert Iranian limb-severer would be flown in to remove some agreed portion of his anatomy – say the right arm. The problem is not that it is hard to think of compromises, as Taylor suggests. The problem is, rather, that it would be utterly revolting, from a liberal point of view, to compromise on the proposition that Rushdie should not suffer a legal penalty for writing *The Satanic Verses*. Compromise over liberal principles is not, and cannot be, a liberal value.

According to Taylor, the problem with saying 'This is the way we do things here' as a justification for imposing liberal norms is that 'the attitude presumed by the reply is seen as one of contempt'. He adds, rather mysteriously: 'often, in fact, this presumption is correct. Thus we arrive again at the issue of recognition.'[99] Taken literally, what this says is that the presumption that non-liberal ideas should be treated with contempt is correct. But this hardly fits in with Taylor's apparently genuine regret that compromise is not possible because 'one either forbids murder or allows it'. What I think Taylor actually means is that, often, those who see the reply as presuming an attitude of contempt are correct in their perception. And then 'we arrive again at the issue of recognition', I suppose, because this presumption is the opposite of the one that Taylor recommends, namely, the presumption that all cultures are of equal value.

Taylor gives the impression that 'This is the way we do things here' presumes an attitude of contempt only when liberals say it. (He does not tell us what attitude is presumed by anti-liberals who say it.) Thus, he says, the 'context' in which 'the reply "this is how we do things here" can seem crude and insensitive' is 'the issue of multiculturalism as it is often debated today'.[100] With characteristic imprecision, he explains that this 'has a lot to do with the imposition of some cultures on others, and with the assumed superiority that powers [*sic*] this imposition'.[101] Never mind the brutal cultural imposition that is going on in places such as Tibet and the Sudan. It turns out to be 'western liberal societies' that 'are thought to be supremely guilty in this regard, partly because of their colonial past, and 'partly because of their marginalization of segments of their populations that stem from other cultures'.[102] But 'western liberal societies' are scarcely the only ones with a 'colonial past', and it is grotesque to suggest that they are unique in their 'marginalization of segments of their population that come from other cultures': the term 'marginalization' would be far too weak, in fact, to describe the fate of such minorities in most of the rest of the world, where 'ethnic cleansing' and genocide are rather more typical responses. Indeed, western liberal societies may be the only ones in which it has ever been widely believed that there is anything wrong in treating outsiders less well than the already established population. Robert Hughes has epitomized this kind of claptrap as: 'Oppression is what we do in the West. What they do in the Middle East is "their culture."' '[103]

Leaving all that aside, Taylor's entire discussion of the issue is based on the false assumption that what western liberals want to say in defence of their institutions is 'This is the way we do things here.' Maybe some apologists of authoritarian governments will attempt to shield them from external criticism by saying 'This is the way we do things here', though others will surely wish to claim that (say) 'Asian values' are superior to western liberal values. But what is perfectly clear is that, outside the ranks of the political philosophers who have succumbed to cultural relativism, that is not how anybody thinks liberal institutions are to be defended. The foundational documents of liberalism are the French Declaration of the Rights of Man and of the Citizen and the American Declaration of Independence. These make universalistic claims, as does, of course, the United Nations Universal Declaration of Human Rights. Thus, the correct defence of the British government's not punishing Rushdie or handing him over to others for punishment (whether within some legal process or outside it) is not 'This is the way we do things here.' It is, rather, that this is the way things ought to be done everywhere: we do things that way here not because it is a part of our culture but because it is the right thing to do.

## 6.   The Limits of Universalism

Martha Nussbaum tells of a conference she attended at which a French anthropologist gave a paper saying that the eradication of smallpox in India was to be regretted because it had 'eradicated the cult of Sittala Devi, the goddess to whom one used to pray in order to avert smallpox'.[104] Since the goddess had manifestly been less efficacious in warding off smallpox than vaccination turned out to be, one might have concluded that her discrediting was to be welcomed, but the anthropologist concluded that this was 'another example of Western neglect of difference'.[105] The objection was made 'that it is surely better to be healthy rather than ill, to live rather than die'. The answer came back that this is a typical piece of Western essentialist thinking, 'which conceives of things in terms of binary oppositions'.[106]

Well, I think that there is much to be said for *some* binary oppositions, and I do not believe that there is anything inherently western about binary oppositions as such. It is better to be alive than dead. It is better to be free than to be a slave. It is better to be healthy than sick. It is better to be adequately nourished than malnourished. It is better to drink pure water than contaminated water. It is better to have effective sanitation than to live over an open sewer. It is better to have a roof over your head than to sleep in the street. It is better to be well educated than to be illiterate and ignorant. It is better to be able to practise the form of worship prescribed by your religion than to be prevented from doing so. It is better to be able to speak freely and be able to join social and political organizations of your choice than to fear that, if your activities attract the disfavour of the regime, you face arbitrary arrest, torture or 'disappearance' at the hands of bodies organized by or connived at by the state. And so on.

It is, of course, a massive understatement to say that the first alternative in each of these binary oppositions is merely preferable to the second. Rather, the first item in each pair constitutes a basic interest of every human being. Together they make up the preconditions (or at any rate a number of the most important preconditions) for what we may describe as a minimally decent human life. And by saying *human* life I wish to emphasize that I am making a claim with cross-cultural scope.

There are a variety of ways in which we might support the claim that such interests are universal. One would be to argue that there is a universal human nature which gives rise to certain physiological and psychological needs. I see no reason why this argument should not be carried through successfully, but I suggest that it may usefully be supplemented by an appeal to the choices actually made by people in a position to make choices. Thus, with rare exceptions that can normally be explained by highly unusual beliefs or circumstances, people strongly prefer life to death, freedom to slavery, and health to sickness. It is worth observing, incidentally, that the devotees of Sittala Devi were no exception: what motivated her worshippers was the hope that she would protect them from smallpox. It was the anthropologist, not the people involved, who elevated the value of cultural diversity above that of health.

Similarly, we can assert with confidence that, if people have the resources to provide themselves with housing, pure water, sanitation and a nourishing diet, they place a very high priority on securing them. Few people choose illiteracy and ignorance for themselves if the choice is open to them; that some choose ignorance for others (e.g. men for their daughters in some societies) is not relevant, since the criterion appealed to is the choices that people make for themselves. In the same way, an authoritarian father may well try to force the members of his family into conformity with his religious beliefs, but he is likely to place a very high value on his own ability to follow the form of religious worship prescribed by his own religion. What is, indeed, remarkable is the willingness of people to face severe sanctions rather than give up the practice of their religious beliefs.

It may be said that this argument is valid so far, but that it runs out when we get to the claim that being able to speak freely and join social and political organizations of one's choice is universally important. However, we must understand the claim correctly. It does not have to be valid unconditionally to be valid universally. Thus, being alive is a necessary condition of wanting anything at all. We can quite reasonably allow for further levels of hierarchy among interests. It may be that people who are only barely alive, suffering from persistent malnutrition and illness, and subsisting under degrading physical conditions, cannot afford the energy to do anything except struggle on from day to day. They are even less likely to aspire to express themselves or take part in the social and political life of their society if, in addition to their other woes, they are illiterate and ignorant. But that does nothing to impugn the claim that freedom of expression and association, and security against state-organized or state-sponsored repression, are highly valued all over the world and their loss widely mourned among people whose other vital interests are being satisfied.

Let me assume that, even if what I have said is not enough to make the case for liberal universalism, the case can be made by elaborating the sketch of an argument that I have offered. This then brings us to the question: what kinds of local variation are consistent with liberal universalism? There are some cases in which 'This is the way we do things here' is an adequate response. For example, 'When in Rome do as the Romans do' is a maxim that applies to the conventions that obtain in the Eternal City with regard to pedestrians and traffic. Even when a pedestrian is standing at a marked crossing, the traffic in Rome will not stop or slow down. It is necessary to set off across the road, daring motorists to run you down, and then the traffic will stop. This may not be ideal, but it is the way in which things work, and anybody who waited for the traffic to stop before crossing the road would be condemned to staying perpetually on the same block.

For obvious reasons, rules of the road are the most often cited example of a convention. Norms of politeness and decorum are similarly conventional. In some societies, belching at the end of a meal is regarded as a polite way of expressing appreciation for the food. In others this is not so. There is no absolute right or wrong about this sort of thing: what is generally regarded as polite and what really is polite are one and the same thing. To say 'They think it's polite but they're wrong' would simply be a mistake in logic. Similarly, whether or not a woman is well dressed to go shopping in only a skirt depends on the local conventions. There may or may not be islands in the South Seas where this is still customary, but there are undoubtedly private beach clubs where it would be in accordance with convention, and others where it would be considered overdressed. Tunbridge Wells High Street, on the other hand, is not such a place. There is no supra-conventional standard of propriety here. One of the complaints about Victorian 'cultural imperialism' which is well founded is that Europeans (especially missionaries) tended to attribute universal moral significance to what in fact were simply the sartorial customs familiar to them from their own culture. The insistence that Christian converts should wear Mother Hubbards, as if Christianity were inextricably tied in with a certain conception of modesty in dress, is a good example of this fault.

Only a misunderstanding of the nature of liberal principles could lead anyone to imagine that they cannot countenance the legal enforcement of conventional norms. Where the general observance of a norm creates a public good that benefits most of the population – and especially where non-compliance with the norm by even a small number destroys the benefit – it is perfectly reasonable to enforce it on all, including those whose culture is such that they do not appreciate the benefit. Nobody (aside from the libertarian lunatic fringe) doubts that the public good of clean streets is sufficiently valuable to underwrite compulsory contributions to the cost of collecting household refuse. Precisely the same public good is served by imposing legal penalties on those who dump discarded mattresses or refrigerators in the street. It would not be a good excuse for breaking the law to say that disposing of unwanted objects in this way was 'a part of your culture', even if this claim was correct. We have here a typical case in which 'This is the way we do things here' is a sufficient basis for the legitimacy of majoritarian collective decision-making with no provision for exceptions.

Notice that temporal priority plays an important part in examples of this kind. People who move into a village sometimes complain about the noise of bell-ringing, and people who move into the country sometimes complain of being kept awake by the crowing of cockerels and the lowing of cattle. (These are real examples from England.) Such people are, quite properly, told that this sort of thing has been going on for a very long time and that it was up to them to check out well-established features of country life such as these before moving into the area. We may contrast this with the situation that would arise if somebody one day decided to raise cockerels in the middle of a suburban residential neighbourhood. Even if the gardens were big enough to obviate any legitimate objections to keeping chickens at all (so that hens might be acceptable), the neighbours could still reasonably object to the prospect of being awakened at the crack of dawn every day by raucous crowing. For they could argue that they had moved into the area with certain expectations about the kinds of activity that people might legitimately undertake in their gardens, and that these expectations had hitherto been satisfied. If persuasion failed to work, they would have a case for asking the local authority to give their expectations the force of law.

I thus take issue with the Dutch sociologist Veit Bader, who writes: 'The "law of the land" [in liberal democracies] differs considerably from the "thin moral code" of public morality in liberal theory. In most states it is still thick or pregnant with illegitimate, even stupid, ethnocentrism, particularly when it comes to unspecified general norms (what is public order, decency, etc.) and administrative, executive rulings and practices.'[107] It goes without saying that illegitimate or stupid ethnocentrism is to be rejected. But what I read Bader as condemning is any filling out of the liberal 'thin moral code' in accordance with local norms that give a specific content to 'public order' or 'decency'. It is no objection that this will involve the enforcement of conventions: we are talking here of cases in which 'This is the way we do things here' comes into its own.

It is interesting to observe that Michael Walzer shares Bader's belief that a commitment to liberalism is incompatible with support for the enforcement of any norms falling outside the ' "thin moral code" of public morality in liberal theory'. Unlike Bader, however, he maintains that liberal principles are defective precisely because they do not lend themselves to 'customization' – in the dual sense of adaptation to the idiosyncrasies of the consumers and the peculiarities of their customs. According to Walzer, 'minimalist universalism' can be compared to a set of blueprints for building identical hotel rooms all over the world in a basic, stripped-down 'international style'.[108] This analogy is based on a complete misapprehension of the role played by liberal principles. They do not tell people what to do; rather, they simply set limits on what they can do to further their ends politically. As Charles Jones has suggested, a better analogy than Walzer's would be with a set of safety regulations that specify the minimum requirements that buildings should satisfy before people can reasonably be expected to occupy them.[109]

Excluding as illegitimate any conceptions of public order or decency that are not universally applicable would mean that there could be virtually no permissible regulations framed in terms of those values. The whole point of concepts such as 'public order' and 'decency' is that they are simply placeholders waiting to be fleshed out by giving them a content derived from local norms. Decency may be, as I have suggested, entirely conventional. Western liberal societies are already a great deal more tolerant of variations in dress than are the great mass of other societies: churches, workplaces, restaurants or even shops may have their own rules, but I doubt if you could be arrested for public indecency for wearing a bikini on the streets of London, however inappropriate this might be both climatically and socially. There are, however, other conventions about public decency that would probably be enforced, such as that prohibiting the practice (common in some cultures) of defecating in public. It might be claimed that this is not simply a question of a norm of public decency because it is a public health issue. That it is not (or not primarily) a public health issue is shown by the fact that following the example of socially responsible dog owners and picking up after yourself would not prevent public defecation from being an offence.

Public order, in contrast to decency, clearly has some non-conventional elements: no state will openly countenance riots, for example. Nevertheless, much of what is taken to constitute a public order depends on local conventions about acceptable behaviour. Norms concerning noise in residential neighbourhoods, for example, appear to vary widely from culture to culture. There are, or so it is said, societies in which it is acceptable to hold noisy parties through the night, with a lot of loud music, shouting and singing. But it is quite reasonable for a society in which this is not the norm to treat this as an illegal disturbance of the peace. It may be noted, incidentally, that such legislation would not prevent the inhabitants of a culturally homogeneous neighbourhood made up of people with the party-going norm from practising it: if nobody objected, there would be no complaints for the police or the local authority to act on.

A case from Western Australia offers an instructive example of conflict between the norms of an established community and those of somebody from a different culture. The origin of the case was as follows:

> Homeswest, the West Australian state housing authority, forced Joan Martin, 56, to leave her small cottage [in Perth] for overcrowding it with 16 relatives....White neighbours lobbied politicians to demand [the Martins'] eviction, flooding the media and police with complaints about unruly behaviour by Mrs Martin's grandchildren.[110]

The report of the case does not anywhere suggest that these complaints of unruly behaviour were unfounded. At any rate, the decision was compatible with their being well founded, since its rationale was that the neighbours would have to put up with the consequences of respecting the Aboriginal cultural norms that resulted in Mrs Martin's having charge of so many children.

> Mrs Martin . . . claimed that she was a victim of racial discrimination, since she was upholding Aboriginal tradition by taking in her homeless children and grandchildren. West Australia's Equal Opportunity Tribunal rejected her case, but last week the Perth Supreme Court ruled she had suffered indirect racial discrimination by Homeswest and ordered it to pay A$20,000 (£8,400) damages. Hannah McGlade, a human rights specialist at Murdoch University law school in Perth, described the judgement as a landmark in Australian law. 'It is an important recognition of cultural differences,' she said.[111]

There is no denying that. But was it an appropriate recognition of cultural differences? I think not. This was, I wish to argue, a case in which 'This is the way we do things here' should have counted as a valid move.

Let me qualify this. In as far as the issue was one of overcrowding, it can be said with much plausibility that Homeswest had it in its power to solve the problem by knocking together two (or even more) houses to accommodate Mrs Martin's brood. This is, for example, what British housing authorities do for very large nuclear families and also for the extended families of Asian citizens when these form a single household unit. With more space, the children might not have engaged in the unruly behaviour that was complained of by the neighbours. The question of eviction would not then have arisen. Suppose, however, that this kind of accommodation of a cultural norm was not enough. Let us assume, in other words, that the underlying problem was that Mrs Martin was simply not able to exert adequate control over the behaviour of such a large number of children. Then the eviction would have been justified on the ground that nobody should be permitted to make the lives of their neighbours miserable by engaging in antisocial activity, according to the prevailing local standards of what constitutes antisocial activity.

What made the Australian case a 'landmark' is that the court apparently took the line that, if it was an Aboriginal custom to gather together all one's children and grandchildren, this had to be upheld regardless of the consequences for others living in the vicinity. Applied in Britain, the same reasoning would eviscerate the powers that local councils have been given by legislation to evict tenants for persistent antisocial behaviour. To resist eviction successfully, it would only be necessary to show that an important part of your culture was (say) keeping pigs in your back garden or that your culture placed a great emphasis on scrap metal-working as a household activity.[112] The neighbours would then simply have to put up with it. It should be observed that the Australian decision goes way beyond anything called for by the International Covenant on Civil and Political Rights. Article 12 (2) of this provides that: 'Everyone lawfully within the territory of a state shall, within that territory, have the right to liberty of movement and freedom to choose his residence.' As I mentioned in the previous chapter, however, all such rights are 'subject to any restrictions... which are... necessary to protect... public order... or the rights and freedoms of others, and are consistent with the other rights in the Covenant'.[113] Thus, norms of civility and good order can trump the right to live anywhere you choose to live, and do anything you choose to do, as long as you can show that it forms a part of your culture.

Liberal principles, nevertheless, impose firm constraints on the way in which claims of amenity can be deployed. If disapproval of an activity that did no harm to those participating in it or to others were deemed sufficient to underwrite its suppression, the basic Millian position on freedom of association would be left in tatters. If an activity is to be complained about legitimately, this must be in virtue of its tangible impact on neighbours. Thus, people in a neighbourhood could not invoke a local norm disapproving of witchcraft as a basis upon which to create a Wicca-free zone. They would have a valid objection only if its practice created spillovers of a kind that could be objected to regardless of the nature of the activity giving rise to them. Examples would be the actuality or a demonstrably high risk of noise, smell, fumes, damage to property or personal injury.

The upshot of this argument is, then, that it is no objection to the legal enforcement of norms of civility and good order that they have a substantial element of convention about them. The whole point of this discussion is to emphasize that these norms emerge from the practice of some actual community. Thus, for example, it would be absurd to suggest that there is anything intrinsically immoral about keeping pigs in your back garden. If it is the local norm then everybody mucks in, as it were. Similarly, in a gypsy encampment, everybody presumably accepts the noise and noxious fumes that arise from breaking up cars and burning the tyres and upholstery, because that is part of the way of life. The same kind of point may be made about the Australian case. Within an Aboriginal community, the behaviour complained of as 'unruly' might be coded as 'high-spirited'. Or perhaps Aboriginal communities are more spread out, so that the same behaviour would not create the same problems as in a densely populated tract of housing. What I am saying is, simply, that the stringency or laxity of the local norms is a fact, and a fact that has moral significance. It creates a strong presumption that the norms should be complied with and if necessary enforced.

# 8

## The Politics of
## Multiculturalism

### I.  The Curious Political Success of Multiculturalism

As we have seen in this book, a number of multiculturalist policies have been adopted in countries such as the United Kingdom, the United States and Canada. How are we to account for the success of the multiculturalist cause? One obvious answer would be that it is a cause that finds favour with the public and that politicians respond to its popularity by enacting multiculturalist legislation. The trouble with this explanation is that the evidence fails to support any such claim about the state of public opinion.

Of the three countries that I have mentioned, only one has a practice of direct voting on ordinary legislation, as against constitutional issues or international treaties. In the United States, a number of States (especially in the western part of the country) have a provision for referenda by popular initiative. One such referendum, in 1998, 'abolished almost all bilingual education programs in public schools' in California.[1] The majority in favour was 61 per cent, and among ethnic minority voters the measure was supported by 37 per cent of Hispanics and 57 per cent of Asians.[2] With that exception, we have to rely on survey data. Here, a noteworthy finding was provided by a public opinion poll conducted in Canada in 1993, which showed 'nearly three quarters of respondents rejecting the idea that Canada is a multicultural nation'.[3]

This result is especially striking because it amounts to a direct repudiation of the Canadian Multiculturalism Act which was passed in 1988.[4] When we examine the wording of this Act, we immediately notice that it exemplifies a phenomenon on which I commented in chapter 2: the tendency among the proponents of multiculturalism to use the term equivocally. Thus, in section 3 (1) of the Canadian Multiculturalism Act, clause (a) says that it is government policy to 'recognize and promote the understanding that multiculturalism reflects the cultural and racial diversity of Canadian society'.[5] Here, 'multiculturalism' must refer to a set of policies. For it is described as 'reflecting' a condition of diversity, and a reflection cannot be identical to the object reflected. This interpretation is confirmed by the rest of the clause, according to which 'multiculturalism...acknowledges the freedom of all members of Canadian society to preserve, enhance and share their cultural heritage'.[6] Thus, the claim being made in clause (a) is that the appropriate way in which to respond to 'cultural and racial diversity' is to pursue multiculturalist policies. This claim is contestable – and I have been contesting it – but it is at any rate intelligible. Clause (b), however, switches the meaning of 'multiculturalism' by committing the government to 'recogniz[ing] and promot[ing] the understanding that multiculturalism is a fundamental characteristic of the Canadian heritage and identity and that it provides an invaluable resource in the shaping of Canada's future'.[7] Here, 'multiculturalism' makes sense only as a synonym for what in the previous clause was called 'cultural and racial diversity'. The result of this legerdemain is to make it conceptually impossible to acknowledge the fact of diversity while rejecting the policies advanced under the name of multiculturalism. We can therefore be confident that the three-to-one majority of Canadians who rejected the proposition that they 'lived in a multicultural nation' were rejecting the entire tenor of the Canadian Multiculturalism Act five years after its passage.

Will Kymlicka has conceded in his recent book *Finding Our Way* that 'more and more Canadians themselves are disillusioned with the basic institutions and principles that underlie the Canadian model'.[8] This, he complains, puts him in 'a paradoxical position...and an increasingly untenable one'.[9] For it means that he has been put 'in the position of trying to encourage foreign audiences to take seriously a set of practices and principles that are increasingly dismissed and derided at home'.[10] What deepens the paradox for Kymlicka is, he says, that ' "the Canadian model" of ethnocultural relations' offers 'one area' in which 'Canada is an internationally recognized leader, in terms not only of specific public policies, but also of the judicial decisions and [he adds modestly] academic studies that analyse and evaluate these policies'.[11] Kymlicka goes on to comment, rather wistfully, that, in contrast to the chilly reception of multiculturalism in Canada, 'audiences in other countries – whether the US, Britain, Australia, the Netherlands, Spain, Italy, Austria, Latvia, or Ukraine – seem genuinely interested in Canada's successes in this area'.[12] The seeming paradox can easily be dissolved by noticing that Kymlicka is not comparing like with like. I have no doubt at all that these 'foreign audiences' to which he has presented the 'Canadian model' were composed in the same way as his audiences in Canada: of academics, lawyers, politicians, civil servants and officials from think-tanks and quangos. I should be very surprised if either in Canada or abroad Kymlicka has ever roused a large public gathering to enthusiasm for multiculturalism.[13]

Multiculturalism in Canada is sustained by 'a fluid interchange of talent and legal resources among... governmental agencies [advocating legal reform and sponsoring test cases], the law schools, and private rights advocacy organizations'.[14] Among the activities of this tightly knit group are efforts to change public opinion towards greater acceptance of the policies that they are engaged in pursuing. Thus, Kymlicka's *Finding Our Way* originated in five short papers that were commissioned by 'officials at the Department of Canadian Heritage of the federal government'.[15] They invited Kymlicka to write about what 'debates among political theorists could tell us about public policy in Canada', and specifically public policy with respect to multiculturalism.[16] Since these officials must have been aware of Kymlicka's role as a tireless promoter of Canadian multiculturalism, they can hardly have been surprised if his version of the debate had the multiculturalists coming out on top. *Finding Our Way* itself is, Kymlicka says, intended in part 'to provide a kind of reality check'.[17] This claim rests on the patronizing assumption that the unpopularity of multiculturalism stems from a lack of information: if Canadians had a better sense of reality they would change their minds. More likely, it is precisely because the Canadian public is, by international standards, familiar with both the theory and practice of multiculturalism that it is so markedly hostile to it.

As far as practices are concerned, Canada may have gone further along the path of multiculturalism than Britain or the United States, but if so there is not an enormous amount in it. The really significant difference is that neither Britain nor the United States has anything corresponding to the Canadian Multiculturalism Act. The consequence of the Act is that in Canada multiculturalism as a whole approach to politics is established as a topic in the public domain, and specific policies promoting the multiculturalist agenda can be seen as aspects of a larger strategy. Contrast this with the position in Britain and the United States, where there is no public debate about the general idea of multiculturalism because there is no focus for such a debate. It is true that there has been a lively (and at times rancorous) debate in America about the content of school textbooks in history and social studies, and this is (as we saw in chapter 6) identified by some Americans with the entire issue of multiculturalism. To the extent, however, that this dispute concerns the substance of a common curriculum intended for all the children in the public schools, it is irrelevant to 'the politics of difference', which is defined by the demand that different people should be treated differently in accordance with their distinctive cultures. Outside the network of academics, lawyers and officials directly involved, it is doubtful that many people in Britain or the United States are aware of multiculturalism as a challenge to the whole idea that equal treatment means treating people in the same way. The result is that there is nothing around which the diffuse discontent with specific multiculturalist policies can coalesce.

Sebastian Poulter argued in the concluding chapter of his book on ethnicity and the law in England that 'some considered thought should be given to the adoption of a clear public agenda for promoting the future of a plural society in Britain, perhaps culminating in the enactment of a Multiculturalism Act', but warned that 'considerable opposition can be expected, as the Canadian experience demonstrates'.[18] Precisely for that reason, it can be predicted with confidence that the policy community committed to the multiculturalist cause in Britain will not be pressing in the foreseeable future for any such 'clear public agenda'. On the contrary, this is the last thing they would wish to see. Adrian Favell has pointed out that adopting 'a formal minority rights structure' in Britain 'would entail scrapping the complex arrangements that currently exist'.[19] He adds that the crisis precipitated by the publication of *The Satanic Verses* led not to the conclusion that such a formal structure was needed but rather to a resolve to hang on at all costs to the existing arrangements. 'Political actors involved on all sides – politicians, religious and cultural representatives, the race relations lobby – were in fact at pains, after the Rushdie case, to re-establish the merits of the existing mechanism for managing ethnic diversity.'[20] You bet they were! Among the 'political actors' enumerated by Favell, one set is conspicuously lacking: anybody representing the interests of the wider public. The Rushdie affair threatened to blow open the cosy circle constituted by these managers of ethnic diversity. It is scarcely surprising that, faced with the risk that multiculturalism might become a subject of public debate, they closed ranks.

It is not simply that debate on the general principles of multiculturalism is strenuously avoided. In addition to that, the specific fixes that constitute practical multiculturalism are negotiated behind closed doors. The public at large is kept in the dark, and even organizations that might rock the boat because they do not belong to the multiculturalist club are excluded from consultation. A perfect example of this process of multiculturalism by stealth is provided by the case of ritual slaughter. As I recounted in chapter 2, the government's own advisory committee, the Farm Animal Welfare Council, issued a report in 1985 recommending that kosher/halal butchery should be prohibited on the ground that it inevitably entails unnecessary animal suffering. I want to focus here on what happened next. Was the report regarded by the government as an ideal opportunity to initiate a wide-ranging public debate on a matter of legitimate concern to all citizens? The answer will come as no surprise. The government could not avoid any response at all to the Council's report. But it gave it in the form least likely to attract public attention: a prepared ministerial reply to a planted parliamentary question.

The matter of the government's response was even more remarkable than its manner. The government, it ran, had 'had an opportunity to consult Jewish and Muslim leaders in great detail on the question'.[21] It had not, be it noted, taken the opportunity to consult any of the organizations concerned with animal welfare, let alone invited any input from the general public. The substance of the reply simply retailed the objections to the Council's report made by these religious leaders. They 'rejected the Council's assessment of the welfare implications of religious slaughter', the government reported.[22] To give this as a reason for rejecting the Council's recommendation was tantamount to conceding that the government had abandoned all canons of rational decision-making. What else could be said about a reason for in-action that consists of citing the fact that the scientific basis of the proposed action was disputed by people who could be counted on without fail to dispute it? It might be argued, indeed, that the Jewish and Muslim leaders consulted by the government would have been guilty of negligence in the pursuit of their constituents' interests if they had refrained from disputing the evidence. Since, however, these leaders had an entrenched position based on religious belief and no credentials as scientists, their objections should have been dismissed. The government also reported the claim by the Jewish and Muslim leaders that 'their slaughter requirements are fundamental obligations'.[23] Here, the government might have pointed out that eating meat is not a religious obligation or that kosher butchery has been declared not to be a religious obligation in countries that have made it illegal. Merely citing the objection as if it were decisive was, in effect, to turn the powers of government over to a pressure group.

Poulter, in the course of recounting the growing opposition to ritual slaughter in Britain, led by bodies such as the RSPCA, the Humane Slaughter Association and Compassion in World Farming, mentions that 'by 1983 a National Opinion Poll revealed that 77 per cent of respondents were altogether opposed to religious slaughter'.[24] It could, of course, be argued that this very large majority rested on lack of information, and that if there had been full public debate on the issue more than one-third of those opposed to religious slaughter would have changed their minds, producing a majority in favour of retaining the exemption. The only way of testing this speculation would be actually to have such a debate. For what it is worth, however, my own impression is that (outside the ranks of those already committed for religious reasons) greater knowledge of the facts intensifies opposition to ritual slaughter.

In the case of the exemption to the crash helmet law that was introduced in 1976 to accommodate turbanned Sikhs riding motorcycles, the government of the day formally abdicated responsibility and adopted an officially neutral attitude to a private member's bill. 'Curiously, the bill was never debated on the floor of the House of Commons itself, partly for obscure procedural reasons, but there was full discussion in the relevant Standing Committee and subsequently in two short debates in the House of Lords.'[25] Given that a piece of primary legislation was involved, it would have been impossible to stifle informed public debate of an important road safety issue more effectively than to relegate debate to two bodies guaranteed to produce paralysing boredom in the public: the House of Lords and a committee of the House of Commons. Once again, however, the only opinion poll evidence offered by Poulter (which was cited in the House of Lords) suggested that 69 per cent of respondents were opposed to a special exemption for Sikhs.[26] It could be argued here too that a full public debate might have induced a big shift in sentiment. My own view is, however, that the more one thinks about the question the less convincing the case for a general rule with a special exemption becomes, for the reasons that I laid out in chapter 2.

Other concessions to demands made on religious and cultural grounds take place even more out of the public eye. Thus, it appears from occasional newspaper items (supported by anecdotal evidence from schoolteachers) that schools all over Britain are acceding to demands by parents that their children should be withdrawn from central parts of the curriculum: the example most commonly mentioned is permission for Muslim girls to be excluded from biology lessons. Left to their own devices, it is hardly surprising if head teachers opt for a quiet life and accommodate parental demands, however educationally harmful they may be. In Britain, the incentives facing head teachers are further skewed by the quasi-market in the state school system introduced by the Conservatives and developed further by Labour, which forces schools to compete for pupils in order to avoid bankruptcy. In the absence of any authoritative ruling, schools that do not give in to educationally deleterious demands face the threat that dissatisfied parents will shift their children to schools that are more accommodating. It is, clearly, the job of public authorities, accountable to the wider public that has a legitimate stake in the education received by all children, to take a position.

For the reasons that I put forward in chapter 6, I do not believe that a policy of allowing parents to pick and choose among subjects in the core academic curriculum could withstand public scrutiny. As far as I am aware, no local authority in Britain has formulated and defended publicly such a policy explicitly; exemptions take place on an *ad hoc* basis in a policy vacuum. In the United States, we know from the *Mozert* case (discussed in chapter 6) about one county's educational authority that refused to allow parents to withdraw their children from part of the school curriculum. It appears from the record of the case, however, that a number of schools in

Hawkins County had acceded to parental demands like those of the *Mozert* parents and would no doubt have continued to do so if the School Board had not acted to pre-empt the schools' discretion by taking the decision that precipitated the case. It may well be that schools all over the United States are yielding to similar pressures from parents to circumscribe their children's education, in the absence of an authoritative ruling prohibiting them from doing so.

The jewel in the multiculturalist crown in America has been bilingual/bicultural education. This too has tended to be adopted by collaboration among elites – advocacy groups, judges and educational bureaucrats – rather than as a result of broad public support. I mentioned in chapter 6 that, in New York State, compulsory bilingual education was imposed by the courts at the behest of a Puerto Rican lobbying group. I may add that, since this group's activities were financed by the Ford and Rockefeller Foundations, it did not even need broadly based support among Puerto Ricans. If we go right back to the early days of the Federal Government's involvement with bilingual/bicultural education, we discover bureaucrats and judges making policy between them, and in the process creating something that was far from the kind of scheme called for by the covering legislation. 'The Bilingual Education Act was created in January 1968 as Title VII of the Elementary and Secondary Education Act [as] a small, exploratory measure aimed at "limited English-speaking" pupils who were falling badly behind in school or dropping out altogether.'[27] The rationale was explicitly that the money was to be used to experiment with alternative ways of helping these children learn English, so that they could join 'mainstream' classes conducted in English. Transitional education in their mother tongue was one, but only one, of the methods whose efficacy was to be investigated.

In the event, however, the implementation of the Title VII programme, which expanded rapidly, was totally at odds with the rationale that the Congress had accepted. Thus, a study carried out in 1974 by the Congressional Accounting Office found that 87 per cent of the programmes funded under Title VII were dedicated to maintaining a minority language and were not designed to enable students to move into an English-speaking environment to complete their education.[28] Even if students in bilingual educational programmes did learn enough English to be able to function in classes taught in English, it was found by another study that '86 per cent of the Title VII project directors interviewed said that they had a policy of keeping students in [Spanish-speaking] classes after they could learn in English'.[29] Even more remarkably, the study by the Congressional Accounting Office found that 'many Title VII programs were made up largely of English-dominant students of Hispanic origin'.[30] The schools were thus maintaining the ancestral language of these students but not their actual language. In any case, such students had no place in any Title VII programme, under the official rationale, because this was intended exclusively for students whose English was deficient. We can understand why the objectives of the programme were subverted by the agency appointed to implement it when we discover that it was headed at this stage by somebody who had previously testified to Congress that he foresaw the United States following Canada in having two official languages – in the American case, English and Spanish.[31]

Parallel to this use of the carrot in the form of special funds dedicated – in practice – to linguistic and cultural maintenance programmes, the Office of Civil Rights (OCR) wielded the stick by threatening to withdraw all federal school aid from 334 school districts unless they introduced bilingual education programmes.[32] These moves, and others along similar lines, had no legislative basis. The OCR claimed that its policy was licensed by the Supreme Court's decision in the case of *Lau* v. *Nichols*. But this case, which originated in San Francisco, simply held that throwing Chinese-speaking children into an English-speaking classroom with no preparation did not constitute 'equality of treatment'.[33] The Court explicitly eschewed any prescription of the means that should be employed to educate these children, leaving open the options of transitional instruction in Chinese, an intensive course in English, or indeed a properly managed 'immersion' programme. However, a 'task force' assembled by the OCR drew up so-called 'Lau remedies' that ignored the Supreme Court's focus on the rights solely of children who could not speak English, and decreed that school districts with more than twenty students whose native language was not English must put them in bilingual programmes, regardless of the adequacy of their English.[34] This clearly turned *Lau* into a mandate for maintaining children in 'their' language as an end in itself. The objectives of the 'task force' become manifest when we observe that they also prescribed bicultural education (an issue that the Supreme Court did not even address), in the obnoxious form of a special curriculum for each ethnic group, reflecting its own 'contributions' to American history.[35] This is, again, a clear case of successful bureaucratic politics in pursuit of a goal other than that mandated by the Congress or the courts.

## 2.  Multiculturalism versus Democracy

That multiculturalist policies continue to be pursued in the face of a high degree of public hostility is a remarkable tribute to the effectiveness of the elites who are committed to them. Should we be concerned about this? If the premises supporting multiculturalism are well founded, the kind of behind-the-scenes manipulation that I have been describing needs no apology. For these premises have strongly anti-majoritarian implications. Many multiculturalists (as we saw in the previous chapter) maintain that each cultural group within a polity constitutes a source of values for its members, and that the values of different groups are incommensurable. On this view, a society with a single set of rules applying to all its members is bound to be oppressive to cultural minorities, because the rules will simply reflect the culture of the majority. The very possibility of arguing that some rules have more to be said for them than that they articulate majority values is simply dismissed in advance as a piece of sophistry. Not all multiculturalists subscribe to this brand of moral nihilism. But even those who are prepared to accept that it makes sense to talk about the right policies to pursue are still likely to accord only very little legitimacy to majoritarian decision-making. For the whole point of the 'politics of difference' is to assert that the right answer is for each cultural group to have public policies tailored to meet its specific demands. It is plausible that this can be achieved only by ensuring that members of cultural minorities are able to control public policies affecting them, either by having political power devolved on them or by being granted some kind of special status in relation to the process by which policies are formulated.

The 'politics of difference' thus rests on a rejection of what we may call, in contrast, the politics of solidarity. On this alternative conception of politics, sketched in chapter 3, citizens belong to a single society and share a common fate. Political disagreements, according to this approach, stem from differing ideas among citizens about the direction to be taken in future by their society. We may expect them to disagree on the policies that will most effectively further the common good and most fairly distribute the benefits and burdens arising from the working of their common institutions. If we conceive of political conflict as predominantly taking this form, we have a clear prima facie case for resolving disputes by adopting the policy favoured by the majority. In matters of common concern, it is hard to see why each person should not have an equal say in the outcome. Where a minority is constituted out of those who are on the losing side in a disagreement about the future of the institutions they share with the majority, there appears to be no case for building in special protections for the minority. It would surely be absurd to say that a minority defined in this way should have a veto on the policy favoured by a majority, or that its members should be able to demand that the policy with which they disagree should not apply to them.

This way of looking at politics is altogether different from the one characteristic of multiculturalists. For them, there is 'no such thing as society' – not in the sense intended by Margaret Thatcher (who added that there were only individuals and families) but in the sense that a society is to be conceived of as a fictitious body whose real constituents are communities. We saw in chapter 5 how the English pluralists in the early years of the twentieth century argued that communities were a valid source of authority and should share sovereignty with the state. Prior to that, in chapter 3, we came across Horace Kallen, the opponent of the 'melting pot' ideal who maintained in the 1920s that ethnically defined communities were destined (apparently by biology) to go on reproducing cultural differences into the indefinite future, and drew from this the conclusion that they should be seen as the building-blocks of society. Throughout the book, we have seen these ideas echoed in the work of contemporary multiculturalists, for whom group identities and group loyalties have primacy over any broader, society-wide identity and loyalty. Bhikhu Parekh, whose ideas I discussed in chapters 2 and 3, is an excellent example. Similarly, Iris Young has suggested that 'in the twentieth century the ideal state is composed of a plurality of nations or cultural groups, with a degree of self-determination and autonomy compatible with federated equal rights and obligations of citizenship'.[36] (But maybe things should be different in the twenty-first?)

Young devotes a chapter of *Justice and the Politics of Difference*, entitled 'The Ideal of Impartiality and the Civic Public', to trashing 'the Enlightenment ideal of the public realm of politics as attaining the universality of a general will that leaves difference, particularity, and the body behind in the private realms of family and civil society'.[37] Young's conception of 'the ideal of impartiality' and of 'the civic public' is the caricature of the Enlightenment typical among multiculturalists that I criticized in chapter 1.[38] She suggests that political theorists such as Benjamin Barber, who wish for a reinvigoration of democratic decision-making, are 'call[ing] for a reinstitution of a civic public in which citizens transcend their particular contexts, needs, and interests to address the common good'.[39] But nobody is proposing that 'particular contexts, needs and interests' cannot be advanced in democratic decision-making. On the contrary, the substance of debate in a democratic society should be, precisely, about the way in which differences of these kinds are to be dealt with by public policy. Indeed, Young herself accurately paraphrases Barber's own view in a way that actually undermines her conclusions about its import: 'The pursuit of particular interests, the pressing of the claims of particular groups, all must take place within a framework of community and common vision established by the public realm.'[40]

Eliminating an element of hyperbole which is not present in Barber's text, what this comes down to is the claim that political life presupposes citizens who think of themselves as contributing to a common discourse about their shared institutions. But this public debate must, of course, address itself to the 'particular contexts, needs and interests' of different people. It does not require, as Young suggests, 'the submerging of social differences'.[41] Let me pick up again an example that I used in chapter 1. Saying that there ought to be a uniform system of taxation within a country simply means that everyone should face the same set of rules; it does not imply that everybody should pay the same amount of tax. The rules themselves can be as differentiated as you like to accommodate claims for special treatment. The point is that all such claims have to be couched in terms of publicly defensible conceptions of equity and efficiency. What is not admissible is to argue that you should get special treatment in virtue of your belonging to a minority (whether culturally defined or not) that has different ideas about the right system of taxation from the ideas of the majority.

In contrast to this conception of politics as a society-wide conversation about questions of common concern, Young posits 'the ideal of a hetero- geneous public, in which persons stand forth with their differences acknow- ledged and respected, though perhaps not completely understood, by others'.[42] The implications of this picture of a society made up of groups whose demands may not even be mutually intelligible are, needless to say, strongly anti-majoritarian. It therefore comes as no surprise when Young suggests later that 'oppressed or disadvantaged' groups should have special representation and 'group veto power regarding specific policies that affect a group directly'.[43] The only two examples of this veto power that she offers are of radically different kinds: one is 'land use policy for Indian reserva- tions'; the other is 'reproductive rights policy for women'.[44]

As far as the first is concerned, it is hard to see that a power of veto over generally applicable public policies has much relevance. What Native Americans presumably want – and, in fact, have – is autonomous decision- making authority over land use within the territory comprising the reserva- tion.[45] It is also puzzling that Young talks about a veto in cases involving generally applicable public policies. For a veto (as in the Security Council) simply blocks change, thus perpetuating the status quo. Since the groups to be granted veto power are, by stipulation, 'oppressed or disadvantaged', having a veto would enable them only to prevent changes that would be deleterious to their perceived interests. Veto power would do nothing to put them in a position to insist on measures to improve their lot. It may be that Young did not feel comfortable about demanding the right of 'oppressed or disadvantaged' groups simply to decide what public policy should be in matters that 'affect them directly'. If the object is to give them a chance to escape from their disadvantaged condition, however, nothing less makes any sense.

Whether groups are to have a veto on policies that affect them directly or are to be granted stronger powers, Young's proposal can be implemented only if we have an answer to a prior question: who is to determine what matters affect groups directly, and on what criteria? Consider Young's own example of 'reproductive rights policy'. She does not explain what she has in mind when she claims that this policy should be controlled exclusively by women. I surmise, however, that she intends to refer primarily to abortion, because other matters falling within the realm of 'reproductive rights policy', such as the terms on which fertility treatment and contraception are to be available, are less plausibly seen as ones in which only women have a legitimate stake. Even if we make the presumption that 'reproductive rights policy' means policy on abortion, though, the example still illustrates what is wrong (or at any rate one of the things that is wrong) with Young's proposal. For the terminology of 'reproductive rights' already takes for granted one view of what is at issue: that abortion is entirely a question about the right of a woman to control her fertility. Moreover, it is only on the basis of this presupposition that abortion can be classified as a matter that exclusively affects women, so that they should have the exclusive power to decide public policy about it.

Whether or not some issue affects only the members of a certain group is itself normally a matter of controversy, and that controversy is itself one on which everyone can properly take a position. Thus, for example, there are not many people who would regard it as axiomatic that public policy on the withholding of life-saving medical treatment from children by their parents should be decided by a vote in which only Jehovah's Witnesses and Christian Scientists have an opportunity to participate. Similarly, few would accept that public policy on female genital mutilation should be turned over to a vote among those for whom it is a culturally prescribed norm.[46] Why is it that not everybody is likely to agree that these are 'specific policies that affect a group directly', and that in consequence the members of the group in question can properly demand the sole right to determine their content? Obviously, reluctance to delegate such decisions to religious or cultural minorities stems from a conviction that all citizens have a stake in public policies affecting the physical well-being and the lives of children, and a suspicion that the parents are not in cases like these trustworthy guardians of their children's interests.

I argued along the same lines in chapter 6 against the view that parents are the only people with a stake in their children's education. All the members of a society, I suggested, have a legitimate concern for the way in which the next generation turns out. On the basis of this, I took exception to the current rule in Britain that confines the right to vote on secondary school reorganization to the parents of children in the secondary schools within an area or attending primary schools within the catchment area of the secondary schools. My account in the previous section of the British government's decision-making process with regard to kosher/halal butchery can also be brought to bear here. *De facto*, if not *de jure*, the government followed the procedure recommended by Young, in that it treated Jews and Muslims as the 'directly affected' groups and took the opposition of the representatives of those groups to the recommendations of the Farm Animal Welfare Council as constituting a veto. But this simply ignored the legitimate interest that the general public has in the protection of non-human animals from excessive suffering.

The upshot of this discussion is that it is a mistake to think of Jehovah's Witnesses, Christian Scientists, Jews and Muslims or parents of children in the state educational system as having special interests that need to be constitutionally protected against majoritarian oppression. Rather, we should conceive of collective decisions about the treatment of children and non-human animals as ones in which all citizens are entitled to participate. Those who wish, on the basis of minority religious beliefs or cultural norms, to engage in practices that would be illegal in the absence of a special exemption should be free to join in the public debate and do their best to convince as many of their fellow citizens as they can of the merits of their case. There is no reason for expecting them to 'transcend their particular contexts, needs and interests', as Young suggests. At the same time, however, they should not be regarded as having some kind of privileged status in relation to decision-making on 'their' issues. It is scarcely necessary, perhaps, to spell out the relevance of these examples to Young's chosen case of abortion. For it is surely clear that her assumption that women have an exclusive interest in public policy on abortion, and should therefore be the only people with a say on what the policy is to be, simply presupposes the falsity of the view that a foetus (or 'unborn baby', as pro-life advocates like to describe it) is worthy of legal protection. It is not necessary to agree with that view to accept that there can be no justification for creating a system for deciding public policy on abortion that is at the outset built on the assumption that it is false.

Women are, of course, related to the question in a different way from men, in that it is their pregnancies that either are or are not terminated. But that does not turn them into a special interest group with a distinctive group policy preference – which Young assumes will be in favour of 'reproductive rights'. That women are involved with abortions in a way that men are not does not in itself entail that women will support liberal abortion laws disproportionately; a priori it is just as likely that women will put a greater emphasis on the value of motherhood, and on the strength of that be more antagonistic to abortion. In practice, women tend to be more active than men on both sides of the issue, and surveys suggest that the distribution of opinion among women and men tends to be quite similar.[47] This is consistent with the proposition that the degree (if any) to which the law should protect foetuses is a question on which people can and should deliberate in their capacity as citizens. It is worth insisting again, however, that Young is quite wrong to suggest that this precludes women from making arguments that derive from their distinctive perspective as the half of the human race capable of bearing children. What it does mean is that they make these arguments in the public forum – and, by the same token, that men can make arguments reflecting *their* distinctive position as the half of the human race that is not capable of bearing children.

It would be absurd to suggest that majorities are incapable of oppression, and I have no intention of suggesting it. But minorities are capable of oppression, too: how else are we to describe the withholding of life-saving medical treatment from children by their parents and the infliction of genital mutilation on young girls at the behest of their parents? The best safeguard against the unjust use of political power is not to parcel it up among minorities committed to practices abhorrent to the majority, but to put some questions beyond the reach of ordinary decision-making procedures. Thus, anti-discrimination provisions such as those imposed by the European Court of Justice on states within the European Union can be highly effective in preventing public policy from treating people unequally on the basis of characteristics such as age, gender and sexual orientation. It has to be conceded that judicial enforcement of equal treatment does not meet the demands of multiculturalists. For the whole point of the 'politics of difference' is that different groups should be treated differently. But the logic of my argument is that, if cultural minorities are to be granted exemptions from generally applicable laws, this should come about as a result of a decision-making process in which all citizens are entitled to take part on equal terms.

## 3.   If Multiculturalism Is the Answer, What Was the Question?

In the course of this book, I have criticized multiculturalism on a variety of counts. I shall not attempt to summarize these criticisms here. The ideas and policies that come under the multiculturalist umbrella are far too heterogeneous to permit my objections to them to be condensed into a few pages. There is, however, one pervasive flaw in multiculturalism that goes a long way to accounting for its irrelevance to most of the problems that members of minority groups characteristically face in contemporary western societies. I have drawn attention to it on a number of separate occasions, but I believe that it is sufficiently significant to warrant some systematic attention in this concluding chapter. The error that I have in mind, which underlies the multiculturalist diagnosis and therefore invalidates its proposed cures, is the endemic tendency to assume that distinctive cultural attributes are the defining feature of all groups. This assumption leads to the conclusion that whatever problems a group may face are bound to arise in some way from its distinctive cultural attributes. The consequence of this 'culturalization' of group identities is the systematic neglect of alternative causes of group disadvantage. Thus, the members of a group may suffer not because they have distinctive culturally derived goals but because they do poorly in achieving generally shared objectives such as a good education, desirable and well-paid jobs (or perhaps any job at all), a safe and salubrious neighbourhood in which to live and enough income to enable them to be adequately housed, clothed and fed and to participate in the social, economic and political life of their society.

Before entering into my bill of particulars, let me introduce the discussion by giving an example of what I have in mind. One of the most serious mistakes made by multiculturalists is to misunderstand the plight of American blacks. As Kwame Anthony Appiah has said,

> it is not black culture that the racist disdains, but blacks. There is no conflict of visions between black and white cultures that is the source of racial discord. No amount of knowledge of the architectural achievements of Nubia or Kush guarantees respect for African-Americans. No African-American is entitled to greater concern because he is descended from a people who created jazz or produced Toni Morrison. Culture is not the problem, and it is not the solution.[48]

The scope of Appiah's remark can, I suggest, be extended beyond its original context. Sometimes, indeed, culture is the problem and culture is the solution. But this is a much more rare occurrence than one would gather from the work of the multiculturalists.

I shall illustrate my thesis by drawing on the writings of Iris Young and Will Kymlicka. They are especially suitable for my purposes because they are exceptionally explicit in 'culturalizing' groups. I am confident, however, that all the advocates of multiculturalism discussed in this book could be shown to rely on a similar kind of analysis, which gives rise to similar policy prescriptions. I shall begin with Young, and I can make what I have to say fairly brief because I have already laid the groundwork in chapter 3. 'Among others', it may be recalled, the oppressed include 'women, Blacks, Chicanos, Puerto Ricans and other Spanish-speaking Americans, American Indians, Jews, lesbians, gay men, Arabs, Asians, old people, working-class people, and the physically and mentally disabled.'[49] This implies that about 90 per cent of Americans are oppressed.[50] It is, she says, 'new social movements in the United States since the 1960s' that claim these groups to be oppressed; but she adds that her aim is 'to systematize the meaning of the concept of oppression as used by these diverse political movements, and to provide normative argument to clarify the wrongs the term names'.[51]

I am concerned here not with Young's concept of oppression but with her concept of a group. ( I discussed her concept of oppression in chapter 3.) Although she says that oppression takes different forms, her analysis is compromised from the outset by her definition of a group as 'a collective of persons differentiated from at least one other group by cultural forms, practices, or way of life'.[52] This makes the possession of a distinctive culture the feature that defines somebody as a member of any group. Yet we can identify people as women, blacks or gays without having to know anything much about their culture. Even if we want to say that there is a women's culture, a black culture or a gay culture, the extent to which members of the group identify with such a distinctive group culture varies greatly from one member to another. And discrimination may well be based on sheer identity as a woman, a black or a gay rather than on any associated cultural attributes. There are also those groups whose members suffer discrimination or other disadvantage but are not marked by any common cultural characteristics at all. Thus, the physically disabled suffer from the unavoidable effects of their disability, plus unfair job discrimination, and the failure of institutions to adapt to their needs. If, however, we leave aside the special case of the deaf (and in particular those who are profoundly deaf from birth, as against those who lose their hearing later in life), there is no 'disabled culture'. On the contrary, what most disabled people want is to be integrated into society and treated as normal members of it. Similarly, there are the inherent disadvantages of growing older, and there is without doubt serious job discrimination on the basis of age, but there is not an 'old culture'.

It is not clear that all the groups listed by Young suffer from oppression at all. Whether or not being Jewish in the United States is necessarily associated with distinctive 'cultural forms, practices, or way of life', I would question Young's assertion that Jews as a group are subject to oppression in any sense, though I concede that my impression is drawn from having lived in the three largest cities. These, however, contain a large proportion of the American Jewish population in America. Along similar lines, the extraordinary success of Asians (especially in California) must make it doubtful that they are, considered as a group, oppressed. Moreover, it is surely clear that 'Asians' do not constitute a group at all, on Young's definition of a group, since there is nothing in the way of 'cultural forms, practices, or way of life' common to all and only Asians.

None of this, to repeat, is intended to deny that there are groups whose members lack the resources (including human capital) necessary for full participation in their society's institutions. Nor is it to downplay the extent to which group members may be subjected to systematic ill-treatment by police and other public officials. And it is certainly not to slight the importance of group-based discrimination as a source of disadvantage in education and employment. My point is simply that the source of bad or unfair treatment may well be group membership as such, identified by skin colour, ethnic descent, sex, and so on. In terms of the distinction introduced in chapter 2, we are talking here about direct rather than indirect discrimination. Indirect discrimination, it may be recalled, exists where there are rules set out in neutral terms which, nevertheless, render compliance more costly for members of some group in virtue of their distinctive culture, and cannot be justified as necessary for the conduct of the school, firm, government service, and so on. We saw in chapter 2 that indirect discrimination is a real possibility, and that anti-discrimination legislation needs to cover it as well as direct discrimination. My complaint is that the 'culturalization' of groups inevitably leads to the conclusion that all disadvantage stems from the 'misrecognition' of a group's culture. This way of thinking leads those who indulge in it to be blind to the most important causes of group disadvantage, as I shall seek to show later in this section.

I turn now to Will Kymlicka's book *Multicultural Citizenship*. The first point to notice about this is that, despite its title, it has virtually no overlap in subject-matter with Young's book. Kymlicka concedes – unwisely, if I am right – that 'there is a sense in which gays and lesbians, women, and the disabled form separate cultures within the larger society'.[53] But he goes on to say that 'this is very different from the sense in which the Québécois form a separate culture within Canada', and tells us that he 'will not describe all of these groups as "cultures" or "subcultures"'.[54] In a footnote directed specifically at Young, he adds that 'some advocates of a "politics of difference", whose focus is primarily on disadvantaged groups, obscure the distinctive demands of national groups. . . . While [Young] ostensibly includes the demands of American Indians and New Zealand Maori in her account of group-differentiated citizenship, she in fact misinterprets their demands by treating them as a marginalized group, rather than as self-governing nations.'[55] Kymlicka will not, he tells us, 'use "multiculturalism" as an umbrella term for every group-related difference in moral perspective or personal identity'.[56] What then is multiculturalism, on his conception? We can see at once from the terms in which the issue is posed that 'multiculturalism' is going to be defined in a way that makes it refer to some (alleged) facts about the existence of group-related differences. Thus, we can say that the word 'multiculturalism' is not going to be used to refer to a political programme. What forms of cultural diversity, then, are to be included within Kymlicka's conception of multiculturalism? He tells us that he is 'using "a culture" as synonymous with "a nation" or "a people" – that is, as an intergenerational community, more or less institutionally complete, occupying a given territory or homeland, sharing a distinct language and history'.[57]

What this means is that Kymlicka is simply equating nationhood and cultural distinctiveness by definitional fiat: there is no way of challenging the assumption that what makes a nation is primarily a culture common to its members but not shared by others. The idea that a nation is defined by its culture arose as a reaction in Germany against Enlightenment universalism, as we saw in the previous chapter. Later in the nineteenth century, the doctrine spread to the Balkans and Central Europe, where it underwrote internal repression in pursuit of national unity and external aggression in pursuit of irredentist claims. Meanwhile, Bismarck deployed it to marginalize the forces of liberalism within Prussia and then the German Empire, and it was invoked by German nationalists to legitimate the seizure of Alsace after the Franco-Prussian war of 1870. In the twentieth century, it underwrote Hitler's *Anschluss* with Austria and his demand for control of the Sudetenland. Bearing in mind the history of romantic nationalist doctrine, it is scarcely surprising that Kymlicka's attempt to found an allegedly liberal theory on it is unsuccessful. Liberalism is not a theory of politics that is applicable in all possible worlds. (Nor is any other political theory.) If the presuppositions of romantic nationalism were correct, there would be no place for liberalism. Fortunately, they are not.

I have already mentioned more than once in this book the way in which the discussion of multiculturalism has been skewed by (one interpretation of) the Canadian case. Thus, Kymlicka writes that 'Quebec sought exclusive jurisdiction over culture' in the negotiations that led up to the Charlottestown Accord, a proposed constitutional settlement whose failure to gain acceptance I shall analyse below. Kymlicka explains that Quebec's demand is 'understandable' because 'possessing a societal culture is the essence of sociological nationhood, and the reproduction of that societal culture is one of the essential goals of nationalism'.[58] This universal claim is simply an unfounded generalization from the particular case of Quebec. If there are any essential goals of nationalism, the preservation and reproduction of a distinctive societal culture is certainly not one of them. I am inclined to think that the only thing shared by nationalist movements is a demand for some kind of control (which may fall far short of sovereign statehood) over the collective affairs of those who are said to belong to the nation. But there is no one purpose that all those who make such a demand must wish to pursue, and it is not necessary that in every case there must be any specific purpose behind the demand for a degree of national autonomy.

It is not, therefore, surprising that Kymlicka is unable to come to terms with the United Kingdom. (In what he does say about it, he treats 'England' and 'Britain' as interchangeable and does not refer to Scotland or Wales at all.[59]) For the United Kingdom is without doubt a multinational state, but one in which national identifications have a very low cultural component. In particular, Scottish nationalism is a well-established phenomenon whose political success is indicated less by the vote for the Scottish National Party than by the Labour Party's reluctant electoral commitment to a referendum in Scotland on devolution and the large majority in favour of Scottish devolution in that referendum.[60] Yet the key to the pervasiveness of national sentiment in Scotland has been the way in which Scottish identity has been carefully detached from any distinctive language and customs. To be a Scot in good standing it is not necessary to speak Gaelic (or even regret the inability to do so), to wear a kilt or to enjoy the music of the bagpipes. Of course, those who buy into Kymlicka's idea that a nation must be characterized by a distinctive language and culture may attempt to make it true even if it is not, so that Croats purge Serbo-Croat of allegedly Serbian encroach-ments and invent a national character for themselves that distinguishes them from Serbs, while Serbs return the compliment. The point is, however, that this is a product of a sense of national identity and is not constitutive of it.

Having defined 'a culture' as 'a nation' or 'a people', Kymlicka goes on to define a state as 'multicultural if its members either belong to different nations (a multination state), or have emigrated from different nations (a polyethnic state), and if this fact is an important aspect of personal identity and political life'.[61] I shall take up in turn these two aspects of a multi-cultural state (as defined by Kymlicka), beginning with the first. We have already seen the way in which Kymlicka's 'culturalist' conception of nation-ality skews his analysis of the phenomenon. His whole approach is shaped by the debate about Quebec within Canada, and in this debate he is strongly committed to one side. Thus, he denounces with vigour the Constitution Act of 1982, which incorporated Pierre Trudeau's vision of 'a pan-Canadian identity based on equal citizenship rights'.[62] Integral to Trudeau's project was the Canadian Charter of Rights and Freedoms, and Kymlicka quotes another writer as saying that 'at the popular level in English-speaking Canada, Trudeau's attempt to make the Charter the acid test of Canadian nationality had succeeded'.[63]

This is precisely the kind of 'liberal constitutionalism' that, as we saw in the previous chapter, is the object of James Tully's ire. Kymlicka, too, regards it as wholly inappropriate to Canadian conditions. Instead, he supports the demand for Quebec to be recognized as a 'distinct society' within the Canadian federation, and on the strength of that to be granted extensive home rule powers in addition to those enjoyed by any of the other provinces – 'asymmetric federalism'. These demands are legitimate, he says, because 'for national minorities like the Québécois, federalism implies, first and foremost, a federation of *peoples*, and decisions regarding the powers of federal subunits should recognize and affirm the equal status of the founding peoples'.[64] According to Kymlicka, 'asymmetrical federalism follows almost necessarily from the idea that Canada is a multination state'.[65] What Quebec nationalists want is not simply more power for Quebec, if that arrangement simply forms part of 'some decentralizing formula applied to all prov-inces'.[66] What they demand is more power than the other provinces have, however much that may be: they 'want asymmetry for its own sake, as a symbolic recognition that Quebec alone is a nationality-based unit within Canada'.[67] (This is rather reminiscent of the diva who said she did not mind how much she was paid for appearing in an opera as long as it was more than anybody else got.)

Kymlicka concedes that 'the overwhelming majority of English-speaking Canadians reject the idea of a "special status" for Quebec'.[68] Indeed, he cites a poll 'showing 83 per cent opposition to special status'.[69] As usual, however, he attributes this opposition to 'confused moral thinking'.[70] The antagonism to the proposal 'to grant special rights to one province' stems, he claims, from the belief that this 'is somehow to denigrate the other provinces and to create two classes of citizens'.[71] While admitting that 'English-speaking Canadians view special status [for Quebec] as unfair', Kymlicka refuses to take this charge seriously.[72] Critics have, he claims, failed 'to identify the nature of the inequality – to determine who gained an unfair advantage, or suffered from some unfair burden, as a result of asymmetry'.[73] This is sheer bluff. Never once in the two chapters in which Kymlicka puts forward his defence of 'asymmetrical federalism' does he mention, let alone address, the obvious inequity inherent in allowing Quebec to opt out of institutions that operate in all the other provinces.[74] This is that representatives from Quebec take part in voting in the national parliament on issues that do not affect their constituents, because whatever legislation is enacted will not apply in Quebec.

This objection to asymmetry is known in Britain as 'the East Lothian question', because the MP for that constituency, Tam Dalyell, goes around asking – to the intense irritation of everybody else – why he should have a vote on matters that, under the provisions of Scottish devolution, do not affect his constituents in Scotland. The Scottish population is smaller in relation to that of the UK than that of Quebec in relation to the Canadian population, and the Scottish opt-out (at present, anyway) covers only a quite limited range of topics. Even so, Neil MacCormick has suggested that, because this 'anomaly' is 'highly visible', it 'seems unlikely to endure long as originally designed'.[75] Kymlicka clearly envisages that the powers to be transferred from the national government to Quebec should be massively expanded beyond their present level, and this would enormously exacerbate the Canadian equivalent of 'the East Lothian question'.

A natural suggestion to deal with the problem is that the representatives of Quebec should abstain from voting whenever an issue that does not affect their constituents comes up. But their abstention could easily result in a majority among the rest for a policy contrary to that supported by the government party or parties. To have two different majorities within the same legislature – one on issues that affected Quebec and another for ones that did not – would manifestly be a recipe for chaos.[76] This dilemma could be resolved if all the provinces except Quebec (Rest of Canada – ROC, in the usual vocabulary) had their own legislature and their own government resting on a majority of representatives within it. That is (as I shall argue in a moment) the true implication of Kymlicka's position, but it is quite different from the 'asymmetrical federalism' for which he argues. The model that he advocates has room for only one legislature, which has to take decisions both for the whole country and the country minus Quebec. The complaint, dismissed by Kymlicka, that asymmetry 'create[s] two classes of citizens' seems to me completely valid. On one side, there are those citizens who determine their own affairs in some matters and in other matters play a part in determining the affairs of everybody else as well. On the other side, there are those citizens who determine their own affairs in some matters and in other matters are unable to determine their own affairs because some other people who have no business taking part in decisions on them have a right to do so. This looks to me like two classes of citizens with unequal rights, if anything does.

Suppose we follow Kymlicka in holding that Canada is the home of two nations – Quebec and ROC – and also adhere to his ideas about what nations can legitimately claim. We can then deduce three propositions. The first is that the Québécois should, as far as possible, determine their own future without interference from outsiders. The second is that ROC should likewise, as far as possible, be able to determine its own future without interference from outsiders. The third is that the remaining issues (presumably foreign policy, defence and some matters of macroeconomic management) should not be decided in a forum in which Quebec, as the minority nationality within Canada, can be outvoted. Rather, they should be settled by negotiation between leaders representing the two nations. For, according to Kymlicka, a 'function of the language of nationhood is to equalize the bargaining power between a majority and national minorities. . . . [B]y defining the minority as a nation, it converts superiority/inferiority into a co-equal partnership.'[77]

Of these three desiderata, 'asymmetric federalism' satisfies the first while failing miserably on the second and third. It subjects ROC to the illegitimate power of representatives of Quebec. At the same time it does not allow Quebec 'recognition' as a co-equal nation in determining Canada-wide public policy, since that is made by a legislature in which Quebec has only a quarter of the votes and by a government resting on the support of a majority of that legislature. As proof of the confusion shown by critics of asymmetry, Kymlicka says that 'some claimed that asymmetry gives Quebecers more rights than other Canadians, others argued that asymmetry would give Quebecers fewer rights than other Canadians, and yet others alternated between the two views'.[78] The right answer was, on Kymlicka's own premises, that both criticisms were well-founded: in one respect asymmetry gave Quebec more than equality and in another respect less than equality.

The country that most closely approximates the model pointed to by Kymlicka's premises – autonomy for two national groups plus bargaining over state-wide policies – is Belgium.[79] But the endless process of haggling that is Belgian politics is so nauseating to all concerned that it is widely thought that the country would already have broken up if it were not for the problem posed by Brussels – a Francophone enclave in Flemish territory that is too big a prize for either side to be willing to relinquish. In the absence of this kind of problem, why should either side wish to maintain a vestigial Canadian state? It seems hard to resist the answer that there may as well be two countries, whose defence policies are co-ordinated by NATO and whose economic policies are co-ordinated by NAFTA and the WTO.

At the beginning of *Finding Our Way*, Kymlicka writes: 'I firmly believe that other countries can learn from our experience, and that we can help other peoples avoid unnecessary conflicts and injustices.'[80] If what I have just been saying is right, however, 'asymmetric federalism' is no more attractive than the rest of the multiculturalist programme. Here, as elsewhere, other countries would be unwise to take the 'Canadian model' as a blueprint. More than that, though, it seems clear that 'asymmetric federalism' is not even a good idea for Canada, especially in the very extensive form advocated by Kymlicka. Once the bulk of the decisions taken at a Canada-wide level did not apply to Quebec, it is hard to imagine that a system of government that gave representatives from Quebec a vote on these decisions could remain legitimate in the eyes of those living in the other nine provinces.

It may reasonably be asked how it is that Canada does as well as it does if its political class is as misguided as I am suggesting it is. One answer is that 'there is a lot of ruin in a nation', especially one whose land and coastal waters contain some of the richest natural resources in the world and whose history has been one of permanent peace with the only country with which it shares a land border. Another answer would appeal to precisely the phenomenon bemoaned by Kymlicka: the steadfast refusal of the Canadian citizenry to be persuaded by their leaders that they are headed in the right direction. Perhaps the best illustration of the way in which the electorate has saved the day is provided by the history of the Charlottestown Accord, the most recent of the ill-starred attempts to create a new constitutional settlement for Canada. The Conservative Prime Minister, Brian Mulroney, was so desperate to come up with an agreed formula that he made concessions to every interest group in sight, as well as giving in to the leap-frogging demands of the provincial premiers and the leaders of Native American groups.[81] Despite all this,

> by the time the [Accord] emerged as the product of demands (in some cases implicit) by interest groups and [provincial] premiers, it could not satisfy the final and most important challenger to mobilize: the general public in each province.... [D]espite virtually unanimous ... support from members of the political élite – including all ten provincial premiers, both representatives of the northern territories, and the leaders of four prominent aboriginal organizations – most provinces produced a majority vote against the Charlottestown Accord.[82]

The integrity of the Canadian state was salvaged by the voters in the teeth of the best efforts of the politicians to destroy it.

So far, I have been addressing multiculturalism as multinationalism, where 'a multination state' is defined as one whose members 'belong to different nations'. We may recall, however, that Kymlicka distinguishes a second variety of multiculturalism in the form of polyethnicity, where 'a polyethnic state' is defined as one whose 'members have emigrated from different nations'.[83] Clearly, this definition makes sense only in relation to New World countries settled by Europeans from a number of different nationalities, thus defining a universe consisting of the United States, Canada and Australia – and the last two only for the past thirty or forty years. But it becomes even more parochial when we factor in Kymlicka's 'culturalist' conception of nationality. As we saw in chapter 3, ethnicity in the United States is not essentially a cultural phenomenon. From the mid-nineteenth to the mid-twentieth century, the most important function of ethnic identities was to constitute the building-blocks of electoral competition in the major cities: if the Irish could control the Democratic machine, they could monopolize the patronage that was at the disposal of City Hall; if the Italians organized to the extent that they had to be put on the Democratic ticket, they got cut in when the time came to share the spoils, and so on. But apart from whatever permits were required for parades on St Patrick's Day or Columbus Day, they made no demands on public policy based on cultural distinctiveness. Nor would they have had any reason for doing so. Thus, the politicization of ethnicity was an instrument in the struggle for more of the goods that are sought by almost everybody, such as secure and (in relation to the skills required) well-paid jobs. It was not about making demands on the polity to ensure the ability to pursue idiosyncratic goals generated by cultural peculiarities.[84]

The political situation in Canada was different from that in the United States, and this gave ethnicity a somewhat different flavour. There, politics was dominated, at the local as well as the national level, by the two 'founding peoples'. Even in the cities, therefore, ethnic coalition-building in pursuit of power had no place. As a consequence, the folkloric aspect of ethnicity was bound to loom larger in Canada by default. But there is another reason for the greater importance of the cultural component in ethnicity, and this is that in Canada there is money in it. Leaving aside minuscule funds allocated by the National Endowment for the Arts, there are no programmes in the United States for subsidizing the cultural activities of ethnic groups whose national origins are in Europe. In Canada, by contrast, governments at all levels provide financial support for ethnically based cultural manifestations. This means that people have a financial incentive to identify with their ethnic community. Even more (as I pointed out in the first section of chapter 6), the existence of those programmes creates a motive for ethnic entrepreneurs to stimulate ethnocultural consciousness. For the bigger the group they can claim, the more money is likely to be forthcoming, even if the basis of allocation is not strictly pro rata. There is an important lesson to be drawn here. This is that multiculturalist policies are not simply a passive adaptation to an ineluctable fact of cultural diversity. Rather, multiculturalism actually creates the reality which is then, in a circular process of self-reinforcement, appealed to as a justification for a further extension of multiculturalist policies.

The upshot of what I have said so far might appear to be that Kymlicka's analysis of what he calls polyethnicity is valid for Canada, even though his claim that it has wider relevance must be rejected. This, however, would still be too favourable a judgement. The veteran British sociologist John Rex has put forward some reservations that seem to me apt about the applicability of the 'Canadian model' even within Canada:

> Canadians sometimes suggest that they have much to teach other countries who face severe problems of ethnic conflict. Perhaps, indeed, they do, but... they will have more to teach if they do not base their case on a somewhat simplistic model of the support of ethnic minorities on a purely cultural level. On the other hand, Europeans and Americans who have faced up to some of the difficult problems of intergroup relationships and who have experience in dealing with these problems may have discovered approaches highly relevant to the Canadian situation.[85]

What Kymlicka's analysis of ethnicity as a purely cultural phenomenon cannot accommodate, as Rex suggests, is any form of group disadvantage that arises from any source except the group's distinctive culture. As I have already argued in criticizing Iris Young's 'culturalization' of group identities, groups can suffer from material deprivation, lack of equal opportunity and direct discrimination, and there is no reason for supposing these disadvantages to flow from their possession of a distinctive culture, even where they have one (which in some cases they will not).

If we want an example of a group subject to deprivation, lack of opportunity and discrimination for whom 'culture is not the problem, and culture is not the solution', we can do no better than go back to the group to which Appiah's statement was originally intended to apply. Adrian Favell has pointed out that 'the culturally focused stress of Kymlicka's framework' entails that he cannot make sense of 'what is still the most important ethnic problem in the US: the ongoing classic "American dilemma" of the black population in the US'. For 'of all the cases Kymlicka mentions, the impossibility of fitting the non-indigenous but non-immigrant American blacks in his distinction between national and immigrant minorities is the most obvious. After some troubling with it, he leaves it aside as an extraordinary exception.'[86] In fact, Kymlicka devotes one section of just two pages and a bit in *Multicultural Citizenship* to the topic of 'Racial Desegregation in the United States'.[87] In this he concedes that, where American blacks are concerned, it is appropriate to apply the principle that 'injustice is a matter of arbitrary exclusion from the dominant institutions of society, and equality is a matter of non-discrimination and equal opportunity to participate'.[88] Having got this over with in the first paragraph of the section, however, he devotes all the remainder of his discussion to the implications of his thesis that 'the historical situation and present circumstances of African-Americans are virtually unique in the world'.[89] It follows, he says, that 'there is no reason to think that policies which are appropriate for them would be appropriate for either national minorities or voluntary immigrants (or vice versa)'.[90]

According to Kymlicka, then, the notion that equal treatment means treating people in the same way has to yield to the 'politics of difference' in all cases except this one, because in all other cases complaints about unequal treatment can arise only if public policy has failed to recognize the claims of culturally distinct national minorities or culturally distinct ethnic groups. On the basis of this extraordinarily sweeping contention, Kymlicka condemns all attempts to extend the formula appropriate to the situation of American blacks – which defines equal treatment as non-discrimination plus equal opportunity – to any other group, either within the United States or anywhere else in the world. A moment's thought should be enough to reveal this for the nonsense it is. Let us for the sake of argument agree with Kymlicka that the history and current situation of American blacks is not precisely reproduced among other groups in the United States or in any other country. (At some level of analysis, this is probably true of the history and current situation of every group in every country.) It is an obvious fallacy to conclude that American blacks are the only group anywhere in the world whose members aspire to achieve the same educational and occupational goals as the majority but are held back by discrimination and exclusion or by lack of resources. Minority groups suffering these disadvantages may, in addition to pursuing mainstream goals, wish to maintain a certain degree of cultural distinctiveness. But this need not, where it does occur, lead to their making any special demands on the polity. Like the ethnic groups in America that I have just discussed, they may be quite happy to maintain certain cultural traits within families, churches and clubs. They may also choose to patronize shops, restaurants and performances that cater to their tastes. All of these opportunities can be pursued within the common legal framework of liberal equality.

The implication of this is that the kind of tough and enforceable anti-discrimination legislation pioneered in the United States should form an element in every country's response to the existence of groups differentiated by ethnicity or 'race'. And, as the quotation from Rex implies, there is no reason for imagining Canada to be the one great exception. In fact, it is interesting to note that, in the four years between *Multicultural Citizenship* and *Finding Our Way*, Kymlicka seems to have come round to the view that there really is a problem of discrimination against blacks in Canada that is not reducible to a cultural issue. However, he still expresses the hope that, with a nudge in the right direction, black Canadians will follow the path of other immigrant groups and take their place as yet another element in the polyethnic mosaic. The title of the chapter in which he discusses the question is 'A Crossroads in Race Relations', and this 'ethnic' model of race relations is one of the possible directions in which he thinks things can go, the other apparently being one in which the issue of 'race' refuses to go away and perhaps becomes more salient.[91] But this analysis continues to miss the point, because Kymlicka's 'culturalist' understanding of ethnicity implies that, if they were free from discrimination, black Canadians would still suffer from unfair treatment unless public policy accommodated their distinctive culture.

Most Canadian blacks are, as Kymlicka says, Afro-Caribbeans, and there is no reason for supposing that they need to have all kinds of special provision laid on by the national or provincial government to ensure equality, any more than their counterparts in Britain do. Of course, if things are already set up so that every minority group can get money out of the government, it is only fair that they should get their share of whatever is going. But it remains true that 'culture is not the problem, and culture is not the solution'. Ill-conceived public policies can *make* culture into a problem, as here, by gratuitously turning it into a form of pork-barrel politics. But that is another matter, and it is one that I shall address, among others, in the next section of this chapter, which brings the book to a close.

## 4.   Culture versus Equality

If not culture, what is the problem and what is the solution? In many cases, there is no problem in the first place, so no solution is called for. As far as most culturally distinctive groups are concerned, a framework of egalitarian liberal laws leaves them free to pursue their ends either individually or in association with one another. The problem is invented out of nothing by multiculturalists, who assume that equal treatment for minorities is merely an arbitrary point on a continuum between specially adverse treatment and specially favourable treatment, with neutrality having nothing in particular to commend it. Kymlicka explicitly argues along these lines in *Finding Our Way*. He first says that it became accepted, 'beginning in the 1970s' (in Canada, Australia and the United States), 'that immigrants should be free to maintain some of their old customs regarding food, dress, religion, and recreation, and to associate with each other for those purposes'.[92] I criticized this passage in chapter 3, especially with regard to the United States.[93] If the descendants of immigrants from Italy were, as Kymlicka implies, not free before the 1970s to eat pasta, practise Roman Catholicism and play *bocce*, one can only say that they seem to have circumvented this lack of freedom pretty successfully.

Let us leave the truth of Kymlicka's statement on one side. What is of concern here is his next move. 'The demand for multiculturalism was a natural extension of this change. If it is acceptable for immigrants to maintain pride in their ethnic identity, then it is natural to expect that public institutions will be adapted to accommodate this diversity.'[94] The only way in which this progression might be regarded as 'natural' is by seeing it in the light of the maxim: 'If you think you're on to a good thing, there's no harm in trying to push it along.' Otherwise, it is simply a *non sequitur* to suggest that there is a 'natural' development from a regime of freedom to live within a framework of uniform laws to a regime in which every ethnic group demands, and gets, some special deal in the form of quotas, earmarked subsidies or exemptions from rules that apply to everybody else. Kymlicka's whole discussion of the issue rests, of course, on the assumption that ethnicity is primarily or exclusively a cultural phenomenon. I shall not repeat my criticisms of that. Let us, for the sake of argument, postulate a case in which there is a genuine cultural component in an ethnic group's identity. My point is that this fact does not in general give rise to valid claims for special treatment, because within a liberal state all groups are free to deploy their energies and resources in pursuit of culturally derived objectives on the same terms.

Another category of demands that should be resisted are those that would put the force of the state behind the infliction of physical injury (up to and including death, at any rate by omission) or behind systems of personal law that generate systematically unequal rights. Here culture is, indeed, the problem – in the sense that the demand arises out of some ethnocultural norm or religious belief – but culture is not the solution, because meeting the culturally based demand would require the state to violate its basic duty to protect its citizens from injury and to guarantee them equality before the law. Some examples of the things I have in mind here have already come up in this chapter. Thus, we saw in section 2 how the state might withdraw its protection from the children of some minority groups by permitting their parents to mutilate them with impunity or even fail to act when parents let their children die as a result of lack of medical care. In chapter 4, I discussed the proposal put forward by Chandran Kukathas that the multiculturalist solution should be generalized, so that the law would not punish any parents, with or without some warrant from their culture, who mutilated their children or allowed them to die preventable deaths. I quoted him there as saying that the consequence of his approach would be that 'significant harms' could 'be inflicted (by the dominant powers in the group) on the most vulnerable members of a minority community – usually women, children and dissenters'.[95] This is an unusually frank avowal of the human costs of multiculturalism. In my view it is a decisive reason for rejecting the policies that create these costs.

So far we have been dealing with cases in which the state has negative responsibility for bringing about outcomes in that it fails to do its job of preventing people from bringing them about – at any rate to the extent that attaching legal sanctions to the acts resulting in those outcomes can prevent them from occurring. The other class of demands made in the name of culture that I claim should be rejected consists of demands for the incorporation into the law of the land of systems of personal law that offend against fundamental principles of equality before the law. I discussed in chapter 5 as examples of this the demands of some Jewish and Muslim leaders in Britain to have Jewish and Muslim personal law given legal effect, so as to form an alternative to the civil law valid for the rest of the population. As I pointed out there, the result of this would be to give effect to grossly inequitable rules regarding divorce. It would also permit a man to have any number of wives up to four, adding wives *ad lib* without having to obtain the agreement of the existing one(s).[96] In the case of Muslim personal law, it would also permit a parent or guardian to marry off a minor child without the consent of the child. I need not rehearse the arguments that can be made against these proposals. Suffice to say that acceding to such demands would be a wholly inappropriate form of deference to minority cultures.

If we rule out all the non-starters, what are we left with? Contrary to what one might gather from the writings of the multiculturalists, the answer is: not much. So far from finding every ethnic group making demands for some kind of special treatment, what we actually discover is that almost all demands arise in virtue of subscription to a non-Christian religion and focus in one country after another around the same handful of issues. Wherever Jews and Muslims are established in a country, they will predictably press for an exemption from humane slaughter laws to enable them to kill animals while they are still conscious. Sikhs will want exemptions from laws that prevent them from wearing turbans while riding motorcycles or working on construction sites. They will also want to be allowed to wear a *kirpan*, or dirk, even if everybody else is prohibited from carrying offensive weapons in public. Muslims, especially if they originate in conservative rural areas of their own countries, will want women to wear head coverings and perhaps other traditional garments in public, and this is likely to lead to demands on educational institutions and employers to accommodate this.

Following my discussion of such cases in chapter 2 (and the auxiliary discussion in the context of the *Smith* case in chapter 5), I suggest that we should draw a sharp distinction between cases in which what is being asked for is a waiver of the application of the criminal law and cases in which what is being asked for is relief from the demands made by educational institutions or employers, whether public or private. Cases of the second kind fall under a principle of non-discrimination. This principle is often given legal effect in a document with special status, such as the Canadian Charter of Rights and Freedoms or the European Convention on Human Rights. Alternatively, or additionally, the principle of non-discrimination may be embodied in ordinary legislation such as the Civil Rights Act in the United States or the Race Relations Act in Britain. Either way, courts are charged with adjudicating claims of discrimination, which may originate in some quasi-judicial body (such as an industrial tribunal or some kind of administrative review body) or come directly to them. What the courts are asked to do here is to decide whether people who are put at a disadvantage by some demand (by, for example, an employer) in virtue of their cultural norms or religious beliefs are suffering from unfair treatment or whether the demand is justified. In reaching its judgement, a court must exercise some discretion: it must decide, for example, if an employer can reasonably require those engaged in work of a certain kind to wear a hard hat, or if a school can reasonably demand that a boy wear the cap that forms part of the school uniform rather than a turban. But it is a bounded discretion. (I discussed such cases in chapter 2.)

In taking account of cultural norms and religious beliefs in such cases, courts are doing what they are required by the legislature to do if they are to carry out the law. In chapter 5, I quoted Justice Scalia's argument to this effect in his judgement in the *Smith* case. The context that he cited there was eligibility for unemployment benefits: 'The statutory conditions provided that a person was not eligible for unemployment benefits if, "without good cause," he had quit work or refused available work. The "good cause" standard created a mechanism for individualized exemptions.'[97] Only someone with strict sabbatarian beliefs could 'with good cause' refuse to do a job that sometimes required working on a certain day of the week (the *Sherbert* case), and only a pacifist could 'with good cause' quit his job when assigned to making gun turrets for tanks (the *Thomas* case). Hence, as Justice Scalia said, 'the Sherbert test...was developed in a context that lent itself to individualized government assessment of the particular circumstances behind an applicant's unemployment'.[98]

The point of Justice Scalia's remarks is that in cases such as these it is entirely appropriate to individuate the application of the law so as to give weight to an employee's idiosyncratic scruples about working on Saturdays or making parts for tanks. For this is precisely what the even-handed application of the law calls for. It was, he suggested, an unwarranted extension of these cases to found upon them a general presumption that anybody who is discommoded by a generally applicable law should be able to gain a waiver from the courts in the name of religious freedom or equal treatment. This, he argued, would throw into the arms of judges decisions of a kind that were the proper province of legislatures. Courts, he said, should not create a situation 'in which each conscience is a law unto itself or in which judges weigh the importance of all laws against the centrality of all religious beliefs'.[99] An example of this kind of judicial usurpation that I gave in chapter 6 was the decision of the Minnesota Supreme Court that reflective silver tape outlining the back of a buggy would be an adequate warning of its presence on the road at night, in lieu of the reflective triangle normally required to be fixed to the back of a slow-moving vehicle. In doing so, the court simply substituted its own unsubstantiated opinion for the determination of the legislature that a reflective triangle was essential – a judgement which was based on the counsel of road safety experts and the testimony of drivers who had had close calls with Amish buggies in the dark.

There is no principle of justice mandating exemptions to generally applicable laws for those who find compliance burdensome in virtue of their cultural norms or religious beliefs. No contemplation of the concept of equal treatment will tell us whether ritual slaughter should be allowed or whether it imposes an unacceptable degree of suffering on the beasts subjected to it. No more will it tell us whether the paternalistic societal interest in preventing road deaths and injuries should or should not outweigh the desire of some Sikhs to ride motorcycles while wearing turbans. There are considerations of some weight on both sides and the only appropriate forum for casting up the balance is a publicly accountable one: a process in which the public at large is, ideally, consulted and (in the absence of compelling reasons for believing that the majority view rests on misinformation or prejudice) heeded. I have argued in this book that, with almost no exceptions, either there is a good enough case for having a law to foreclose exemptions or alternatively the case for having a law is not strong enough to justify its existence at all. I do not wish to insist on that conclusion here. Nothing in my larger argument turns on it. Even if there is more to be said for exemptions to accommodate cultural and religious minorities than I am inclined to believe there is, we should still resist being bullied by the multiculturalists into thinking that we are not entitled to form our own views about the pros and cons. There is no overriding demand of justice that preempts our decision.

The upshot of what has been said so far might seem to be that multiculturalism is a sideshow that should never have got the main billing. It is all of that, but the more substantial objection to it is that it actually directs attention away from more important problems. Let me return to the case of inner-city American blacks. As Adrian Favell writes, the issues involved need to be disassociated entirely from the problematic of multicultural citizenship, which wrongly raises the question in cultural terms when the significance of racial and cultural factors [is] in decline. . . . If it in fact proves to be socio-economic structural and class factors that are most significant in the integration failure of American blacks, it may well be harmful to their cause that the question has so often been merged in the great multiculturalism debate in the US, with inappropriate 'citizenship' issues raised more often by immigration or middle class campus politics.[100]

Thus, William Julius Wilson, to whom Favell refers here, has argued that the migration of jobs to the suburbs has made it physically difficult for the residents of the ghetto to get to them, especially if they do not run a car – and without a job in the first place there is no legal way of paying for one. Equally important is the way in which the social isolation of the ghetto means that its denizens are not in everyday contact with people who do have jobs. They are thus excluded from the personal networks through which many jobs are filled.[101] Moreover, changes in technology have made jobs for which the only requirement is physical strength increasingly scarce, yet the educational attainments of blacks have not kept pace with the demands of the economy.

There are several reasons for this lag in educational attainment. One is that funding for schools tends to be local, so that schools in poor areas are poorly funded. Another is that the multiple social pathologies of the ghetto are not conducive to steady application. Parental poverty itself is no doubt also a contributory factor, since it makes it unlikely that a child will have access to a quiet room in which to do homework or will be given the books and the computer that middle-class parents can come up with. But the help that middle-class parents are able to give their children is not just material. Parents who are themselves ill-educated are not well placed to give their children good strategic advice about courses of study or talk them through problems with their work. Indeed, the intergenerational transmission of educational disadvantage begins well before children start attending school. The cumulative tendency of recent research (such as that to which I referred in chapter 3) is to suggest that the most significant contributions that middle-class parents make to their children's preparedness to benefit from schooling is to deploy an extensive vocabulary with them. The scale of the disparity is illustrated by the finding in one study 'that 3-year-olds in families with professional parents used more extensive vocabularies in daily interactions than did mothers on welfare – not to mention the children of those mothers'.[102]

This is yet another instance in which the invocation of 'culture' would lead to a misdiagnosis of the problem. It is true that we could loosely describe the educational disadvantage of black children as arising from 'cultural deprivation'. But this has almost nothing to do with the cultural differences that drive the multiculturalist agenda. There is 'no conflict of visions between black and white cultures' here, to refer again to my quotation in the previous section from Anthony Appiah. Rather, we are talking about a deficit that is more aptly compared to a physical disability or treated as equivalent to lacking a certain kind of non-material resource. Indeed, it was precisely this sort of disadvantage that I had in mind when I said earlier that some groups are short of both material resources and human capital. 'Like other forms of capital, [human capital] accumulates over generations; it is a thing that parents "give" to their children through their upbringing, and that children then successfully deploy in school, allowing them to bequeath more human capital to their children.'[103]

Thinking of the situation in this way prompts us to ask about possible methods for boosting human capital. Our attention will thus be directed towards strategies such as intensive pre-school education and after-school facilities that are attractive, well-equipped and well-staffed.[104] More radically, we might follow up the idea mooted by the head teacher of an inner-city school in Hartford, Connecticut 'that the Hartford schools should simply be shut down, and the children dispersed into the surrounding suburbs'.[105] The rationale of this is that, if an inner-city child interacts only with children like itself, it is simply going to reproduce the same self-defeating patterns.[106] More radically still, the families themselves could be provided with the resources to enable them to move to the suburbs. The most striking illustration of this strategy at work has been 'the famous Gautreaux experiment in Chicago, in which families were given subsidies to move from high-poverty neighbourhoods to the suburbs; studies have found that children in these families were far more successful academically than would have otherwise been predicted'.[107] These remedies are potentially relevant wherever there is an identifiable group whose members tend to transmit from generation to generation a lack of human capital. Thus, W. G. Runciman has written, with Britain in mind:

> If families are relocated from an inner-city area to a socially integrated suburb, the children may be less likely to drop out of school, fail to find employment, and become engaged in activities socially defined as 'delinquent'. Even if they go on living where they do but go to a school in a different area, their chances of individual intergenerational mobility may be increased.[108]

The alternative 'culturalist' diagnosis of the plight of those lacking human capital would be that what they need is the reinforcement of 'their culture'. This might include, in the American case, the recognition of 'black English' or 'ebonics' by the schools as a valid form of English, and in the British case the recognition of Afro-Caribbean English. No doubt both variants are, as linguists insist, dialects with a consistent set of syntactical rules. But the fact remains that no employer in the mainstream economy would employ anybody in a capacity that required communication with the public who lacked a command of standard English. Like knowing only Spanish, being able to speak and write only in a non-standard form of English is a one-way trip to a dead-end job. This is not to say that schools should conceive it as their job to prevent children from speaking in the form of English used in their home or community, any more than it should be the job of the schools to prevent children from speaking Spanish. Their task should be to attempt to make their pupils fluent in standard English as well.

The notion that one can maintain two versions of the same language, and that these versions have different occasions for use, seems to be much more easily accepted by speakers of languages other than English. Perhaps the explanation is that in the case of other languages – German, for example – the variants tend to be regionally based, whereas in England (especially southern England) it is location in the class structure that is, in Orwell's memorable phrase, 'branded on the tongue'.[109] Similarly, to the extent that there is a distinctive black accent and syntax in the United States (though not, of course, one spoken by all blacks), it is a characteristic of a status group rather than a region. If I am right about this, the implication is that it is especially important here not to suggest that the non-standard variant is 'wrong' or inferior. But there is no escaping the conclusion that, if they are not to short-change their pupils, the schools should try to ensure that by the time they leave they are equipped with a command of the standard form of the language.

We can add the abuse of 'culture' I have just been discussing to those dissected in the previous chapter. On the basis of such an approach, the Indian government could defend itself from criticism for its failure to get the literacy rate above 50 per cent by saying that it is not 'part of the culture' of a large proportion of the population to read, and that it is carrying out its multiculturalist duty by arranging things so that they are able to maintain their culture of illiteracy. In case this sounds far-fetched, let me remind the reader that, in chapter 6, we saw Chandran Kukathas claiming in the name of 'cultural toleration' that gypsies should be free to keep their children illiterate. Kukathas's argument that even rudimentary formal education is not necessary to enable children to pursue the 'traditional' life of a gypsy could no doubt be said with equal validity of the requirements for living the life of a hereditary crossing-sweeper or night-soil collector in India.

What is conspicuously missing from all this is any concern for the interests of the children themselves. I argued in chapter 6 that states have an obligation both to the children and to the citizenry in general to ensure that as far as possible all children should leave school capable of doing a good job of raising children of their own, being gainfully employed in the mainstream economy and protecting their legal interests in private transactions. I also suggested that schools should provide their pupils with the skills necessary for dealing with public officials and taking part in the public life of their society. I argued, finally, that we should conceive of access to the common heritage of humanity in the form of the arts and sciences as the birthright of every child. Parents should not be able to block their children's access to it by saying that bigotry or ignorance are 'a part of their culture', any more than they should be able to keep them in straitjackets or locked rooms.

'In my beginning is my end.'[110] I want to draw this discussion to a conclusion by returning to a theme that I first sounded in the first chapter. Pursuit of the multiculturalist agenda makes the achievement of broadly based egalitarian policies more difficult in two ways. At the minimum, it diverts political effort away from universalistic goals. But a more serious problem is that multiculturalism may very well destroy the conditions for putting together a coalition in favour of across-the-board equalization of opportunities and resources. To her credit, Iris Marion Young has recognized the existence of a problem. In an article written subsequently to *Justice and the Politics of Difference*, she acknowledges the case for 'universal public programmes of economic restructuring and redistribution', again citing the work of William Julius Wilson.[111] She clings, however, to the belief that 'a group differentiated politics' is also required to 'recognize the justice of group based claims of ... oppressed people to specific needs [*sic*] and compensatory benefits'.[112] She adds that 'it is not obvious how both kinds of politics can occur'.[113] I have to say that after reading the article it is no more obvious to me than it ever was. It is easy to understand this lack of persuasiveness if we recognize that pursuing group-differentiated policies really is inimical to the pursuit of the 'programme of universal material benefits to which all citizens have potential access' advocated by Young.[114]

Let me first take up the less severe form of the tension between them. Suppose a certain pot of money is set aside for the support of minority cultural activities. This sets the stage for a struggle between ethnocultural entrepreneurs for a share of the funds, so that efforts that might have been devoted to more broad-based causes are dissipated on turf wars. Even where the pursuit of special group-based objectives does not have this zero-sum feature, the results are going to be similar. Cultural minorities might be non-competitive in getting publicly funded schools of their own or perhaps (*à la* Parekh) having other bits of public provision put under their control. But this kind of particularistic focus will still tend to make cultural minorities weak partners in endeavours to redistribute income from rich to poor across the board or to improve the quality of schools and other public services generally.

The more severe form of the conflict between group-based and universalistic policies arises where group-based policies split the potential coalition for broad-based egalitarian reform down the middle. I pointed out in chapter 3 that a system of preferential admission to college for minorities tends not to displace the children of affluent whites whose children attend high-quality public schools or private schools. Rather, those who lose out are those whose scores and school records would just barely push them over the line in the absence of a preferential system, and these are likely to be the children of relatively unprivileged non-minority parents. I also argued that Orlando Patterson's proposal of a permanent system of preferences for the children of a minority consisting of the poorest parents would create, if it were adopted, a conflict between those whose children met the criteria for inclusion in the programme and those in very similar material circumstances who just failed to do so. Special preferences of either sort would have the effect of pitting against one another the potential constituency for universalistic policies aimed at benefiting all those below the median income.[115] The point about group-based preferences can be generalized. At best, all they can ever do is achieve a minor reshuffling of the characteristics of the individuals occupying different locations in an unchanged structure that creates grossly unequal incomes and opportunities. In Todd Gitlin's felicitous phrase, 'the politics of identity...struggles to change the color of inequality'.[116] Not only does it do nothing to change the structure of unequal opportunities and outcomes, it actually entrenches it by embroiling those in the lower reaches of the distribution in internecine warfare.

Undoubtedly, a significant source of support for the multiculturalist cause has been despair at the prospects of getting broad-based egalitarian policies adopted. But it is a fallacy to suppose that the 'politics of difference' is any kind of substitute. Imagine for a moment that the wildest dreams of every supporter of the 'politics of difference' were realized – to the extent that their maximal demands are compatible with one another. Would this transform the lives of members of cultural minorities? I think the answer is that it would make a profound difference to the lives of many, but not in ways that they would all experience as liberating. The whole thrust of the 'politics of difference', as we have seen in one context after another, is that it seeks to withdraw from individual members of minority groups the protections that are normally offered by liberal states. Where a group qualifies as a national minority within a liberal state, multiculturalists commonly propose that it should be free to make its own laws, perhaps within a decision-making system that gives male elders a monopoly of power. These laws, they suggest, should not have to conform to the norms of 'liberal constitutionalism', and should be able to discriminate with impunity against women or adherents of religions other than that of the majority. As we saw in chapter 4, Will Kymlicka argues that the reasons for not invading Saudi Arabia in an attempt to improve its human rights record are equally valid in showing why Québécois or Native American groups should not be required to adhere to basic liberal principles concerning such matters as freedom of religion or non-discrimination.

Even where the power of collective decision-making is not turned over wholesale to possibly illiberal groups, the point of multiculturalism is still to insist that liberal protections for individuals should be withdrawn wherever they interfere with a minority's ability to live according to its culture. Kukathas, as we have seen, concedes that the chief sufferers would be women, children and dissidents, as a consequence of the free rein that would be given to traditional patriarchal and authoritarian cultural norms. Children would be liable to mutilation, lack of medical care or education, and could be married without their consent. The traditional norms of religious and cultural groups would be incorporated into the laws governing marriage and divorce, and women who stepped out of line would be subject to sanctions imposed by (normally male) communal authorities. Again, many minorities are characterized by deep-seated hostility to homosexuality. 'In June [1999] a gay ball planned near Leicester by Asians had to be cancelled at the insistence of local community leaders. . . . The few clubs that cater for black and Asian homosexuals are secret places.'[117] The accommodation of 'deep diversity' among groups thus goes along with the suppression of diversity within groups. Woe betide anyone who has the misfortune to be a member of a minority whose behaviour contravenes the norms of an intolerant cultural minority!

The destruction of the 'myth of merit', as advocated by Iris Young, might seem at first glance more unequivocally beneficial to cultural minorities, or at any rate those whose members are disproportionately ill-educated or lacking in command of the established language of business and public life. But this becomes more doubtful when we bear in mind that, even among the population of working age (that is, leaving out those who are 'oppressed' in virtue of being either young or old), only about one-fifth are not members of oppressed groups, as defined by Young. She proposes that, in the politicization of the process of recruitment to desirable jobs, the non-oppressed should not be permitted to do favours for one another. But as far as everybody else is concerned, it is to be a free-for-all with no ground rules. The less-advantaged groups within the 80 per cent of the 'oppressed' population could easily be driven to the wall under this regime, and might well finish up worse off than they would be in a system that awarded jobs to those qualified to do them. Moreover, even though it might be gratifying to obtain a job for which one had no qualifications on the basis of a vote among the other employees, this would have to be offset against the drawback that the hospitals and the schools (and the universities), the banks and the shops, the firms and the public services would all be run by people who had got where they were without needing any qualifications. Under these conditions, the case for giving jobs to those qualified to do them might perhaps come to look quite persuasive even to those who were themselves unqualified to do the jobs they were doing.

On rather similar lines, it is bound to be prima facie attractive to members of any given cultural minority to be able to indulge in antisocial behaviour if it is 'part of their culture'. But enthusiasm for such a regime may well be attenuated as a result of experiencing the uses made of the same privilege by members of other cultural minorities. While, for example, you may appreciate being able to cut the throats of goats in your back garden for culturally prescribed ritual purposes, you may be given pause if your next-door neighbour on one side has collected together the children of several relatives and allows them to run riot (as in the Western Australian case considered in chapter 7) and your neighbour on the other side follows the 'traditional' practice of breaking up old cars and burning the tyres and upholstery.

Again, it may at first blush seem advantageous (however obnoxious it may be from a liberal standard) to a member of a cultural minority for it to be illegal for anyone to disparage the beliefs or the way of life of anybody else. But most members of cultural minorities are strongly inclined to disapprove of the beliefs and ways of life of many other groups in their society. Unless they watch their tongues carefully in trains and buses, in restaurants and shops, and in streets and parks, they are liable to be hauled up before the Commissioners of Political Correctness. On reflection, calling off the Politically Correct Thought Police altogether may appear to be the better option.

I could go on, but I hope that what I have said is enough to suggest that the full implementation of the multiculturalist programme would be at best a mixed blessing even for its intended beneficiaries. Multiculturalists will no doubt complain that I have been unfair to them because nobody is in favour of every single element in the programme. But whether this is true or not is irrelevant. My purpose has been simply to suggest that, administered in doses of any strength you like, multiculturalism poses as many problems as it solves. And, to return to my theme for the last time, it cannot in the nature of the case address the huge inequalities in opportunities and resources that disfigure – and increasingly dominate – societies such as those of Britain and the United States.

# Notes

## Preface

1 Jo Ellen Jacobs, ed., *The Complete Works of Harriet Taylor Mill* (Bloomingdale, Ind.: Indiana University Press, 1998), p. 291; the text of the dedication is on pp. 291–2.
2 Ibid., letter on p. 472.
3 Ibid., letter on pp. 472–3.
4 Caroline Alexander, *Mrs Chippy's Last Expedition: The Remarkable Journal of Shackleton's Polar-Bound Cat* (London: Bloomsbury, 1997).
5 David Laitin, *Identity in Transition: The Russian-Speaking Populations in the Near Abroad* (Ithaca, NY: Cornell University Press, 1998).

## Chapter 1 Introduction

1 Karl Marx and Friedrich Engels, *Manifesto of the Communist Party*, pp. 469–500 in Robert C. Tucker, ed., *The Marx-Engels Reader* (2nd edn, New York: W. W. Norton, 1978), p. 473.
2 Will Kymlicka, 'Introduction: An Emerging Consensus?', *Ethical Theory and Moral Practice* 1 (1998), 143–57, p. 147, emphasis suppressed.
3 Ibid., p. 148.
4 Robert Hughes, *Culture of Complaint: The Fraying of America* (New York: Oxford University Press, 1993); Todd Gitlin, *The Twilight of Common Dreams: Why America is Wracked by Culture Wars* (New York: Henry Holt, 1995).
5 Kymlicka, 'Introduction: An Emerging Consensus?', p. 149.
6 John Rawls, *A Theory of Justice* (Cambridge, Mass.: Harvard University Press, 1971).

7 See for an example John Gray, *Enlightenment's Wake: Politics and Culture at the Close of the Modern Age* (London: Routledge, 1995). I shall discuss this book in chapter 7.

8 James Schmidt, 'Civility and Society at the Century's End' (paper delivered at UNESCO conference on *Ethics of the Future*, Rio de Janeiro, June 1997), p. 7.

9 Ibid.

10 James C. Scott, *Seeing Like a State: How Certain Schemes to Improve the Human Condition Have Failed* (New Haven, Conn.: Yale University Press, 1998), p. 32.

11 James Tully, *Strange Multiplicity: Constitutionalism in an Age of Diversity* (Cambridge: Cambridge University Press, 1995), pp. 58–9 and 62.

12 Ibid., p. 66.

13 Ibid.

14 See especially Iris Marion Young, *Justice and the Politics of Difference* (Princeton, NJ: Princeton University Press, 1990), ch. 4.

15 G. Baumann, 'Dominant and Demotic Discourses of Culture: Their Relevance to Multi-Ethnic Alliances', pp. 209–25 in P. Werbner and T. Modood, eds, *Debating Cultural Hybridity: Multi-Cultural Identities and the Politics of Anti-Racism* (London: Zed Books, 1997), p. 222, quoted in R. D. Grillo, *Pluralism and the Politics of Difference: State, Culture, and Ethnicity in Comparative Perspective* (Oxford: Clarendon Press, 1998), p. 196.

16 Alison M. Jaggar, 'Multicultural Democracy', *The Journal of Philosophy* 7 (1999), 308–29, p. 314. Young explicitly repudiates this conception of groups in *Justice and the Politics of Difference*. Jaggar's point is, however, that it is required as a rationale for group representation: if the members of a group (women, say, or gays) have nothing in common *qua* members of the group, why should they be represented as a group – and how can they be?

17 Richard A. Lebrun, ed., Joseph de Maistre, *Considerations on France* (Cambridge: Cambridge University Press, 1994), p. 53.

18 Grillo, *Pluralism and the Politics of Difference*, p. 200.

19 See ibid., pp. 200–1.

20 See 'Sketch for a Historical Picture of the Progress of the Human Mind', pp. 209–82 in Keith Baker, ed., *Condorcet: Selected Writings* (Indianapolis: Bobbs-Merrill, 1976). (In his Introduction, Keith Baker says that this work is 'often regarded as the very epitome of Enlightenment thought'. Ibid., p. vii.)

21 Karl Marx, 'On the Jewish Question', pp. 137–50 in Jeremy Waldron, ed., *'Nonsense upon Stilts?' Bentham, Burke and Marx on the Rights of Man* (London: Methuen, 1987), p. 149. This is a notoriously obscure text: it is something of an understatement to say, as Waldron does, that 'Marx's views on rights were never formulated with the clarity or unequivocality that modern analysis presupposes'. Ibid., p. 135. Nevertheless, as Waldron adds, the general tenor of Marx's writings on the subject evinces an 'attitude...that explains the lack of emphasis on rights in the Marxian tradition'. Ibid., pp. 135–6.

22 Young, *Justice and the Politics of Difference*, p. 10.

23 Ibid., p. 9.

24   Nathaniel Hawthorne, *The Scarlet Letter*, pp. 289–546 in Malcolm Cowley, ed., *The Portable Hawthorne* (New York: The Viking Press, 1969 [1948]); Jung Chang, *Wild Swans* (London: Flamingo, 1993 [1991]).

25   See Young, *Justice and the Politics of Difference*, pp. 152–5, (section entitled 'Justice and Cultural Revolution'), quotation from p. 153. Orwell's account of the constant monitoring and self-monitoring in the society of *Nineteen Eighty-Four* runs as follows: 'A Party member lives from birth to death under the eye of the Thought Police.... His friendships, his relaxations, his behaviour towards his wife and children, the expression on his face when he is alone, the words he mutters in sleep, even the characteristic movements of his body, are all jealously scrutinized.' George Orwell, *Nineteen Eighty-Four* (London: Secker and Warburg, 1949), p. 216.

26   Schmidt, 'Civility and Society', p. 19. See also Dorinda Outram, *The Enlightenment* (Cambridge: Cambridge University Press, 1995), which is organized around the idea that asking 'What is enlightenment?' was itself the characteristic activity of the Enlightenment.

27   Rawls has by now abandoned most of the ideas that made *A Theory of Justice* worthwhile. I have no interest in defending anything Rawls has written since about 1975, including his subsequent interpretations of *A Theory of Justice* or his revisions of its text. Rawls's current position, embodied in *The Law of Peoples* (Cambridge, Mass.: Harvard University Press, 1999), amounts to a rather muddled version of Michael Walzer's anti-Enlightenment particularism, which I discuss in chapter 4.

## Chapter 2   The Strategy of Privatization

1   Ivan Hannaford, *Race: the History of an Idea in the West* (Washington, DC: The Woodrow Wilson Center Press, 1996), p. 356.

2   Will Kymlicka, 'Introduction: An Emerging Consensus?', *Ethical Theory and Moral Practice* 1 (1998), 143–57, p. 149.

3   Will Kymlicka, *Multicultural Citizenship: A Liberal Theory of Minority Rights* (Oxford: Clarendon Press, 1995).

4   Eliezer Ben-Rafael, 'The Israeli Experience in Multiculturalism', pp. 111–41 in Rainer Bauböck and John Rundell, eds, *Blurred Boundaries: Migration, Ethnicity, Citizenship* (Aldershot: Ashgate, 1998), p. 111, citations suppressed.

5   Charles Westin, 'Temporal and Spatial Aspects of Multiculturality', pp. 53–84 in Bauböck and Rundell, eds, *Blurred Boundaries*, p. 56.

6   Charles Taylor, 'The Politics of Recognition', pp. 25–73 in Amy Gutmann, ed., *Multiculturalism: Examining the Politics of Recognition* (Princeton, NJ: Princeton University Press, 1994), cited in Ben-Rafael, 'The Israeli Experience', p. 111.

7   Danielle Juteau, Marie McAndrew and Linda Pietrantonio, 'Multiculturalism à la Canadian and Intégration à la Québécoise. Transcending their Limits', pp. 95–110 in Bauböck and Rundell, eds, *Blurred Boundaries*, p. 95.

8   Westin, 'Temporal and Spatial Aspects', p. 57.

9   M. G. Smith, *The Plural Society in the British West Indies* (Berkeley and Los Angeles: University of California Press, 1965), p. 14.

10   Edward Gibbon, *The Decline and Fall of the Roman Empire*, abridged by D. M. Low (London: Chatto and Windus, 1960), p. 11 (ch. 2).

11   Ibid.

12   See Samuel P. Huntington, *The Clash of Civilizations and the Remaking of World Order* (New York: Touchstone Books, 1997).

13   John Julius Norwich, *Byzantium: The Early Centuries* (London: Penguin, 1990 [1988]), p. 379.

14   Gibbon, *Decline and Fall*, p. 639.

15   T. N. Madan, 'Secularism In Its Place', pp. 297–320 in Rajeev Bhargava, ed., *Secularism and Its Critics* (Delhi: Oxford University Press, 1998), p. 319.

16   Stanley J. Tambiah, 'The Crisis of Secularism in India', pp. 418–53 in Bhargava, ed., *Secularism and Its Critics*, p. 445, emphasis in original.

17   The self-conscious reintroduction of barbarous punishments, for example, is not simply behaving traditionally, any more than a shop that says it sells 'traditional fish and chips' can be a traditional fish and chip shop. There is also quite commonly the familiar phenomenon of the 'invention of tradition'. The brutal elimination of women from the public sphere by the Taliban, for example, is not a return to former Afghan customs but an imposition by zealots trained up in Pakistan.

18   A leading contemporary Muslim scholar maintains, for example, that the Koran provides the answers to questions 'of administration, property and legitimate politics'. More sweepingly, he says: 'Islam declares openly that it includes all aspects of human life: material and spiritual, individual and social.' Youssef Qaradawi, *Islam and 'Almaniya: Face to Face* (Cairo: Maktaba Wahba, 1998), pp. 48–9, and 93. I am grateful to Scott Morrison for the reference and the translation, drawn from his Columbia PhD dissertation in progress.

19   The force of this would be weakened if it could be said that stable liberal democracies have occurred only in countries that are Christian (or ex-Christian). However, if we are prepared to count Israel, India and Japan, the peculiarity of Islam stands out.

20   Taylor, 'The Politics of Recognition', p. 62. (Kymlicka similarly says that the 'traditional pretensions' of the model of unitary citizenship 'to ethnocultural neutrality can no longer be sustained'. 'Introduction: An Emerging Consensus?', p. 149.)

21   Ibid.

22   Ibid.

23   Tariq Modood, 'Anti-Essentialism, Multiculturalism and the "Recognition" of Religious Groups', *Journal of Political Philosophy* 6 (1998), 378–99, p. 393.

24   Ibid., p. 394.

25   Peter Jones, 'Rushdie, Race and Religion', *Political Studies* 38 (1990), 687–94, pp. 690–1.

26   Quoted in Philip Thody, *Don't Do That: A Dictionary of the Forbidden* (London: Athlone Press, 1997), p. 201.

27   Jones, 'Rushdie, Race and Religion', p. 689. (This is set forth as a possible view; it is not that of the author.)

28  Bhikhu Parekh, 'The Rushdie Affair: Research Agenda for Political Philosophy', *Political Studies* 38 (1990), 695–709, p. 708.
29  Both quotations from ibid., p. 707.
30  Ibid., p. 708.
31  Ibid., p. 709.
32  Bhikhu Parekh, 'Superior People: The Narrowness of Liberalism from Mill to Rawls', *Times Literary Supplement*, 25 February 1994, pp. 11–13, p. 13.
33  Jones, 'Rushdie, Race and Religion', p. 694.
34  'The Sikh's turban no longer remains a cultural symbol, which is what it largely is, and becomes a religious requirement.' Bhikhu Parekh, 'Cultural Diversity and Liberal Democracy', pp. 202–27 in Gurpreet Mahajan, ed., *Democracy, Difference and Social Justice* (Delhi: Oxford University Press, 1998), p. 208.
35  Sebastian Poulter, *Ethnicity, Law and Human Rights: The English Experience* (Oxford: Clarendon Press, 1988), pp. 294–5.
36  Peter Singer, *Animal Liberation* (London: HarperCollins, 2nd edn, 1991), p. 154.
37  Yael Tamir, *Liberal Nationalism* (Princeton, NJ: Princeton University Press, 1993), p. 39.
38  See especially Michael Sandel, *Democracy's Discontent* (Cambridge, Mass.: Harvard University Press, 1996).
39  Bhikhu Parekh, 'Equality in a Multiracial Society', pp. 123–55 in Jane Franklin, ed., *Equality* (London: Institute for Public Policy Research, 1997), p. 135.
40  Ibid., pp. 150–1.
41  See *The Oxford English Dictionary* under 'Opportune' and, for more information about Portunus, Manfred Lurker, *Dictionary of Gods and Goddesses, Devils and Demons* (London and New York: Routledge and Kegan Paul, 1987), p. 286.
42  Poulter, *Ethnicity, Law and Human Rights*, p. 322, n. 271. See also p. 48.
43  Parekh, 'Equality in a Multiracial Society', p. 135.
44  Ibid.
45  Poulter, *Ethnicity, Law and Human Rights*, p. 356.
46  This thought was anticipated by A. E. Housman when he wrote in the penultimate poem in *A Shropshire Lad* (62) that 'malt does more than Milton can / To justify God's ways to man.'
47  Poulter, *Ethnicity, Law and Human Rights*, pp. 372–3.
48  Dissent by Justices Blackmun, Brennan and Marshall in *Employment Division, Department of Human Resources of Oregon et al.* v. *Alfred L. Smith et al.*, 494 US 872 (1990), p. 918.
49  Poulter, *Ethnicity, Law and Human Rights*, pp. 366–9.
50  Parekh, 'The Rushdie Affair', p. 704.
51  Poulter, *Ethnicity, Law and Human Rights*, pp. 136–7.
52  Singer, *Animal Liberation*, p. 155.
53  Poulter, *Ethnicity, Law and Human Rights*, p. 134.
54  Ibid., p. 135.
55  Ibid., p. 136.
56  Ibid., p. 139.
57  'Six years ago I gave up the academic life and went to live near Malmesbury [in Wiltshire] . . . . I was ignorant of country ways and ashamed of it. But within

months I had come to see how far removed is the countryside from the culture of cities.' 'We're the Law Out Here, Stranger: Faced with a Crime Invasion, Rural Communities Have Every Right to Protect Themselves, Says the Philosopher Roger Scruton.' *Sunday Times*, 23 April 2000, News Review, p. 6. As an earnest of his intention to go thoroughly native, Scruton maintains in this article that farmers should, as the title suggests, be a law unto themselves, in that they should be able to kill intruders without incurring any legal penalties. Thus, a farmer, Tony Martin, who did just that, and was convicted of murder, is described as 'a martyr', apparently because where Scruton lives 'farmers... would almost certainly behave as Martin did, were they faced with a nocturnal intruder'. Ibid. The claim that people should be able to break the law without suffering punishment if it conflicts with their culture can be seen as a radical extension of the claim for an exemption from the law. This so-called 'cultural defence' has been put forward in a number of court cases in Britain and the United States and has found favour with some theorists of multiculturalism. I do not discuss it in this book because, if I am right in claiming that justice does not require exemptions to accommodate cultural norms, it must follow that it does not require the acquittal of those who break the law, on condition that there are sound reasons for having the law in the first place (a condition that I take to be met by the law prohibiting murder).

58  Poulter, *Ethnicity, Law and Human Rights*, p. 142.
59  Sebastian Poulter, 'Ethnic Minority Customs, English Law and Human Rights', *International and Comparative Law Quarterly* 36 (1987), 589–615, p. 612.
60  Poulter, *Ethnicity, Law and Human Rights*, p. 295.
61  Ibid., p. 293.
62  Ibid., p. 324.
63  Ibid.
64  Ibid., p. 293.
65  Ibid.
66  Ibid., p. 295.
67  Parekh, 'Equality in a Multiracial Society', p. 128.
68  Ibid.
69  Poulter, *Ethnicity, Law and Human Rights*, p. 295.
70  Ibid.
71  Ibid., p. 292.
72  Ibid., p. 295.
73  Ibid., p. 329.
74  Parekh, 'Equality in a Multiracial Society', p. 129.
75  Poulter, *Ethnicity, Law and Human Rights*, p. 319, n. 245.
76  Ibid., p. 314, citing Health and Safety Commission Consultative Paper (1986).
77  Ibid., pp. 326–7.
78  Ibid.
79  Ibid., p. 282. (Sikhs are not a census category.)
80  Ibid., p. 314.
81  In 1986, only 30 per cent of workers were estimated to be wearing safety helmets. Ibid., p. 313.

82  Ibid., p. 322, n. 271.
83  Ibid.
84  'Excalibur Regained as Arthur Pulls it Off', *Guardian*, 6 November 1997, p. 1.
85  Gustav Niebuhr, 'Witches Cast as the Neo-Pagans Next Door', *New York Times*, 30 October 1999, pp. 1 and 30, p. 30.
86  Ibid., p. 1.
87  John Harlow, 'Pagans Stripped of Charity Status', *Sunday Times*, 31 October 1999, p. 11.
88  Ibid.
89  Ibid.
90  Ibid. 'In 1990 there were 5,000 practising British pagans; now, according to a study by Newcastle University, there are 100,000.' Ibid. In relation to the population, this makes paganism bigger in Britain than even the high estimate would make it for the USA.
91  Ibid.
92  Ibid.
93  Ibid.
94  Ibid.
95  Poulter, *Ethnicity, Law and Human Rights*, pp. 37–8.
96  Ibid., p. 49.
97  Professor Gordon Conway, letter to the *Independent*, 25 October 1997, p. 20. (The author was the chairman of a Runnymede Trust Commission on British Muslims and Islamophobia.)
98  Poulter, *Ethnicity, Law and Human Rights*, p. 354.
99  Joseph H. Carens and Melissa S. Williams, 'Muslim Minorities in Liberal Democracies: The Politics of Misrecognition', pp. 137–73 in Bhargava, ed., *Secularism and Its Critics*, p. 161.
100 The best discussion of the role of *laïcité* in French public life that I know is Jean Bauberot, 'The Two Thresholds of Laïcization', pp. 94–136 in Bhargava, ed., *Secularism and Its Critics*.
101 Poulter, *Ethnicity, Law and Human Rights*, p. 306.
102 Ibid., pp. 302–4.
103 Ibid., p. 306.
104 Ibid.
105 Ibid.

## Chapter 3   The Dynamics of Identity

1  Charles Taylor, 'The Politics of Recognition', pp. 25–73 in Amy Gutmann, ed., *Multiculturalism: Examining the Politics of Recognition* (Princeton, NJ: Princeton University Press, 1994), p. 62.
2  Todd Gitlin, *The Twilight of Common Dreams: Why America is Wracked by Culture Wars* (New York: Henry Holt, 1995), pp. 236–7.
3  David Cay Johnston, 'Gap between Rich and Poor Found Substantially Wider', *New York Times*, 5 September 1999, p. 16, data from Congressional Budget Office.

4   John Cassidy, 'Wall Street Follies', *New Yorker*, 13 September 1999, p. 32, data from 'a new study published jointly by the Washington-based Institute for Policy Studies and the advocacy group United for a Fair Economy'.

5   Ibid.

6   Gitlin, *Twilight of Common Dreams*, p. 225, emphasis suppressed.

7   Taylor, 'The Politics of Recognition', p. 60.

8   Ibid., p. 61.

9   Ibid.

10  Ibid., p. 58.

11  Ibid.

12  Ibid.

13  Gitlin, *Twilight of Common Dreams*, p. 126.

14  See John Tomasi, 'Kymlicka, Liberalism and Respect for Cultural Minorities', *Ethics* 105 (1995), 580–603, p. 585.

15  Taylor, 'The Politics of Recognition', p. 40.

16  Ibid., p. 41, n. 16.

17  Will Kymlicka, ed., *The Rights of Minority Cultures* (Oxford: Oxford University Press, 1995).

18  Peter Jones, 'Political Theory and Cultural Diversity', *Critical Review of International Social and Political Philosophy* 1 (1998), 28–62, p. 36.

19  Michael Hartney, 'Some Confusions Concerning Collective Rights', pp. 202–27 in Kymlicka, ed., *The Rights of Minority Cultures*, p. 222, emphasis in original.

20  Ibid.

21  'Man emancipates himself politically from religion by banishing it from the field of public law and making it a private right.... It is still only the abstract recognition of a particular perversion, private whim, and arbitrariness. For example, the infinite splintering of religion in North America already gives it the exterior form of a purely individual affair.... The ... displacement of religion from the state to civil society ... thus does not abolish or even try to abolish the actual religiosity of man.' Karl Marx, 'On the Jewish Question', pp. 137–50 in Jeremy Waldron, ed., *'Nonsense upon Stilts?' Bentham, Burke and Marx on the Rights of Man* (London: Methuen, 1987), p. 142.

22  It is unnecessary to give references to instances of such a pervasive line of criticism, but among the usual suspects are (in alphabetical order) Alasdair MacIntyre, Michael Sandel, Michael Walzer and Iris Marion Young.

23  John Rawls, *A Theory of Justice* (Cambridge, Mass.: Harvard University Press, 1971), esp. ch. 3.

24  I discuss this question in some detail in *Justice as Impartiality* (Oxford: Clarendon Press, 1995), ch. 3.

25  Iris Marion Young, *Justice and the Politics of Difference* (Princeton: Princeton University Press, 1990), p. 158.

26  See 'Racism and Sexism', pp. 11–50 in Richard A. Wasserstrom, *Philosophy and Social Issues* (Notre Dame, Ind.: Notre Dame University Press, 1980), esp. p. 25.

27  Young, *Justice and the Politics of Difference*, p. 158.

28  Ibid.

29  Wasserstrom, *Philosophy and Social Issues*, p. 26.

30 Iris Marion Young, 'Together in Difference: Transforming the Logic of Group Political Conflict', pp. 155–76 in Kymlicka, ed., *The Rights of Minority Cultures*, p. 162. (Pages 162–3 contain a succinct statement of Young's position.)

31 Ibid., p. 163.

32 Eliezer Ben-Rafael, 'The Israeli Experience in Multiculturalism', pp. 111–41 in Rainer Bauböck and John Rundell, eds, *Blurred Boundaries: Migration, Ethnicity, Citizenship* (Aldershot: Ashgate, 1998), p. 115.

33 Rainer Bauböck, 'The Crossing and Blurring of Boundaries in International Migration. Challenges for Social and Political Theory', pp. 17–52 in Bauböck and Rundell, eds, *Blurred Boundaries*, p. 42.

34 Ibid., p. 40.

35 The Nazi programme drawn up in 1920 'established the principle in Article IV that a "citizen" was a member of the German race.... A citizen was a person of German blood and descent ... thus no Jew could be a citizen, and the article explicitly said so.' Ivan Hannaford, *Race: The History of an Idea in the West* (Washington, DC: The Woodrow Wilson Center Press, 1996), p. 365.

36 *Show Boat*, book and lyrics by Oscar Hammerstein II, Act 1, Scene 4. The 'one drop' rule, still notionally applicable in census classifications, 'merely reflects racism and power relationships'. Dirk Hoerder, 'Segmented Macrosystems, Networking Individuals, Cultural Change: Balancing Processes and Interactive Change in Migration', pp. 81–95 in Veit Bader, ed., *Citizenship and Exclusion* (London: Macmillan, 1997), p. 94.

37 *Show Boat*, Act I, Scenes 2 and 4.

38 Alec de Waal, 'Group Identity and Rational Choice', *Critical Review* 11 (1997), 279–89, p. 283.

39 John Pilger, 'Australia', *Observer Review*, 22 March 1995, p. 5.

40 Bauböck, 'The Crossing and Blurring of Boundaries', p. 35.

41 Alfred Stepan, 'Modern Multinational Democracies: Transcending a Gellnerian Oxymoron', pp. 219–39 in John A. Hall, ed., *The State of the Nation: Ernest Gellner and the Theory of Nationalism* (Cambridge: Cambridge University Press, 1998), p. 223.

42 Joseph Raz, 'Multiculturalism', *Ratio Juris* 11 (1998), 193–205, p. 203.

43 For amplification of this see Brian Barry, *Justice as Impartiality* (Oxford: Clarendon Press, 1995), pp. 99–111.

44 See Raz, 'Multiculturalism', p. 202.

45 Andrew Mason, 'Political Community, Liberal-Nationalism and the Ethics of Assimilation', *Ethics* 109 (1999), 261–86, pp. 278–9.

46 Wsevolod W. Isajiw, 'On the Concept and Theory of Social Incorporation', pp. 79–102 in Wsevolod W. Isijiw, ed., *Multiculturalism in North America and Europe: Comparative Perspectives on Interethnic Relations and Social Incorporation* (Toronto: Canadian Scholars' Press, 1997), p. 83.

47 Aristide R. Zolberg, 'Modes of Incorporation: Toward a Comparative Framework', pp. 139–54 in Bader, ed., *Citizenship and Exclusion*, p. 151.

48 Bauböck, 'The Crossing and Blurring of Boundaries', p. 43.

49 Zolberg, 'Modes of Incorporation', p. 151.

50    'The rates of intermarriage among all European ethnic groups are very
      high...[so] it will become increasingly less clear to any individual what his
      ethnic group is and how it is to be defined.' Indeed, the whole notion of
      belonging to *an* ethnic group is breaking down: 'in the Census two-fifths of
      Americans gave multiple ancestries.' Nathan Glazer, *We Are All Multicultural-
      ists Now* (Cambridge, Mass.: Harvard University Press, 1997), pp. 119, 120.

51    Will Kymlicka, 'Ethnic Associations and Democratic Citizenship', pp. 177–213
      in Amy Gutmann, ed., *Freedom of Association* (Princeton, NJ: Princeton Uni-
      versity Press, 1998), p. 197.

52    The same passage appears in an almost identical form on p. 44 of Will Kymlicka,
      *Finding Our Way* (Toronto: Oxford University Press, 1998), with the exception
      that 'un-American' is replaced by 'un-Canadian' (this time in quotation
      marks). It may be that Kymlicka's claim has more substance in relation to
      Canada, where 'French-Canadians developed an organicist and ethnic model
      of the national community', while 'English Canada developed a national
      model akin to the French *Staatsnation*, the state actively pursuing its goal of
      nation-building.... Oriented toward the construction and imposition of a British
      model of identity and symbolic system, it allowed for the hegemony of Nativism,
      Anglo-conformity, and assimilationism.' Danielle Juteau, 'Multicultural Cit-
      izenship: The Challenge of Pluralism in Canada', pp. 96–112 in Bader, ed.,
      *Citizenship and Exclusion*, p. 102. An explicit contrast between on one hand
      pressure towards cultural assimilation in Canada (and Australia) until the 1970s
      and on the other hand a more relaxed attitude to the retention of immigrant
      cultures in the United States is made by Stephen Castles in 'Multicultural
      Citizenship: The Australian Experience', pp. 113–38 in Bader, ed., *Citizenship
      and Exclusion*, p. 118.

53    Michael Ignatieff, 'The Narcissism of Minor Differences', pp. 34–71 in his *The
      Warrior's Honor: Ethnic War and the Modern Conscience* (New York: Henry
      Holt, 1997).

54    Zolberg, 'Modes of Incorporation', p. 149.

55    Ibid.

56    Ibid.

57    See Linda Colley, *Britons: Forging the Nation 1707–1837* (New Haven, Conn.:
      Yale University Press, 1992), esp. pp. 374–5.

58    Tariq Modood, 'Anti-Essentialism, Multiculturalism and the "Recognition" of
      Religious Groups', *Journal of Political Philosophy* 6 (1998), 378–99, pp. 384 and
      385.

59    See John McGarry, ' "Orphans of Secession": National Pluralism in Secessionist
      Regions and Post-Secession States', pp. 215–32 in Margaret Moore, ed.,
      *National Self-Determination and Secession* (New York: Oxford University
      Press, 1998).

60    Enoch Powell, quoted in R. D. Grillo, *Pluralism and the Politics of Difference:
      State, Culture and Ethnicity in Comparative Perspective* (Oxford: Clarendon
      Press, 1998), p. 174.

61    It should be said that sympathy with the Stuart cause had several sources,
      including the principle of historical legitimacy that animated Boswell and John-

son. But it is significant in the present context that, by the time Boswell came to write his *Life*, he apparently anticipated no harm to Johnson's reputation or his own social standing by revealing in print what were, after all, treasonous sentiments.

62 Horace Kallen, *Culture and Democracy: Studies in the Group Psychologies of the American Peoples* (New York: Boni and Liveright, 1924). The expression 'a democracy of nationalities' occurs on p. 124; cited by Jeff Spinner, *The Boundaries of Citizenship: Race, Ethnicity, and Nationality in the Liberal State* (Baltimore: The Johns Hopkins University Press, 1994), p. 61.

63 Ibid., p. 115, cited in Spinner, *The Boundaries of Citizenship*, p. 61.

64 Horace Kallen, ' "Americanization" and the Cultural Prospect', pp. 176–7 in Kallen, *Culture and Democracy*, cited in Spinner, *The Boundaries of Citizenship*, p. 64. Kallen's ideas were put into effect in the implementation of the 1924 Immigration Act, which was supposed to tie immigration quotas from each country to the proportion of citizens from that country. Joseph Hill, who was in charge of making the estimates, explained that 'the great mixture of nationalities through inter-marriage' was to be dealt with by counting 'four people each of whom had three English grandparents and one German grandparent' as 'the equivalent of three English inhabitants and one German inhabitant'. Thus, 'the Quota Board assumed that [,] even if nationalit[ies] combined through inter-marriage, they did not mix but remained in descendants as discrete, unalloyed parts that could be tallied as fractional equivalents.' Mae M. Ngai, 'The Architecture of Race in American Immigration Law: A Reexamination of the Immigration Act of 1924', *Journal of American History* 86 (1999), 67–92, p. 79.

65 Spinner, *The Boundaries of Citizenship*, p. 196, n. 9.

66 Jules Michelet, *The People* (Urbana: University of Illinois Press, 1973 [1846]), p. 93, cited in Grillo, *Pluralism and the Politics of Difference*, p. 134.

67 Hannaford, *Race*, p. 323.

68 Grillo, *Pluralism and the Politics of Difference*, p. 135.

69 Maurice Barrès, *Scènes et doctrines de nationalisme* (Paris: Plon, 1925 [1902]), p. 161: cited (in translation) by Grillo, *Pluralism and the Politics of Difference*, p. 135.

70 Ibid., p. 162, cited (in translation) by Grillo, *Pluralism and the Politics of Difference*, p. 136.

71 George Orwell, 'As I Please', 6 December 1946, pp. 291–5 in Sonia Orwell and Ian Angus, eds, *The Collected Essays, Journalism and Letters of George Orwell*, vol. 4 (Harmondsworth, Mddx: Penguin, 1970[1968]), p. 293.

72 'London Letter to *Partisan Review*', July–August 1943, pp. 327–34 in vol. 2 of *Collected Essays*, p. 333. Max Beerbohm, in an essay published in 1923 but based on experience of English life dating from before the First World War, claimed that there were only fourteen topics that were regarded as funny by the English public, one of which was Jews. His tentative explanation of the humourousness of Jews is revealing: 'Jews, are, after all, foreigners, strangers, and the public has never got used to them.' Max Beerbohm, 'The Humour of the Public', pp. 209–18 in David Cecil, ed., *Max Beerbohm: Selected Prose* (Boston: Little, Brown, 1970), p. 217.

73    More remarkably, perhaps, the same trend is strongly apparent in France: in the Paris region 'one of eight marriages was mixed in 1935; this had increased to one of three in the late 1950s and to every other marriage in the early 1980s.' Gérard Noiriel, *The French Melting Pot: Immigration and National Identity* (Minneapolis: University of Minnesota Press, 1996), p. 179.

74    'Newspapers like the Sunday Times denounce it as "spouting the fantasies of racial purity" to say that a child born of English parents in Peking is not Chinese but English, or that a child born of Indian parents in Birmingham is not English but Indian. It is even heresy to assert the plain fact that the English are a white nation.' Enoch Powell, quoted in Grillo, *Pluralism and the Politics of Difference*, pp. 174–5. It is worth bearing in mind, incidentally, that 'whiteness' is itself a socially constructed category. In earlier times, for example, neither Greek nor Jews counted as 'white' in the United States, whereas this is now unquestioned.

75    Modood, 'Anti-Essentialism', p. 385.

76    Ibid., p. 387. The comparable figures for Indian and African Asian men are one-fifth, and for Pakistani and Bangladeshi men one-tenth; 'very few South Asian women had a white partner' (ibid).

77    Gitlin, *Twilight of Common Dreams*, p. 236.

78    James D. Fearon and David D. Laitin, 'Explaining Interethnic Cooperation', *American Political Science Review* 90 (1996), 715–35, p. 730.

79    Grillo, *Pluralism and the Politics of Difference*, p. 75, internal quotation from P. F. Sugar, *Southeastern Europe under Ottoman Rule, 1354–1804* (Seattle: University of Washington Press, 1977), p. 3.

80    Tom R. Tyler, Robert J. Boeckman, Heather J. Smith and Yuen J. Huo, *Social Justice in a Diverse Society* (Boulder, Colo.: Westview Press, 1997) p. 260.

81    Ibid., p. 182, referring to M. Sherif, O. J. Harvey, B. J. White, W. R. Hood and C. W. Sherif, *Intergroup Conflict and Cooperation: The Robber's Cave Experiment* (Norman, Okla.: University of Oklahoma Book Exchange, 1961).

82    Ibid.

83    Bhikhu Parekh, 'Cultural Diversity and Liberal Democracy', pp. 202–27 in Gurpreet Mahajan, ed., *Democracy, Difference and Social Justice* (Delhi: Oxford University Press, 1998), p. 217.

84    Ibid.

85    See James B. Jacobs and Kimberly Potter, *Hate Crimes: Criminal Law and Identity Politics* (New York: Oxford University Press, 1998) for a loosely argued attack on 'hate crime' statutes that nevertheless manages to illustrate some of the problems inherent in their formulation and application.

86    Glazer, *We Are All Multiculturalists Now*, p. 119, quoting Read Lewis, 'Americanization', in *Encyclopedia of the Social Sciences*, (New York: Macmillan, 1930), vol. 2, p. 34.

87    Young, *Justice and the Politics of Difference*, p. 195.

88    Ibid.

89    Ibid., p. 29.

90    John Stuart Mill, *The Subjection of Women*, in Stefan Collini, ed., *On Liberty and Other Writings* (Cambridge: Cambridge University Press, 1989), p. 168.

91   Ibid., p. 144.
92   Ibid., p. 167.
93   Ibid., p. 144.
94   Susan Moller Okin, *Women in Western Political Thought* (Princeton, NJ: Princeton University Press), p. 229.
95   Young, *Justice and the Politics of Difference*, p. 162.
96   Ibid., p. 199.
97   Ibid.
98   Lewis Carroll, *Alice's Adventures in Wonderland*, in *The Complete Works of Lewis Carroll* (New York: Vintage Books, 1976), p. 38.
99   Young, *Justice and the Politics of Difference*, p. 175, quoting Kenneth Karst, 'Paths to Belonging: The Constitution and Cultural Identity', *North Carolina Law Review* 64 (1984), 303–77, p. 337.
100  Ibid.
101  Ibid., p. 43 (see also p. 186).
102  'The Deaf movement, barely a generation old, is representative of the strengths of post-1960's "ethnicization." The practice of capitalizing Deaf signifies more than a new respect for those who cannot hear: it has become a sign of activism, with a popular base, with heroes and histories. It includes a commitment to American Sign Language, an active bilingualism, a call for representation (marked in 1988 by the successful demand that the incoming president of Gallaudet University in Washington [an institution for the deaf] be a deaf person). It extends as far as the rejection of cochlear implants intended to restore a certain degree of hearing. The claim to a Deaf culture is, today, no laughing matter.' Gitlin, *Twilight of Common Dreams*, pp. 162–3.
103  Young, *Justice and the Politics of Difference*, p. 196.
104  Ibid.
105  Ibid., p. 198.
106  Orlando Patterson, *The Ordeal of Integration* (Washington, DC: Civitas/Counterpoint, 1997), p. 35.
107  This is put forward by Christopher Jencks in his *Rethinking Social Policy: Race, Poverty and the Underclass* (New York: HarperCollins, 1993), pp. 128–9.
108  This suggestion was made by William Julius Wilson in a lecture delivered at the London School of Economics on 27 June 1998.
109  Young, *Justice and the Politics of Difference*, p. 202.
110  Ibid., p. 206.
111  Ibid., p. 207.
112  *Griggs* v. *Duke Power Co.*, 401 US 424 (1971), decision printed as pp. 111–21 in Gertrude Ezorsky, *Racism and Justice: The Case for Affirmative Action* (Ithaca: Cornell University Press, 1991).
113  Ezorsky, *Racism and Justice*, pp. 113–14.
114  Ibid., p. 117.
115  Ibid., p. 117, n. 7.
116  Ibid., pp. 116–17.
117  Ibid., p. 116.

118 According to Ezorsky, one of the effects of the *Griggs* decision was that employers began 'identify[ing] minority persons with borderline qualifications but who, with relevant skill training, [could] become competent workers.' Ibid., p. 40.

119 See ibid., p. 50 for the later history.

120 Christopher Jencks and Meredith Phillips, 'The Black–White Test Score Gap: An Introduction', pp. 1–51 in Christopher Jencks and Meredith Phillips, eds, *The Black–White Test-Score Gap* (Washington, DC: Brookings Institution Press, 1998), p. 15.

121 The cumulative effect of the sophisticated research reported in the volume edited by Jencks and Phillips is for the most part to undermine a number of popular (and in some cases intuitively quite plausible) explanations of the persistence of the black–white test score gap. The one that (almost by default) is left standing is the speculation that there is something about black child-rearing practices that inhibits academic achievement. (I shall return to this issue in chapter 8.)

122 Christopher Jencks, 'Racial Bias in Testing', pp. 55–85 in Jencks and Phillips, eds, *The Black–White Test-Score Gap*, p. 80.

123 Jencks and Phillips, 'The Black–White Test-Score Gap', pp. 14–15.

124 Ibid., p. 15.

125 Ezorsky, *Racism and Justice*, p. 116.

126 Ibid., p. 121.

127 Young, *Justice and the Politics of Difference*, p. 21.

128 Ibid., p. 212.

129 Ibid.

130 Young, *Justice and the Politics of Difference*, p. 160.

131 Ibid., p. 181.

132 It should be emphasized that to say 'a country' provides equal opportunities for speakers of more than one language does not mean that opportunities for a speaker of a given language are equal within the whole territory of the country. (As far as I am aware, there is no country in the world that provides equal opportunities in that sense.) Rather, what it means is simply that the range of jobs open within Belgium to French-speakers in the French-speaking part of the country is roughly equivalent to the range of jobs open within Belgium to Dutch-speakers in the Dutch-speaking part of the country. The same goes for French and German in Switzerland and for French and English in Canada.

133 Bhikhu Parekh, 'Equality in a Multiracial Society', pp. 123–55 in Jane Franklin, ed., *Equality* (London: Institute for Public Policy Research, 1997), pp. 150–1.

134 See Russell Hardin, *One for All: The Logic of Group Conflict* (Princeton, NJ: Princeton University Press, 1995), pp. 219–20.

135 Claus Offe, ' "Homogeneity" and Constitutional Democracy: Coping with Identity Conflicts through Group Rights', *Journal of Political Philosophy* 6 (1998), 131–41, p. 134.

136 Richard Jenkins, *Rethinking Ethnicity: Arguments and Explorations* (London: Sage, 1997), p. 148.

137 Ibid., p. 149.

138 Ibid.

139 Thus, in the United States at any rate, 'evidence...suggests that congenial relations at work have more influence than income levels over people's job satisfaction'. Robert E. Lane, *The Loss of Happiness in Market Democracies* (New Haven, Conn.: Yale University Press, 2000), p. 126.

### Chapter 4  Theories of Group Rights

1 Bhikhu Parekh, 'The Rushdie Affair: Research Agenda for Political Philosophy', *Political Studies* 38 (1990), 695–709, p. 704, emphasis suppressed.

2 Jacob T. Levy, 'Classifying Cultural Rights', pp. 22–66 in Ian Shapiro and Will Kymlicka, eds, NOMOS 39: *Ethnicity and Group Rights*, (New York: New York University Press, 1997), pp. 25 and 28.

3 The distinction between the operation of a quota system and the operation of a preference system would disappear if the weighting was adjusted each year so as to bring about a predetermined outcome after the field of applicants was already known. This is why I stipulated that it is the size of the bonus that must be predetermined. Provided this is reviewed only at intervals of several years, there can be fluctuations in proportions from year to year depending on the relative strengths of the minority and majority applicants. The current position of the Supreme Court, which turns on the distinction between quotas and preferences, has been much criticized as a fudge. My suggestion is that whether this is so or not depends on the precise way in which a preference system is implemented. For a discussion of university admission policies in practice, see Patricia Conley, 'The Allocation of College Admissions', pp. 25–79 in Jon Elster, ed., *Local Justice in America* (New York: The Russell Sage Foundation, 1995), esp. pp. 59–64.

4 William Julius Wilson, *The Truly Disadvantaged* (Chicago: University of Chicago Press, 1987).

5 Orlando Patterson, *The Ordeal of Integration* (Washington, DC: Civitas/Counterpoint, 1997), pp. 4–5.

6 Ibid., p. 193.

7 Ibid.

8 William A. Galston, 'Two Concepts of Liberalism', *Ethics* 105 (1995), 516–34, quotations from p. 521.

9 Will Kymlicka, *Multicultural Citizenship: A Liberal Theory of Minority Rights* (Oxford: Clarendon Press, 1995), p. 154.

10 John Stuart Mill, *On Liberty*, in Stefan Collini, ed., *On Liberty and Other Writings* (Cambridge: Cambridge University Press, 1989), p. 59.

11 Ibid., p. 107.

12 Ibid.

13 Ibid.

14 Ibid.

15 The most eminent of the culprits is John Rawls. Mill's actual position is sometimes acknowledged: thus Amy Gutmann has noted that Mill was opposed to

what she calls 'state-enforced civic education', including one 'intended to teach children...to choose for themselves among different ways of life'. Amy Gutmann, 'Civic Education and Social Diversity', *Ethics* 105 (1995), 557–79, p. 562. Despite this, she persistently refers to 'Millian liberalism' as a synonym for 'comprehensive liberalism', where both terms are understood to include in their definition the demand that the state should enforce 'teaching children to live self-directing or autonomous lives'. Ibid., p. 576.

16   Andreas Føllesdal, 'Minority Rights: A Liberal Contractualist Case', pp. 59–83 in Julia Raikka, ed., *Do We Need Minority Rights? Conceptual Issues* (The Hague: Martinus Nijhoff, 1996), p. 69.

17   Ibid.

18   I have developed this argument in *Justice as Impartiality* (Oxford: Clarendon Press, 1995), and defended it at some length against critics in 'Something in the Disputation not Unpleasant', pp. 186–256 in Paul Kelly, ed., *Impartiality, Neutrality and Justice: Re-reading Brian Barry's Justice as Impartiality* (Edinburgh: Edinburgh University Press, 1998).

19   Bhikhu Parekh, 'Superior People: The Narrowness of Liberalism from Mill to Rawls', *Times Literary Supplement*, 25 February 1994, pp. 11–13, p. 13.

20   Charles Taylor, 'The Politics of Recognition', pp. 25–73 in Amy Gutmann, ed., *Multiculturalism: Examining the Politics of Difference* (Princeton, NJ: Princeton University Press, 1994), p. 58.

21   Galston, 'Two Concepts of Liberalism', p. 525.

22   Carter Lindberg, *The European Reformations* (Oxford: Blackwell, 1996), p. xii.

23   Ibid., p. 366.

24   Ibid., p. 363.

25   Harro Höpfl, ed., *Luther and Calvin on Secular Authority* (Cambridge: Cambridge University Press, 1991), Introduction, pp. viii–ix.

26   Lindberg, *The European Reformations*, p. 269.

27   Ibid., p. 370.

28   Ibid., pp. 307 and 308, internal quotation from p. 490 of James D. Tracy, 'Public Church, *Gemeente Christi*, or *Volkerk*', pp. 487–510 in Hans R. Guggisberg and Gottfried Krodel, eds, *The Reformation in Germany and Europe: Interpretations and Issues* (Gütersloh: Gütersloher Verlagshaus, 1993).

29   Mill, *On Liberty*, p. 11.

30   Höpfl, *Luther and Calvin*, p. viii.

31   Lindberg, *The European Reformations*, p. 246.

32   See ibid., p. 247.

33   Ibid.

34   Parekh, 'Superior People', p. 13. The same claim is made (in the same words) in Bhikhu Parekh, 'Cultural Diversity and Liberal Democracy', pp. 202–27 in Gurpreet Mahajan, ed., *Democracy, Difference and Social Justice* (Delhi: Oxford University Press, 1998), p. 206.

35   James Tully, *Strange Multiplicity: Constitutionalism in an Age of Diversity* (Cambridge: Cambridge University Press, 1995), esp. pp. 1–17 and pp. 188–91.

36   Yael Tamir, 'Who Do You Trust?', *Boston Review* 22 (October/November 1997), 32–3, p. 33.

37  Chandran Kukathas, 'Multiculturalism as Fairness: Will Kymlicka's *Multicultural Citizenship*', *Journal of Political Philosophy* 5 (1997), 406–27, p. 426.
38  Parekh, 'Cultural Diversity and Liberal Democracy', p. 207.
39  Ibid., p. 212.
40  R. D. Grillo, *Pluralism and the Politics of Difference: State, Culture and Ethnicity in Comparative Perspective* (Oxford: Clarendon Press, 1998), p. 212; internal quotation from N. Yuval-Davis, 'Fundamentalism, Multiculturalism and Women in Britain', pp. 278–91 in J. Donald and A. Rattansi, eds, *'Race', Culture and Difference* (London: Sage, 1992), p. 283.
41  Mill, *On Liberty*, p. 72.
42  Ibid., p. 63.
43  Taylor, 'The Politics of Recognition', p. 58.
44  Parekh, 'Superior People', p. 12, emphasis in original.
45  Ibid.
46  Parekh, 'Cultural Diversity and Liberal Democracy', p. 207.
47  John Stuart Mill, *The Subjection of Women*, in Collini, ed., *On Liberty and Other Writings*, pp. 146–7.
48  Mill, *On Liberty*, pp. 104 5.
49  Chandran Kukathas, 'Cultural Toleration', pp. 69–104 in Shapiro and Kymlicka, eds, *Ethnicity and Group Rights*, p. 99.
50  Chandran Kukathas, 'Are There any Cultural Rights?', pp. 228–56 in Will Kymlicka, ed., *The Rights of Minority Cultures* (Oxford: Oxford University Press, 1995), p. 239.
51  Kukathas, 'Multiculturalism as Fairness', p. 426.
52  Kukathas, 'Are There any Cultural Rights?', p. 251.
53  Ibid.
54  Parekh, 'Cultural Diversity and Liberal Democracy', p. 207.
55  Ibid.
56  Ibid.
57  Kukathas, 'Cultural Toleration', p. 84.
58  Ibid.
59  Ibid.
60  Daniel Weinstock, 'The Graying of Berlin', *Critical Review* 11 (1997), 481–501, p. 493, internal quotation from John Gray, *Isaiah Berlin* (Princeton, NJ: Princeton University Press, 1996), p. 152.
61  Ibid.
62  'The liberal view advanced here . . . begins with the relatively innocuous, shared assumption that moral evaluation is individualistic in the sense that what counts, ultimately, is how the lives of actual individuals are affected.' Kukathas, 'Are There any Cultural Rights?', p. 246.
63  Parekh, 'Superior People', p. 13.
64  Bryan G. Norton, 'On the Inherent Danger of Undervaluing Species', pp. 110–37 in Bryan G. Norton, ed., *The Preservation of Species: The Value of Biological Diversity* (Princeton, NJ: Princeton University Press, 1986), p. 118.
65  Kukathas, 'Cultural Toleration', p. 97.
66  Ibid.

67 Michael Walzer, 'The Moral Standing of States: A Response to Four Critics', *Philosophy & Public Affairs* 9 (1980), 209–25, esp. pp. 210–12.

68 David Miller, 'Introduction' to David Miller and Michael Walzer, eds, *Pluralism, Justice and Equality* (Oxford: Clarendon Press, 1995), p. 2.

69 Michael Walzer, *Spheres of Justice: A Defense of Pluralism and Equality* (New York: Basic Books, 1983), p. 313. Slavery and genocide can be ruled out consistently with this doctrine, because the chance of there being a consensus on them within a society is extremely remote. This theory was internally coherent, if implausible. Since then, Walzer has enhanced its plausibility, but at the expense of coherence. He now says that 'murder, torture, and enslavement are wrongful features of any distributive process – and they are wrong for reasons that have little to do with the meaning of social goods'. Michael Walzer, 'Response', pp. 281–97 in Miller and Walzer, eds, *Pluralism, Justice and Equality*, p. 293. But this is pure fiat on his part: he lacks the theoretical resources to explain why it is true. I mentioned in the last note in chapter 1 that Rawls's current position is a muddled version of Walzer's. So, it can now be added, is Walzer's. He and Rawls have now converged. If anything, they have gone past one another, travelling in opposite directions, calling to mind Mark Twain's story about the two drunks who fought so hard that they finished up by struggling into one another's overcoats. For an astute critique of the recent evolution of Walzer's ideas, see Charles Jones, *Global Justice: Defending Cosmopolitanism* (New York: Oxford University Press, 1999), ch. 7 (pp. 173–202).

70 'The social world does not divide at its joints into perspicuous we's with whom we can empathize ... and enigmatical they's with whom we cannot. ... The wogs begin long before Calaise.'. Clifford Geertz, *Available Light: Anthropological Reflections on Philosophical Topics* (Princeton, NJ: Princeton University Press, 2000), p. 76.

71 Kymlicka, *Multicultural Citizenship*, p. 234, n. 17.

72 See David Luban, 'The Romance of the Nation-State', *Philosophy & Public Affairs* 9 (1980), 292–7.

73 In 1985, 'an amendment to the Basic Law [was adopted] which bars Knesset lists that do not expressly "recognize the state of Israel as the state of the Jewish people"; alternative wording proposed by Knesset members, to the effect that the state of Israel is "the state of its citizens" or "the state of the Jewish people and its Arab citizens", were voted down.' See As'ad Ghanam, 'State and Minority in Israel: The Case of the Ethnic State and the Predicament of Its Minority', *Ethnic and Racial Studies* 21 (1998), 428–48, p. 432. For further discussion see Gershon Shafir and Yoav Peled, 'Citizenship and Stratification in an Ethnic Democracy', *Ethnic and Racial Studies* 21 (1998), 408–27, p. 414.

74 Rogers Brubaker, 'Myths and Misconceptions in the Study of Nationalism', pp. 272–306 in John A. Hall, ed., *The State of the Nation: Ernest Gellner and the Theory of Nationalism* (Cambridge: Cambridge University Press, 1998), p. 280.

75 Kymlicka, *Multicultural Citizenship*, p. 165.

76 Ibid.

77 Ibid., p. 167.

78 Ibid., p. 165.

79  Ibid., p. 168.
80  Kukathas, 'Cultural Toleration', p. 70.
81  Ibid., pp. 70–1.
82  Ibid., p. 88.
83  Ibid.
84  Ibid., p. 70.
85  Susan Moller Okin, 'Is Multiculturalism Bad for Women?', pp. 9–24 in Susan Moller Okin with Respondents, *Is Multiculturalism Bad for Women?*, ed. Joshua Cohen, Matthew Howard and Martha C. Nussbaum (Princeton, NJ: Princeton University Press, 1999), p. 18. The father and the two husbands, charged with child abuse and statutory rape respectively, resorted to the 'cultural defence', claiming that this was all 'part of their cultural marriage practices'. Ibid.
86  Where Muslim law has legal validity, the issue of 'forcing' does not even arise, because the state recognizes the marriage without requiring the child's consent: 'a minor child may be validly married simply on the basis of his or her guardian's consent, without the minor having any voice in the matter. Where such a marriage does occur Muslim law grants the child "the option of puberty" which means that upon subsequently attaining puberty [defined as twelve years old for boys and nine years old for girls] the minor may elect to have the marriage set aside, provided the marriage has not yet been affirmed by voluntary consummation. However, under the Hanafi school of Islamic jurisprudence, as applied in the Indian subcontinent, this option is only available to a child that has been married off by a guardian other than the father or grandfather.' Sebastian Poulter, *Ethnicity, Law and Human Rights: The English Experience* (Oxford: Clarendon Press, 1998), p. 207. (There is, incidentally, an obvious question about the application of the term 'voluntary' to any act performed by a girl and a boy before the ages of nine or twelve respectively.)
87  Martha C. Nussbaum, *Sex and Social Justice* (New York: Oxford University Press, 1999), p. 119; internal quotation from Nahid Toubia, *Female Genital Mutilation: A Call for Global Action* (New York: UNICEF, 1995), p. 5.
88  Both quotations from Kukathas, 'Cultural Toleration', pp. 70–1.
89  Daniel M. Weinstock, 'How can Collective Rights and Liberalism Be Reconciled?', pp. 281–304 in Rainer Bauböck and John Rundell, eds, *Blurred Boundaries: Migration, Ethnicity, Citizenship* (Aldershot: Ashgate, 1998), p. 296.
90  'The essential ethic of BDSM [Bondage, Discipline and Sado-Masochism] is mutual consent. . . . Salon Kitty's, in line with the entire BDSM scene[,] does not condone any act that does not have the explicit consent of the submissive partner.' (From the Salon Kitty [Australia] website.) I am grateful to Vittorio Bufacchi for sharing his research on the ethics of sado-masochism.
91  Salon Kitty acknowledges that long-term interests trump consent: 'It is . . . the responsibility of the dominant to ensure that a submissive is not consenting to an act that is not in his or her best long-run interest.' The state has, I suggest, a role in defining 'long-run interest' and punishing violations, in as far as they come to the attention of the police.
92  Ian Shapiro, *Democracy's Place* (Ithaca: Cornell University Press, 1996), p. 231.

93 Colin Bird, *The Myth of Liberal Individualism* (Cambridge: Cambridge University Press, 1999), p. 207, citing Daniel Bell, *Communitarianism and its Critics* (Oxford: Clarendon Press, 1993), p. 4 (quotation corrected).

94 Stuart White, 'Freedom of Association and the Right to Exclude', *Journal of Political Philosophy* 5 (1997), 373–91, p. 373.

95 Ibid., p. 377, italics in original. There is, of course, something of an irony here in that 'catholic' *means* 'universal' or 'all-embracing'. (The *Oxford English Dictionary* devotes over a page to variations on this before giving a final column to senses associated with Roman Catholicism.) But the Roman Catholic Church's claim to universality has never (either before or after the Reformation) been intended to mean that people could belong on their own terms; rather, it was the claim that everybody should belong on its terms. The Roman Catholic Church can still define the terms on which people belong to it; but today, despite its name, it functions in most of the countries in which it has adherents simply as one Christian denomination among others.

96 The American Supreme Court has declined to review decisions made by religious bodies, on the ground that it would be illegitimate intervention in an internal dispute. Justice Rehnquist, however, disagreed with this decision and took the line that 'consent to membership in a religious body does not extend to clerical action in violation of its constitution'. Judicial intervention would not involve 'imposing alien external rules' but would simply entail that 'where religious procedures exist, and where members lodge a civil complaint against church authorities for failing to adhere to them, courts should consider the merits of the case and uphold these rules'. Nancy Rosenblum, *Membership and Morals: The Personal Uses of Pluralism in America* (Princeton, NJ: Princeton University Press, 1998), p. 82.

## Chapter 5   Liberal States and Illiberal Religions

1 Nancy L. Rosenblum, *Membership and Morals: The Personal Uses of Pluralism in America* (Princeton, NJ: Princeton University Press, 1998), p. 87. The issue that galvanized the English pluralists arose out of the secession of the 'Wee Frees' from the Free Church of Scotland when it formed a union with the United Presbyterian Church. See Denise G. Réaume, 'Common-Law Constructions of Group Autonomy: A Case Study', pp. 257–89 in Ian Shapiro and Will Kymlicka, eds, NOMOS 39: *Ethnicity and Group Rights* (New York: New York University Press, 1997).

2 Ibid.

3 Ibid.

4 Ibid.

5 Sebastian Poulter, *Ethnicity, Law and Human Rights: The English Experience* (Oxford: Clarendon Press, 1998), p. 217.

6 Ibid.

7 Oonagh Reitman, personal communication.

8 Oonagh Reitman, 'Cultural Accommodation in Family Law: Jewish Divorce in England', paper delivered at ECPR Joint Sessions of Workshops, University of

Warwick, March 1998. I am much indebted to this unpublished paper, and am grateful for permission to quote from it.

9   Sophie Goodchild and Gloria Tessler, 'Jewish Women Fight Veto on Divorce', *Independent on Sunday*, 10 October 1999, p. 13.

10  The author is Judith Rotem, *Distant Sisters: The Women I Left Behind* (Philadelphia: The Jewish Publication Society, 1997), pp. 95–6; quotation in text from Rietman, 'Cultural Accommodation', p. 8.

11  Reitman, 'Cultural Accommodation', p. 8.

12  Poulter, *Ethnicity, Law and Human Rights*, pp. 201–2.

13  Reitman, 'Cultural Accommodation', p. 15.

14  Church of England vicars have always been registrars as well. Weddings solemnized according to the rites of the Church of England do not therefore require any additional ceremony to be legally valid. Despite this, the Church of England does not permit people who are divorced to remarry in church, except for those who live in a parish where experimental diocesan guidelines are being followed, in which case a marriage in church may take place at the discretion of 'the minister...in consultation with the bishop'. House of Bishops, *Marriage* (London: Church House Publishing, 1999), p. 24. There is a body of opinion in favour of further liberalization, but nobody makes the argument that, because Church of England marriages have legal force, the Church is obliged to bring its practice in conformity with the law and treat legally divorced people on the same footing as those who have not previously been married. I am grateful to the Revd Michael Day for assistance on this point.

15  Rosenblum, *Membership and Morals*, p. 84.

16  Reitman, 'Cultural Accommodation', p. 12, n. 84.

17  'This year, the Chief Rabbi, Jonathan Sacks, announced he was taking steps to see if a way can be found to help the agunot [literally "chained" – i.e. women denied a divorce by their husbands], but that effort seems to have run into the sand.' James Meek, 'Rabbi Plans to Shame Husbands', *Guardian*, 30 October 1999, p. 9.

18  Rosenblum, *Membership and Morals*, p. 85.

19  Kent Greenawalt, 'Freedom of Association and Religious Association', pp. 109–44 in Amy Gutmann, ed., *Freedom of Association* (Princeton, NJ: Princeton University Press, 1998), p. 129.

20  Ibid., internal quotation from *Guinn* v. *Church of Christ*, 775 P. 2d 766 (1989), p. 768.

21  Ibid., pp. 129–30.

22  *Guinn*, p. 768, cited in Greenawalt, 'Freedom of Association', pp. 129–30.

23  Thus, for example, 'the Agunot Campaign, which is working to change the rules' is targeting the Chief Rabbi, not parliament: according to Goodchild and Tessler, a number of its members recently chained themselves to the railings outside his office in Finchley.

24  'Between the years 1948 and 1986, the courts used the power to compel the *get* a mere fourteen times in cases involving a recalcitrant husband.' Reitman, 'Cultural Accommodation', p. 6.

25  Ayelet Schachar, 'Group Identity and Women's Rights in Family Law: The Perils of Multicultural Accommodation', *Journal of Political Philosophy* 6 (1998), 285–305, p. 291.

26  Ibid., p. 291, n. 21, quoting Martin Edelman, *Courts, Politics, and Culture in Israel* (Charlottesville, Va.: University Press of Virginia, 1994), p. 121.

27  Ibid., p. 291.

28  Reitman, 'Cultural Accommodation', p. 5, n. 26.

29  Ibid.

30  Reitman, 'Cultural Accommodation', p. 5.

31  Meek, 'Rabbi Plans to Shame Husbands'.

32  Schachar, 'Group Identity', p. 302, n. 62.

33  Reitman, 'Cultural Accommodation', p. 8.

34  Ibid., p. 10.

35  Ibid., p. 9.

36  Ibid., pp. 9–10, internal quotation from Section 56 Family Law Act.

37  Will Kymlicka, *Multicultural Citizenship: A Liberal Theory of Minority Rights* (Oxford: Clarendon Press, 1995), p. 161. Some of this discussion is couched in terms of the implications of Rawls's 'political liberalism', but it is clear that Kymlicka regards the implications he draws from it as entailed by liberalism on his own understanding of it.

38  Ibid.

39  Ibid.

40  Jacob T. Levy, 'Classifying Cultural Rights', pp. 24–66 in Shapiro and Kymlicka, eds, *Ethnicity and Group Rights*, p. 64, n. 67.

41  Kymlicka, *Multicultural Citizenship*, p. 161.

42  Ibid.

43  Ibid.

44  Levy, 'Classifying Cultural Rights', p. 42.

45  Ibid., p. 64, n. 67, italics in original.

46  'And unto the angel of the Church of the Laodiceans write; . . . I know thy works, that thou art neither cold nor hot: I would thou wert cold or hot. So then because thou art lukewarm, and neither cold nor hot, I will spue thee out of my mouth.' Revelation 3: 14–16.

47  Amy Gutmann, *Democratic Education* (Princeton, NJ: Princeton University Press, 2nd edn 1999 [1987]), p. 121. The President of Bob Jones University, Bob Jones 3rd, announced on a talk show on the evening 3 March 2000 that the University had that afternoon ended the policy of prohibiting interracial dating. Gustav Niebuhr, 'Bob Jones U. Drops its Ban on Interracial Student Dates', *New York Times*, 4 March 2000, p. A11.

48  Amy Gutmann, 'Freedom of Association: An Introductory Essay', pp. 3–32 in Gutmann, ed., *Freedom of Association*, p. 6.

49  Ibid., pp. 7–8.

50  William A. Galston, 'Two Concepts of Liberalism', *Ethics* 105 (1995), 516–34, p. 532.

51  Rosenblum, *Membership and Morals*, p. 44.

52  Ibid., p. 89.

53 Greenawalt, 'Freedom of Association', p. 119.
54 Rosenblum, *Membership and Morals*, p. 89.
55 Greenawalt, 'Freedom of Association', p. 120.
56 Quoted in Rosenblum, *Membership and Morals*, p. 90.
57 Quoted at ibid.
58 Ibid., p. 92.
59 Ibid., punctuation in original.
60 Ian Shapiro, *Democracy's Place* (Ithaca: Cornell University Press, 1996), p. 244.
61 Cass R. Sunstein, 'Should Sex Equality Law Apply to Religious Institutions?', pp. 85–94 in Susan Moller Okin with Respondents, *Is Multiculturalism Bad for Women?*, ed. Joshua Cohen, Matthew Howard and Martha C. Nussbaum (Princeton, NJ: Princeton University Press, 1999), p. 93.
62 Ibid., n. 2.
63 *Employment Division, Department of Human Resources* v. *Smith*, 494 US 872 (1990).
64 Sunstein, 'Should Sex Equality Law Apply?', n. 13.
65 *Smith*, p. 874.
66 Ibid., p. 875.
67 Ibid., p. 876 (citation omitted).
68 Ibid., p. 890.
69 See ibid., p. 891.
70 Poulter, *Ethnicity, Law and Human Rights*, p. 370, nn. 277–9.
71 *Smith*, p. 890 (citations omitted).
72 Stephen Macedo, 'Liberal Civic Education and Religious Fundamentalism: The Case of God v. John Rawls', *Ethics* 105 (1995), 468–96, p. 489.
73 Ibid., p. 490.
74 Ibid., p. 489.
75 *Smith*, pp. 888–9 (citations omitted).
76 Ibid., p. 889, n. 5.
77 Ibid., p. 890.
78 Sunstein, 'Should Sex Equality Law Apply?', n. 13.
79 Ibid., p. 91.
80 'The prohibition [on employment discrimination] is generally inapplicable "to a religious corporation, association, educational institution, or society with respect to the employment of individuals of a particular religion to perform work connected with the carrying on by such corporation, association, educational institution, or society of its activities."' Ibid., n. 3.
81 Ibid.
82 Poulter, *Ethnicity, Law and Human Rights*, p. 264.
83 Ibid., internal quotation from *ISKCON* v. *UK* (1994) 76 – A, Dec & Rep 90, p. 107.
84 See the Inspector's description of the impact of the proposed development at ibid., p. 256.
85 Quoted in Rosenblum, *Membership and Morals*, p. 89.
86 See, for example, Mary Fainsod Katzenstein, *Faithful and Fearless: Moving Feminist Protest inside the Church and the Military* (Princeton, NJ: Princeton University Press, 1998), chs 5 and 6.

87  'The cardinals who elected Karol Wojtyla 20 years ago wanted a strong Pope. They got one, but cannot have foreseen the rest. They did not guess that riding on the back of a centralised papal authority, the papal civil service would sometimes treat them, in the words of one American cardinal, "like altar boys." ' John Wilkins, 'The Vatican's Inflexible Champion of the·Faith', *Manchester Guardian Weekly*, 18 October 1998, p. 12. (The writer is editor of *The Tablet*, a long-established Roman Catholic journal.) Many of the women studied by Katzenstein are much more radical in their aims, seeking to overthrow hierarchy altogether (see *Faithful and Fearless*, esp. pp. 107–8).

88  Robert L. Kidder, 'The Role of Outsiders', pp. 213–33 in Donald B. Kraybill, ed., *The Amish and the State* (Baltimore: The Johns Hopkins University Press, 1993), p. 223.

89  Donald B. Kraybill, 'Negotiating with Caesar', pp. 3–20 in Kraybill, ed., *The Amish and the State*, p. 5.

90  Ibid.

91  Paton Yoder, 'The Amish View of the State', pp. 23–40 in Kraybill, ed., *The Amish and the State*, p. 24.

92  Ibid., p. 25.

93  Ibid., p. 26.

94  Kraybill, 'Negotiating with Caesar', p. 6.

95  Macedo, 'Liberal Civic Education', p. 472.

96  Ibid., p. 489.

97  Albert N. Keim, 'Military Service and Conscription', pp. 43–64 in Kraybill, ed., *The Amish and the State*, p. 49.

98  Yoder, 'The Amish View of the State', pp. 30–1 (citations omitted).

99  See ibid., pp. 32–6.

100  Ibid., p. 36.

101  Ibid., p. 37.

102  Ibid., pp. 37–8.

103  Kidder, 'The Role of Outsiders', p. 215.

104  Yoder, 'The Amish View of the State', p. 38.

105  Ibid.

106  Peter J. Ferrera, 'Social Security and Taxes', pp. 125–43 in Kraybill, ed., *The Amish and the State*, p. 142.

107  Kidder, 'The Role of Outsiders', p. 220.

108  Ibid.

109  See the chapter by its founder, William C. Lindholm, 'The National Committee for Amish Religious Freedom', pp. 109–23 in Kraybill, ed., *The Amish and the State*.

110  The only exception to uncritical advocacy is the chapter by Kidder on 'The Role of Outsiders'.

111  Kraybill, 'Negotiating with Caesar', p. 4.

112  Kidder, 'The Role of Outsiders', p. 216.

113  Elizabeth Place, 'Land Use', pp. 191–210 in Kraybill, ed., *The Amish and the State*, esp. p. 194.

114  Kidder, 'The Role of Outsiders', pp. 216–17.

115 *Wisconsin* v. *Yoder*, 406 US 205 (1972), p. 216.
116 William B. Ball, 'First Amendment Issues', pp. 251–62 in Kraybill, ed., *The Amish and the State*, p. 255.
117 Ibid.
118 *US* v. *Lee*, 455 US 252 (1982).
119 Sunstein, 'Should Sexual Equality Law Apply?', p. 92.
120 Quoted in Rosenblum, *Membership and Morals*, p. 90.
121 *Smith*, p. 10, n. 4.
122 Sunstein, 'Should Sexual Equality Law Apply?', p. 92.
123 Elizabeth Place, 'Significant Legal Cases', pp. 263–73 in Kraybill, ed., *The Amish and the State*, p. 268, summarizing *Sherbert* v. *Verner*, 374 US 398 (1963), in which the Court 'found that the denial of unemployment compensation benefits to a Seventh Day Adventist who was discharged for refusing to work on Saturday, her Sabbath, burdened the free exercise of her religion by requiring her either to forgo benefits or to abandon her religious beliefs in order to accept employment' (ibid.).
124 *Smith*, p. 10, n. 4.
125 Lee J. Zook, 'Slow-Moving Vehicles', pp. 145–60 in Kraybill, ed., *The Amish and the State*, p. 149.
126 Ibid., pp. 147–8.
127 Ibid., p. 149. See also p. 156 for the author's testimony on these lines in the *Hershberger* case.
128 Ibid., p. 155.
129 Ibid., p. 157.
130 *State* v. *Hershberger* (*Hershberger I*), 444 NW 2d 282 (Minn. 1989).
131 Zook, 'Slow-Moving Vehicles', p. 158.
132 *Hershberger I*, p. 286, citing *Thomas* v. *Review Board of the Indiana Employment Security Division*, 450 US 707 (1981), p. 714.
133 Ibid., citing *Thomas*, p. 715.
134 *Bowen* v. *Roy*, 476 US 693 (1986), p. 708, quoted in *Smith*, p. 884, interpolation in square brackets in text of *Smith*.
135 *Smith*, p. 884.
136 *State* v. *Hershberger* (*Hershberger II*), 462 NW 2d 393 (Minn. 1990).
137 See, for example, *Smith*, p. 879.
138 Zook, 'Slow-Moving Vehicles', pp. 156–7.
139 *Hershberger I*, p. 288.
140 Ibid., p. 289.
141 Levy, 'Classifying Cultural Rights', p. 51.
142 Ibid., citing Allen Buchanan, *Secession: The Legitimacy of Political Divorce* (Boulder, Colo.: Westview Press, 1991), p. 59.
143 Ibid., p. 60, n. 40.
144 Ibid.
145 Ibid., p. 51.
146 Kymlicka, *Multicultural Citizenship*, p. 40.
147 Iris Marion Young, *Justice and the Politics of Difference* (Princeton, NJ: Princeton University Press, 1990), p. 183.

148 Chandran Kukathas, 'Are There any Cultural Rights?' , pp. 228–56 in Will Kymlicka, ed., *The Rights of Minority Cultures* (Oxford: Clarendon Press, 1995), p. 242.
149 Levy, 'Classifying Cultural Rights', p. 51; see also p. 42.
150 Kraybill, 'Negotiating with Caesar', p. 5.
151 Ibid., p. 6.
152 Greenawalt, 'Freedom of Association', p. 127.
153 Kidder, 'The Role of Outsiders', p. 215.
154 *Bear* v. *Reformed Mennonite Church*, 462 Pa. 330, 341 A 2d 105 (1975), p. 106, quoted in Greenawalt, 'Freedom of Association', p. 128.
155 Greenawalt, 'Freedom of Association', p. 128.
156 Ibid., p. 129.
157 Place, 'Land Use', pp. 205–6.
158 Kidder, 'The Role of Outsiders', pp. 231–2.
159 Place, 'Land Use', pp. 199–201.
160 Ibid., p. 208.
161 'Further subdivision of many farms for the upcoming generation is not economically feasible, and many young farmers are prevented from buying new land by prohibitive land prices.' Ibid., p. 199.
162 Ferrera, 'Social Security and Taxes', p. 129.
163 Ibid., p. 136.
164 Ibid.
165 Ibid.
166 'Decisions about [lobbying, negotiating and fighting court cases] do not emerge from consensual meetings of congregations. Instead, long-term strategy and day-to-day decisions are guided by lay leaders with specialized abilities and political connections. The results of their work often affect all Amish congregations across North America.' Kidder, 'The Role of Outsiders', p. 220.
167 Ferrera, 'Social Security and Taxes', p. 137.
168 Ibid., p. 136.

## Chapter 6   The Public Stake in the Arts and Education

1 Michael Walzer, *Spheres of Justice: A Defence of Pluralism and Equality* (New York: Basic Books, 1983).
2 Veit Bader, 'Egalitarian Multiculturalism: Institutional Separation and Cultural Pluralism', pp. 185–220 in Rainer Bauböck and John Rundell, eds, *Blurred Boundaries: Migration, Ethnicity, Citizenship* (Aldershot: Ashgate, 1998), p. 189.
3 Ibid.
4 Robert Hughes, *Culture of Complaint: The Fraying of America* (New York: Oxford University Press, 1993), p. 199.
5 Ibid.
6 Ibid.
7 John Stuart Mill, *On Liberty*, in Stefan Collini, ed., *On Liberty and Other Writings* (Cambridge: Cambridge University Press, 1989), p. 105. This must, incidentally,

be one of the few occurrences of an exclamation mark in the whole corpus of writings intended by Mill for publication.

8   Sanford Levinson, 'Is Liberal Nationalism an Oxymoron? An Essay for Judith Shklar', *Ethics* 105 (1995), 626–45, p. 642.

9   This famous phrase is quoted in the present context by Susan Moller Okin in her *Justice, Gender and the Family* (New York: Basic Books, 1989), p. 21.

10   Ibid., p. 9.

11   Charles Fried, *Right and Wrong* (Cambridge, Mass.: Harvard University Press, 1978), p. 152.

12   Ibid., p. 154.

13   Mill, *On Liberty*, p. 104.

14   Amy Gutmann, *Democratic Education* (Princeton, NJ: Princeton University Press, 2nd edn, 1999 [1987]), p. 299; internal quotation from Stephen G. Gilles, 'On Educating Children: A Parentalist Manifesto', *University of Chicago Law Review* 63 (1996), 937–1034, p. 1018. See also Stephen G. Gilles, 'Why Parents Should Choose', pp. 395–407 in Paul E. Peterson and Bryan C. Hassel, eds, *Learning from School Choice* (Washington, DC: Brookings Institution Press, 1998).

15   Ibid.

16   *Wisconsin* v. *Yoder*, 406 US 205 (1972), p. 219.

17   Richard Arneson and Ian Shapiro, 'Democratic Autonomy and Religious Freedom: A Critique of *Wisconsin v. Yoder*', pp. 356–411 in Ian Shapiro and Russell Hardin, eds, NOMOS 38: *Political Order* (New York: New York University Press, 1996), p. 380, emphasis in original.

18   See ibid., pp. 380–1.

19   Mill, *On Liberty*, pp. 104–5.

20   Arneson and Shapiro, 'Democratic Autonomy', p. 366.

21   Ibid., p. 381.

22   Paul Myers, 'Alternative Cure "Zealot" Jailed for Daughter's Death', *Guardian*, 6 November 1996, p. 1.

23   Ibid.

24   Arneson and Shapiro, 'Democratic Autonomy', p. 382.

25   Gutmann, *Democratic Education*, pp. 299–300.

26   See for a discussion of funding limits Harry Brighouse, 'Egalitarian Liberals and School Choice', *Politics and Society* 24 (1996), 457–86.

27   Levinson, 'Is Liberal Nationalism an Oxymoron?' p. 634.

28   Amy Gutmann, 'Civic Education and Social Diversity', *Ethics* 105 (1995), 557–79, p. 570.

29   For a description, see Thomas J. Meyers, 'Education and Schooling', pp. 87–106 in Donald B. Kraybill, ed., *The Amish and the State* (Baltimore: The Johns Hopkins University Press, 1993), p. 91.

30   *Employment Division, Department of Human Resources of Oregon, et al.*, v. *Alfred L. Smith et al.*, 494 US 872 (1990), p. 881.

31   Kent Greenawalt, 'Freedom of Association and Religious Association', pp. 109–44 in Amy Gutmann, ed., *Freedom of Association* (Princeton, NJ: Princeton University Press, 1998), p. 126.

32    *Yoder*, pp. 230–1.

33    Ibid., p. 232.

34    Greenawalt, 'Freedom of Association', p. 125.

35    Gertrude Enders Huntington, 'Health Care', pp. 163–89 in Kraybill, ed., *The Amish and the State*, p. 178.

36    Donald B. Kraybill, 'Negotiating with Caesar', pp. 3–20 in Kraybill, ed., *The Amish and the State*, p. 10.

37    Genesis 27: 22.

38    Mill, *On Liberty*, p. 105.

39    Shelley Burtt, 'In Defense of *Yoder*: Parental Authority and the Public Schools', pp. 412–37 in Hardin and Shapiro, eds, *Public Order*, pp. 419–20 (Word order rearranged: in the original, the phrase inserted in brackets occurred at the end of the sentence.)

40    Kenneth J. Meier and Joseph Stewart, Jr., *The Politics of Hispanic Education: Un Paso Pa'lante y Dos Pa'tras* (Albany, NY: State University of New York Press, 1991), p. 78.

41    Jennifer L. Hochschild and Nathan Scovronick, 'One, Some and Many: The Problems of Democracy in Education Policy', paper presented at the annual meeting of the American Political Science Association, Boston, September 1998, p. 16.

42    Meier and Stewart, *The Politics of Hispanic Education*, p. 78.

43    Peter D. Salins, *Assimilation, American Style* (New York: Basic Books, 1997), p. 74.

44    Ibid.

45    Ibid., p. 75.

46    Ibid.

47    Meier and Stewart, *The Politics of Hispanic Education*, p. 78.

48    Salins, *Assimilation*, p. 74.

49    A study in 1977 found that 'less than 30 percent of the participating children were actually limited in their English-speaking ability and that approximately 86 percent of the projects tended to keep children in bilingual education programs long after they were able to move into regular English-language classrooms.' Quoted in Meier and Stewart, *The Politics of Hispanic Education*, p. 23.

50    Salins, *Assimilation*, p. 75.

51    Meier and Stewart, *The Politics of Hispanic Education*, p. 38.

52    Will Kymlicka, *Multicultural Citizenship: A Liberal Theory of Minority Rights* (Oxford: Clarendon Press, 1995), p. 10.

53    Ibid., p. 16.

54    Meier and Stewart, *The Politics of Hispanic Education*, p. 66.

55    Kymlicka, *Multicultural Citizenship*, p. 16.

56    Meier and Stewart, *The Politics of Hispanic Education*, p. 73.

57    Ibid. (Note that the evidence cited dates back to 1983, so the proportion is bound to be higher now.)

58    Kymlicka, *Multicultural Citizenship*, p. 16.

59    Meier and Stewart, *The Politics of Hispanic Education*, p. 38.

60 Ibid., p. 73.

61 Ibid., p. 77.

62 Ibid., p. 82 (citation omitted).

63 Harry Brighouse, 'Educational Equality and the Value of the Family" (unpublished paper), p. 4.

64 Martha C. Nussbaum, *Cultivating Humanity: A Classical Defense of Reform in Liberal Education* (Cambridge, Mass.: Harvard University Press, 1997), p. 85.

65 Amy Gutmann, 'Children, Paternalism, and Education', *Philosophy & Public Affairs* 9 (1980), 338–58, p. 349. People who exhibit a high degree of autonomy, as that is understood by Galston, Kymlicka, Gutmann and other contemporary political theorists, might well be regarded as psychologically disturbed by the American Psychiatric Association. According to the latest edition of its Diagnostic and Statistical Manual (DSM–IV), 'the symptoms of Identity Problem (313.82)' include 'uncertainty about . . . long-term goals, career choice, friendship patterns, sexual orientation and behavior, moral values and group loyalties'. Joe Sharkey, 'Word for Word: Mental Disorders. Defining the Line between Behavior that's Vexing and Certifiable', *New York Times*, 19 December 1999, Section 4, p. 7.

66 Ibid., p. 351.

67 John Rawls, *Political Liberalism* ( New York: Columbia University Press, 1993), p. 200.

68 Gutmann, *Democratic Education*, p. 13, quoting John Dewey, *'The Child and the Curriculum' and 'The School and Society'* (Chicago: University of Chicago Press, 1956), p. 7.

69 Ibid., p. 14.

70 Ibid., p. 39.

71 Ibid.

72 Ibid., p. 287.

73 Harry Brighouse, 'Civic Education and Liberal Legitimacy', *Ethics* 108 (1998), 719–45, p. 734, emphases in original.

74 Ibid., p. 731.

75 Nussbaum, *Cultivating Humanity*, esp. pp. 33–5.

76 James Traub, 'Back to School', *New York Times Book Review*, 19 September 1999, p. 16; internal quotation from Alfie Kohn, *The Schools Our Children Deserve: Moving Beyond Traditional Classrooms and 'Tougher Standards'* (Boston: Houghton Mifflin, 1999).

77 Ibid.

78 Gutmann, *Democratic Education*, p. 111.

79 Vivian S. Toy, 'Crew Wants Sex Offender Photos Removed', *New York Times*, 21 November 1998, p. B3.

80 See Will Kymlicka, *Finding Our Way: Rethinking Ethnocultural Relations in Canada* (Toronto: Oxford University Press, 1998), esp. p. 162.

81 Maureen Covell, 'Belgium: The Variability of Ethnic Relations', pp. 275–95 in John McGarry and Brendan O'Leary, eds, *The Politics of Ethnic Conflict Regulation: Case Studies of Protracted Ethnic Conflicts* (London: Routledge, 1993), p. 294.

82   Kent Greenawalt, 'Quo Vadis: The Status and Prospects of "Tests" under the Religion Clause', *The Supreme Court Review 1995* (Chicago: University of Chicago Press, 1996), 323–91, p. 347.

83   Ibid.

84   Ibid.

85   Gutmann, *Democratic Education*, p. 287.

86   Ibid., p. 136.

87   Ibid., pp. 287–8.

88   Ibid., p. 298.

89   Ibid., p. 287.

90   Hochschild and Scovronick, 'One, Some and Many', p. 9.

91   Ibid.

92   William Galston, *Liberal Purposes* (Cambridge: Cambridge University Press, 1992), p. 221.

93   Ibid., pp. 243–4.

94   Brighouse, 'Civic Education and Liberal Legitimacy', pp. 724–5.

95   Galston, *Liberal Purposes*, p. 244.

96   Salins, *Assimilation*, p. 81.

97   Ibid., pp. 81–2.

98   For the first, see chapter 1 of Todd Gitlin, *The Twilight of Common Dreams: Why America is Wracked by Culture Wars* (New York: Henry Holt, 1995); for the second, see Nathan Glazer, *We Are All Multiculturalists Now* (Cambridge, Mass.: Harvard University Press, 1997), esp. ch. 2.

99   Glazer, *We Are All Multiculturalists Now*, p. 76.

100  'In the New York State syllabus there is a reference to the influence of the Iroquois or Hodenosaunee federation on the framers of the Constitution.' Ibid., p. 41.

101  Ibid., p. 54.

102  Jeff Spinner, *The Boundaries of Citizenship: Race, Ethnicity, and Nationality in the Liberal State* (Baltimore: The Johns Hopkins University Press, 1994), p. 181.

103  Glazer, *We Are All Multiculturalists Now*, pp. 13–14.

104  Ibid., pp. 12–13.

105  Ibid.

106  Hochschild and Scovronick, 'One, Some and Many', p. 13.

107  Glazer, *We Are All Multiculturalists Now*, p. 160, emphasis in original.

108  Hochschild and Scovronick, 'One, Some and Many', p. 9.

109  R. D. Grillo, *Pluralism and the Politics of Difference: State, Culture, and Ethnicity in Comparative Perspective* (Oxford: Clarendon Press, 1998), p. 197, citing L. Black, *New Ethnicities and Urban Culture: Racisms and Multiculture in Young Lives* (London: UCL Press, 1996), p. 152.

110  Hochschild and Scovronick, 'One, Some and Many', p. 7.

111  Ibid.

112  Ibid.

113  Ibid., p. 15.

114  The equivocal nature of 'multicultural education' is emphasized by Nussbaum, *Cultivating Humanity*, pp. 109–12.

115  Hochschild and Scovronick, 'One, Some and Many', p. 14.
116  Chandran Kukathas, 'Are There any Cultural Rights?', pp. 228–56 in Will Kymlicka, ed., *The Rights of Minority Cultures* (Oxford: Oxford University Press, 1995), p. 248.
117  Ibid., p. 247.
118  Ibid., internal quotations from Sebastian Poulter, 'Ethnic Minority Customs, English Law and Human Rights', *International and Comparative Law Quarterly* 36 (1987), 589–615, pp. 600–1.
119  Sebastian Poulter, *Ethnicity, Law and Human Rights: The English Experience* (Oxford: Clarendon Press, 1998), p. 151.
120  Ibid., p. 152.
121  Yael Tamir, 'Siding with the Underdogs', pp. 47–52 in Susan Moller Okin with Respondents, *Is Multiculturalism Bad for Women?*, ed. Joshua Cohen, Matthew Howard and Martha C. Nussbaum (Princeton, NJ: Princeton University Press, 1999), p. 51.
122  Poulter, *Ethnicity, Law and Human Rights*, pp. 191–2.
123  Ibid., p. 100.
124  Ibid., p. 101.
125  Stephen Macedo, 'Liberal Civic Education and Religious Fundamentalism: The Case of God v. John Rawls', *Ethics* 105 (1995), 468–96, p. 489.
126  Spinner, *The Boundaries of Citizenship*, p. 102.
127  Macedo, 'Liberal Civil Education', p. 489.
128  Spinner, *The Boundaries of Citizenship*, p. 102.
129  Thus, Spinner (ibid., pp. 105–8) argues that the Amish should be regarded as 'partial citizens' and on this basis exempted from the education for citizenship that he otherwise advocates.
130  Galston, *Liberal Purposes*, p. 255.
131  Burtt, 'In Defense of *Yoder*', p. 426.
132  Ibid.
133  Ibid.
134  *Mozert* v. *Hawkins County Board of Education*, 827 F 2d 1058 (6th Circuit, 1987).
135  Gutmann, 'Civic Education and Social Diversity', pp. 556–7.
136  Ibid.
137  Ibid.: as the Lollards (almost) asked: 'When Adam cooked / And Eve read / Who was then the gently bred?'
138  Ibid.
139  *Mozert* v. *Hawkins*, p. 1077.
140  Ibid., p. 1080.
141  Macedo, 'Liberal Civil Education', p. 471.
142  Spinner, *The Boundaries of Citizenship*, p. 107.
143  Gutmann, *Democratic Education*, p. 298, referring to Galston, *Liberal Purposes*, pp. 224–7.
144  Ibid.
145  Ibid.
146  Ibid., p. 101.

147  Ibid.
148  Ibid., pp. 103–4.
149  Ibid., p. 102.
150  Ibid., p. 102, internal quotation from Larry Laudan, 'Appendix B, Science at the Bar: Causes for Concern', pp. 149–54 in Jeffrie G. Murphy, *Evolution, Morality and the Meaning of Life* (Totowa, NJ: Rowman and Littlefield, 1982), p. 154 (citation in Gutmann corrected).
151  Stephen Holmes, 'Gag Rules or the Politics of Omission', pp. 19–58 in Jon Elster and Rune Slagstad, *Constitutionalism and Democracy* (Cambridge: Cambridge University Press, 1988), pp. 54–5.
152  Ibid., p. 55.
153  'Alabama biology textbooks ... must carry a warning that reads in part: "No one was present when life first appeared on earth. Therefore, any statement about life's origins should be considered as theory, not fact." ' James Glanz, 'Science vs. the Bible: Debate Moves to the Cosmos', *New York Times*, 12 October 1999, pp. 1, 40, p. 40.
154  Albert J. Menendez, *Visions of Reality: What Fundamentalist Schools Teach* (Buffalo, NY: Prometheus Books, 1993), p. 1.
155  Ibid., p. 120, internal quotation from William S. Pinkston, Jr., *Biology for Christian Schools, Teacher's Edition* (Greenville, SC: Bob Jones University Press, 1991), Book 1, p. 169.
156  Pinkston, *Biology for Christian Schools*, Book 2, p. 612, cited on p. 122 of Menendez, *Visions of Reality*. (This looks suspiciously like the Manichean heresy, but the orthodoxy or otherwise of Bob Jones University theology is not my present concern.)
157  Ibid., Book 1, p. 169, cited on p. 120 of Menendez, *Visions of Reality*.
158  Jan Anderson and Laurel Hicks, *Beginnings of American Literature, Classics for Christians*, vol. 3 (Pensacola, Fla.: Pensacola Christian College, A Beka Book Production, 1982), p. 385, quoted in Menendez, *Visions of Reality*, p. 96.
159  Menendez, *Visions of Reality*, ch. 4, pp. 79–117.
160  Ibid., p. 64, quoting from Glen Chambers and Gene Fisher, *United States History for Christian Schools* (Greenville, SC: Bob Jones University Press, 1982), p. 559.
161  Chambers and Fisher, *United States History*, p. 543. Prior to the abrupt reversal of its ban on interracial dating on 3 March 2000, Bob Jones University was defending the policy by citing God's intentions, as manifested in the destruction of the Tower of Babel. ' "God made racial differences as He made gender differences," said a statement the University posted on its Internet site. But, the statement added, when God stopped humans from building The Tower of Babel ... [He] did so to prevent them from creating "one-world government." Based on the biblical account (Genesis 10 and 11), the statement said, "the university wishes to give God the benefit of any doubt and avoid pursuing any direction that would give assistance to the renewed efforts of man to create a one-world community consisting of one religion, one economy, one government and one race." ' Gustav Niebuhr, 'Bob Jones U. Drops its Ban on Interracial Student Dates', *New York Times*, 4 March 2000, p. A11. This shows

that the condemnation of the United Nations in the history textbook put out by the University was no mere aberration but reflected one of its core doctrines.

162   *State* v. *Whisner*, 47 Ohio St. 2d. 181 (1976); summarized in Elizabeth Place, 'Significant Legal Cases', pp. 263–73 in Kraybill, ed., *The Amish and the State*, pp. 270–1.

## Chapter 7   The Abuse of 'Culture'

1   See Brian Barry, *Sociologists, Economists and Democracy* (Chicago: University of Chicago Press, 1978 [reprint]) for a critique of 'culture' as explanation.
2   Jared Diamond, *Guns, Germs and Steel* (London: Vintage, 1998), p. 53.
3   Ibid., pp. 53–4.
4   Ibid., p. 53.
5   'Hunters Put a Spin on the Seal Market', *Independent*, 11 March 1998, p. 11.
6   'Whalers Take Aim at Ban', *Guardian*, 20 October 1997, p. 11. The whales are killed, incidentally, in a peculiarly horrible way because, according to the same report, the Chukchi have lost the art of projecting a harpoon into the whale's heart – and presumably cannot be bothered to reacquire it. Instead, they pump round after round of bullets from old Soviet machine guns into the hapless creatures until they eventually die.
7   Ibid.
8   BBC Online Network, 24 May 1999, 'UK Urges Whaling Ban'. (I am grateful to Philip Parvin for this item.)
9   'Whalers Take Aim at Ban.'
10   Ibid.
11   James Tully, *Strange Multiplicity: Constitutionalism in an Age of Diversity* (Cambridge: Cambridge University Press, 1995), p. 172.
12   Ibid.
13   'It is generally accepted that cultures are not rigid monoliths given once and for all, as National Romanticism of the nineteenth century would have it, but receptive and responsive ways of constructing meaning, continuously battered by requirements to change and develop, and by counter-forces stressing ideals of purism, opposing newfangled expressions and interpretations.' Charles Westin, 'Temporal and Spatial Aspects of Multiculturality', pp. 53–84 in Rainer Bauböck and John Rundell, eds, *Blurred Boundaries: Migration, Ethnicity, Citizenship* (Aldershot: Ashgate, 1998), p. 61.
14   Tully, *Strange Multiplicity*, p. 172, internal quotations from Avigail Eisenberg, 'The Politics of Individual and Group Difference in Canadian Jurisprudence', *Canadian Journal of Political Science* 27 (1994), 3–21, p. 18.
15   Ibid.
16   Ian Shapiro, 'Group Aspirations and Democratic Politics', pp. 210–21 in Ian Shapiro and Casiano Hacker-Cordón, eds, *Democracy's Edges* (Cambridge: Cambridge University Press, 1999), p. 220.
17   'Anger Greets March Proposal', *Independent*, 18 October 1997, p. 12.
18   Westin, 'Temporal and Spatial Aspects', p. 56.

19  Jürgen Habermas, 'Struggles for Recognition in the Democratic Constitutional State', pp. 107–48 in Amy Gutmann, ed., *Multiculturalism: Examining the Politics of Recognition* (Princeton, NJ: Princeton University Press, 1994), p. 132.

20  Dennis H. Wrong, 'Cultural Relativism as Ideology', *Critical Review* 11 (1997), 291–300, pp. 292–3.

21  'The notion of *Kultur* developed in tension with the concept of a universal civilization that was associated with France. What the French understood to be a transnational civilization was regarded in Germany as a source of danger to distinctive local cultures.' Adam Kuper, *Culture: The Anthropologists' Account* (Cambridge, Mass.: Harvard University Press, 1999), p. 31.

22  Daniel Weinstock, 'The Graying of Berlin', *Critical Review* 11 (1997), 481–501, p. 486.

23  Arthur Gobineau, *Essai sur l'inégalité des races humaines* (1853–5), trans. *The Inequality of Human Races* (New York: G.P. Putnam's Sons, 1915 ).

24  Wrong, 'Cultural Relativism', p. 293.

25  Todd Gitlin, *The Twilight of Common Dreams: Why America is Wracked by Culture Wars* (New York: Henry Holt, 1995), pp. 164–5.

26  Kuper, *Culture*, p. 241.

27  Gitlin, *The Twilight of Common Dreams*, p. 84.

28  Tully, *Strange Multiplicity*, p. 17.

29  Ibid., p. 203.

30  Ibid., p. 204.

31  Thomas Nagel, 'MacIntyre versus the Enlightenment', pp. 203–9 in Thomas Nagel, *Other Minds: Critical Essays 1969–1994* (New York: Oxford University Press, 1995), p. 206.

32  Tully, *Strange Multiplicity*, p. 186.

33  Peter Jones, 'Political Theory and Cultural Diversity', *Critical Review of International Social and Political Philosophy* 1 (1998), 28–62, p. 44.

34  'The incommensurability that I will be concerned with is the incommensurability of value: the possibility that the value of two items, or that the goodness of two options, is incommensurate, in that neither of them is better than the other nor are they of equal value.' Joseph Raz, 'Incommensurability and Agency', pp. 110–50 in Ruth Chang, ed., *Incommensurability, Incomparability and Practical Reason* (Cambridge, Mass.: Harvard University Press, 1997), p. 110.

35  Quotations from John Gray, *Enlightenment's Wake: Politics and Culture at the Close of the Modern Age* (London: Routledge, 1995), p. 79.

36  Ibid., p. 127.

37  Ibid., p. 133.

38  Ibid., pp. 133, 83. It should be mentioned that, like Michael Walzer, Gray qualifies his radical particularism by invoking a 'minimum universal content to morality'. Unlike Walzer, however, he says explicitly that he has no intention of trying to explain where it comes from, and is remarkably coy about what the content might be (ibid., p. 81). But since he does say that the current regime in mainland China is one of the 'regimes that clearly meet the minimum universal content of morality' (ibid., p. 83), it need not detain us long.

39 For an acknowledgement of the influence of Herder, see Charles Taylor, *Reconciling the Solitudes: Essays on Canadian Federalism and Nationalism*, ed. Guy Laforest (Montreal and Kingston: McGill/Queen's University Press, 1993), p. 136.

40 Charles Taylor, 'The Politics of Recognition', pp. 25–73 in Gutmann, ed., *Multiculturalism*, p. 41, emphasis in original.

41 Ibid.

42 Ibid., p. 42.

43 Ibid., pp. 66–71.

44 Ibid., p. 42.

45 Ibid., p. 71, emphasis in original.

46 Ibid., emphasis in original.

47 Ibid., p. 67.

48 Robert Hughes, *Culture of Complaint: The Fraying of America* (New York: Oxford University Press, 1993), pp. 201–2.

49 Iris Marion Young, *Justice and the Politics of Difference* (Princeton, NJ: Princeton University Press, 1990), p. 174.

50 Tully, *Strange Multiplicity*, p. 190.

51 Ibid., p. 189.

52 Ibid.

53 John Rawls, *A Theory of Justice* (Cambridge, Mass: Harvard University Press, 1971), p. 441.

54 Daniel Weinstock, 'How Can Collective Rights and Liberalism Be Reconciled?', pp. 281–304 in Bauböck and Rundell, eds, *Blurred Boundaries*, p. 298.

55 Tully, *Strange Multiplicity*, p. 190, emphasis supplied.

56 Rawls, *A Theory of Justice*, p. 441.

57 Nancy L. Rosenblum, *Membership and Morals: The Personal Uses of Pluralism in America* (Princeton, NJ: Princeton University Press, 1998), p. 353, emphasis in original.

58 Ibid., p. 355.

59 Ibid.

60 Chapter 1 of Young's book is entitled 'Displacing the Distributive Paradigm'.

61 Young, *Justice and the Politics of Difference*, p. 152.

62 Ibid., p. 23.

63 Ibid., p. 87.

64 Ibid., p. 120, my emphasis.

65 Robert Fullinwider, 'Citizenship, Individualism and Democratic Politics', *Ethics* 105 (1995), 497–515, p. 503.

66 This story is told by Hughes in *Culture of Complaint*, pp. 200–1.

67 Fullinwider, 'Citizenship', p. 52.

68 Jones, 'Political Theory', p. 45.

69 Young, *Justice and the Politics of Difference*, p. 16.

70 Ibid.

71 Ibid., p. 25.

72 Ibid.

73 Ibid.

74   Ibid.
75   Ibid.
76   Ibid., p. 26.
77   Ibid.
78   Ibid., p. 161.
79   Ibid.
80   Ibid.
81   This 'medicalization' of opposition to homosexuality is matched by the 'medicalization' of homosexuality itself, which gave rise to an advertising campaign by the Christian Right in America in 1997 'in defence of "curing" homosexuals', who were 'portrayed as sick and needing therapy'. Andrew Sullivan, 'Going Down Screaming', *New York Times Magazine*, 11 October 1998, pp. 46–91, p. 49.
82   Nancy Fraser, 'From Redistribution to Recognition? Dilemmas of Justice in a "Post-Socialist" Age', *New Left Review* 212 (July/August 1995), 68–93, p. 75.
83   Ibid.
84   Ibid., pp. 77–8.
85   Sullivan, 'Going Down Screaming', p. 49.
86   Ibid., p. 48.
87   Young, *Justice and the Politics of Difference*, p. 120.
88   Christine Di Stefano, 'Feminist Attitudes towards Ethical Pluralism', paper delivered at the Ethikon Institute Conference on Ethical Pluralism, Civil Society, and Political Culture at La Jolla, California, 25–27 June 1999, p. 23.
89   Ibid.
90   Andrew Sullivan, 'What's so Bad about Hate?' *New York Times Magazine*, 26 September 1999, pp. 50–7, p. 54.
91   Young, *Justice and the Politics of Difference*, p. 162.
92   Taylor, 'The Politics of Recognition', p. 63.
93   Ibid.
94   Ibid.
95   See Richard Hofstadter, *Social Darwinism in American Thought* (Boston, Mass.: Beacon Press, rev. edn, 1955), esp. ch. 9.
96   Matthew Arnold, *Culture and Anarchy*, in Stefan Collini, ed., *Culture and Anarchy and Other Writings* (Cambridge: Cambridge University Press, 1993), pp. 64–5.
97   See Gray, *Enlightenment's Wake*, pp. 83, 127; emphasis in original.
98   Taylor, 'The Politics of Recognition' p. 63.
99   Ibid.
100  Ibid.
101  Ibid.
102  Ibid.
103  Hughes, *Culture of Complaint*, p. 115.
104  Martha C. Nussbaum, 'Human Capabilities, Female Human Beings', pp. 61–104 in Martha C. Nussbaum and Jonathan Glover, eds, *Women, Culture and Development: A Study of Human Capabilities* (Oxford: Clarendon Press, 1955), quotation from p. 65. The same passage is repeated in Martha C.

Nussbaum, *Sex and Social Justice* (New York: Oxford University Press, 1999), p. 35.
105  Ibid.
106  Ibid.
107  Veit Bader, 'Egalitarian Multiculturalism: Institutional Separation and Cultural Pluralism', pp. 185–220 in Bauböck and Rundell, eds, *Blurred Boundaries*, p. 201.
108  Michael Walzer, *Thick and Thin: Moral Argument at Home and Abroad* (Notre Dame, Ind.: University of Notre Dame Press, 1994), p. 52; for a more elaborate presentation of the analogy, see Michael Walzer, *Interpretation and Social Criticism* (Cambridge, Mass.: Harvard University Press, 1987), pp. 14–16.
109  Charles Jones, *Global Justice: Defending Cosmopolitanism* (Oxford: Oxford University Press, 1999), p. 194, n. 45.
110  Jan Mayman, 'Aboriginal Artist Wins Race Case', *Independent on Sunday*, 22 March 1998, p. 17.
111  Ibid.
112  See Sebastian Poulter, *Ethnicity, Law and Human Rights: The English Experience* (Oxford: Clarendon Press, 1998), p. 185: 'Pressures to move into housing seem certain to be resisted by the vast majority of gypsies currently living in caravans. [There is not much available housing.] Nor would the gardens of most houses be suitable for gypsies to carry on their traditional economic activities, such as scrap-metal work.'
113  Ibid., pp. 191–2.

### Chapter 8   The Politics of Multiculturalism

1  Jennifer L. Hochschild and Nathan Scovronick, 'One, Some, and Many: The Problems of Democracy in Education Policy', paper presented at the annual meeting of the American Political Science Association, Boston, September 1998, p. 18, n. 49.
2  Ibid.
3  Sebastian Poulter, *Ethnicity, Law and Human Rights: The English Experience* (Oxford: Clarendon Press, 1998), p. 385.
4  The Canadian Multiculturalism Act is excerpted as Appendix A, pp. 184–6 in Will Kymlicka, *Finding Our Way: Rethinking Ethnocultural Relations in Canada* (Toronto: Oxford University Press, 1998). (See also Poulter, *Ethnicity, Law and Human Rights*, pp. 382–3.)
5  Kymlicka, *Finding Our Way*, p. 185.
6  Ibid.
7  Ibid.
8  Ibid., p. 4.
9  Ibid.
10  Ibid.
11  Ibid., pp. 3–4.
12  Ibid., p. 4.
13  The esoteric nature of Kymlicka's influence is emphasized in an article in the *Wall Street Journal* for 27 March 2000, pp. B1 and B4, which goes under the title

'A Philosopher in Red Sneakers Gains Influence as a Global Guru: From Estonia to New Zealand, Nations with Ethnic Strife Turn to Will Kymlicka' (written by G. Pascal Zachary). For 'nations', read 'politicians': 'Though closely studied by academics, Mr Kymlicka is virtually unknown to the wider public. But... politicians in Europe, Asia and North America are starting to draw inspiration from his ideas on how best nations can meet minority demands.' Quotation from p. B1.

14 Charles R. Epp, 'Do Bills of Rights Matter? The Canadian Charter of Rights and Freedoms', *American Political Science Review* 90 (1996), 765–79, p. 770.

15 Kymlicka, *Finding Our Way*, p. vii.

16 Ibid.

17 Ibid., p. 5.

18 Poulter, *Ethnicity, Law and Human Rights*, p. 385.

19 Adrian Favell, 'Applied Political Philosophy at the Rubicon: Will Kymlicka's *Multicultural Citizenship*', *Ethical Theory and Moral Practice* 1 (1998), 255–78, pp. 262–3.

20 Ibid., p. 263.

21 Poulter, *Ethnicity, Law and Human Rights*, p. 137.

22 Ibid.

23 Ibid.

24 Ibid., p. 134.

25 Ibid., p. 294.

26 Ibid., p. 295, n. 134.

27 Noel Epstein, 'Bilingual Education in the United States: the "Either/Or" Mistake', pp. 85–109 in D. J. R. Bruckner, ed., *Politics and Language: Spanish and English in the United States* (Chicago: The University of Chicago Center for Public Policy, 1980), p. 87.

28 Ibid., p. 99

29 Ibid.

30 Ibid., p. 89.

31 Ibid., p. 103.

32 Ibid., p. 92.

33 Ibid., p. 93.

34 Ibid.

35 Ibid., p. 94.

36 Iris Marion Young, *Justice and the Politics of Difference* (Princeton, NJ: Princeton University Press, 1990), pp. 179–80.

37 Ibid., p. 97.

38 For a far more gross caricature, see John Gray, *Enlightenment's Wake: Politics and Culture at the Close of the Modern Age* (London: Routledge, 1995), ch. 1.

39 Young, *Justice and Politics of Difference*, p. 118.

40 Ibid., p. 117, referring to Benjamin R. Barber, *Strong Democracy: Participatory Politics for a New Age* (Berkeley and Los Angeles: University of California Press, 1984).

41 Ibid.

42 Ibid., p. 119.

43   Ibid., p. 184.
44   Ibid.
45   It seems to me questionable that Indian reservations should be free, as they are under federal law, to disregard the general land use regulations of the State within which they are situated. But that is presumably the position that Young wishes to endorse.
46   It is true that Chandran Kukathas's version of libertarianism would give such parents a free hand in all these matters and others, though by a different means: in his ideal society, all parents would have a right to dispose of their children as they wished. As I argued in chapter 4, however, Kukathas's theory becomes grossly implausible once its implications are fully grasped.
47   As a matter of fact, men in the United States are slightly more 'pro-choice' than women. (I am indebted to my colleague Robert Shapiro for this information.)
48   K. Anthony Appiah, 'Multicultural Misunderstanding', *New York Review of Books* 44, 9 October 1997, p. 36.
49   Young, *Justice and the Politics of Difference*, p. 40.
50   Will Kymlicka has suggested that Young's 'list of "oppressed groups" in the United States would seem to include 80 per cent of the population'. Will Kymlicka, *Multicultural Citizenship: A Liberal Theory of Minority Rights* (Oxford: Clarendon Press, 1995). But this still appears to me to be a substantial underestimate of the extent of oppression, according to Young's criteria. Women constitute over half the population. If we define young and old as those below the age of majority (18) and above the age of eligibility for a social security pension (65), the proportion of males who fall into one or the other category approaches a half. Of the remaining quarter or so of the population, about a third belong to one or other of the ethnic or racial groups described by Young as oppressed. (It should be borne in mind that her list includes groups such as Jews whose members are not normally counted as ethnic minorities – whether oppressed or not.) If, from the sixth of the population left, we subtract the gays and the disabled, and then reckon about a quarter of the rest to belong to the working class, we end up with a figure around 10 per cent of the total population constituting the non-oppressed.
51   Ibid.
52   Ibid., p. 43.
53   Kymlicka, *Multicultural Citizenship*, p. 19.
54   Ibid.
55   Ibid., p. 199, n. 10.
56   Ibid., p. 19.
57   Ibid., p. 18.
58   Kymlicka, *Finding Our Way*, p. 157.
59   Kymlicka, *Multicultural Citizenship*, pp. 54–5.
60   As Neil MacCormick writes, 'although little rewarded in terms of Parliamentary seats won, the SNP remained after 1979 a substantial electoral force in Scottish politics . . . and this was what imposed the political necessity on the Labour Party to uphold a commitment to Scottish devolution towards which its London-

based leadership frequently seemed at best tepid in enthusiasm.' Neil MacCormick, 'The English Constitution, the British State, and the Scottish Anomaly', pp. 289–306 in *Proceedings of the British Academy* 101 (Oxford: Oxford University Press, 1999), p. 304.

61  Ibid., p. 18.
62  Kymlicka, *Finding Our Way*, p. 149.
63  Ibid., p. 142, quoting Jeremy Webber, *Reimagining Canada: Language, Culture, and Community and the Canadian Constitution* (Montreal: McGill/Queen's University Press, 1994), pp. 142–3.
64  Ibid., p. 143.
65  Ibid.
66  Ibid., quoted from Philip Resnick, 'Toward a Multination Federalism', in Leslie Seidle, ed., *Seeking a New Canadian Partnership: Asymmetrical and Confederal Options* (Montreal: Institute for Research on Public Policy, 1994), p. 77.
67  Ibid.
68  Ibid., p. 141.
69  Ibid., p. 207, n. 22.
70  Ibid., p. 141.
71  Ibid.
72  Ibid., p. 154.
73  Ibid., p. 142.
74  Chapters 10 and 11 of *Finding Our Way* are devoted to 'asymmetry', apart from a section on aboriginal rights.
75  MacCormick, 'The English Constitution', p. 305.
76  Similarly, MacCormick argues that Scottish MPs cannot plausibly refuse to take part in decisions that do not affect their constituents: 'parliamentary arithmetic will sometimes make it necessary for them also to play a decisive role in purely English matters, if a government is in power without a majority among the representatives of English constituencies.' Ibid.
77  Kymlicka, *Finding Our Way*, p. 132.
78  Ibid., p. 142.
79  There is no constitutional mechanism guaranteeing that Belgium-wide policies reflect concurrent Flemish and Walloon majorities. But there is a strong convention to this effect, which is built into the process of government-formation. (See the discussion of Belgium in section 6 of chapter 6.)
80  Kymlicka, *Finding Our Way*, p. 4.
81  For an analysis of the Charlottestown Accord on these lines, see Patrick James, 'The Chain Store Paradox and Constitutional Politics in Canada', *Journal of Theoretical Politics* 11 (1999), 5–36.
82  Ibid., pp. 29–30. 'Seven out of ten provinces [were] either evenly divided or opposed.' Ibid., p. 25.
83  Kymlicka, *Multicultural Citizenship*, p. 18.
84  Ethnicity was also an organizing factor in some occupations within the private sector, entry to which could be controlled by an apprenticeship system or a union closed shop. Again, however, the objective was economic advantage rather than the maintenance of a distinctive culture.

85  John Rex, 'Multiculturalism in Europe and North America', pp. 15–33 in Wsevolod W. Isajiw, ed., *Multiculturalism in North America and Europe: Comparative Perspectives on Interethnic Relations and Social Incorporation* (Toronto: Canadian Scholars' Press, 1997), p. 31.

86  Favell, 'Applied Political Philosophy', p. 267.

87  Kymlicka, *Multicultural Citizenship*, pp. 58–60.

88  Ibid., p. 59.

89  Ibid., p. 60; see also p. 25.

90  Ibid.

91  See Kymlicka, *Finding Our Way*, ch. 5.

92  Ibid., p. 44.

93  I allowed in a note (ch. 3, n. 52) that there might be more truth in Kymlicka's claim with respect to Canada and Australia, though even in relation to them it is surely overstated.

94  Kymlicka, *Finding Our Way*, p. 44.

95  Chandran Kukathas, 'Cultural Toleration', pp. 69–104 in Ian Shapiro and Will Kymlicka, eds, NOMOS 39: *Ethnicity and Group Rights* (New York: New York University Press, 1997), p. 88.

96  I mentioned in the Preface that the *reductio ad absurdum* is a difficult argument to deploy against multiculturalists, because there is almost no proposal so daft that some multiculturalists will not embrace it. Arguing that 'it is not clear how [the prohibition of polygamy] fits with the general principle that adults should normally be able to enter into whatever contracts or personal relationships they choose', two Canadian political theorists have suggested that 'if the issue is asymmetry between men and women, that would appear to be remedied by a legal regime that permitted women as well as men to have multiple spouses, even if, among Muslims, only men availed themselves of this opportunity.' Joseph H. Carens and Melissa S. Williams, 'Muslim Minorities in Liberal Democracies: The Politics of Misrecognition', pp. 137–73 in Rajeev Bhargava, ed., *Secularism and Its Critics* (Delhi: Oxford University Press, 1998), pp. 155, 156. The objectionable asymmetry is, however, the inequality of power *within* a polygamous marriage (whether polygynous or polyandrous). Contrary to the authors' assertion, people in western liberal societies are free to form any personal relationships they like, subject to the prohibition on incest. The question is what forms of relationship should be defined as constituting marriage for legal purposes, and the argument against polygamy is that systematically unequal forms should not be recognized. What is wrong with slavery is that it is a legally unequal relationship. Getting rid of the 'asymmetry' that only whites could be owners and only blacks could be slaves would not, as the authors' argument implies, have made slavery acceptable. The essence of polygamy in its usual form (polygyny) is that the husband can take additional wives without the consent of existing ones and divorce any wife without the consent of the others. Even if each wife had a right to divorce on the same terms as the husband, there would still be a structural asymmetry because no wife could 'divorce' another wife if she found that this other wife made the marriage intolerable. Exactly how this inherently unequal system could be extended so that it was available to both

men and women is not at all apparent. Assuming that a marriage could be either polygynous or polyandrous, but not both simultaneously, would the first spouse to add another one on his or her sole initiative thereby assume all the rights of the man under the standard form of polygyny? If not, what? It is possible to conceive of a genuinely egalitarian alternative in which either spouse could add others and they in turn could bring in more, and so on *ad infinitum*. But it is not necessary to have a PhD in social choice theory to see why this is not a good plan, especially if we ask how equal rights to divorce might work within such an arrangement. Could any member of this collectivity made up of a number of men and a number of women initiate proceedings to expel any other member? Would everybody have to agree, except the proposed expellee? Or would the decision go by majority vote? The whole idea of egalitarian polygamy is manifest nonsense.

97    *Employment Division, Department of Human Resources* v. *Smith*, 494 US 872 (1990), p. 884.

98    Ibid.

99    Ibid., p. 890

100    Favell, 'Applied Political Philosophy', p. 267.

101    See especially William Julius Wilson, *The Truly Disadvantaged: The Inner City, the Underclass and Public Policy* (Chicago: University of Chicago Press, 1987).

102    James Traub, 'Schools are not the Answer', *New York Times Magazine*, 16 January 2000, pp. 52–91, p. 57.

103    Ibid.

104    See ibid., p. 81.

105    Ibid., p. 91.

106    'At bottom, the reason the kids at McDonough [the school whose head teacher was quoted in the text] and practically every other elementary school in Hartford were failing, while the kids in the wealthy suburbs that began just on the other side of West Hartford were thriving, was not that the schools in Hartford were bad and the schools in the suburbs were good, but that each set of children was repeating patterns, and following trajectories, established before they arrived at school.' Ibid.

107    Ibid., p. 90.

108    W. G. Runciman, 'Is There Always an Underclass?', pp. 273–87 in *Proceedings of the British Academy* 101, p. 286.

109    Orwell himself attributed the phrase to D. B. Wyndham Lewis: 'The English working class, as Mr Wyndham Lewis has put it, are "branded on the tongue".' George Orwell, 'The English People', pp. 16–56 in Sonia Orwell and Ian Angus, eds, *The Collected Essays, Journalism and Letters of George Orwell*, vol. 3 (Harmondsworth, Mddx: Penguin Books, 1970 [1968]), p. 19. The expression is now, however, firmly associated with Orwell – who does not, incidentally, provide a citation to the work by Lewis in which it first appeared.

110    T. S. Eliot, *Four Quartets*, 'East Coker' (London: Faber and Faber, 1959), p. 23.

111    Iris Marion Young, 'Together in Difference: Transforming the Logic of Group Political Conflict', pp. 155–76 in Will Kymlicka, ed., *The Rights of Minority Cultures* (Oxford: Oxford University Press, 1995), p. 155.

112 Ibid., p. 156.
113 Ibid.
114 Ibid., p. 155.
115 The political problem would not occur if the scheme of preferential admissions encompassed the children of over half the parents in the population. But the benefits of such a scheme would scarcely flow at all to the children of the poorest parents, who would then be competing with a lot of much better prepared candidates. It is clear, in any case, that Patterson envisages the system of preferential admissions as covering a relatively small minority – perhaps the poorest 10 or 15 per cent of the population.
116 Todd Gitlin, *The Twilight of Common Dreams: Why America is Wracked by Culture Wars* (New York: Henry Holt, 1995), p. 237.
117 Yasmin Alibhai-Brown, 'Some of the Worst Prejudice Can Be Found among the Ethnic Minorities', *Independent*, 10 February 2000, p. 11.

# Index